The American Journalist
PARADOX OF THE PRESS

4920 Strathmore Avenue

D1411874

A.J. Liebling dissects the press in Jacob Burck's 1948 cartoon (after the Rembrandt). Originally published in the "Page One" annual of the Chicago Newspaper Guild.

The American Journalist

PARADOX OF THE PRESS

Loren Ghiglione

17768

WASHINGTON, 1990

LIBRARY OF CONGRESS

Published by the Library of Congress in cooperation with
the American Society of Newspaper Editors, and made possible
by a grant from the Gannett Foundation

Library of Congress Cataloging-in-Publication Data

Ghiglione, Loren.
    The American Journalist: Paradox of the Press/Loren
Ghiglione.
        p.   cm.
    Includes bibliographical references (p.
    ISBN 0-8444-0701-1
    1. Journalism—United States—History.   I. Title.
PN4855.G48   1990
071'.3'09—dc20   89-600392
                                                      CIP

Design: A D R I A N N E   O N D E R D O N K   D U D D E N

To Nancy, Jessica and Laura,
who paid more than the cover price

Contents

THE JOURNALIST OF FICTION
Fun-house mirror reflection of reality   97

THE JOURNALIST OF TOMORROW
Into the world of science fiction   163

Mural by Frank McNitt in the office of the editor, *The News,* Southbridge, Massachusetts, depicts the newsroom and composing room of the paper as the artist saw them in 1935

Preface

Looking down on me as I type these words is a mural painted in 1935 by Frank McNitt, a Yale art student who later, despite his better judgment, became publisher of the *Southbridge* (Massachusetts) *Evening News*. The mural portrays the newsroom and composing room of the *News*, then a struggling two-thousand-circulation daily (today it's a struggling seven-thousand circulation daily).

To an outsider, the mural may look like a Norman Rockwell magazine cover, mixing fact and fiction. Andrew Tully, the sportwriter/proofreader just out of high school, wears a hat while he types, as if trying to imitate a reporter he saw in *The Front Page*. Leo LaFortune, who began working at the *News* in 1927 at age fourteen, concentrates on putting the lines of metal type in a page form. LaFortune rose from printer's devil to compositor to production manager. Today, sixty-two years after he began at the *News*, he still helps produce the paper each day, as if working in the *News* composing room has been for him an inky drink from a mythical fountain of youth.

The myth as well as the reality represented by McNitt's mural help explain my enthusiasm for writing about the American journalist. My American journalist is less the magazine writer, wire-service reporter, television anchor or corporate media boss, and more the daily newspaper reporter, photographer or editor.

Any description of the American journalist needs to go beyond the 56,000 news staffers at the nation's 1,642 daily newspapers. An equally large number of newspeople—often with greater visibility and more influence—work for broadcast networks, television stations, radio stations, wire services, weekly newspapers, and news magazines. But a scribbler for twenty years at a daily newspaper chooses, I admit, to devote more attention to the daily newspaper journalist.

Having confessed my bias, let me also acknowledge my debts. This book and the companion exhibit on the American journalist—produced by the Library of Congress in cooperation with the American Society of Newspaper Editors—would not exist without a generous grant to the Library from the Gannett Foundation. My deep appreciation goes to Eugene Dorsey, president, Calvin Mayne, vice president/grants administration, Gerald M. Sass, vice president/education, and Tracy A. Quinn, vice president/communications.

A grant from a press-related foundation to a book and exhibit on the American journalist could appear to be a conflict of interest. For that reason I have refrained, in the book and the exhibit, from noting the achievements of any Gannett journalists. The Gannett Foundation, however, could not have been more supportive or more scrupulous, giving me a free hand to write this book and to shape the exhibit.

I am equally indebted to the Library of Congress. Ruth Ann Stewart, formerly assistant librarian for national programs, shepherded the exhibit through the Library. William Miner, then exhibits officer, developed the basic structure of the exhibit. Diantha Schull, interpretive programs officer in 1988–89, helped staff the project.

As guest curator, I have been ably assisted on the book as well as on the exhibit by David F. Halaas, exhibit curator. From beginning to end, the project has relied on his determination and knowledge of journalism history.

In 1989, he was joined by a talented team: Sara Day, associate curator; Corinne Szabo, audio-visual editor; Joanne Freeman, administive coordinator; Reid S. Baker and James R. Higgins, Jr., photographers; Nancy Bush, information officer; and Benjamin Lawless and Jan Adkins, exhibit designers.

Charles W. Bailey, Peter Braestrup, Michael Gartner, Gene Giancarlo, and S. Branson Marley improved the text by their editing. Dana Pratt, the Library's director of publishing, Staffan Rosenborg, editor, Johanna Craig, production manager, Victoria L. Agee, indexer,

This book focuses on daily newspaper journalists, the kind who occupied the city room of the Los Angeles *Times*, 1922. Photograph by George Watson. Courtesy The Los Angeles *Times* History Center

Holly Cutting Baker, proofreader, and Adrianne Onderdonk Dudden, designer, played major roles in the book's production.

Also crucial to the project was the leadership of Lee Stinnett, executive director of the American Society of Newspaper Editors, and of John Seigenthaler, who advanced his ASNE presidency by one year so that I could complete the book and exhibit. Susan H. Miller, who chaired the 1990 ASNE convention committee, successfully integrated the exhibit opening into the ASNE convention.

I owe a special debt to Everette Dennis and the Gannett Center for Media Studies at Columbia University's Graduate School of Journalism. Without my fellowship year, 1987–88, the research and writing for this book and exhibit would never have started.

The writing of the book would not have been finished without the assistance and encouragement of Marvin Kalb, director of the Joan Shorenstein Barone Center on Press, Politics and Public Policy at Harvard University's John F. Kennedy School of Government, who arranged for a fellowship at the Center during 1988–89.

A deep bow goes to Doris Mittasch, my executive assistant, who worked early, late and on weekends to locate missing sources, eliminate my mistakes, suggest improvements, and get the book manuscript and exhibit materials to the Library of Congress.

I also wish to mention Helen Rhodes, Jackie Hemeon, Bryan P. Hori, and all the other people at Worcester County Newspapers who covered for me. The biggest burden fell on the top management—Chris Nesbitt, Mike Simon, and Ron Tremblay—but everyone in the company made a difference.

Finally, as always, I want to thank Nancy, my wife, who read and edited book drafts at every stage. She and our daughters—Jessica and Laura—offered encouragement and made extraordinary sacrifices. Without their support, this book and the accompanying exhibit would not exist.

Loren Ghiglione
Editor, *The News*
Southbridge, Massachusetts
September 20, 1989

The American Journalist
PARADOX OF THE PRESS

Numb. 1.

PUBLICK OCCURRENCES

Both *FORREIGN* and *DOMESTICK.*

Boston, Thursday *Sept.* 25th. 1690.

IT is designed, that the Countrey shall be furnished once a moneth (or if any Glut of Occurrences happen, oftener,) with an Account of such considerable things as have arrived unto our Notice.

In order hereunto, the Publisher will take what pains he can to obtain a Faithful Relation of all such things; and will particularly make himself beholden to such Persons in Boston whom he knows to have been for their own use the diligent Observers of such matters.

That which is herein proposed, is, First, That Memorable Occurrents of Divine Providence may not be neglected or forgotten, as they too often are. Secondly, That people every where may better understand the Circumstances of Publique Affairs, both abroad and at home; which may not only direct their Thoughts at all times, but at some times also to assist their Businesses and Negotiations.

Thirdly, That some thing may be done towards the Curing, or at least the Charming of that Spirit of Lying, which prevails amongst us, wherefore nothing shall be entered, but what we have reason to believe is true, repairing to the best fountains for our Information. And when there appears any material mistake in any thing that is collected, it shall be corrected in the next.

Moreover, the Publisher of these Occurrences is willing to engage, that whereas, there are many False Reports, maliciously made, and spread among us, if any well-minded person will be at the pains to trace any such false Report so far as to find out and Convict the First Raiser of it, he will in this Paper (unless just Advice be given to to the contrary) expose the Name of such person, as A malicious Raiser of a false Report. It is suppos'd that none will dislike this Proposal, but such as intend to be guilty of so villanous a Crime.

THE Christianized *Indians* in some parts of *Plimouth*, have newly appointed a day of Thanksgiving to God for his Mercy in supplying their extream and pinching Necessities under their late want of Corn, & for His giving them now a prospect of a very *Comfortable Harvest.* Their Example may be worth Mentioning.

'Tis observed by the Husbandmen, that altho' the With-draw of so great a strength from them, as what is in the Forces lately gone for *Canada*, made them think it almost impossible for them to get well through the Affairs of their Husbandry at this time of the year, yet the Season has been so unusually favourable that they scarce find any want of the many hundreds of hands, that are gone from them; which is looked upon as a Merciful Providence.

While the barbarous *Indians* were lurking about *Chelmsford*, there were missing about the beginning of this month a couple of Children belonging to a man of that Town, one of them aged about eleven, the other aged about nine years, both of them supposed to be fallen into the hands of the *Indians.*

A very *Tragical Accident* happened at *Water-Town*, the beginning of this Month, an *Old man*, that was of somewhat a Silent and Morose Temper, but one that had long Enjoyed the reputation of a *Sober* and a *Pious Man*, having newly buried his Wife, The Devil took advantage of the Melancholy which he thereupon fell into, his Wives discretion and industry had long been the support of his Family, and he seemed hurried with an impertinent fear that he should now come to want before he dyed, though he had very careful friends to look after him who kept a strict eye upon him, least he should do himself any harm. But one evening escaping from them into the Cow-house, they there quickly followed him, found him *hanging by a Rope*, which they had used to tye their *Calves* withal, he was dead with his feet near touching the Ground.

Epidemical *Fevers* and *Agues* grow very common, in some parts of the Country, whereof, tho' many dye not, yet they are sorely unfitted for their imployments; but in some parts a more *malignant Fever* seems to prevail in such sort that it usually goes thro' a Family where it comes, and proves *Mortal* unto many.

The *Small-pox* which has been raging in *Boston*, after a manner very Extraordinary is now very much abated. It is thought that far more have been sick of it then were visited with it, when it raged so much twelve years ago, nevertheless it has not been so *Mortal*, The number of them that have

Introduction

Three hundred years ago Boston's Benjamin Harris published *Publick Occurrences Both Forreign and Domestick*, a newspaper that would cure, he promised, "that Spirit of Lying, which prevails amongst us."[1] Harris's paper for September 25, 1690, was scrawny—three printed pages and a blank one—but jammed with news.

The paper reported a suicide by hanging, the spread of a smallpox epidemic, and developments in the French and Indian wars. The Indians were described as "those miserable Salvages."[2]

The paper also reported a rumor about improprieties by the King of France. The Massachusetts government, opposed to Harris's unauthorized printing of "Reflections of a very high nature,"[3] suppressed the paper. The man who wanted to cure the lying spirit ended his career in England hawking "Angelical Pills" and other patent medicines.[4]

Harris's *Publick Occurrences*, North America's first newspaper,[5] is often described by historians as the opening chapter in the evolution of the American journalist—an evolution marked by at least three kinds of change.

First, technological improvements have made the dictionary definition of news—"report of a recent event"—mean something quite different today than it meant three hundred years ago. During the late seventeenth century, news from Europe reached American audiences months after the event. Today television and radio reporters often broadcast news from Europe—or almost anyplace else—as the event unfolds.

Technological change has also transformed the journalist's work. Isaiah Thomas and other colonial printers set type by hand, one letter at a time, and pulled newspapers off their manual presses at the rate of only one hundred to two hundred sheets an hour. Much faster power presses of the early nineteenth century resulted in penny papers for almost everyone. They spurred the growth of armies of reporters who could fill the papers with fresh news. The telegraph, trans-Atlantic cable, wireless, telephone, computer, and communications satellite accelerated the pace of reporting. Developments in picture-making—from wood engraving to halftone to today's four-color electronic still video photography—enhanced the accuracy, availability, and freshness of images. And the ubiquity of radio and television led to July 21, 1969—the day pictures from the moon were first broadcast live.

The second kind of change has expanded journalists' freedom. In the era of Benjamin Harris, free speech had no legal standing. The trial, in 1735, of John Peter Zenger, editor and publisher of the *New York Weekly Journal*, focused attention on the principles of freedom of the press and the journalist's right to criticize government.[6] Guarantees of press freedom were written into nine of the first thirteen state constitutions and into the First Amendment to the U.S. Constitution.

Attacks on press freedom have been a constant of American history—from the suppression of *Publick Occurrences* to the Alien and Sedition Acts of 1798 to the latest police searches of newsrooms for photos, videotapes and reporters' notes.[7] But usually such attacks have been rebuffed by the Supreme Court. In this generation, *Times v. Sullivan* (1964) and the Pentagon Papers case (1971) have reestablished the principle that plaintiffs in libel suits and governmental attempts at prior restraint must bear a heavy burden—in the interests of press freedom. By 1980, lawyer Floyd Abrams could conclude: "The American press has never been more free, never been more uninhibited, and—most important—never been better protected by law."[8]

Published by Benjamin Harris in 1690, *Publick Occurrences* was North America's first newspaper. The Public Record Office, London, possesses the only known original. Photo courtesy of Public Record Office

Circulated much as a news report, Paul Revere's engraving of the Boston Massacre was a powerful weapon in the hands of Patriot propagandists, who put partisanship ahead of journalistic professionalism. Library of Congress, Prints and Photographs Division

The third kind of change has affected the journalist's position in society. The American journalist, it could be said, began as a part-time amateur who put partisanship ahead of professionalism. Sam Adams and his fellow propagandists for the American Revolution were followed by John Fenno, Philip Freneau, and other mouthpieces for political parties. By the middle of the nineteenth century, however, the journalist saw himself less as opinion maker and more as news reporter. The chroniclers of the Civil War, the reporters covering sports, business, religion, and the courts for James Gordon Bennett's New York *Herald*, the country editors detailing crop problems, local deaths, and other bulletin-board news, the muckrakers exposing big-city corruption—all emphasized the importance of the journalist as an autonomous, full-time, professional monitor of the world.

The portrayal of the journalist as an increasingly professional, increasingly objective, increasingly important chronicler who has benefited from greater press freedom and accelerating technological change, masks certain realities. It hides the paradoxical nature of the American journalist.

The American journalist resembles a description of Ernest Hemingway—himself once a journalist—by his first wife, Hadley: "So many sides to him you could hardly make a sketch of him in a geometry book."[9]

Any generalization about journalists of this generation meets with a counter-generalization. Media mottos—the New York *Times*'s slogan of "All the News That's Fit to Print," and the sign-off of "And that's the way it is" by CBS's Walter Cronkite, dean emeritus of newscasters—declare, in effect, that the American journalist's work is comprehensive, accurate, and authoritative.

But social scientists and even some newspeople do not see the journalist telling it as it is. Sociologist Michael Schudson says the journalist is "attuned to the conventional wisdom, serving the political culture of media institutions, and committed to a narrow range of public, literary expression."[10] David Broder, the Washington *Post*'s national political correspondent, describes the newspaper that journalists create daily as "a partial, hasty, incomplete, inevitably somewhat flawed and inaccurate rendering of some of the things we've heard about in the past 24 hours . . . ."[11]

Richard Viguerie, William Rusher, and other conservatives cite surveys that indicate journalists who see themselves as liberals outnumber those who see themselves as conservatives by three to one.[12] Rusher, publisher of the *National Review*, describes the news media as "a bunch of slanted liberals who have deliberately, systematically, over a long period of time delivered the liberal line."[13]

But others describe journalists, whatever

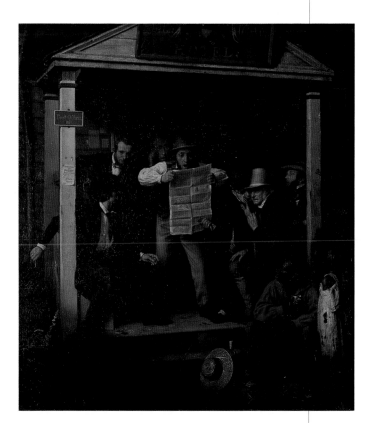

Whatever the failings of journalists, they have provided news that has left the public open-mouthed with wonderment or worry. *War News from Mexico*, painting by Richard Caton Woodville, 1848. Courtesy National Academy of Design, New York City

their politics, as following a middle-of-the-road to conservative course, influenced by the giant conglomerates that increasingly own the media. Ben Bagdikian, a Washington *Post* editor who became dean of journalism at the University of California at Berkeley, says: "The news media . . . suffer from built-in biases that protect corporate power . . . . These biases in favor of the status quo . . . do not seem to change materially over time."[14]

Some contend that the journalist has an obligation to serve as society's watchdog. Broadcast journalist Roger Mudd once said: "The national media, and mainly television, . . . believe that their chief duty is to put before the nation its unfinished business: pollution, the Vietnam War, discrimination, continuing violence, motor traffic, slums. The media have become the nation's critics . . . ."[15]

But other journalists contend that the press really acts less as critic—as agent of change—than as passive puppet. Walter Karp writes that "the press, strictly speaking, can scarcely be said to do anything. It does not act, it is acted upon."[16]

Press critics complain about a trend toward good-news journalism—less coverage of social ills, and more emphasis on uncritical reporting. Jonathan Kozol, author of *Illiterate America*, attacks the "compulsively upbeat" coverage of literacy, the formula story about the illiterate, who, after slogging through adult literacy classes, is now "off welfare and soon to get a job at IBM."[17]

But other observers criticize the press for overdoing bad news. Corporate executives, says Louis Banks, a former *Fortune* editor, berate "the persistent drumbeat of media oversimplification, exaggerated fault-finding, and antagonistic news selection."[18] Eugene H. Methvin, a senior editor of *Reader's Digest*, goes so far as to call for a "journalism of affirmation . . . seeking out and 'playing' stories of success, selfless devotion to the public weal, and the like, as well as scandal, malfeasance and nonfeasance."[19]

The aggressiveness of the reporter, some

claim, helps keep government honest. Lowell Weicker, the former U.S. senator from Connecticut, asserts that "every major scandal of the past twenty years [has] been uncovered by the press."[20]

But others insist the press is an investigative pussycat—a timid lackey of the "state propaganda system"[21]—regurgitating the viewpoints of government officials. One study of the Washington press corps concludes that officials, often in conflict, act as sources for three-quarters of what these journalists routinely report.[22]

Today's reporters see themselves as more neutral and less biased than their predecessors. They avoid obvious conflicts of interest. They refrain from political activity. Some even refuse on principle to vote.

But some press observers detect bias inherent in the neutrality journalists espouse. Political scientist W. Lance Bennett argues that journalists' work "is not biased in spite of, but precisely be-

James Gordon Bennett, Jr., in *Vanity Fair*, November 15, 1884. Library of Congress, General Collections

cause of, the professional journalism standards intended to prevent bias."[25] Journalists who adhere to neutrality standards give greater credence than deserved, these observers contend, to the declarations—and deceptions—of public officials.

Today's journalists are better educated, less reprobate, and more respectable than those of previous generations. In *The Imperial Media*, columnist Joseph Kraft wrote, "We [journalists] have enjoyed a huge rise in income, in status and in power . . . . We have advanced almost overnight from the bottom to the top; from the scum of the earth . . . to the seats of the high and mighty."[24]

But journalists have dropped in public esteem, scoring well below bankers,[25] and, some would say, not far ahead of used car salesmen. The National Opinion Research Center reported in 1976 that 29 percent of Americans had "a great deal of confidence" in the press.[26] By 1983 the confidence level had been cut in half, dropping to 13.7 percent, the lowest ever.[27]

No simple answer exists for the paradoxes that surround the journalists and their craft. Three explanations, however, stand out. First, not one but many journalists exist. The motivation and methods of the war correspondent are not those of the gossip columnist, or the editorial cartoonist, or the television talk-show host. For that reason this book describes eight journalistic types—from the street reporter to the exploiter to the entertainer.

The second explanation for the contrasts that mark journalists involves the journalists themselves. To some degree, all journalists are actors who play different roles depending on their employer, the story, and the circumstances. They are both neutral and partisan, insider and outsider, truth-teller and liar.

Newsday columnist Sydney Schanberg focuses on one ethical dimension. The journalist is, at the same time, a member of the human race and a paid, professional observer: "You run to the scene, and some people are dead or

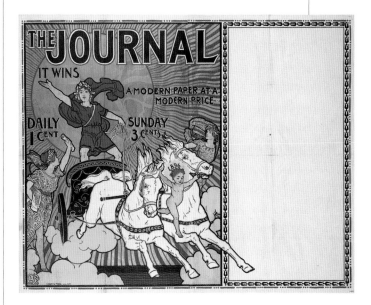

The journalist is entertainer as well as explicator, as made clear by advertising posters from the "Yellow Journalism Wars," c. 1896. Library of Congress, Prints and Photographs Division

wounded. You scribble notes and snap pictures and at some point you try to decide what you must do. Do you minister to the wounded? Do you give blood? You're required to go back and write a story. Your function is to tell people where you were today, to communicate a scene to them. That is your unspoken oath. But how do you do that and stay human?"[28]

A third explanation of the contradictions in journalistic behavior points to the profession's

The paradoxical journalist sometimes produces a strong reaction. In a speech before the White House News Photographers Association in 1983, President Reagan expressed his attitude toward the press, saying "I've been waiting years to do this." UPI/Bettmann Newsphotos

inconsistent self-image—based partly on reality and partly on fiction. Despite the derring-do of fictional journalists, the work of real editors and reporters is not usually risky. Their death rate ranks below those of architects and funeral directors.[29] The typical journalist, sociologists report, "is a white Protestant male who has a bachelor's degree, is married and has children, is middle-of-the-road politically . . . ."[30] Trade magazines publish stories—"When MBAs rule the newsroom"[31]—that describe journalists as organization men and women.

But journalists prefer not to see themselves that way. They favor two other self-images. First, they enjoy regarding themselves, writes Robert C. Christopher, administrator of the Pulitzer Prizes, as "the keepers of society's conscience and hence at least indirectly as social and political engineers."[32] Ben Bradlee, executive editor of the Washington *Post*, acknowledges that

Lanny Budd, a crusading weekly editor in an Upton Sinclair story, piqued his early interest: "The calls to Lanny from the President to solve this or that problem which all the President's men found too tough was one of the early and great fantasies."[33]

The other self-image that journalists still savor—based more on the fictional newspeople of *The Front Page* than on reality—is the hard-living, fun-loving reporter, a member of a unique fraternity. They enter journalism dreaming, as Tom Wolfe fantasized about his first newspaper job, of "[d]runken reporters out on the ledge of the *News* peeing into the Chicago River at dawn. . . . Nights down at the detective bureau." Wolfe sought "the whole movie, nothing left out."[34]

Early in his career, CBS television anchor Dan Rather also revealed the impact of *The Front Page*: "The average journalist, including myself, is a whiskey-breathed, nicotine-stained, stubble-bearded guy. . . ."[35] Frederick Taylor, former executive editor of the *Wall Street Jour-*

Or he may be this

In Illustrations for Will Irwin's 1911 series on the American newspaper in *Collier's*, Art Young depicted the journalist as not only a "servant of truth" but as a privacy-invading peepholer. Library of Congress, General Collections

nal, said, "It probably is embarrassing to admit it, but as a kid I saw the movie, *The Front Page,* (the original version) and said to myself, 'That looks like fun.'"[36]

The Front Page has become a kind of icon for many journalists. Charles Anderson, editor of the Wilmington (North Carolina) *Star-News,* recalls giving tickets to two young reporters. "You must see this play. You will love it. *It is about newspapering.* Come back and tell me about it." The reporters returned, surprised at Anderson's enthusiasm for *The Front Page.* "I immediately formed a professional opinion that both lacked the souls of reporters," Anderson says. "It was substantiated some months later when one left for PR work and the second went into business with his dad, selling advertisements for matchbook covers."[37]

The Front Page, like many plays, movies, and novels about journalists, was written by ex-journalists. Journalists—all of us—invent versions of ourselves that contain what psychoana-

Some journalists have savored a self-image based partly on fiction. Arthur Fellig ("Weegee the Famous"), a New York freelance news photographer of the 1930s and 1940s, resembled the Hollywood stereotype of the press photographer. Courtesy Wilma Wilcox

The press has benefited from the public perception of the journalist as a David, not as a Goliath, though that perception may be changing. Here Kuniko Terasawa, 93, works on her four-page Japanese-language newspaper, Salt Lake City's *Utah Nippo.* Photo by Taro Yamasaki/People Weekly © 1989 The Time Inc. Magazine Company.

The rule of the journalist as sensationalist is apparent in the front page of William Randolph Hearst's New York *Journal*, with drawing by Homer Davenport. Library of Congress, Serial and Government Publications Division

lysts call "personal myths"[38] and "fictive personalities."[39] Many journalists imitate mythic journalists, some from reality and some from fiction. Real journalists realize, as psychoanalyst Jay Martin writes, that "life without imitation is impossible and unthinkable."[40] The distinction between real journalist and imaginary journalist blurs.

Fiction's journalist provides at least a different way of understanding the American journalist, as myth as well as reality. For that reason, this book follows its description of eight types of

real journalists with a section on fictional newspeople.

The book focuses, for instance, on the real big-city street reporter and, later, on the fictional counterpart as amateur detective. The real reporter sometimes has played sleuth. William Randolph Hearst's New York *Journal* formed a special "murder squad."[41] Reporters at Joseph Pulitzer's New York *World* sent a number of criminals to prison, including an astrologer who ran a white-slave trade.[42] But the reporter-sleuths of fiction have gone beyond reporting and occasional snooping. They prefer to spend all their time capturing bribers and murderers or undertaking the bribing and murdering themselves.[43]

Some journalists fear that the public, exposed to the excesses of newspeople in fiction and film, will become increasingly hostile to the freedom granted real journalists. After surveying four decades of newspaper films, Nora Sayre, critic for the New York *Times*, wrote: "Small wonder that many moviegoers don't love or trust newspaper people . . . movies have stated that reporters blithely invent the news while ignoring what really happened, and that the newsroom is a giant nursery seething with infantile beings."[44] Ron Dorfman ended a review of the movie *Under Fire* by worrying that the film "will produce a more hospitable public climate for claims that real journalists have all along been feeding us misinformation"[45] and that they should have their freedom curtailed.

The journalists' problem goes deeper than unflattering portraits produced by moviemakers. The public today perceives journalists not as Davids but as Goliaths—part of the third largest U.S. industry, which is profitable, powerful, and privileged. The press often cites its privileged status, arguing for confidentiality of sources and for shield laws, proclaiming "the public's right to know," and wrapping itself in the First Amendment.

The press also uses its First Amendment prerogatives as reason to discourage criticism. Journalists attack press councils and other mechanisms proposed for evaluating journalistic performance. Newspeople huddle, wrote Harry S. Ashmore, former editor of the Arkansas *Gazette*, "rumps together, horns out, in the immemorial manner of, say, the National Association of Manufacturers faced by a threat of regulated prices."[46] While journalists argue passionately for the right to examine all of society's institutions, they accept as "the most sacred cow in journalism's holy credo"[47] the right to reject any examination of their own performance.

The public, when it gets the opportunity, does not refrain from passing judgment on journalists. Juries make million-dollar libel awards against newspapers. "Juries are the American people," explained Eugene Patterson, former chairman of the St. Petersburg (Florida) *Times*. "They want to punish us."[48]

Judging from opinion polls, a majority of Americans now support laws—laws that would violate the First Amendment—against journalists who slant the news.[49] Those who remember Mr. Dooley's epigram about the Supreme Court following the election returns, worry that the Court, using national security, the right to privacy, or some other rationale, will restrict press freedom. Or they fear that, as Walter Lippmann warned seventy years ago, "Congress, in a fit of temper, egged on by an outraged public opinion, will operate on the press with an axe."[50]

Three centuries after the birth of the first American newspaper, the public is still deciding what kind of journalist it wants and what kind of freedom it will grant that journalist. A tug-of-war continues between the advocates of greater press freedom and those who prefer a less pugnacious, more "responsible" press.[51]

What this future holds for newspeople is the subject of this book's final section, "The Journalist of Tomorrow." Reporters will have to learn to live not only with space-age gadgetry—global computers and sophisticated central data banks—but also with the possibility of intense public pressure to restrict their freedom.

In *The Federalist Papers*, Alexander Hamilton wrote that the survival of the press's liberty "must altogether depend on public opinion, and on the general spirit of the people and of the government."[52] What freedom the public gives journalists, the public can take away. But the ultimate irony may be that insofar as the public chooses to restrict its journalists' freedom, the public restricts its own freedoms. Journalists who can no longer attempt to cure "that Spirit of Lying," as did Benjamin Harris three hundred years ago, can no longer fully serve the public.

"The News, -Which?" Another Art Young illustration for Will Irwin's series in *Collier's,* January 21, 1911. Library of Congress, General Collections

Collier's

THE NATIONAL WEEKLY

The
Reporter
and the News

Seventh Article
in the Series

The AMERICAN
NEWSPAPER

By

WILL IRWIN

The Journalist of Fact

A "troublemaker" as diverse as the news itself

Think of the American journalist as Edna Buchanan, a Pulitzer Prize-winning Miami *Herald* police reporter who lives with four stray cats, a dog named Rocky Rowf, and a gun or two. She writes staccato opening paragraphs. She begins a story about a woman accused of a murder conspiracy: "Bad things happen to the husbands of the Widow Elkin."[1]

Or think of the American journalist as James Russell Wiggins, who never went to college but served as executive editor of the Washington *Post*, then U.S. Ambassador to the United Nations. Today, at 86, he edits the weekly *American* in Ellsworth, Maine. A front-page story on a pet snake carries the headline: "Police put permitless pet python in pen."[2]

Or think of the American journalist as Michael Fancher, executive editor of the Seattle (Washington) *Times.* In addition to a B.A. and an M.S. in communications, he holds a Master of Business Administration. Were it not for his gray beard and mustache, one might mistake him for an insurance company president—button-down collar, paisley tie, and gray suit.

Or think of the American journalist as Terry Anderson, former Marine staff sergeant and chief Middle East correspondent for Associated Press, kidnapped at gunpoint March 16, 1985, on a Beirut street. He had said earlier about the dangers facing a journalist in Lebanon: "There's no story worth getting killed for."[3]

Or think of the American journalist as Wilbert Rideau No. 75546, the self-taught editor of the *Angolite*, the inmate magazine at Louisiana State Prison. Rideau, serving a life sentence for a 1961 murder, won the prestigious George Polk Award in 1980 for exposing systematic rape at the prison.

The journalist, unlike the lawyer and doctor, cannot be defined in terms of educational attainment, state certification, or professional standards. The variety of the American journalist is a primary focus of this book.[4] As Buchanan, Wiggins, Fancher, Anderson, and Rideau suggest, the American journalist works in many different worlds and performs a multitude of functions. There remains, however, one constant. The American journalist continues to enlarge the definition of news.

The categories of journalists that follow—street reporter, persuader, crusader, investigator, exploiter, entertainer, war correspondent, broadcast journalist—suggest the range of roles.

In his 1911 *Collier's* series on the American press, **Will Irwin** argued that the power of the press rested with the street reporter. *Collier's*, April 22, 1911. Library of Congress, General Collections

And yet these categories also suggest the limitations that invariably characterize descriptions of the people Robert Rutland called the "troublemakers in American history."[5]

First, the history of the journalist inevitably gets written in terms of big-city notables. Such bias is not irrational: Talented, ambitious reporters in smaller towns have traditionally moved to the metropolis to test their skills, expand their audiences, and enlarge their paychecks. But journalism history perhaps overemphasizes newspeople in metropolitan media—primarily New York newspapers—just as business history focuses on Wall Street, and the history of the theater centers on Broadway.

Overlooked have been the small-town successes—for example, the triumph of Edith O'Keefe Susong, a divorced woman with two children and a four-thousand-dollar mortgage, who in October 1916 took over a struggling weekly in Greeneville, Tennessee. She wrote the articles, sold the advertising, kept the books, helped run the two-page flatbed press, folded and addressed copies by hand, and lugged the papers to the post office for mailing to 650 subscribers. One of the two competing weeklies huffed: "The Greeneville *Democrat* is now being managed by a woman. It will not be alive when the roses bloom again."[6] But Susong bought out her two weekly competitors and consolidated them into a daily—the Greeneville *Sun*. At her death in 1974, after fifty-eight years as reporter and editor, she left to the next generation of her family a daily with one of the highest circulation/household ratios in the country.[7]

Second, it is difficult when choosing from hundreds of thousands of journalists to resist naming those who won—those who scooped the competition, pioneered in newsgathering techniques, or helped establish important First Amendment principles.

But recognition should also go to the many talented newspeople who—often because of their unflinching devotion to principle—struggled unsuccessfully to survive. We should remember Hodding Carter, the small-town Mississippi editor who opposed racism during the 1940s and 1950s and still was able to keep publishing. But we also should remember three other anti-segregationist Mississippi editors who, despite all the journalism awards they won, were driven from their papers. Ira B. Harkey, Jr., the Pulitzer Prize-winning editor of the seven-thousand-circulation Pascagoula *Chronicle*, "could not bear to exist in the vacuum of . . . ostracism."[8] Pulitzer Prize winner Hazel Brannon Smith, who put out the Lexington *Advertiser* and three neighboring weeklies, faced boycotts orchestrated by the White Citizens Council, and eventually suffered financial defeat.[9] And P. D. East, editor of *The Petal Paper*, lost all two thousand of his subscribers, almost all his advertisers, and then, finally, his weekly.[10]

Third, journalism history—like all history—favors those who represent change: the first sportswriter to get a by-line, the first woman war correspondent, the first police reporter. Reflecting a prejudice of the press, historians give little weight to the absence of change. The importance of continuity—of preserving worthwhile elements of the status quo, of reaffirming the best traditions of journalism history—often is overlooked.

Eleanor Roosevelt holds a press conference in the Monroe Room of the White House, March 13, 1933—one in a series of Monday morning press conferences for women only. These were instituted by Mrs. Roosevelt to emphasize the value of continuing to employ female journalists and to encourage other papers without women reporters to hire them. Courtesy Historical Pictures Service, Chicago

Journalism history could be written in terms of repetition and cycles. Is the "tabloid television" journalism of today placed in a more revealing perspective if compared not only to the sensationalism of 1920s tabloids but to the journalism of *Publick Occurrences*'s Benjamin Harris—and to the gossipy reporting of legendary Anne Royall? Known as the "widow with the serpent's tongue," Royall published the first issue of her Washington, D.C. paper, *Paul Pry*, in 1831. She let no one, including the president, escape her questioning. She sat on John Quincy Adams's clothes while he bathed in the Potomac—so the story goes[11]—until he agreed to an interview. At sixty, she was arrested and found guilty of being a common scold, avoiding the ducking stool only because of her age.[12] Consider her, perhaps, the spiritual grandmother of New York columnist Walter Winchell—and the spiritual great-grandmother of television's Geraldo Rivera.

Fourth, it is difficult to avoid emphasizing white males in a book about journalism—a craft, like others, that for much of its history has been inhospitable to women,[13] African Americans, and others. Beginning with the Indians—the first Americans[14]—virtually every ethnic and racial minority has boasted influential journalists who have produced spirited newspapers aimed primarily at their own people. While this book for space reasons has not focused on journalists of the ethnic and racial press,[15] it is Elias Boudinot, Francisco Ramirez, Fred Makino, Lucile Bluford, and other members of this press who have compensated for the stereotypical reporting, limited coverage, and employment discrimination by mainstream newspapers.

In 1828, Boudinot, a Cherokee schoolteacher and missionary, began putting out the first Indian newspaper, the *Cherokee Phoenix* (renamed a year later *Cherokee Phoenix and Indian Advocate*), in New Echota, Georgia. Printed in English and Cherokee, the four-page newspaper published Cherokee laws and described persistent alcoholism and other problems. In his first issue, Boudinot called for a time when "all the Indian tribes of America shall rise, Phoenix-like, from their ashes, and when terms like 'Indian depredations,' 'war whoops,' 'scalping knife,' and the like shall become obsolete and forever buried 'under deep ground.'"[16] Boudinot earned three hundred dollars a year for his work; the newspaper's printer, three hundred fifty dollars. The printer, apparently, was judged more valuable than the journalist.[17]

Lucile Bluford interviews a soldier at Fort Riley, Kansas, in the 1940s. Courtesy Kansas City *Call*

In 1832, Cherokees divided over accepting payment to move west—to abandon their homes and ancestral gravesites as well as to leave behind regular raids against them by marauding whites. Boudinot was ordered by the Cherokee Nation to keep reports of the division out of the paper. He resigned instead. The paper closed. For supporting a treaty that led to the removal of the Cherokees to the West, Boudinot was later axed to death.

Ramirez, while still a teen-ager, founded *El Clamor Publico,* a four-page Los Angeles tabloid, in 1855. When Anglo mobs began lynching native Californios, Ramirez editorially attacked "the pirate instincts of the Anglo-Saxons"[18] and proposed that the U.S. democracy be re-named "lynchocracy."[19] Ramirez's Spanish-language weekly called for Chicanos to resist Anglo indignities and even proposed return to Mexico as a response to those "who treat us worse than slaves."[20]

Makino, born in Japan of an English father and a Japanese mother, immigrated to Hawaii and founded *The Hawaii Hochi* in 1912. The viewpoints of his nonpartisan, independent newspaper landed him in jail. To counter the plantations' exploitation of the Japanese, he helped them establish unions. To combat Hawaii's effort to control the 180 Japanese-language schools, he mounted a challenge that led to a U.S. Supreme Court decision in 1927: Hawaii's law to control the schools was unconstitutional.[21]

Bluford became a reporter at the Kansas City *Call,* a black weekly, in 1932, shortly after earning a bachelor's degree from the University of Kansas. Between 1939 and 1942, she tried eleven times to gain admission to the graduate school of journalism at the University of Missouri–Columbia. Later she said her purpose was not primarily to obtain a master's degree but "to break down that separate but equal business, which was never equal."[22] The university refused her admission and, to maintain segregation, encouraged the state to establish a school of journalism at nearby Lincoln University, a historically black institution. A half-century later, the university that had turned away Bluford awarded her an honorary doctorate of humanities. Still working at the *Call*—as its editor, publisher, and majority owner—Bluford accepted the 1989 University of Missouri degree "for the thousands of black students who suffered discrimination all those years."[23]

Finally, the title of this book—*The American Journalist*—emphasizes the individual. The focus underplays journalism's dependence on teamwork, on commercial imperatives, on the marketplace. However superb the newspaper reporter's work, it goes virtually unread in most cities if an army of children fails to deliver the newspaper to the doorsteps of subscribers who, whatever their reservations about the paper, remain willing to pay for it.

These five points are made to explain the prism through which this book views the journalist. To identify some of the ways in which the prism distorts the view is to appreciate more fully the diversity of American journalists and the range of their reporting.

1 Street Reporter

Largely Unsung and Often Unknown

Local reporters and photographers cover the full spectrum of life, from the arrest of the man lying drunk in the gutter, to the mayor's speech at city hall, from the first baby born in town this year, to the Spanish-American War veteran who died in his sleep. These journalists create the images that people have of their communities and of themselves. Yet these reporters and photographers remain largely unsung and often unknown.

Even as journalism textbooks immortalize Benjamin Day as the founder in 1833 of the New York *Sun*, America's first successful penny paper, they often overlook George Wisner, the *Sun*'s twenty-one-year-old police reporter. Yet it was Wisner's coverage of everyday dramas— crime, cholera, and corruption—that made the *Sun*'s motto of "all the news of the day" credible. "[I]t was Wisner, rather than Day," writes James Stanford Bradshaw, "who gave the *Sun* its high popular appeal, and made the American newspaper one for the masses . . . ."[1]

Wisner used colloquial language to capture tragicomedy. In his "Police Office" reports, Wisner quoted a drunk who admitted that he "could not see a hole through a ladder"[2] and a woman who said "she felt as happy as a singed cat."[3] Wisner criticized his competitors' clichés: "Are people married now-a-days? No, they are always led to the 'hymnal altar.' Are they hanged? By no means; they are 'launched into eternity.'"[4]

Wisner's stories were concise: "Mary Ann Coburn was found drunk in the street. She said she was not in the habit of getting intoxicated, but her husband, God Bless him, had just returned from a five years' voyage—and although she had been married two or three times during

his absence, yet she was so much rejoiced on seeing him again, that she went right down to Water Street, and drank three glasses of rum. Magistrate: Why I think your husband would have refused to live with you after such conduct on your part. Prisoner: I'll tell you what it is—he likes drink as well as I do."[5]

Not everyone, especially those identified by name in Wisner's articles, admired his reporting. The *Sun* acknowledged "some 20 or 30" libel suits in 1834. But Wisner's new brand of personal journalism attracted readers. And his ruinous habits, which led him to leave the *Sun* after only twenty-one months, presaged that of generations of hard-living street reporters.

Reporters in the nineteenth century worked seventeen-hour days. As late as the 1880s, they labored, Samuel Blythe wrote, "until four o'clock in the morning for from ten to fifteen dollars a week, doing anything that came along from a state convention to a church wedding."[6] They were assigned up to fifteen stories a day and paid on "space rates"—the payment depending on the length of the published story— which encouraged windiness. Their newspapers only reimbursed them for carfare, Will Irwin recalled, "if the trip was longer than eight city blocks . . . . City Hall, the Hall of Justice, the city jail, and the morgue, the places where reporters went most often, lay about seven blocks away from the office."[7]

Insecurity haunted street reporters. Amid the newspaper circulation wars, editors came and went; at the beginning of the 1900s, twenty-seven people occupied the city editor's chair at the Chicago *Evening American* in thirty-seven months. A change of editor often meant massive layoffs. Edwin L. Shuman's how-to journalism guide described the reporter's tenure in 1894 as "so precarious that he is supposed never to pass the waste-basket without looking in to see if his head is there."[8]

With notebook in hand and press card in hat, Meyer Berger of the New York *Times* typifies the street reporter at work in the early 1950s. Courtesy The New York *Times* Archives

The street reporter, nevertheless, not only survived as a species but often turned out prose that showed considerable mastery of the English language. After working as a journeyman printer and running his own short-lived weekly, Walt Whitman, not yet twenty-two in 1841, began reporting for New York dailies. He tried to write what he called "pictures of life as it is."[9]

In the New York *Aurora*, he described the "heterogeneous mass" at the New York Market: "There comes a journeyman mason (we know him by his *limy* dress) . . . . With what an independent air the mason looks around upon the fleshy wares; the secret of the matter is, that he has his past week's wages in his pocket, and therefore puts he on that devil-may-care countenance. So marvellous an influence hath money in making a man feel valiant and as good as his neighbor."[10]

Whitman often failed to give the addresses, names, and other facts that competing reporters

Walt Whitman in 1855, the year *Leaves of Grass* first appeared. Library of Congress, Prints and Photographs Division

provided. But, as is apparent in an *Aurora* account of a fire that left hundreds of people without a home, he made readers feel as if they were watching the event: "Puddles of water and frequent lengths of hose-pipe endangered the pedestrian's safety; and the hubbub, the trumpets of the engine foreman, the crackling of the flames, the lamentations of those who were made homeless by the conflagration—all sounded louder and louder as we approached, and at last grew to one continued and deafening din."[11]

Both the journeyman mason and the fire would find their way into "Song of Myself," published in Whitman's *Leaves of Grass* (1855). After his stint at the *Aurora*, Whitman worked at ten other newspapers before becoming editor of the Brooklyn *Daily Eagle* in 1846.[12] Eventually Whitman the journalist grew into Whitman the poet. The mood pieces by Whitman the journalist, pictures of his time, became in the hands of Whitman the poet images for all time.[13]

Some two generations later, in 1889, Annie Laurie, whose real name was Winifred Black, began her career as a street reporter more inauspiciously than Whitman had begun his. Her editor at the San Francisco *Chronicle* tore up her first article: "This is a bad story . . . . We don't want fine writing in a newspaper . . . . There's a gripman on the Powell Street line—he takes his car out at three o'clock in the morning, and while he's waiting for the signals, he opens the morning paper. . . . Don't write a single word he can't understand and wouldn't read."[14]

Black became famous in the trade for eyewitness exposés. To get a hospital story, she dressed as a bag lady with drops of belladonna in her eyes, making her look desperate. She pretended to faint on a San Francisco street. She was thrown into a prison horse cart, roughly dragged inside the hospital, and given an emetic. Her account of hospital conditions led to staff dismissals, better treatment of women, and the creation of an ambulance service.

Black's vivid prose and her boldness as a

Winifred ("Annie Laurie") Black, c. 1912. Library of Congress, Prints and Photographs Division

street reporter caused William Randolph Hearst to send her everywhere. She wrote from England about suffragettes who kicked policemen in the groin. She exposed Chicago's malfunctioning juvenile court system. She hid on a presidential train to extract an exclusive interview from President Benjamin Harrison. Dressed as a boy to get past police emergency lines, she covered a Texas tidal wave disaster that took seven thousand lives.

In forty years she rarely missed an important murder trial. She covered the trial of Harry Thaw—Thaw was charged with killing architect Stanford White—at which a famous phrase originated. Black sat at the press table with Dorothy Dix, Ada Patterson, and Nixola Greeley-Smith. Irvin Cobb wrote about the four "Sob Sisters." Their function, as Ishbel Ross explained, "was to watch for the tear-filled eye, the widow's veil, the quivering lip, the lump in the throat, the trembling hand."[15] But Black shot back: "I am not a 'Sob Sister' . . . I'm just a plain, practical all-around newspaper woman. That is my profession and that is my pride."[16]

Equally effective as street reporters were two men who both grew up on New York's Lower East Side and who both quit school at fourteen to go to work. Meyer Berger, one of eleven children, started paying his way at eight, selling newspapers. His first job as a journalist was as a police reporter for the New York *World*. In 1928, he moved to the New York *Times*. There he not only covered the trials of Al Capone and Dutch Schultz, but also wrote prose poems.

One such poem began: "New York's voice speaks mystery . . . . It has a soft, weird music, a symphony of wind at high altitudes, of muted traffic in endless serpentine twisting over city hills and grades, of jet hiss and propeller thrum, of the hoarse call of tugs on many waters, of great liners standing in from the broad sea . . . ."[17]

Berger's speed as a writer—always a prized virtue in journalists—made him a legend. In 1949, Howard Unruh, a crazed World War II veteran, shot thirteen people on the streets of Camden, New Jersey, before giving himself up to police. Berger retraced Unruh's rampage, interviewed fifty witnesses, and then recreated the tragedy in a four-thousand-word story that took him only two and one-half hours to write.

Berger captured the victims' panic and shock: "Unruh first walked into John Pilarchik's shoe repair shop . . . . The cobbler, a twenty-seven-year-old man who lives in Pennsauken Township, looked up open-mouthed as Unruh came to within a yard of him. The cobbler started up from his bench but went down with a bullet in his stomach. A little boy who was in the shop ran behind the counter and crouched there in terror. Unruh walked out into the sunlit street . . . ."[18] The story earned Berger the Pulitzer Prize for local reporting. He delivered the one-thousand-dollar prize money to Unruh's mother.

Berger wrote an official history of the *Times*,[19] three other books, and a celebrated "About New York" column from 1953 until his death in 1959. But he said he preferred being a reporter.

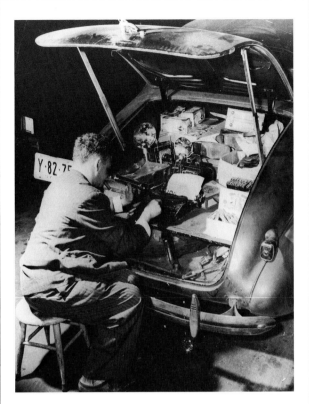

"Weegee at the trunk of his Chevrolet," 1942. Courtesy Wilma Wilcox

"Asleep on Fire Escape During Heat Spell," by Arthur Fellig ("Weegee the Famous"), 1938. Courtesy Wilma Wilcox

The second product of the Lower East Side, Arthur Fellig, stamped his life as well as his photographs "Credit Weegee the Famous." After leaving home at fourteen to work as a busboy, day laborer, dishwasher, and candy peddler, Weegee spent his twenties as a darkroom developer for Acme News Service. That time in the darkroom led to a career as a New York freelance news photographer. Equipping his Chevrolet with a two-way police radio (the first allowed to be used in New York by an ordinary citizen) he captured the city's dark side from midnight to dawn.

Weegee gained his nickname from the Ouija board. He seemed clairvoyant, as if he knew in advance where a crime would occur.[20] Weegee never thought about art.[21] But his five-dollars-a-print photographs of five thousand murders and other mayhem created enduring portraits of New York street life during the 1940s. "Asleep on Fire Escape During Heat Spell" proved his vision was not limited to corpses and killers.

Weegee looked the very image of the New York news photographer: a fat mouth stuffed with a cigar, a hand clutching a Speed Graphic, a crumpled fedora, and a baggy suit that he may have slept in. In 1946, he published *Naked City* (the title was later sold to Mark Hellinger for a movie), a photo collection that brought him modest fame. He pursued "lush living" in Hollywood and turned out *Naked Hollywood*, which he dismissed as "a bad book."[22] In the "Land of the Zombies," as he called Hollywood, his work became zombielike.[23]

Alternative reporters: catalysts for cultural— and journalistic—change

Reporters for the alternative press—for the hundreds of dissident papers in the 1960s that focused on civil rights, Vietnam, feminism, ecology, peace, sexual liberation, and New Age spirituality—did more than redefine news.

They lived the new counterculture, promoting and attacking its ideas, creating media events, and plugging themselves into a street life foreign to many journalists. They openly practiced "deliberate bias."[1] Police officers were called "pigs," the governor of California was labeled "Rat Fink Reagan," and establishment leaders were identified as "the MAN."

Alternative journalists often could not rely on the underground press to provide a living. Publication was irregular—an editor of *Black Panther* described the paper as "a weekly, man, but it's just that some weeks are longer than others"[2]—and papers often ignored sound business practices. Making money, however, was not the purpose of most alternative journalists.

They sought subjects ("All the News That's Unfit to Print") and styles more personal and provocative than traditional newswriting permitted. Norman Mailer, part-owner of the *Village Voice*, the thirty-five-year-old father of alternative papers, launched attacks on orthodoxy— "the declaration of my private war on American journalism, mass communications, and the totalitarianism of totally pleasant personality."[3] He parodied mainstream columnists. Ed Sullivan was "Ed Sullen-Vain on C's of B.S.," and Walter Winchell of the *Mirror* became "Voltaire Vein-Chill in the N.Y. Daily Rimmer."[4]

Horseshit, published by Scum Press in California, indicated by its name one feature of the underground press:

It reported without any restrictions on language. But the alternative press also offered different heroes (Timothy Leary and Che Guevara), different heels (university administrations and the CIA), different front-page news (rock music and radical politics), and different features. The Chicago *Seed* and the *Rat* not only reported the 1968 Democratic National Convention in Chicago, they published survival-guide issues. Dr. Hippocrates, a humorously hip Dear Abby, specialized in advice on aberrant sexual practices. By 1969, the mainstream San Francisco *Chronicle* was publishing the column.

Artists, cartoonists, and designers also provided highly individualistic—sometimes psychedelic—work that complemented the occasionally scatological, do-your-own-thing writing. Ron Cobb's political cartoons savaged the establishment. Walt Crowley satirized comics and the accepted soft porn of automobile advertising in his underground "comix" for Milwaukee's *Kaleidoscope.* The cover design of *Avatar* and *The East Village Other* displayed a freedom uncharacteristic of the overground press (one *East Village Other* cover featured a Nazi stormtrooper's body topped by President Johnson's head).

But anti-establishment as the alternative reporters and artists were, they resembled their mainstream counterparts in one important respect: they expanded the permissible agenda of news. In effect, alternative journalists presented new ideas, styles, trends, and values to the establishment press and the larger society.[5] They broadened Americans' definition of news, expanded their public vocabulary, and gave them new images for understanding the world.

Front page of *The East Village Other,* with collage by San Francisco artist Sätty. Courtesy Journalism Library, University of Missouri–Columbia

One news photographer who managed to capture Hollywood was George Watson. He joined the Los Angeles *Times* as its first full-time photographer in 1917. He caught the daffy quality of Southern California: Albert Einstein walking arm-in-arm with Charlie Chaplin; eighteen starlets kicking Rockette-style on an airplane's wing; Robert Wadlow, eight feet, eight and one-half inches tall, promoting a Poppy Day sale; and evangelist Aimee Semple McPherson explaining her sensational "kidnapping" (cynics described it as a tryst) to ten thousand fans.

But Watson's photos also chronicled Southern California's economic boom, the growth of the aviation industry, the development of Hollywood as a center for film and radio, and even the birth of atomic energy. In 1924, he photographed a machine at the California Institute of Technology that, he was told, would split the atom and revolutionize science. Watson did not give the photo much thought until a generation later when the United States dropped an A-bomb on Hiroshima.

Watson often relied on impertinence to get the pictures he wanted. He startled fellow journalists by yelling at Belgium's monarch, Albert I, "Hey, King, take off your hat!"[24] The king complied. In 1919, Watson wangled a ride in a biplane to take the first aerial shots of Los Angeles. To photograph a murder-trial autopsy from which the press was excluded, he persuaded a sheriff to deputize him. And he developed a miniature camera—hidden inside a hat with a lens-sized trap door—to capture dramatic courtroom scenes.

George Watson, the first full-time photographer for the Los Angeles *Times*, in 1917. A Delmar Watson Los Angeles Historical Archives photograph

George Watson captured an Odd Couple in 1935—physicist Albert Einstein and comedian Charlie Chaplin. Mrs. Einstein is on the right. A Delmar Watson Los Angeles Historical Archives photograph

Photographer R. C. Hickman, 1949, by unknown photographer. Courtesy Barker Texas History Center, The University of Texas at Austin

"Buddies in the Army can't be Buddies in the Melba," Melba Theater, Dallas, Texas, March 1955. Photograph by R. C. Hickman. Courtesy Barker Texas History Center, The University of Texas at Austin

Another kind of drama was caught by R. C. Hickman of Mineola, Texas. After serving as an Army photographer during World War II, Hickman returned to Texas, worked as a darkroom technician, took a photography course, and began recording life in the African American community for the Dallas *Express*, Kansas City *Call*, and Dallas *Star Post*. In addition, he freelanced for *Jet* magazine, several Eastern newspapers, and the National Association for the Advancement of Colored People.

While Dallas's mainstream media usually failed to report demonstrations against racial segregation, Hickman documented the events with his Speed Graphic, despite the danger. "I stood with one foot on the running board of a Buick and one on the ground. I had my camera cocked and the engine running."[25] Once a car full of white racists chased him from Mansfield to Fort Worth. He escaped by dashing into a friend's funeral home.

Hickman not only caught the demonstrations and the car wrecks but the visits of such celebrities as Joe Louis, Nat King Cole, and Martin Luther King, Jr., who, because of racial discrimination by local hotels, stayed in private homes. Hickman also captured ordinary people— "Bobbie the Newsboy" delivering the *Star Post*, a Navy son arriving home, friends around a piano singing Christmas carols, men working at Mac's Texaco station.

Two generations after Hickman entered journalism, photographer Michel duCille, also black, could gain wide recognition of his talents. DuCille left his hometown of Kingston, Jamaica, at fifteen, worked as a photographer for the *Times*, Gainesville, Georgia, during high school, graduated from Indiana University, and joined the Miami *Herald* as an intern in May 1980, just in time for a real trial by fire. "I arrived on the 16th," duCille said. "The [Liberty City] riots started the 17th."[26]

His skill as a street reporter led to assignments abroad—the invasion of Grenada and a volcano disaster in Colombia for which he (along with Carol Guzy) was awarded a Pulitzer Prize in 1986. But he retained a fondness for portraying city life. "I like the beach area because it has so much diversity. It has old people, a very small group of blacks, [and] Mariels."[27]

In 1987, convinced that the *Herald*'s coverage of cocaine abuse had dealt too exclusively with the excesses of white professionals, he undertook an essay about the drug's impact on one public housing project called the Graveyard. He moved in, became just another black face, and took photos for weeks. The resulting essay not only won duCille a second Pulitzer Prize but caused the transformation of the housing project and even affected the lives of some of the addicts. On November 8, 1987, Judy Williams, a crack addict described in "The Graveyard" essay, graduated from a six-month drug rehabilitation program.[28]

The 1972 reporting of the Washington *Post*'s Robert Woodward and Carl Bernstein on the Watergate scandal developed links between President Richard Nixon's aides and a burglary at Democratic National Committee headquarters. Nicholas Gage, formerly an investigative reporter for the New York *Times*, said: "The reason the other papers missed out on Watergate, in my opinion, is that they tried to cover it like any other story—on the phone—whereas Woodward and Bernstein were out there ringing doorbells."[29] Bernstein agreed: "For every sale, you had fifty rejects. . . . We went back to several places several times, were thrown out again and again, and then maybe on the fourth time, they will say, 'Okay, we'll talk to you.'"[30]

The reporters whose work tormented the Nixon Administration were an odd couple: Woodward, middle-class son of an Illinois judge, Yale graduate, veteran of five years in the Navy, only nine months of daily newspaper experience; Bernstein, son of a Communist Party union man, college dropout, long-haired rebel, all-night carouser who had written his first newspaper article at age sixteen. "There are only two similarities between me and Woodward," Bernstein

Michel duCille won a second Pulitzer Prize for his photographic essay on drug abuse in a Miami public housing project. Courtesy of The Miami *Herald*

Bob Woodward and Carl Bernstein, two largely unknown street reporters who helped fell a President. Photograph by Ken Feil. **Courtesy The Washington** *Post*

said. "One thing is that neither of us ever takes 'no' for an answer. And the other is that we usually made up our own assignments. Long before Watergate."[31]

But editors saw two other similarities. Leonard Downie, now the *Post*'s managing editor, spoke of a drive born of insecurity to write stories that would make the front page.[32] Though Woodward was stuck with the 7 P.M.-to-3 A.M. beat at police headquarters, he earned more Page One by-lines than any other reporter on the metropolitan staff.

Downie also mentioned guile. Woodward and Bernstein visited the homes of employees of the Committee to Re-Elect the President. The reporters told the employees that other unnamed CREEP personnel said they might be willing to talk. That was a lie, but it began useful conversations. "You act differently with different people,"

Bernstein explained. "You adapt different roles and ploys depending on who you're talking to. You get to know their prejudices and play to them. You've got to bullshit some."[33]

Most important, Woodstein, as the two reporters came to be called, unearthed elements of the Watergate scandal in the manner of regular street reporters, not White House correspondents. They bird-dogged from the bottom up, Bernstein said, "finding secretaries, clerks, and middle-level aides . . . [V]ery often you will get a much better version of the truth from them than you would get from their superiors or the target you're after."[34]

Harry Rosenfeld, the *Post* editor who ran the metropolitan staff, said: "It wasn't an accident that the metro staff got the Watergate story."[35] Watergate required the shoeleather of the street reporter.

2 Persuader

Shaping the Issues of the Day

Persuaders offer opinion and interpret news. They provide images in words and pictures that often influence our thinking and our understanding of events. Persuaders are editorialists, cartoonists, photographers, columnists, and, as in the case of Horace Greeley, editors who are as eccentric as they are eloquent.

In the spring of 1862, Greeley, editor of the New York *Tribune*, worried about how the Civil War would end. General George B. McClellan, whom Greeley had touted as a "young Napoleon," was promising Union victories—but delivering none. With war costs at two million to three million dollars a day, the Lincoln Administration was heading toward insolvency. Britian and France seemed ready to recognize the Confederacy as a separate nation.

Greeley wanted the immediate emancipation of the slaves. He liked a law Congress had just passed: Slaves who came under Union military control were confiscated. If the North adopted that policy everywhere, Greeley thought, the Union armies' ranks would be swelled by four hundred thousand black men. And the British and French, who despised slavery, would see that the North was really fighting a crusade to free the slaves.[1]

But President Lincoln and his commanders shied away from using the confiscation law. Greeley presented a case for emancipation designed to persuade, not antagonize, Lincoln. An editorial campaign culminated on August 20 in a dramatic open letter to the president. Entitled "The Prayer of Twenty Millions," the open letter pleaded with Lincoln to enforce the confiscation law. Twenty million northerners, Greeley contended, were praying for the president to put an

end to slavery. The editorial had the effect of nudging the president, who already had drafted the Emancipation Proclamation, to act. "It is the beginning of the new life of the nation," the *Tribune* cheered, "GOD BLESS ABRAHAM LINCOLN!"[2]

Horace Greeley may have been beloved in his native America, but in England he was regarded as a backwoods bumpkin. *Vanity Fair*, an English publication, made Greeley a target during his 1872 campaign for the presidency. Library of Congress, General Collections

Picketing a Hearst newspaper, Heywood Broun epitomized the persuader as daringly direct outsider. Courtesy Wide World

Judge Magazine artist Grant E. Hamilton begs help of Henry Watterson in this watercolor cartoon, dated June 7, 1909. Library of Congress, Manuscript Division

The open letter's success signaled Greeley's influence. His weekly and daily *Tribune* reached one and a half million Americans.[3] Emerson joked that Greeley provided all the "thinking and theory" for midwestern farmers "at two dollars a year."[4]

The open letter also was characteristic of two Greeleys. First, there was Greeley the showman-soul-saver who used a simple, logical writing style to preach the gospel of reform. He rejected slavery and capital punishment. He advocated labor unions, serving as the first president of the New York Printers' Union. He promoted a homestead law and other measures that would allow the poor to settle the West. He opposed the sale of liquor. He favored keeping public schools open day and night so that all could attend.

Second, the open letter on freeing the slaves showed Greeley the man of contradictions; less than two years earlier, he had argued for letting the slave-holding South leave the Union in peace. He exhibited other paradoxes too. He hired Margaret Fuller, the first woman to serve as a regular staffer on a major American newspaper. But he offered no support to women's suffrage. He preached conservative Whiggism. Yet he embraced a form of socialism that led him to offer shares in the *Tribune* for sale to its staff. He preached pacifism. But, when it came to the Civil War, his paper roared: "Forward to Richmond! Forward to Richmond!"[5]

Nevertheless, Greeley raised the art of writing editorials—which occupied up to one-quarter of the nonadvertising space in the *Tribune*—to a new level of advocacy.[6]

He was not alone. After the Civil War, Henry Watterson and Joel Chandler Harris were loyal Southerners who came to write persuasively about the change required in the New South if the once divided nation was to reunite.

A rebel by his Tennessee heritage, Watterson served briefly in the Confederate army from 1861 to 1862. He then became editor of the Chattanooga *Rebel*. Candid war reporting and flamboyant editorials—Watterson berated Lincoln as "a rude, vulgar, obscure, backwoods pettifogger"[7]—made the *Rebel* the paper most widely read by Confederate soldiers.

In 1865, Watterson helped resuscitate the *Republican Banner* in Nashville. He editorialized in favor of national reconciliation and proposed "The New Departure"—diversified farming and northern investment to stimulate southern development. His success with the *Banner* led in 1868 to his editorship (and one-third ownership) of the Louisville *Courier-Journal*, a paper he edited for fifty-one years. Watterson's view of the paper as persuader was reflected in its staffing: the *Courier-Journal* had ten editorial writers, more than the number of reporters.

Watterson successfully fought a state law that barred testimony by African Americans against whites. He doubted the wisdom of social equality, but argued for acceptance of the Fourteenth and Fifteenth Amendments, seeing them as "the real Treaty of Peace between the North and South . . . . The political emancipation of the blacks was essential to the moral emancipation of the whites."[8] His lecture tours, which described "The Comicalities and Whimsicalities of Southern Life," dismissed the differences between Northerners and Southerners as "purely exterior." All Americans were alike.

That was Joel Chandler Harris's message too, communicated through the dialect stories of Uncle Remus and other characters from the Old and New South. Harris entered journalism at age thirteen as a typesetter for *The Countryman*, the first plantation newspaper. The year was 1862 and Turnwold in rural Georgia was unable to escape the trauma of the Civil War. Another fourteen years would pass before Harris, as associate editor of the Atlanta *Constitution*, would transform his Turnwold experiences into Uncle Remus stories.

The *Constitution* was the South's leading voice in the 1870s in favor of an economic and literary renaissance. Associate Editor Henry W. Grady pushed for industrial growth. Harris called for a new literature of the South—"an enlarged vision, broad sympathies and national views . . . absolutely removed from . . . the prejudices to which sectionalism gives rise."[9] Harris concluded: "The result must . . . be American, otherwise it will not survive."[10]

Harris wrote dozens of editorial-page stories—and eighteen books—about Uncle Remus and friends before his retirement from the *Constitution* in 1900. He actually created two Uncle Remuses. The first struggled to survive postwar Atlanta and regularly visited the *Constitution* office where he expounded on party politics, the Ku Klux Klan, and current events. The second, a plantation slave with great wit and wisdom, evolved into the teller of African American folk tales. The image of the second Uncle Remus might suggest that Harris was only demeaning African Americans. The old man says education would ruin his people; a beating is better than book-learning.[11] But Harris's intent was to promote the reconciliation of North and South.

An 1887 story capsulized Harris's position.[12] In "Aunt Fountain's Prisoner," Ferris Trunion, a disabled Union soldier brought back to health in the South, stays there to rebuild a war-devastated plantation—"a practical illustration of the fact that one may be a Yankee and a Southerner too simply by being a large-hearted, whole-souled American."[13]

The creator of "Uncle Remus," Joel Chandler Harris. Photograph by Frances B. Johnston, 1906. Library of Congress, Prints and Photographs Division

Homer Davenport was the persuader as editorial cartoonist. Born in Silverton, Oregon, he trained for cartooning by working as a jockey, circus clown, and railroad engine wiper. By 1892, at age twenty-five, he was drawing at ten dollars a week for the San Francisco *Examiner*, making suggestions for cartoons that were, a fellow staffer recalled, "really ten years ahead of the times."[14] Davenport's biting caricatures caught William Randolph Hearst's eye. After Hearst purchased the New York *Journal*, he invited Davenport east in 1895.

Hearst alone among the publishers of the most important eastern papers supported Democrat William Jennings Bryan for the presidency in 1896. The *Journal* editorially lynched Bryan's Republican opponent, William McKinley, by charging that he was the tool of Mark Hanna, a millionaire industrialist from Cleveland. Hearst's most effective weapon was Davenport's cartoons—McKinley, the "syndicate-owned

Republican campaign manager Mark Hanna, Homer Davenport's favorite target, is said to have cried out, "It hurts . . . I tell you it hurts." Davenport drawing in *The New York Journal*, November 8, 1896. Library of Congress, Prints and Photographs Division

MARK HANNA AS HE IS AND AS DAVENPORT MADE HIM.

candidate" as Hanna's slave, and Hanna as the gargantuan monster, his clothes covered with dollar signs, his eyes reduced to tiny dots, his ears almost as large as a baby elephant's.

Davenport became New York's best-paid cartoonist.[15] His cartoons brought Hanna to tears: "That hurts . . . to be held up to the gaze of the world as a murderer of women and children. I tell you it hurts."[16] After the 1896 election, Hanna visited Davenport at his home in East Orange, New Jersey, pleading without success for him to at least excise the dollar signs from the cartoons. At their first public meeting, Hanna said, "I admire your genius and execution, but damn your conception."[17]

Davenport's other memorable caricatures included a sympathetic rendition of Uncle Sam and a personification of the trusts as muscle-bound behemoths wearing grass skirts and carrying blacksnake whips. When the coal operators agreed to arbitration with the union, Davenport drew the coal trust gorilla flattened and helpless, with a petite miner's daughter walking over his prone form carrying a full coal scuttle.

In 1904, a one-thousand-dollars-a-week salary lured Davenport to the Republican New York *Evening Mail*. With Hanna on his death bed, Davenport drew a sentimental scene, a concerned Uncle Sam taking Hanna's pulse. He also drew "He's good enough for me"—"the greatest vote-getting cartoon in American history"[18]— depicting Uncle Sam with his left hand placed approvingly on the shoulder of Republican presidential candidate Theodore Roosevelt. But Davenport, ally of the Republican establishment, lacked the bite of Davenport, destroyer of Republicans. He returned to cartooning for Hearst. Davenport's death came in 1912, after he worked for a week despite sickness to capture the horror of the Titanic's sinking.

Walter Lippmann and Heywood Broun variously epitomized the persuader as cool, sophisticated insider, and as disheveled, daringly direct outsider. Each man graduated from a New York private school, attended Harvard, class of

1910, and went on to write opinion pieces in the 1920s for the Pulitzer family's New York *World*—"the Great Temple of the newspaper industry."[19] Lippmann, who for forty years would be described as the country's most influential syndicated columnist, dressed the role of the suave insider: well-tailored, pin-striped suit, bowler hat, and walking stick. He wanted the respect—and the ear—of the informed elite, not the "great mass of boobs."[20] He tried behind the scenes to make the system work, helping Woodrow Wilson formulate his Fourteen Points, tutoring Dwight Eisenhower for the presidency, advising President Lyndon Johnson on Vietnam. Lippmann functioned, said one observer, as "a one-man State Department."[21]

Broun, a large, rumpled man, who, it was said, looked like an unmade bed, sipped gin and bitters from a battered flask he carried in his left hip pocket. He was the feisty outsider. He put his career on the line with "It Seems to Me," a col-

Walter Lippmann. Original painting and collage by Al Hirschfeld. Courtesy, Collection of Paul Neely, Chattanooga, Tennessee

umn that, Arthur Krock said, "set the Hudson afire almost every day."[22] And he put others' careers on the line when he founded the American Newspaper Guild. In a Staten Island saloon, he persuaded Alexander Crosby at a meeting of Staten Island *Advance* reporters to raise his hand in favor of the Guild. Crosby was fired shortly thereafter. Broun hired him to choose columns for a book collection.

The differences in the persuader as outsider and the persuader as insider showed themselves in the controversy surrounding Nicola Sacco and Bartolomeo Vanzetti, Italian-born anarchists sentenced to death for two Massachusetts murders. Governor Alvan Fuller appointed a three-man commission headed by A. Lawrence Lowell, president of Harvard, to second the guilty verdict or recommend a new trial or clemency. The commission concurred in the guilty verdict. Lippmann, in the *World*'s lead editorial, applauded the Lowell report for its fairness. But four days later, after being berated by influential friends, Lippmann wrote an editorial asking the Lowell commission to explain why the judge's prejudice did not make a new trial necessary.

Broun, who described Lippmann as the "greatest carrier of water on both shoulders since Rebecca at the well,"[23] growled in his column: "It is not every prisoner who has a President of Harvard University throw on the switch for him."[24] The next day, Broun snapped: "From now on, I want to know, will the institution of learning in Cambridge which once we called Harvard be known as Hangman's House?"[25] The *World*'s publisher, without argument from Lippmann, refused to print any additional Broun columns about the case. Broun sent two more anyway. They were not published.

Broun wrote: "By now I am willing to admit that I am too violent, too ill-disciplined, too indiscreet to fit pleasantly into the *World*'s philosophy of daily journalism."[26] Eventually, following another quarrel, the *World* fired Broun for "disloyalty."[27] Two years later, it promoted Lippmann to executive editor.

No freedom of press about race

Race—slavery, lynching, or segregation—has been an issue about which journalists have either echoed local community opinion or risked ostracism, financial ruin, and even the threat of death.

On October 21, 1835, a Boston mob captured William Lloyd Garrison, editor of the abolitionist *Liberator,* and pulled him through the streets with a rope around his body. Mayor Theodore Lyman halted the mob and helped hustle Garrison into jail, where he spent a night in protective custody.

A Southern editor suspected of "squinting toward abolitionism" could expect to be forced by the Southern code into a duel. Or he could anticipate having his newspaper destroyed. James G. Birney tried in 1835 to start an anti-slavery paper in a half-dozen Kentucky towns. The opposition made sure printers were bought out or coerced. A postmaster told Birney his incendiary paper would be kept from the mail. When Birney began publishing across the Ohio River in Cincinnati, a mob—in full view of the mayor—demolished Birney's printing press.

The Louisville *Journal's* George D. Prentice, one of many Southern editors raised in the North and "originally educated to think slavery wrong,"[1] got the message. He adopted the pro-slavery position of his community.[2] Cassius Clay, a temperate spokesman for "gradual and constitutional emancipation,"[3] outfitted the office of his *True American,* in Lexington, Kentucky, with two brass cannons, a trap door to the roof for escape, and a powder keg positioned to blow up the office and its invaders should they gain control. Despite Clay's precautions, a mob in 1845 removed the *True American's* presses to Cincinnati, effectively killing the newspaper.

The Richmond *Enquirer's* reaction was typical of Southern newspapers. It supported the Kentucky mob and dismissed Clay as a "fiery fanatic."[4] Southern editors did not feel that their freedom of speech was denied, explained historian Clement Eaton, "because they had no desire to publish antislavery articles."[5] On the issue of race, Southern newspapers were, in the words of Hodding Carter, almost unanimously "irreconcilable spokesmen of hate."[6]

That role did not end with the Civil War and the Emancipation Proclamation. As late as the 1960s, a Southern newspaper that went against the segregationist majority faced retaliation, as Harry Golden could attest. Golden kept alive his monthly, *The Carolina Israelite,* from 1942 to 1968, pumping sixty-two thousand dollars of his own money into it during its last three years. Earlier, he had used royalties from such humorous best-sellers as *Only In America* to offset an advertising boycott orchestrated by white supremacists.[7]

Golden's paper was one of only a handful below the Mason-Dixon line to cheer the U.S. Supreme Court's 1954 school desegregation decision. Writing from the paper's offices—two old houses on the edge of downtown Charlotte, North Carolina—he used wit as his weapon. Recognizing that bank counters, supermarkets, and department stores allowed whites and blacks to stand in the same lines, Golden proposed his "Vertical Negro Plan": Take the seats out of schools and have all students stand at their desks.[8]

Golden also implemented his "Out-of-Order Plan" by persuading a department store owner to turn off the water to a "White Only" fountain and slap on an "Out of Order" sign. Within three days, Golden wrote, whites—without even a whimper of complaint—were drinking "segregated water" from the "Negro" fountain.

When asked toward the end of his life why he helped the cause of civil rights for blacks, Golden said, "I didn't do it for the 'Negroes,' I did it for America." But America, as had been apparent to generations of journalists, did not always appreciate the help.

Harry Golden at his desk. Harry Golden Papers. Courtesy Special Collections, J. Murray Atkins Library, the University of North Carolina at Charlotte

Frances Benjamin Johnston was the persuader as photojournalist, making a Progressive's points about America.

Johnston attempted to photograph deep underground a "hopelessly black" coal mine in Shenandoah City, Pennsylvania.[28] Despite the danger from using a magnesium powder flash and despite an atmosphere "fogged and heavy with dampness, smoke, and a fine, gritty dust,"[29] she managed in four hours to get three powerful images of workers—some who looked to be only twelve years old.

She also photographed men mining iron in the Mesabi Range of Minnesota, women making shoes in a Massachusetts factory, students at Hampton Institute in Virginia at work on the stairway of the treasurer's house, and nearby rural blacks—only a generation or two from slavery—who remained unschooled, unskilled, and impoverished.

In addition, Johnston captured the lives of Washington's famous, earning the sobriquet "photographer of the American Court." She undoubtedly was not hurt by her reputation as a bourbon-belting Bohemian who, when it came time for entry to the White House, could transform herself into what one biographer called "a properly conventional Victorian woman."[30]

In this 1896 self-portrait, Frances B. Johnston violates three cardinal Victorian rules. Proper Victorian women were not to reveal their legs, use tobacco, or drink beer. Library of Congress, Prints and Photographs Division

H. L. Mencken, the persuader as venomous
iconoclast, in 1928. Library of Congress, Prints and
Photographs Division

H.L.MENCKEN
1524 HOLLINS ST.
BALTIMORE.

May 5th

Dear Mr. White:-

　　　　The Christian Advocate is right.　From the standpoint
of the average man it is certainly a damned sight better to have
good schools, reliable bichloride tablets, cement sidewalks and
good country butter than it is to have a town full of Beethovens.
Beethoven, as a citizen, was anything but ideal.　He drank too much,
he kept a dirty house, he was forever having lawsuits, and there is
grave ground for suspicion that he sometimes stooped to fornication.
Let us look at the other fellow's viewpoint.　Such things offend him.　No
wonder he is against them.　I believe thoroughly that the Beethovens
are tolerable only to a small minority of men, and admirable only to
a still smaller one.
　　　　I think I'll do a piece on the subject for the Evening
Sunpaper.　The enclosed shows that Maryland takes the same general view
that Kansas takes.　I believe that this Messenger of Federalsburg
is a very typical Marylander.

Sincerely yours,

Mencken reveals his acerbic wit in this letter to William
Allen White, dated May 5, 1922. Library of Congress,
Manuscript Division

H. L. Mencken, Baltimore's best-known
newspaperman, was the persuader as venomous iconoclast. He was, of course, much more—literary critic, political theorist, ethicist, philosopher, and philologist. But his reputation, despite his versatility, rests on what he called "journalism pure and simple—dead almost before the ink which printed it was dry."[31]

A Baltimore *Herald* reporter by the age of eighteen, he became, seven years later, in 1906, city editor of the Baltimore *Sun*, his journalistic home until his death in 1956. (His pro-German views before America's entry into World War I— he wrote in 1917 about the Germans' fight for "freedom and their right to exist as a nation"[32]— forced him to work for the New York *Evening Mail* in 1917–18; following war's end, he was invited to return to the Sunpapers.)

Mencken's *Sun* columns and monthly columns for *The Smart Set* magazine and later the *American Mercury* magazine (both of which he edited) were designed for "stirring up the animals."[33] He stilettoed politicians, preachers, professionals, patriotism, and Puritanism, which he described as "the haunting fear that someone, somewhere, may be happy."[34]

When he was asked to assess the *Sun*'s editorial page, he criticized the editorials in language that explained his own invective: "Too cautious . . . excess of politeness. . . . It is also useful to remember that most men are convinced, not by appeals to their reason, but by appeals to their emotions and prejudices."[35] Mencken chose *Prejudices* as the generic title for six volumes setting forth his opinions. His own prejudices— including anti-Semitism ("dreadful kikes")[36] and racism—were openly expressed in his diary.

An attack on American journalism in *The Smart Set* typified his vituperative tone: "The *average* American newspaper, *especially* of the so-called better sort, has the intelligence of a Baptist evangelist, the courage of a rat, the fairness of a Prohibitionist boob-bumper, the information of a high-school janitor, the taste of a designer of celluloid valentines, and the honor of a police-

Hodding Carter, the country editor as gentle persuader. For his 1955 *Look Magazine* article attacking the Citizens' Councils, Carter was branded a liar by the Mississippi House of Representatives. Courtesy Mitchell Memorial Library, Mississippi State University

station lawyer."[37] Most of the blame, Mencken later wrote, should not be heaped on newspaper owners, but on "the stupidity, cowardice and Philistinism of working newspaper men. The majority of them, in almost every American city, are still ignoramuses, and proud of it."[38]

Hodding Carter of the *Delta Democrat-Times* in Greenville, Mississippi, was the country editor as gentle persuader. In 1932, Carter was told by his Associated Press boss in New Orleans that he "would never make a newspaperman."[39] He and his wife, Betty, returned to Hammond, his hometown sixty miles to the north, and converted a mimeographed, throwaway advertising weekly into a four-page tabloid, the *Daily Courier*.

During a month with a half-dozen murders, he angered locals by suggesting in a front-page editorial that Hammond was the most logical site for a small-arms-and-ammunition plant. All production would be used up locally, guaranteed. Carter himself was forced to pack a gun because of his crusade against Huey Long, potentate of Louisiana politics. The Carters sold their paper in 1936 and moved to Greenville. They started a new afternoon daily, the *Delta Star*, that soon devoured the competing *Democrat-Times*.

The *Delta Democrat-Times* wasn't just "a one-issue newspaper," Betty Carter recalled.[40] But it established a national reputation—its position in the Deep South on race was so unusual—as a voice against segregation and discrimination. Carter won a Pulitzer Prize in 1946 for editorials condemning intolerance. In a moderate's language, he criticized the poll tax, school segregation, and the subjective literacy test that kept black citizens who comprised half of the area's population from voting. Carter also spoke as a moderate about a Southern town's bigotry in his 1941 novel, *The Winds of Fear*: "If you have not lived in Carvell City it is too easy to denounce its masters, forgetting that they are also the slaves of the fear which impels them."[41]

But, as one historian has written, "To be a moderate on segregation was to be radical in the South."[42] In 1955, following *Look* Magazine's publication of an article by Carter critical of the White Citizens Councils, the Mississippi House of Representatives voted—on April 1, appropriately—to declare that he was a liar.

Carter fired off an editorial retort to the lawmakers' 89-to-19 resolution: "I herewith resolve by a vote of 1 to 0 that there are 89 liars in the State Legislature . . . . I am hopeful that this fever[,] like the Ku Kluxism which rose from the same kind of infection, will run its course before too long a time. Meanwhile those 89 character mobbers can go to hell collectively or singly and wait there until I back down. They needn't plan on returning."[43]

Abolitionist crusader Elijah Lovejoy died defending his press. Frontispiece in John F. Trow's *Alton Trials* (New York, 1838). Library of Congress, Rare Book and Special Collections Division

3 Crusader
Renegade, Revolutionary, and Rabble-rouser

The crusaders cut their eye-teeth on causes: abolition, equality for women, a new social order, political revolution. They often worked outside the journalistic mainstream. Sometimes, as with William Lloyd Garrison, moral outrage eclipsed factual reporting.

By 1828, Garrison found himself editing a rural Vermont weekly, *Journal of the Times* (Greeley called it "about the ablest and most interesting newspaper ever issued in Vermont").[1] On the subject of slavery, Garrison felt no need for understatement: "We are resolved to agitate the subject to the utmost; nothing but death shall prevent us from denouncing a crime which has no parallel in human depravity."[2] In 1829, Garrison assumed the co-editorship of a Baltimore weekly, *Genius of Universal Emancipation*. His call for instant, unconditional emancipation without compensation to slaveholders soon landed him in jail for criminal libel. "I am in prison," Garrison responded, "for denouncing slavery in a free country."[3] Released after seven weeks, he was threatened with another libel suit.

Garrison moved to Boston and, at the age of twenty-five, started a weekly, *The Liberator*. At first, the public responded to *The Liberator* with indifference; the paper could claim only five hundred subscribers after a year. But Garrison helped establish the American Anti-Slavery Society, which created 1,350 local branches. Soon laws were passed in the Southern states prohibiting African Americans from receiving *The Liberator*. Georgia placed a five-thousand-dollar bounty on Garrison's head. In Boston, handbills urged his tarring and feathering.

If the Union could not free itself from slavery, Garrison argued, then let it dissolve. In 1845, *The Liberator*'s motto became: "No Union with Slaveholders!"[4] But Garrison, the devoted non-participant in government, spoke out for Lincoln in the presidential campaign of 1860, seeing in his victory emancipation's likely realization. Lincoln's election caused Wendell Phillips to say: "Lincoln is in *place*, Garrison is in *power*."[5] The Thirteenth Amendment, which abolished slavery in 1865, led Garrison to close down *The Liberator* on its thirty-fifth anniversary. The *Nation* called his crusade "perhaps the most remarkable instance on record of a single-hearted devotion to a cause."[6]

Nameplate of *The Liberator*, an Abolitionist weekly started in Boston in 1831 by William Lloyd Garrison. Library of Congress, General Collections

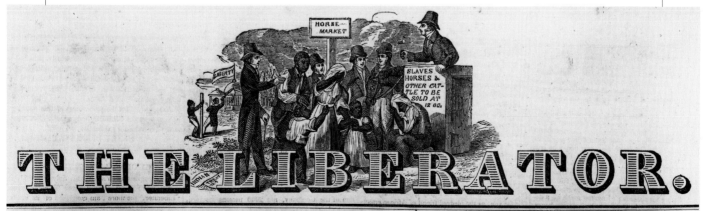

VOL. I.]   WILLIAM LLOYD GARRISON AND ISAAC KNAPP, PUBLISHERS.   [NO. 33.

BOSTON, MASSACHUSETTS.]   OUR COUNTRY IS THE WORLD—OUR COUNTRYMEN ARE MANKIND.   [SATURDAY, AUGUST 13, 1831.

Frederick Douglass escaped slavery via the underground railroad in 1838. Portrait attributed to Elisha Hammond. Courtesy National Portrait Gallery, Smithsonian Institution

Frederick Douglass, when asked where he gained his higher education, answered: "From Massachusetts University, Mr. Garrison, president."[7] Born a slave in 1817, Douglass escaped from Maryland to Massachusetts via the underground railroad in 1838. He promoted the cause of abolition by describing his slave experiences in speeches throughout the East and in England. He wrote an autobiographical *Narrative* in 1845 and, two years later, began publication in Rochester, New York, of a weekly, *The North Star*, later renamed *Frederick Douglass' Paper*, which continued in monthly form until August 1863, midway through the Civil War.

Douglass discontinued his paper, he explained in a "Valedictory," so that he could go south to organize African American soldiers "who shall win for the millions in bondage the inestimable blessings of liberty and country."[8]

Douglass wrote with great clarity. Alain Locke described his style as "pithy prose so different from the polished and often florid periods of his orations, a sort of Negro edition of Ben Franklin, reacting to the issues of his time with truly profound and unbiased sanity."[9] Douglass showed intellectual independence too. While Garrison described the Constitution as a proslavery document, Douglass argued it was "an antislavery instrument, demanding the abolition of slavery as a condition of its own existence as the supreme law of the land."[10]

Despite opposition—the New York *Herald* advised people to dump Douglass's press into Lake Ontario and banish him to Canada—Douglass used his newspaper to speak out on issues other than emancipation. He was also an early advocate of equality for women, equal education (including industrial training) for African Americans, and the right of African Americans to fight in the Civil War and receive the same pay and benefits as white Union soldiers. He took pride in the visits of curious white Southerners, "having, as they said, believed it impossible that an uneducated fugitive slave could write the articles attributed to me."[11]

Another abolitionist, Elijah Lovejoy, a St. Louis editor, started his career as a believer in slavery. However, embracing religion at a church revival, he studied for the Presbyterian ministry at Princeton, and returned home to assume editorship of the St. Louis *Observer*, a Presbyterian weekly, in 1833. His criticism of slavery provoked local mass meetings and charges that such "amalgamationist" talk was "seditious, and calculated to incite insurrection and anarchy."[12] In 1836, when a St. Louis mob burned a black man to death, Lovejoy responded with a furious editorial. A mob smashed his equipment and tossed it in the Mississippi River.

Lovejoy moved across the river to Alton, Illinois, where, again, his printing equipment was dumped in the river. But citizens raised money to buy another press and the first issue of Lovejoy's Alton *Observer* appeared on September 8, 1836. A year later, he advocated the establishment of an Illinois Anti-Slavery Society and addressed the irony of July 4 oratory about freedom—in a nation of slaves: "[E]ven that very flag of freedom that waves over our heads is formed from materials cultivated by slaves, on a soil moistened by their blood, drawn from them by the whip of a republican task-master."[13] Again, a mob demolished his presses.

His admirers raised money for a third press. It too was destroyed by a mob. Friends talked to Lovejoy about the wisdom of leaving Alton. He responded: "If the civil authorities refuse to protect me, I must look to God; and if I die, I have determined to make my grave in Alton."[14] While trying to protect his fourth press against a mob, he was shot five times and killed. The press was destroyed. The killers went unpunished. Garrison wrote: "Lovejoy died the representative of philanthropy and justice, liberty and Christianity: well, therefore, may his fall agitate Heaven and earth."[15]

Women, who had long set type in the back-shop and had kept family newspapers alive after the deaths of their husbands, crusaded for their rights in and out of the newsroom. Jane Grey Swisshelm founded the abolitionist Pittsburgh *Sunday Visiter* (the spelling was a matter of principle) in 1847. When she went to Washington in 1850 to write a column for her paper and for Horace Greeley's New York *Tribune*, she was relegated to the Senate public gallery. She asked Vice President Millard Fillmore for a seat in the Senate press gallery to hear a debate on slavery. He cautioned her that "the place would be very unpleasant for a lady . . . I would not like it."[16] But Swisshelm gained her seat, opening the press gallery to women.

Swisshelm urged that every woman, regardless of race, should be allowed to advance be-

Like many of her fellow crusaders, Jane Grey Swisshelm suffered from mob violence. In 1858 vigilantes destroyed her *St. Cloud Visiter* office, dumped the press in the street, and threw the type into the Mississippi River. Courtesy Minnesota Historical Society

yond menial work and substandard pay. In an 1853 collection of columns, *Letters to Country Girls*, she knifed male condescension: "But let one presume to use her mental powers—let her aspire to turn editor, public speaker, doctor, lawyer—take up any profession or avocation which is deemed honorable and requires talent, and O! bring cologne, get a cambric kerchief and feather fan, unloose his corsets and take off his cravat!"[17]

After giving birth to a child at age forty, Swisshelm resigned from the *Visiter* in 1857 and left her husband. He had given her some cause: He kept pet bears and a panther that once tried to devour her. She wrote about a woman's need,

In 1953, Ethel Payne became one of the first black women accredited to the White House press corps, where her probing questions on segregation soon raised the hackles of President Dwight Eisenhower. Photo from Eleventh Annual Communications Conference, Howard University School of Communications, Washington, D.C., 1982. Courtesy Ethel Payne

after "twenty years without the legal right to be alone one hour," for privacy and for property rights.[18] She moved to Minnesota and started the St. Cloud *Visiter.* After her press and type were destroyed and her business ruined by a libel suit, she launched a new paper, the St. Cloud *Democrat,* which she continued publishing until 1863.

Even after she left full-time journalism, Swisshelm remained a crusader. She traveled to Washington on a lecture tour, speaking against leniency for Sioux Indians charged with massacring white settlers (she advocated using poi-

soned bait to exterminate the "lazy, impudent beggars").[19]

About three generations later, the journalism career of syndicated columnist Ethel Payne began "by accident."[20] In 1948, she started keeping a diary of her experiences as an Army Special Services hostess stationed in a Tokyo quartermaster depot. President Harry Truman's order to integrate the Armed Forces was being ignored in Japan. When the Korean War began in 1950, black soldiers without combat training were pressed into battle. Alex Wilson, a war correspondent for the Chicago *Defender,* an African American weekly, came through Tokyo. He read Payne's diary and encouraged the *Defender* to publish excerpts.

Payne's writing caused an uproar. Allied headquarters, she said, accused her of disrupting troop morale and made her "a scapegoat for what was happening."[21] Her writing also resulted in a job offer from the *Defender.*

Assigned in 1953 to Washington, she became one of the first black women accredited to the White House press corps. In an era when civil rights was "on the back burner,"[22] she gave it high priority. At a White House press conference, she asked President Dwight Eisenhower: "Mr. President, the Interstate Commerce Commission has issued an opinion saying it is time to end segregation in interstate travel. When can we expect that you would give an executive order regarding this?"[23] An angry Eisenhower shot back: "What makes you think I'm going to do anything for any special interest? I am the president of all the people."[24] The Washington *Star* published a front-page article: "Negro Woman Reporter Angers Ike." Payne's mother, a Republican, telephoned: "Sister, I don't think you should be down there making the president mad."[25]

But the Washington *Post*'s Edward T. Folliard, dean of the White House press corps, reassured Payne: "Don't feel bad about what happened. You asked the question that we should have been asking."[26]

Almost three generations earlier, Thomas Nast, the cartoonist, conducted a six-year campaign in *Harper's Weekly* against local graft; he was widely credited with dethroning William Marcy Tweed, boss of New York's Tammany Hall. A draftsman at fifteen for *Frank Leslie's Illustrated Weekly*, Nast had covered Garibaldi's campaign in Italy and the American Civil War by the time he opened fire on the Tweed Ring in 1869. The four Tweed bosses were plundering the city. In only thirty months, they put thirty million dollars in their pockets and added fifty million dollars to the public debt (the work of one plasterer cost the city $2,807,464.06 in nine months).[27] Tweed bought support from much of the press, though early in 1870 the New York *Times* joined Nast in his attack (Tweed's offer of a one-million-dollar bribe to George Jones, manager and owner of the *Times*, was rejected).

To silence Nast, the Tweed Ring stripped Harper Brothers of a lucrative municipal text-book contract. But Fletcher Harper stood behind Nast. A subsequent bribe offer caused Nast to reply, "I shall be busy here for some time getting a gang of thieves behind the bars!"[28]

As the municipal election of 1872 approached, Nast intensified his attack. He achieved his objective—"hit the enemy between the eyes and knock him down"[29]—in two pre-election masterpieces, "A Group of Vultures Waiting for the Storm to 'Blow Over.' 'Let Us Prey'" and "The Tammany Tiger Loose—'What are you going to do about it?'" The public showed what it was going to do in the voting booth. The Tweed Ring, intimidated by a Nast cartoon of citizens placing their ballots in a wastebasket, permitted a relatively honest election. The Ring lost, and its leadership crumbled: some Tweed men confessed their crimes, some fled to Europe, some eventually died in prison.

Nast's Tweed Ring cartoons helped to triple *Harper's* circulation. He continued to find targets

"THE TAMMANY TIGER LOOSE.— **What are you going to do about it?**" Thomas Nast's powerful image of the Tweed Ring appeared in *Harper's Weekly*, November 11, 1871. Library of Congress, Prints and Photographs Division

for his pen in Horace Greeley, President "King Andy" Johnson, and the Catholic Church. His elephant and donkey symbols for the Republican and Democratic parties achieved lasting fame. When he quit *Harper's* in 1887, "Nast lost his forum," Henry Watterson said. "*Harper's Weekly* lost its political influence."[30]

To take on the press requires almost as much nerve as taking on the Tweed Ring. Few newspeople risk ostracism and publicly cite the failings of fellow journalists. Will Irwin and A. J. Liebling were two journalists willing to incur their peers' resentment.

Irwin, reporter of the 1906 San Francisco earthquake, muckraking editor of *McClure's*, and later a correspondent in World War I, wrote regularly about the press from 1909 to 1931. In a fifteen-part series for *Collier's*, Irwin attempted to go beyond "finding shame" to "making discoveries and formulating principles."[31] But he found plenty of shame: corporations subsidizing newspapers; newspapers trading favorable play reviews for full-page advertisements; editors suppressing stories about adulterated beer.

Irwin's pioneering 1911 series—the first on the press published by a mass-circulation magazine—drew attention to news columns supplanting the editorial page as the source of the press's influence. The series also raised questions about the nature of news. "News, as it works out in newspaper practice, amounts to gossip, the impressionist picture of truth," Irwin wrote. "It is gossip organized to our uses, subdued to our hand, and raised to both a science and an art."[32] Irwin did not try to pretend that reporters wrote objectively: "[T]ruth, illumined by a point of view, is the very kernel of the reporter's art . . . ."[33]

As if anticipating the end of the twentieth century, when corporate conglomerates would own three-fourths of the nation's daily newspapers, Irwin worried about the time when an individual proprietor—a Joseph Pulitzer or a William Rockhill Nelson—would give way to ownership by a company with shareholders:

"[W]hen its directors meet but to shave this year's expenses and increase next year's dividends, commercialism usually binds it . . . . If it approximate free journalism, it usually does so only because freedom may pay in the long run."[34] But Irwin was optimistic about the press of tomorrow not losing its independence. "The system will cure itself."[35]

Liebling, who wrote eighty-three "Wayward Press" articles, dozens of other *New Yorker* notes, and three books about the press between 1945 and his death in 1963, did not share Irwin's optimism. A former reporter for the New York *Times*, the Sunday *World*, and the *World-Telegram*, he saw the press as part of a larger social struggle—wealthy vs. poor, employer vs. employee, conservative vs. liberal. The publisher, invariably, was the villain.

Liebling sprinkled his criticism with recommendations: the establishment of foundation-endowed or labor-supported newspapers; the employment of more reporters for better local, Washington, and foreign coverage; the regular publication of corrections; the creation of a control newspaper (to appear hours after other papers and estimate the extent of their bias), and a school for publishers, "failing which, no school of journalism can have meaning."[36]

Liebling himself held out little hope that his advice would be followed: "[T]he longer I criticized the press, the more it disimproved."[37] But he reveled in the dissection. Liebling in 1953, for instance, wrote wittily about the death of Joseph Stalin, who "had the bad taste to die in installments."[38] Liebling compared newspapers' descriptions of Stalin's death: "Within a week after Stalin's announced demise, the American public knew that he had died of natural causes or been murdered subtly, either on the date named by *Pravda*, or several weeks earlier; that the people of Moscow had demonstrated grief but (a *Journal-American* scoop) the demonstration had been a carefully organized fake; that his death portended either a hardening or a softening of policy toward the West, which, in turn, would

E. W. Scripps and Joseph Pulitzer: paradoxical crusaders

E. W. Scripps, Joseph Pulitzer, and other newspaper owners who crusaded on behalf of the working class represented a certain paradox.

While championing the common folk, they indulged themselves with yachts and other trappings of uncommon wealth. While supporting the rights of workers to unionize, they welcomed unions at some of their own newspapers with less than open arms.[1] While dependent on advertising from capitalists, they espoused egalitarian views that those advertisers often interpreted as anti-capitalist.

Pulitzer came by his crusading zeal early. As a young reporter for the *Westliche Post,* a German-language newspaper in St. Louis, Pulitzer worked sixteen-hour days— 10 A.M. to 2 A.M.— trying, as a colleague wrote, "to root out public abuses and expose evildoers."[2]

In 1878, Pulitzer bought the St. Louis *Dispatch* at a sheriff's sale and combined it with the *Post.* The *Post-Dispatch* campaigned for the consumer and attacked monopolies, tax-dodges, illegal gambling, insurance-company scams, and the rental or lease of "homes to the frail sisterhood for immoral purposes."[3]

The New York *World,* which Pulitzer bought in 1883, dedicated itself to people. At the height of the Gilded Age, Pulitzer not only sought immigrants, tenement dwellers, and factory workers as readers, but he crusaded against the conditions that made their lives miserable.[4] As the paper that claimed, "Our aristocracy is the aristocracy of

E. W. Scripps. Courtesy Scripps Howard

John S. Sargent portrait of Joseph Pulitzer. Courtesy Pulitzer Publishing Company

labor,"[5] the *World,* unlike many other New York papers, reported labor news and defended the right of workers to strike, picket, bargain collectively, and impose secondary boycotts.

Edward Wyllis Scripps, born in Rushville, Illinois, in 1854, went from working on the family farm to helping start the *Detroit Evening News* in 1872, to owning a controlling interest, at one time or another, in fifty-two newspapers. With the motto of "Whatever is, is wrong," he saw himself as "the mouthpiece for those who have no other mouthpiece."[6]

Unlike other newspaper people, he carried his concern with the power of advertisers and other members of the "wealthier and more intellectual class"[7] to its logical conclusion. He restricted the quantity of advertising, holding the San Francisco *News,* for example, to three columns of ads. He twice tried to develop an adless newspaper, free from the possibility that advertisers would influence news content.

Scripps is remembered today mainly for being the first major newspaper chain owner and for reveling in his eccentricity. He wore a skullcap indoors to ward off colds. He claimed to smoke forty cigars and drink a gallon of whiskey a day. Prior to his marriage in 1885, he collected mistresses almost as fast as he bought newspapers. But he, like Pulitzer, also deserves to be remembered as that unusual paradox—an owner who amassed his millions by crusading for the millions.

lessen or increase the chances of open war; and that his death would either precipitate an immediate struggle for power among the surviving leaders or impel them to stand together until they got things running smoothly . . . . The subject permitted a rare blend of invective and speculation—both Hearst papers, as I recall, ran cartoons of Stalin being rebuffed at the gates of Heaven, where Hearst has no correspondents—and I have seldom enjoyed a week of newspaper reading more."[39]

A reader of Liebling's essays would not fail to understand that major dailies mutilated or missed important stories. But John Reed and Isidor Feinstein ("Izzy") Stone, examples of the crusader as dissident, targeted important issues overlooked by mainstream media.

Reed wrote for *The Masses*, a radical monthly journal (1911–1917) that focused on the plight of labor and other underpublicized topics, and published political cartoons by Robert Minor, Art Young, and John Sloan. *The Masses* carried Sloan's arresting drawing from the mine strike in Ludlow, Colorado,[40] and Reed's reporting from the silk-mill strike in Paterson, New Jersey. "The magazine of free expression" also charged a major journalistic institution, The Associated Press, with suppressing information in its reports of a West Virginia coal miners' strike. AP sued for libel. The August 1913 issue of *The Masses* requested "that all suits at law be postponed until fall, as our jail editor, John Reed, has gone to Europe."[41] AP eventually dropped its suit.

Reed, who had covered Pancho Villa's forays in Mexico for the El Paso *Herald*, went to Russia in 1917 to report the revolution for *The Masses*. (That year, the Post Office used the Espionage

John Sloan drew the 1914 Ludlow Massacre in Colorado's coal fields. Library of Congress, Prints and Photographs Division

John Reed, who reported the Russian Revolution, is the only American to be buried by the Kremlin wall. Library of Congress, Prints and Photographs Division

I. F. Stone, the crusader as dissident. UPI/Bettmann Newsphotos

Act to declare the magazine "unmailable," forcing it out of business in December 1917.) Writing as a radical partisan ("I have thousands of comrades here"[42]) Reed achieved the status of trusted insider. He was "about the only foreigner," said historian John Hohenberg, "who could work effectively at this period."[43]

I. F. Stone was a Washington gadfly pamphleteer—Henry Steele Commager called him "a modern Tom Paine"[44]—who kept his distance from the political establishment. He operated under the assumption that "every government is run by liars, and nothing they say should be believed."[45] A veteran of the New York Post, The Nation, and PM and its successors, the radical and his wife, Esther, published I. F. Stone's Weekly (and later Bi-Weekly), for almost two decades, 1953–1971. He dug revealing nuggets out of the Congressional Record, official transcripts, unread government documents, and dozens of newspapers, juxtaposing inconsistencies and exposing lies. "People read, but they miss most of what they see," said Peter Osnos, a Stone assistant who went on to the Washington Post. "Izzy misses nothing."[46]

I. F. Stone's Weekly started by assaulting the House Committee on Un-American Activities, the blacklist, and Senator Joseph McCarthy. Later it tackled the Pentagon, U.S. involvement in Vietnam, and the Atomic Energy Commission. In Jerry Bruck, Jr.'s documentary film, I. F. Stone's Weekly, Stone describes how he proved the AEC had lied about a crucial issue in Soviet-American test-ban negotiations. The AEC, apparently interested in undermining the negotiations, said underground tests could not be detected beyond 200 miles. Remembering a New York Times article in which the Soviet Union proposed atomic monitoring stations 580 miles apart, Stone interviewed U.S. government seismologists—"I don't think they'd seen a reporter since Noah"—who described monitoring Nevada tests from Washington, a distance of more than 2000 miles. After Stone published his findings, the AEC publicly confessed that it had lied.

"The establishment reporters know a lot of things I don't know," Stone said. "But a lot of what they know isn't true, and a lot of what they know that is true they can't report."[47] When President John Kennedy was assassinated, few journalists went beyond uncritical eulogy. Stone, noting that "funerals are always occasions for pious lying,"[48] wrote that Kennedy "was a conventional leader, no more than an enlightened conservative, cautious as an old man for all his youth, with a basic distrust of the people . . . ."[49]

Stone's four-page newsletter, which reached a circulation of seventy thousand, was a yardstick for investigative reporters, who, like Stone, saw their work as a crusade.[50]

Elizabeth ("Nellie Bly") Cochrane's investigative stories earned her the reputation of being the "best reporter in America." Library of Congress, Prints and Photographs Division

4 Investigator

Uncovering the Veiled and Hidden

Investigators, reporters with a low threshold of indignation, practice what David Kraslow calls high-risk journalism. For their work—challenging muddy morality, attacking conflicts of interest, uncovering cover-ups—they often are rewarded with greater official secrecy and public indifference.

Elizabeth Cochrane earned her greatest fame for her 1888–1889 trip around the world in seventy-two days, six hours, eleven minutes, and fourteen seconds. The trip culminated in front-page hyperbole by the New York *World* ("FATHER TIME OUTDONE!"), songs that shouted her praise, and games, clothes, and a race horse that bore her pen name: Nellie Bly.

But she also deserves to be remembered for her first-person investigative reporting. She was not only a "stunt girl" who went up in a balloon, down in a diving bell, and around the world, but a skilled I-was-there investigator. To persuade the *World* to hire her in 1887, she faked madness, convinced three doctors that she deserved admittance to Blackwell's Island, and exposed the treatment at the "human rat trap"[1] of an insane asylum. The patients, she wrote, ate garbage. Those in need of a bath were doused with buckets of ice water. A grand jury supported Bly's reports, the asylum overhauled its management, and three million dollars in improvements were made.

In the era of "Fair Woman's World"—a *World* page decorated with flowers, music notes, and a lady with a fan and a bustle—Bly documented the inadequacies of city prisons, free dispensaries, factories, tenements, and nursing homes. She wrote with high moral indignation. A ten-column account in 1893 of her days as a Salvation Army worker resulted in major support for the charity. An exposé about an Albany lobbyist—described as a "briber . . . and boodler"[2]—netted the names of the capital's corruptible politicians.

At age twenty-nine, she married Robert L. Seaman, a seventy-two-year-old hardware manufacturer. After his death in 1904, she tried to run his factory, went bankrupt, and returned to journalism. In a 1920 New York *Journal* story, she dramatized a campaign against capital punishment by detailing the Sing Sing execution of Gordon Hamby. In the style of the twenties, she ended her tale: "The horribleness of life and death. Through my mind flitted the thought that one time this young boy going to the death chair had been welcomed by some fond mother. He had been a babe, lo, loved and cherished. And this is the end . . . ."[3] Two years later, Bly died of pneumonia. The *Evening Journal* said succinctly: "She was the best reporter in America."[4]

Traveling by steamship, railroad, and horse-drawn cart, "Nellie Bly" in 1889 went round the world in just over seventy-two days, easily beating Jules Verne's fictional record. Nellie Bly board game. Courtesy New York Public Library

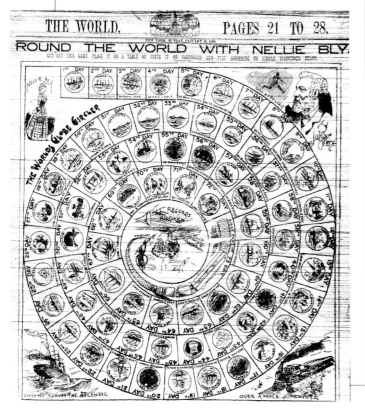

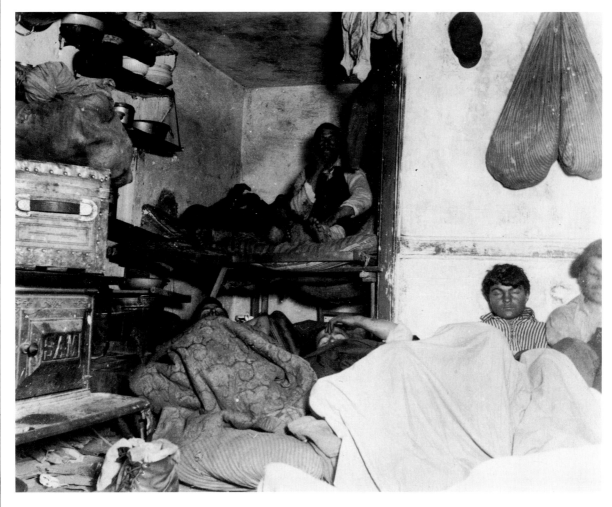

"Five cents a spot," photograph by Jacob Riis or an assistant. Riis exposed the wretched living conditions in New York City's tenement districts. Library of Congress, Prints and Photographs Division

Another New York reporter, Danish immigrant Jacob Riis, turned a mundane newspaper beat—that of the night police reporter—into classic investigations of the city's slums. At the end of the nineteenth century, while others on Riis's beat rewrote police reports, he documented street life for the *Evening Sun*. Each dawn after work he insisted on slowly walking, not riding, through one of the city's most depressing precincts: "I liked to walk, for I saw the slum when off its guard."[5]

"Riis was interested not at all in vice and crime," fellow journalist Lincoln Steffens wrote, but "only in the stories of people and the conditions in which they lived."[6] Riis's *How the Other Half Lives* (1890), based on his first twelve years

as a police reporter, prompted nationwide action: sermons, volunteer house-to-house surveys, and investigations. The book became a call to action for state regulation, slum clearance, and public housing. Theodore Roosevelt called it "an enlightenment and an inspiration."[7]

Riis described the camera as his ally in the fight against the slums. But it was a costly ally: "Twice I set fire to the house with the apparatus, and once to myself."[8] Much of Riis's writing is dated and demeaning. He characterized Italians as "swarthy"[9] and "ignorant,"[10] and Jews as people for whom "[m]oney is . . . God."[11] But his photos are timeless, even though their full force could not be realized in the *Sun*, where they were translated into crude wood engravings.[12] Riis's primitive camera required a shutter speed of a second or more, encouraging a posed woodenness. Yet he captured the darkness and confinement of the narrow alleys, and, in such photos as "Italian Mother and her Baby," and "Street Arabs in the Area of Mulberry Street," he somehow overcame the stiffness of the posed shot.

Ida B. Wells was the investigator as conscience, exposing Americans to the causes and consequences of lynching. Born a slave in Holly Springs, Mississippi, in 1862, the oldest of eight children, Wells became responsible at age sixteen for raising her brothers and sisters. She first attracted public attention in 1884 when she sued the Chesapeake and Ohio Railroad for racial discrimination after being ordered into a separate-but-unequal smoking car. She began writing articles for religious weeklies. Soon she became a full-time journalist, editing and owning one-third of the Memphis *Free Speech*.

The lynching in 1892 of three local blacks provoked her to investigate "every lynching I read about."[13] Sometimes—as with a lynching in Tunica County, Mississippi—she thoroughly researched the circumstances: "The Associated Press reporter said, 'The big burly brute was lynched because he had raped the seven-year-old daughter of the sheriff.' I visited the place afterward and saw the girl, who was a grown woman more than seventeen years old. She had been found in the lynched Negro's cabin by her father, who had led the mob against him in order to save his daughter's reputation. That Negro was a helper on the farm."[14]

Wells not only editorially attacked the lynchers but those in power who had allowed the lynchings: "If Southern white men are not careful they will over-reach themselves and a conclusion will be reached which will be very damaging to the moral reputation of their women."[15] The Memphis *Commercial Appeal* responded: "The black wretch who had written that foul lie should be . . . burned at a stake." A mob wrecked Wells's press and threatened to lynch her if she tried to continue the *Free Speech*.

Wells moved to the New York *Age*, where she renewed her reporting on the lynching of blacks. She published a pamphlet, *Southern Horrors*, lectured in England, organized U.S. anti-lynching committees, and produced another pamphlet, *A Red Record: Tabulated Statistics and Alleged Causes of Lynchings in the United States, 1892-1893-1894*. The pamphlet made clear to Frederick Douglass and others that lynchings were simply a way to "keep the nigger down."[16] Wells's "painful duty" in the pamphlet—a duty she took as her life goal—was "to reproduce a record which shows that a large portion of the American people avow anarchy, condone murder and defy the contempt of civilization."[17]

Ida B. Wells. Photo courtesy of Department of Special Collections, Joseph Regenstein Library, University of Chicago.

Who should watch the watchdog?

The journalist, wrote Janet Malcolm in a 1989 *New Yorker* article, "is a kind of confidence man, preying on people's vanity, ignorance, or loneliness, gaining their trust and betraying them without remorse."[1]

Newspeople responded angrily to Malcolm's criticism. "Outraged Journalists Dispute Cynical Portrayal of Their Craft," read a Washington *Post* headline.[2] It takes a confidence man to know one, barked other journalists.[3] They made it clear that they did not accept Malcolm as a credible critic of the press.

But if the journalist serves as watchdog of the government and other powerful institutions, should not someone watch the watchdog?

Some journalists have argued that the press, for First Amendment reasons, should have no watchdog. In this view, the consumer—the reader who can choose not to buy the newspaper, the viewer who can decide to flip to another channel—is watchdog enough. These anti-watchdog journalists have opposed the National News Council, a nongovernmental forum to air complaints against media news performance, and other efforts to institutionalize scrutiny of the press.[4]

But many newspapers, worried about their credibility, have at least adopted methods for handling errors—through corrections boxes and, in the case of twenty-seven U.S. dailies, through editors called ombudsmen who field readers' complaints and sometimes write columns about their papers' mistakes.[5]

Broadcast news organizations have been less willing to admit error. They prefer to read from listeners' or viewers' letters offering corrections than to write and broadcast corrections themselves. After studying the three major television networks' corrections policies in 1987, the News Study Group at New York University concluded: "[T]he key to on-air corrections too often was whether anyone, inside or outside the news organization, was willing to protest vigorously enough."[6]

Except for *Columbia Journalism Review, Washington Journalism Review, Nieman Reports, Quill,* and a few other limited-circulation magazines of press criticism, the role of watchdog has largely been left by the journalism community to a growing number of outside media-monitoring organizations that often have an ideological agenda.

Accuracy in Media (AIM), concerned about so-called liberal bias, rebutted a thirteen-part 1983 PBS series, "Vietnam: A Television History," with two films of its own: "Vietnam: The Real Story" and "Television's Vietnam: The Impact of the Media." AIM charged that, despite U.S. battlefield victories, the press's biased reporting from Vietnam caused the U.S. government to lose the support of the American public.

From the left end of the ideological spectrum, FAIR (Fairness & Accuracy in Reporting) concerns itself with what Jeff Cohen, its executive director, describes as "corporate concentration and its control over the media and the increasing rightward drift."[7] A FAIR-commissioned survey by Boston College sociologists David Croteau and William Hoynes concluded that ABC News's "Nightline" was partial to guests like former Secretaries of State Henry A. Kissinger and Alexander M. Haig, Jr.—white males identified with the government and corporate establishment.

But the presence of press criticism on the right and left does not satisfy less political press critics. They see a need for academe and the press itself to provide more analysis. Corrections boxes and an occasional column of criticism are not enough.

Richard Harwood, Washington *Post* ombudsman, calls on ombudsmen and other journalists to "establish a tradition of criticism and analysis that goes beyond explanations of why the letter 'r' was omitted from the word "shirt' . . . . We should begin looking at the news business the way we look at the business of politics and government. What ethical and professional standards do we profess, if any, and how often do we violate them?"[8]

But until such a tradition of self-criticism develops, those who assume the role of press watchdog can expect to be greeted by journalists as Janet Malcolm was greeted—with a chorus of catcalls.

The press struggles to examine its own health in Jacob Burck's cartoon. Courtesy Loren Ghiglione

Ida M. Tarbell, the investigator as muckraker. Courtesy Joseph Regenstein Library, The University of Chicago

Another woman investigator, Ida M. Tarbell, raised in the Pennsylvania oil regions, focused her most famous efforts on the Standard Oil Company. Not averse to rummaging through wastebaskets, she developed, nevertheless, a new, more scholarly approach to investigative journalism, based on her training in history at the Sorbonne and on her seven years as editor of the *Chautauquan*.

In 1893, S. S. McClure hired her as contributing editor for his muckraking *McClure's* magazine. After producing biographies of Napoleon and Lincoln, Tarbell spent five years researching and writing her eighteen articles on Standard Oil, published from 1902 to 1904. The indignant

tone of her series made clear she never intended to fall victim to bland objectivity. She attacked blackmail, price-rigging, favoritism, and other illegalities by the "big hand"[18] that controlled ninety percent of the nation's petroleum supply. Standard Oil's competitive moves were conducted, she wrote, "not to save its life, but to build up and sustain a monopoly in the oil industry."[19]

Carefully studying court records, Tarbell supported her charges "by documents and figures."[20] Observers disagree on whether the work of Tarbell and other writers at *McClure's*, which had a circulation of half a million, paved the way for reforms initiated by President Theodore Roosevelt.[21] But historian George Mowry describes the muckrakers' enormous impact: "[F]ew literate Americans could have any real feelings of complacency about their civilization."[22] And other historians acclaim Tarbell's "History of the Standard Oil Company" as "substantially accurate in all but a few minor details."[23]

A half century later, Drew Pearson, the investigator as government watchdog, described Congress as "a gaggle of old men from small towns . . . a council of elders whose only claim to power is their ability to outlive their colleagues."[24] Congress was his favorite target, and his exposés put four Congressmen in jail. Known as the "Scorpion-on-the-Potomac," he humiliated a North Carolina Congressman who padded his payroll by listing a dead person. He destroyed Senator Thomas J. Dodd of Connecticut in 123 columns, relying heavily on six thousand documents stolen, photocopied, and returned to Dodd's files. The Senate censured Dodd in 1967. He lost a re-election bid in 1970 and died the following year.

Pearson's radio program and syndicated "Washington Merry-Go-Round" column (written with Robert S. Allen from 1932-1942) was carried by six hundred newspapers with an aggregate circulation of forty million. The column prompted four presidents to call Pearson a liar. President Truman's description of Pearson as an

S.O.B. led to a letter addressed to "The S.O.B."—
with no name, street, or city on the envelope—
being delivered to Pearson's home.

But an estimated 275 lawsuits for a grand
total of two-hundred million dollars in damages
proved 99.6 percent unsuccessful. Pearson lost
only one case that went to trial, paying forty
thousand dollars. He was not, however, above
blackmailing his way out of lawsuits. He reported in 1932 that General Douglas MacArthur
was responsible for the eviction of twenty thousand homeless veterans camped in Washington
to lobby Congress for a bonus. MacArthur sued
for one million seven-hundred-fifty thousand
dollars. Pearson used informants to track down

the General's former mistress. MacArthur abandoned the suit.

Pearson, like other columnists, let his ideology determine his targets. He supported reform—
civil rights, improved East-West relations, Medi-
care, oil-pipeline safety, welfare programs—and
harassed right-wingers, racists, and Red-baiters.
When Senator Joseph McCarthy made his first
charge in 1950 about "205 members of the
Communist Party . . . in the State Department,"[25] Pearson showed that the loyalty of only
three people on McCarthy's list deserved question. Two had not worked at the State Department for four years, and the third had never
worked there. On Pearson's birthday in 1950,
McCarthy attacked Pearson, landing one punch
to the head and kneeing him in the groin before
Richard Nixon pulled them apart.

Pearson was fond of crediting his sense of
smell for scoops. "If something smells wrong, I
go to work."[26] But most of his major exclusives,
writes biographer Oliver Pilat, "were thrust into
his hands as a reward for taking part in public
quarrels with a high ideological content."[27] As
for his famous predictions, he guessed wrong as
often as right. He crystal-gazed in 1966 that
Vietnam might prevent President Lyndon Johnson from running for re-election. He also predicted that Hitler, close to his final defeat, would
escape to the Alps disguised as a rabbi.

Seymour M. Hersh represents the modern
investigative reporter as maverick. After
stints as editor of a weekly newspaper near Chicago and as United Press International correspondent in Pierre, South Dakota, Hersh worked
two years in Chicago for Associated Press. In
1965, AP sent him to Washington, D.C., and a
year later assigned him to cover the Pentagon.
He once surprised fellow Pentagon correspondents by walking out of an unproductive official
briefing. Some of the Vietnam war briefings, he
said, "were lies."[28]

When officials failed Hersh, he turned to
unofficial sources—"systems analysis guys with
access to the cables." Hersh explained the tech-

Drew Pearson, the investigator as watchdog, interviews Soviet defector Igor Gouzenko on television.
Wide World Photos

Seymour Hersh, the investigator as maverick. Associated Press photo. Courtesy D.C. Public Library

nique he used once of playing off "the Navy against the Army, or tell[ing] the Air Force [source], 'You hit only three bombs on target the other day' so that he'd tell me the truth."[29] Assigned to a new investigative team at AP, Hersh put together a series on U.S. manufacture of biological and chemical weapons. A subsequent article for the *New Republic*, which named universities and corporations performing the work under contract for the government, led a publisher to offer Hersh a contract to write a book. Hersh quit AP in 1967.

As a free-lancer he doggedly pursued a tip about the Army "trying to court martial some guy in secret."[30] He traveled thirty thousand miles, located Lt. William L. Calley, Jr., at Fort Benning, Georgia, and told the tragedy of the 1968 My Lai massacre in Vietnam. Later Hersh would report the recollections of three eyewitnesses and claim that My Lai—the murder of at

least 347 Vietnamese civilians, including women and children—was not an isolated incident. He revealed how Army field officers in Vietnam destroyed records to cover up My Lai and a second, smaller mass murder of civilians nearby.[31] In 1970, he won a Pulitzer Prize for international reporting without having traveled outside the United States.

As a New York *Times* reporter from 1972 to 1979 and as a free-lancer, Hersh focused on the misapplication of government power, what the Washington *Post*'s Bob Woodward described as "the abuse of really big power, concentrated power. . . ."[32] Hersh reported in 1974 that the Central Intelligence Agency, "directly violating its charter, conducted a massive illegal domestic intelligence operation during the Nixon Administration against the antiwar movement and other dissident groups in the United States . . . ."[33] He wrote about the CIA's clandestine campaign to topple Salvador Allende in Chile, and Henry Kissinger's involvement in FBI wiretaps of his aides to locate leaks to the press.

But not even the biggest of investigative blockbusters—My Lai, for example—guaranteed publication in the mainstream media. When Hersh finished his first My Lai article in the autumn of 1969, he offered it to *Life* and *Look* magazines. Both rejected it. The My Lai article was finally printed with the assistance of the little-known Dispatch News Service, with thirty-five of about fifty newspapers approached paying one-hundred dollars each to publish the story.[34]

The press, however, had not aggressively pursued the story. The Associated Press had relayed a brief Army announcement at Ft. Benning, Georgia, about official charges against Lieutenant Calley weeks before Hersh's story, but neither the AP nor its member newspapers had followed up on this announcement. As Hersh noted in his book, *My Lai 4: A Report on the Massacre and the Aftermath*, "there was little investigative reporting on the part of the American press to determine exactly what had happened . . . ."[35]

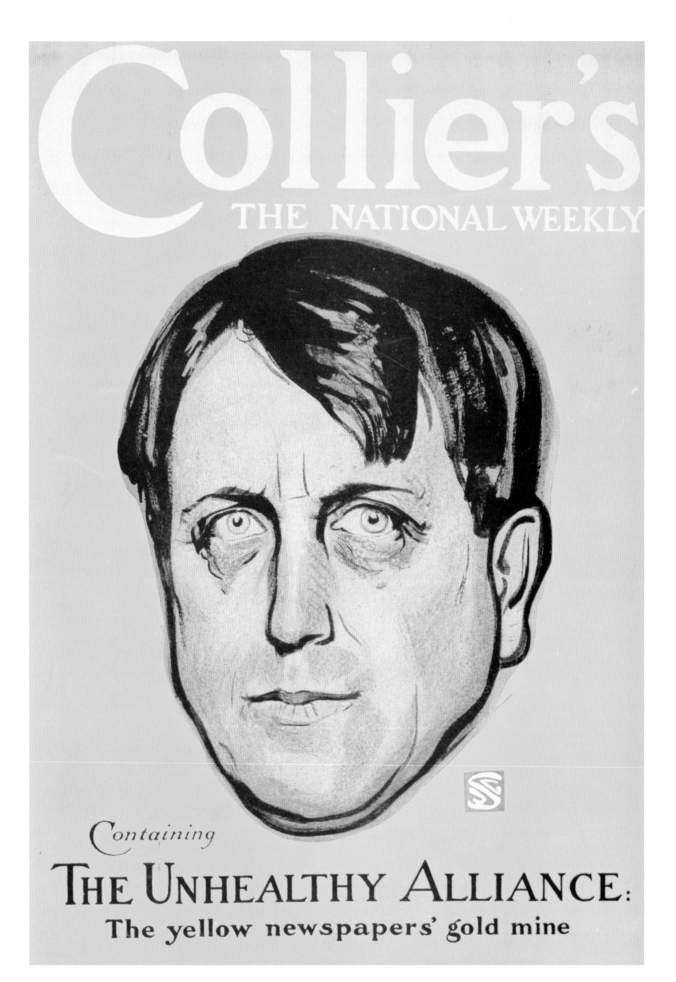

Collier's
THE NATIONAL WEEKLY

Containing

THE UNHEALTHY ALLIANCE:
The yellow newspapers' gold mine

William Randolph Hearst, the exploiter as newsmaker, campaigned for U.S. involvement in the Spanish-American War. *Collier's* cover from Library of Congress, General Collections

5 Exploiter

Sultan of Sensationalism

Exploiters hoax, lie, and commit other sins. But mostly they sensationalize. They turn any story—hard news, human-interest feature, or court report—into the kind of salacious merchandise that nineteenth-century New York newsvendors, eager to sell out early, found especially welcome.

"Here's this morning's *New York Sewer!*" cries a newsboy in Charles Dickens's *Martin Chuzzlewit* (1843–44). "Here's this morning's *New York Stabber!* Here's the *New York Family Spy!* Here's the *New York Private Listener!* Here's the *New York Peeper!* Here's the *New York Plunderer!* Here's the *New York Keyhole Reporter!* Here's the *New York Rowdy Journal!* Here's all the New York papers!"[1]

The heated competition in New York for readership following the founding in 1833 of the first successful penny paper, *The Sun*, brought sensational crime news, spicy scandal, and, on August 21, 1835, something new. *The Sun* published a brief notice reprinted, as was the custom, from the Edinburgh *Courant*. It announced "astronomical discoveries of the most wonderful description" just made by means of "an immense telescope on an entirely new principle." The astronomer, Sir John Herschel, was the son of Sir William Herschel, discoverer of Uranus.

Succeeding stories in *The Sun*, copied from a supplement of the *Edinburgh Journal of Science*, described the life seen on the moon—"a strange amphibious creature of a spherical form, which

Locke's "Moon Hoax" captivated readers, and the New York *Sun*'s daily circulation increased dramatically. Library of Congress, Rare Book and Special Collections Division

rolled with great velocity across the pebbly beach."[2] A fourth installment detailed the "man-bat . . . with a near resemblance to the human figure, wings greatly resembling those of the bat."[3]

Crowds clamored for copies of the next edition. *The Sun*'s circulation shot to nineteen thousand, larger than that of any other newspaper in the world. Competing papers either applauded *The Sun*'s moon articles (*Times:* "an air of intense verisimilitude"[4]) or declared them a hoax, which they were. Eventually reporter Richard Adams Locke, an experienced, Cambridge-

Lydia Thompson, described by Wilbur F. Storey as a "beefy specimen of a heavy class of British barmaids," horsewhipped the editor on a Chicago street in 1870. Photo courtesy Chicago Historical Society

educated writer who had edited London periodicals, confessed to what Frank Luther Mott describes as "probably the greatest 'fake' of our journalistic history."[5] *The Sun* congratulated itself on providing "much intellectual amusement, if not, indeed, much theoretical instruction."[6]

The hoax succeeded as well as it did for two reasons. First, the press had created an atmosphere in which sensationalized coverage, hoaxes, and even lies were not regarded as extraordinary occurrences (a year later, Locke would start the New York *New Era* and publish another hoax about Africa explorer Mungo Park). Second, however often responsible newspeople have decried fabrications, a tradition had been established of such tales in the press. Locke's fantasy was followed by the futuristic fiction of Jules Verne,[7] Edgar Allan Poe,[8] Edward Everett Hale,[9] Robert Duncan Milne,[10] and Mark Twain,[11] by Sanford Jarrell's Prohibition-era phony in the New York *Herald Tribune* about a floating nightclub,[12] and by "Jimmy's World," Janet Cooke's 1980 fake in the Washington *Post* about an eight-year-old heroin addict. The story won Cooke a Pulitzer Prize before proved a hoax.

Wilbur F. Storey represents a different kind of exploiter—the scandalmonger. Storey's Chicago *Times* built a circulation lead in Chicago during the 1870s with seduction stories, lottery drawings, sensationalized reporting, and personal attacks. His favorite advice to reporters pursuing their quarry: "We must cut the gut fat out of him."[13] At one point, Storey faced twenty-four libel suits.

He had bought the *Times* in 1861 for thirteen thousand dollars. No admirer of the Republican party and the Union government, he attacked Lincoln and Union generals, defied military rules regarding coverage of the Civil War, and settled for any war news, accurate or not, that would sell papers. He told his correspondents: "Telegraph fully all news and when there is no news send rumors."[14] In 1864, General Ambrose E. Burnside ordered the seizure and suspension of the *Times* for sedition (after three days, Lincoln rescinded Burnside's order). And Warren Isham, a *Times* war correspondent and Storey's brother-in-law, was courtmartialed and sentenced to prison "for the duration of the war unless released by competent authority."[15]

To beat the competition after the war, Storey encouraged "Holy-cow" headlines. Editorializing, punning alliteration became a trademark— "DEATH'S DEBAUCH" (a railroad wreck story), "JOHN'S JAW" (coverage of a John Logan speech), and "THE HOUSE THAT VANDERBILT" (an article on a Vanderbilt will).[16] For a story about four murderers subjected to public hangmen in the South, the headline read in brassily bold type: "JERKED TO JESUS."[17]

Storey did not let ethics deter him. Plays performed in theaters that did not advertise heavily in his newspaper suffered consistently negative reviews. *Times* staffers were sometimes hired on the basis of nonjournalistic qualifications. Said the city editor: "Two of my men are ex-convicts, ten of them are divorced and not a single one is living with his own wife."[18]

Storey contended that the newspaper's function was to "print the news and raise hell." He added, in words that could serve as his epitaph, "a journalist should not be popular."[19] When the *Times* described women in a burlesque troupe as "large-limbed, beefy specimens of the barmaid class,"[20] two of the women jumped Storey in the street and horsewhipped him.

Storey embraced spiritualism ("an insane delusion," reported the competition)[21] and cavorted with his mistress, wife of a convict. When he divorced his wife and married his mistress, the new couple rewarded invitations to social events with detailed coverage in the *Times*. The Storeys not only appeared first on the list of guests but their names were printed in capital letters.

By 1876, Storey showed signs of insanity, caused by a syphilitic infection. He began building a marble mansion, changing the plans daily, running up a quarter-million dollars in bills, but

Homer Davenport's impish William Randolph Hearst. Library of Congress, General Collections

never completed construction. By 1882, he was hearing "angels' voices" at editorial meetings and publishing gibberish in the editorial space.[22] The words were set in bizarre mixtures of advertising and headline type. He died two years later. Once he had said: "I don't wish to perpetuate my newspaper. *I am the paper!* I wish it to die with me . . . ."[23] He almost got his wish. The *Times* died only a decade later.

William Randolph Hearst was the exploiter as newsmaker. Despite two years at Harvard and the wealth that came with being the son of a silver magnate, Hearst had a keen sense of mass taste. In 1895, after succeeding with the family's San Francisco *Examiner*, he bought the New York *Journal* and began a battle for circulation with Joseph Pulitzer's *World*.

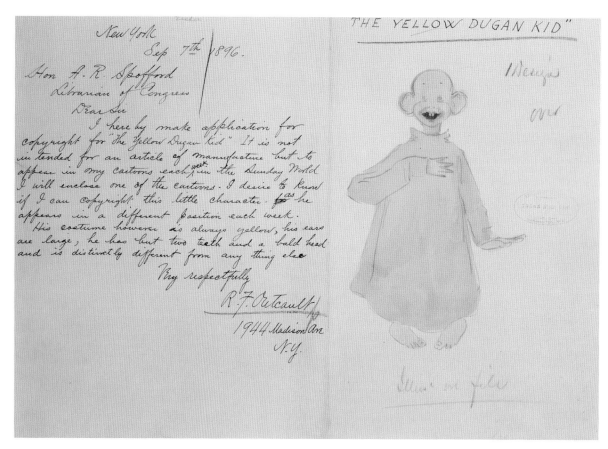

R. F. Outcault's cartoon character "The Yellow Dugan Kid" became the symbol of Hearst's brand of exploitive journalism. From Outcault's copyright application. Library of Congress, Prints and Photographs Division

Hearst looked for events, especially those involving sex and crime, to transform into circulation-building news. The headline and sketches that accompanied Alan Dale's interview with French actress Anna Held—"Mlle. Anna Held Receives Alan Dale, Attired in a Nightie"—precipitated boycotts. *Journal* reporters, ordered into the detective business, solved the "Guldensuppe mystery." Edition after edition milked the discovery in the East River of a headless, armless, legless torso. Hearst's reporters identified the corpse, found the murderers, and trumpeted their success: "MURDER MYSTERY SOLVED BY THE JOURNAL."[24]

To the sex-and-crime sensationalism, Hearst's Sunday paper added a heavy dose of sports, society, supplements (*American Magazine* and *Woman's Home Journal*), pseudo-science, and color comics. A Morrill Goddard story,

based on dinosaur fossils, promised "Real American Monsters and Dragons" and featured a half-page drawing of "The Jumping Laelaps of 5,000 Years Ago."[25] *American Humorist*, Hearst's comic supplement, was advertised as "eight pages of iridescent polychromous effulgence that makes the rainbow look like a lead pipe."[26] Richard F. Outcault's "Yellow Kid," the toothless, smiling star of the comics, became a ubiquitous symbol of Hearst's brand of yellow journalism.

Hearst did not start the Spanish-American War. He may not even have sent the infamous telegram to war artist Frederic Remington, who had requested relief from his Cuban insurrection assignment because nothing was happening. Hearst, so the story goes, cabled back: "Please remain. You furnish the pictures and I'll furnish the war."[27] But Hearst's headlines—"The War

The journalist: exploiter or exploited?

Between the press and Senator Joseph McCarthy (R., Wis.), it was sometimes difficult to tell who was the exploiter and who the exploited.

McCarthy's claim in 1950—at the height of the Cold War—that 205 Communists infested the State Department received heavy press coverage. His allegations about Communist "dupes" and disloyal federal employees continued for four years. Before an accused's denial could catch up with McCarthy's charge, the senator was accusing another government worker of subversion.

Some journalists defended the reporting of McCarthy's "exposés." Walter Lippmann said that when a prominent U.S. senator "makes such attacks . . . it is news which has to be published."[1] George Reedy, a United Press senate correspondent, agreed: "Joe couldn't find a Communist in Red Square . . . he didn't know Karl Marx from Groucho—but he was a United States senator."[2]

Nevertheless, one McCarthy target, Secretary of State Dean Acheson, told the American Society of Newspaper Editors: "You are in a worse situation than I am. I . . . [am] only the intended victim . . . of this mad and vicious operation. But you, unhappily—by reason of your calling—are participants."[3]

Wire-service correspondents—suppliers of close to eighty-five percent of early newspaper reports on McCarthy's charges—felt especially exploited. The pressure to beat the competition, to provide a provocative lead, and to limit oneself to "straight" reporting led the wire-service correspondent to act as "a recording device for Joe," said John L. Steele of the United Press in 1950. "I felt trapped."[4]

William Theis, then chief of the International News Service senate staff, recalled "all three wire services were so goddamn objective that McCarthy got away with everything, bamboozling the editors and the public."[5]

McCarthy tried to intimidate journalists who refused to go along with his tactics. Perhaps as a result, much coverage was timid. Some reporters even invited McCarthy to exploit them. Murrey Marder, who covered McCarthy for the Washington *Post,* recalled, "Milt Kelly [of The Associated Press] or Warren Duffee [United Press] would come and say, 'I must have a story,' and McCarthy would go through his files until he found something. McCarthy learned that on Friday the wire-service reporters were always in need of stories that could be run on Sunday or Monday, the two dead news days, and he saved up tidbits for them."[6]

In the end, however, the press contributed to McCarthy's undoing. In stories about his accusations, some papers provided bracketed inserts that contained facts refuting his charges. The facts suggested McCarthy was a liar. Even the New York *World-Telegram*'s Frederick Woltman—billed as "the premier Red-baiter among American newspaper reporters"—rejected McCarthy as "a major liability to anti-Communism."[7]

McCarthy reminded the press that it had a responsibility to go beyond simple stenography. After surveying more than forty reporters who covered McCarthy, Edwin R. Bayley concluded: "Newspaper people realized that it was not enough simply to tell what happened or what was said, but that they had to tell what it meant and whether or not it was true."[8] Otherwise journalists invited demagogues to exploit them.

As the namesake of "the McCarthy era," the junior senator from Wisconsin inevitably became a focal point of press attention. 1951 photo by Carl Mydans, *Life* magazine, © Time, Inc.

Ship *Maine* was Split in Two by an Enemy's Secret Infernal Machine"—certainly did not discourage U.S. involvement. Indeed several historians, after examining the jingoism of the *Journal,* agree with correspondent James Creelman that "if Hearst had not challenged Pulitzer to a circulation contest at the time of the Cuban insurrection, there would have been no Spanish-American War."[28]

Hearst portrayed Evangelina Cisneros, the imprisoned niece of the leader of the insurrectionists, as an innocent at the mercy of the "lech-

Bernarr Macfadden, owner and publisher of the New York *Evening Graphic*. From Fulton Oursler, *The True Story of Bernarr Macfadden* (New York: Lewis Copeland Company, 1929). Library of Congress, General Collections

erous and foiled scoundral"[29] who ran Cuba. Hearst ordered correspondent Karl Decker to Havana to free Cisneros from prison. Once freed, she was brought to Washington to meet President McKinley. Then, when the U.S. battleship *Maine* was sunk in Havana harbor, a *Journal* banner headline blared: "DESTRUCTION OF THE WAR SHIP MAINE WAS THE WORK OF AN ENEMY."[30] The *Journal* blamed Spain, financed a Congressional investigation, and cheered as the United States declared war.

To Hearst the war was a personal venture. The *Journal*'s front-page ears carried the question: "HOW DO YOU LIKE THE JOURNAL'S WAR?"[31] And Hearst dispatched an army of correspondents, including Creelman, who recalled the time he was wounded: "Opening my eyes, I saw Mr. Hearst . . . . a revolver at his belt, and a pencil and notebook in his hand . . . . Slowly he took down my story of the fight . . . . 'I'm sorry you're hurt, but'—and his face was radiant with enthusiasm—'wasn't it a splendid fight? We must beat every paper in the world!'"[32]

Bernarr Macfadden was the exploiter as faker. A poorly educated Missouri farm boy, Macfadden had made thirty million dollars by publishing *Physical Culture Magazine* and *True Story Magazine.* His chief intellectual gift was, H. L. Mencken said, "a vast and cocksure ignorance."[33] Macfadden decided in 1924 to publish a crusading tabloid for physical fitness, and against "medical ignorance [and] . . . Prurient Prudery."[34] A contest to find ten Apollos and Dianas—"perfect mates for a *new* human race, free of inhibitions and free of the contamination of smallpox vaccine"[35]—paid one thousand dollars to any Apollo and Diana who married.

In addition to such contests, Macfadden's New York *Evening Graphic* (*Pornographic,* said its critics) featured: first-person "news" accounts ("I am Now the Mother of My Sister's Son"); photo-illustrated True Story Serials ("He Pressed Me Tightly Against Him So That I Could Feel the Trembling of His Heartbeats"); play reviews by "common folks," not by experi-

Alice Kip Rhinelander undresses in a judge's chambers in this first New York *Graphic* "composograph." From Lester Cohen, *The New York Graphic* (Philadelphia: Chilton Books, 1964). Library of Congress, General Collections

enced critics; a Physical Culture page; a love diary; crossword puzzle contests; columns by Walter Winchell and Ed Sullivan; and a regular "composograph," a tasteless composite photograph of, for instance, Alice Kip Rhinelander undressing before a jury, or Rudolph Valentino meeting Enrico Caruso in heaven.

Physical culturists helped Emile Gauvreau, Macfadden's first editor, and other professional journalists put out the paper. Gauvreau recalled: "The spectacle of powerful gentlemen, sleeves rolled up to bare bulging muscles, while they tore my telephone books in half with one swipe of the hands, was not uncommon when I entered my office."[36]

Gauvreau also received new ideas from Macfadden after the strongman's brisk, and often barefoot, thirty-mile walk from his home. The *Graphic* ridiculed doctors, promoted "Walk to

Work" clubs, and made up news, hyping a trivial squabble between millionaire Edward "Daddy" Browning and bride Frances "Peaches" Heenan. In reaction, the New York Society for the Suppression of Vice successfully insisted on the arrest of Macfadden and the paper's executives. The *Graphic* earned its reputation as "the most-sued paper in American journalism."[37]

Macfadden's vanity led him to offer readers a Prize Art Portfolio consisting of his muscular poses. It also drove him to buy money-losing papers in Connecticut, Pennsylvania, and Michigan as part of a Macfadden-for-President campaign. The campaign—and the *Graphic*, which cost Macfadden eleven million dollars in losses—died. The final issue in 1932 featured a sizzling serial, "SALLY GETS HOT," causing one editor to remark that the tabloid went out "as it came in, in a blaze of gory."[38]

6 Entertainer

The Lighter Side of News . . . and Nonnews

The entertainer provides gossip, advice to the lovelorn, baseball ballyhoo, and dialect humor, all for fun. Sometimes, as in the case of Samuel Clemens, the public takes the fun too seriously.

The trouble began for Clemens, reporter on Virginia City's *Territorial Enterprise*, in May 1864. Women of the Nevada Territory were fund-raising for the U.S. Sanitary Commission, which aided wounded Union soldiers. Reuel Gridley, an old schoolmate of Clemens's, raised one-hundred-fifty thousand dollars in three months by auctioning and reauctioning a fifty-pound sack of flour.[1] Clemens, ever the entertainer, joked in the *Enterprise*—under the pen name Mark Twain—that some of the money raised actually had gone to "a Miscegenation Society somewhere in the East."[2]

The *Union*, a competing paper, and the women of the Sanitary Commission were not amused. Clemens was described in the *Union* as "an unmitigated liar, a poltroon and a puppy."[3] Clemens responded by calling the *Union*'s publisher "an unmitigated liar"[4] and demanding a duel. But Clemens fled by stagecoach to California on May 29.

The departure of the *Enterprise*'s journalist-entertainer was Virginia City's loss. Clemens had reported everything from fires to the doings of the Nevada legislature and, using the pen name Mark Twain for the first time, had produced amusing satires. A petrification mania had prompted Twain to write about a nose-thumbing stone mummy with a wooden leg discovered near Gravelly Ford.[5] The gullibility of readers about the hoax led Twain to conclude several

years later: "To write a burlesque so wild that its pretended facts will not be accepted in perfect good faith by somebody, is very nearly an impossible thing to do."[6]

Other journalist-entertainers—predecessors of Dear Abby—amused readers with advice to lonelyhearts. When her husband was stricken by an incurable mental illness, Elizabeth Meriwether Gilmer began writing in 1896 for the New Orleans *Picayune*. She developed one of the earliest personal advice columns, "Dorothy Dix Talks." Newspapers, which had long ignored female readers, began to court them. William Randolph Hearst persuaded Dix to join his new acquisition, the New York *Journal*, in 1901. Dix's

Portrait of 28-year old reporter Mark Twain (1863). From the Mark Twain Papers, the Bancroft Library, Berkeley, California.

Covarrubias cartoon of an "impossible interview" between advice columnist Dorothy Dix (left) and six-times-married showgirl Peggy Hopkins Joyce. Library of Congress, Prints and Photographs Division

first major assignment took her to Nebraska to cover the saloon-smashing titan of temperance, Carrie Nation. Dix described her as a "queer, frowzy, fat, unromantic Joan of Arc who heard voices and . . . made no move unless she was spiritually guided."[7]

In addition to covering political conventions, vice investigations, and murder trials where, in the Hearst tradition, she was expected to write sympathetically about the woman in the case, Dix syndicated her advice-to-the-lovelorn column to two hundred newspapers. Often the column relied on humor. A bride wondered whether she should let her groom-to-be know about her false teeth. Dix's advice: "Marry him, and keep your mouth shut."[8]

Dix counseled people to assume control of their lives. She also campaigned for women's suffrage and greater opportunities for women in employment and education. She gained a one-hundred thousand dollars-a-year salary and considerable fame. A roadside Burma Shave sign advised: "Love and Whiskers Do Not Mix—Don't Take Our Word, Ask Dorothy Dix."[9] Her advice column lasted fifty-five years—until 1951—making it America's longest surviving newspaper feature by the same author.

The entertainer who could develop a humorous dialect character often got away with commentary otherwise difficult in newspapers. Finley Peter Dunne had worked for a half-dozen Chicago newspapers by 1893 when he introduced Martin Dooley, the Irish saloon keeper of Archey Road, in a *Sunday Post* piece. The popularity of Mr. Dooley's comments on the Spanish-American War led to *Mr. Dooley in Peace and in War* and other books. Dunne became the "moral censor of the nation,"[10] a skeptical reformer skeptical even about reform.

Government was a favorite Mr. Dooley target: "Th' modhren idee iv governmint is 'Snub th' people, buy th' people, jaw th' people.'"[11] As for the nation's highest court, "Th' supreme coort follows th' iliction returns."[12] Though Mr. Dooley began many a monologue with "I see be

James Montgomery Flagg drawing of Finley Peter Dunne's Mr. Dooley, in *The American Magazine*, October 1909. Library of Congress, General Collections

th' pa-apers," he did not stop short of pricking the press: "There's always wan encouragin' thing about th' sad scientific facts that comes out ivry week in th' pa-apers. They're usually not thrue."[13] The press permitted no privacy: "We march through life an' behin' us marches th' phottygrafter an' th' rayporther."[14] As for an editor's duties: "They'se nawthin' so hard as mindin' ye'er own business an' an iditor niver has to do that."[15]

Will Rogers was the entertainer as humorous commoner. Not only did the one-million-dollar-a-year cowboy philosopher—the Poet Lariat—work as a radio commentator and an actor, but he also wrote. Beginning in 1922, he produced a newspaper column that reached the readers of four hundred newspapers. He insisted on writing in a folksy, ungrammatical style. He said: "Grammar and I get along like a Russian and a Bathtub."[16] When Charles Driscoll, a McNaught Newspaper Syndicate editor, complained about Rogers using "ain't," he replied, "Listen, Driscoll. I know a lot of people that don't say 'ain't that ain't eatin'.'"[17]

At first Rogers imitated Mr. Dooley, but then

he developed his own brand of epigrams and short paragraphs. After invariably starting a column with "Well, all I know is what I read in the papers,"[18] Rogers would good-naturedly demolish the target of the day: "Politics is the best show in America."[19] On the Depression: "We are the first nation in the history of the world to go to the poor house in an automobile."[20] Occasionally he sounded almost nihilistic: "Nothing don't mean anything. We are just here for a spell and pass on . . . . Fords and bathtubs have moved you and cleaned you, but you was just as ignorant when you got there. We know lots of things we used to dinent know but we dont know any way to prevent em happening."[21]

enry Chadwick, Grantland Rice, Red Smith, and Willard Mullin, sports-page entertainers, filled their worlds with heroes and bums. The bums made famous by Mullin—the New York *World-Telegram* cartoonist dubbed by Smith "the sports cartoonist of all human history"[22]—were the Brooklyn Dodgers and their fans.[23] Mullin created not only the lasting image of the Bums with toes winking from half-destroyed shoes, but also the images of the St. Louis Swifty of the Cardinals and the giant oaf of the New York Giants.

When the Dodgers escaped Brooklyn for Los Angeles, the Bums donned sunglasses, Bermuda shorts, and berets. But it wasn't only the carica-

Will Rogers, the entertainer as humorist commoner, lassoing his children, August 13, 1941. Library of Congress, Prints and Photographs Division

When is it necessary to entertain without offending?

In a smaller town, readers like their local newspaper to be entertaining, but preferably not at someone's expense.

The newspaper is expected to publish a flattering review of the community theater group's latest performance, skipping over the plight of the dimwit who forgot half his lines. The sports editor is expected to report thoroughly the heroics of the high school baseball players and, as the season draws to a close, cheer on the team that has lost every game for the third year in a row.

Sherwood Anderson solved the problem of bringing candor and criticism to a small-town newspaper. When he stopped writing fiction in 1927, he bought two country weeklies— one Republican, one Democratic—in Marion, Virginia, population four thousand.[1] In deciding to "return to Winesburg,"[2] Anderson chose to see the world through the eyes of a small-town newsperson. He made himself into two reporters: the real one who gathered news and wrote "What Say!" editorials, and the mythical one— eighteen-year-old Buck Fever of Coon Hollow, Virginia.[3]

"Buck could say

Sherwood Anderson (right), creator of Buck Fever. Courtesy Black Star Publishing Company

things about people, make cracks at them, have fun at people's expense that, had I been writing under my own name, would have at once got me into trouble," Anderson explained.[4] Buck commented on serious subjects—racism as well as the Rotary Club—drawing attention, for example, to a discriminatory system that had white convicts working beside black ones, but sleeping in separate cells.

Buck Fever was more than a critic. He and his imaginary associate, Mrs. Homing Pigeon, undertook to convert a machinery dump into a town park. They wrote about it as if it already existed. "We got our park," Anderson said. "We had fixed the charming little park in the imagined life of the people of the town and, after a time, the fact that it had not been built became unbearable to them."[5]

But Anderson's most important use of his imaginary reporter was to permit coverage of the imprisonment of a local adulteress and other sensitive subjects. Buck Fever made unacceptable opinions and topics acceptable—so acceptable that the townspeople named him honorary president of the Marion town board.

Willard Mullin cartoon about the Brooklyn Dodgers (1955). Courtesy *The Sporting News*.

Red Smith, the entertainer as sports writer, testifies before a House Monopoly Subcommittee investigating baseball in 1951. Photograph from UPI/Bettmann Newsphotos

tures that made Mullin, beginning in 1935, a sports buff's must six days a week for thirty-three years. It was the ideas. Each Mullin cartoon was an editorial. Smith wrote, "I would hate to admit how many times over the years I swiped a whole column from one of his cartoons."[24]

Smith, who wanted to be called a good reporter—"getting as near the truth as possible"[25]—is remembered best for the elegant simplicity of his writing. For much of his fifty-five-year career, he wrote from four to seven columns a week for the New York *Herald Tribune* or the New York *Times*. He worried about treating sports too seriously. His advice: "[W]rite it as entertainment."[26]

Wit was one of Smith's weapons. He rejected track ("If God had intended man to run, He would have given him four legs")[27] and described a sportswriters' interview with Leon Trotsky as probably "the first time in his life any group of interviewers met him on a completely equal footing of understanding; they knew pre-

cisely as much about Communism as he did about baseball."[28] Smith said writing was easy: "All you do is sit down at the typewriter and open a vein."[29]

Grantland Rice really did find writing easy, churning out sixty-seven million words from 1901 to 1954, including twenty-two thousand columns, seven thousand verses, one thousand magazine articles, and numerous sports film scripts. Rice admitted to what Stanley Woodward called "Godding up those ballplayers"[30]—making heroes of sports figures with energy and drive. But Rice didn't apologize, insisting: "Enthusiasm coupled with Purpose was the best Daily Double he'd ever played."[31]

The New York *Clipper* employed sportwriter Henry Chadwick, who did much to standardize the rules of baseball. **Courtesy National Baseball Library, Cooperstown, New York**

He began a 1924 column about a 14-to-7 Notre Dame victory over Army: "Outlined against a blue-gray October sky, the Four Horsemen rode again. In dramatic lore they are known as Famine, Pestilence, Destruction and Death. These are only aliases. Their real names are Stuhldreher, Miller, Crowley and Layden. They formed the crest of the South Bend cyclone before which another fighting Army football team was swept over the precipice at the Polo Grounds yesterday . . . ."[32]

Henry Chadwick, had he been alive in 1924, probably would have chastised Rice. He decried sportswriters' purple prose. Chadwick, one of the earliest by-lined sports columnists, began writing in 1848, contributing to the New York *Times*, the *Tribune*, and the New York *Clipper*, a sports newspaper. In 1869, Chadwick also started publishing baseball guides. They not only satisfied the sports addict's hunger for statistics but helped standardize the game—number of play-

ers, diamond dimensions, equipment—by providing rules.[33]

Honored by President Theodore Roosevelt as the "Father of Baseball,"[34] Chadwick developed the modern method of scoring the game, and campaigned for protective equipment, the professionalization of sportswriting (he organized the first sportswriters' association), and high ethical standards. One chronicler credited Chadwick with keeping baseball free from scandal during his half-century career.[35]

Louella Parsons and Hedda Hopper wrote syndicated Hollywood columns that embraced gossip and scandal. Parsons began at sixteen as a five-dollars-a-week general-assignment reporter in Dixon, Illinois. By 1926, she was movie editor for Hearst's Universal News Service—"the most widely known motion picture critic in the country—the czarina of Hollywood."[36]

Parsons was the first to report Rudolph Valentino's will, the Mary Pickford-Douglas

Fairbanks divorce, and Ingrid Bergman's pregnancy from her affair with Italian director Roberto Rossellini. The speed with which she reported Hollywood breakups earned her the title of Love's Undertaker.

Hedda "the Hat" Hopper, whose hats sometimes resembled Dagwood sandwiches, went from being a mediocre M-G-M actress to rivaling Parsons, scooping her in 1939 on the divorce of James Roosevelt, a son of President Roosevelt. Describing herself as "a ham trying to be a columnist,"[37] Hopper overcame her newspaper inexperience by working 130 hours a week, hiring a writer to turn her dictation into English, and employing two legmen to dig up gossip. Hopper recalled: "The minute I started to trot out the juicy stuff, my phone started to ring."[38]

Hopper earned a reputation as a coldblooded destroyer of those who crossed her. She was especially vindictive toward established stars. She accused Noel Coward and Cary Grant of having a sexual relationship. Following World War II, she turned conservative, urging a boycott of films produced by people with Communist connections. She described her Beverly Hills home as "the house that fear built."[39]

Louella Parsons and Hedda ("the Hat") Hopper, czarinas of filmdom. *Time*, Inc.

WHEN AUTOMOBILE SPEEDS AT FIFTY MILES AN HOUR MOTORCYCLE COP (A) STARTS IN PERSUIT - MOTORCYCLE HITS CAT (B) CAUSING IT TO FALL ON BUTTON (C) WHICH SETS OFF CANNON (D) - CANNON BALL (E) HITS IVORY DOME OF BARBER (F), BOUNCING OFF AND KNOCKING NECK OFF BOTTLE OF STRONG ACID (G) - ACID DROPS ON GOLD NUGGET (H) DISOLVING IT - WEIGHT OF KERNELS OF CORN (J) LOWER BOARD (I) AND FALL INTO FLOWER POT (K) - CORN GROWS TILL IT REACHES HEIGHT (L) - CAN (N) OF LIMA BEANS (M) JUMPS AT CORN ON ACCOUNT OF THE NATURAL AFFINITY FOR SUCCOTASH - STRING ON END OF CAN PULLS LEVER (O) WHICH PUSHES POINTER (P) INTO PAPER TANK (Q) HALF FILLED WITH WATER IN WHICH SARDINE (R) IS SWIMMING - POINTER PUNCTURES PAPER TANK, WATER RUNS OUT AND SARDINE CATCHES SEVERE COLD FROM EXPOSURE - SARDINE CONTRACTS A VERY HIGH FEVER THAT FINALLY SETS FIRE TO PAPER TANK AND LIGHTS CIGAR (S).

Goldberg's "Simple Way to Light a Cigar in an Automobile Traveling Fifty Miles an Hour," 1915. The Bancroft Library, University of California, Berkeley

For his "Inventions" cartoon series, Rube Goldberg became a dictionary word. The Bancroft Library, University of California, Berkeley

Rube Goldberg built his career on destroying fear—the fear Americans had of technology. The most famous of Goldberg's fifty thousand published cartoons made technology a subject of comedy. Many of the complex contraptions in the "Inventions of Professor Lucifer Gorgonzola Butts" series drew upon the simple activities of everyday life. Goldberg, a five-a-day cigar smoker, chose as the subject for one of his earliest "Inventions" cartoons a "Simple Way to Light a Cigar in an Automobile Traveling Fifty Miles an Hour" (1915).

Goldberg produced sixty-one cartoon series, won a Pulitzer Prize for editorial cartooning in 1948, and achieved fame both as a radio and television star and as a sculptor. But the prophetic "Inventions" series was Goldberg's signature. He became so identified with his invented gadgetry, which he drew from 1914 to 1964, that by 1966 "Rube Goldberg" appeared in the Random House dictionary. That made the cartoonist "the only American to have his name a dictionary word while he was alive," says biographer Peter Marzio. "None of his other accomplishments gave him greater satisfaction."[40]

For Brooks Atkinson, the scholarly drama critic of the New York *Times*, satisfaction did not come from the make-or-break impact on Broadway plays of his reviews. Atkinson saw himself not as a reviewer but as a reporter, and he was—a Pulitzer-winning correspondent in China and the Soviet Union during World War

II, and an author of thirteen books on everything from mountain climbing to birds to Thoreau. People on Broadway, however, saw him as Dr. Death—the kind of black-hatted reviewer in Arthur Dove's collage, "The Critic" (1925), who deserved the cord draped around his neck.

Atkinson sought to offer in his reviews, which he began writing in 1925, an honest, independent opinion. He refused to read out-of-town reviews before seeing a New York opening. He avoided friendships with theater people.

He insisted that he did not decide the fate of plays, pointing to box-office hits that he had panned. But theater people contended that his displeasure virtually guaranteed a show's demise. Nevertheless, when Atkinson retired from reviewing plays in 1960, Actors Equity Association, out of affection, made him a life member, and he became the first drama critic to have a Broadway theater named after him.

For every entertainer in journalism who has gotten to see his name in lights or in a dictionary, there have been thousands who have toiled more anonymously, earning perhaps no reward other than readers' amused giggles or angry Bronx cheers.

Theater people insisted a Brooks Atkinson review could make or break a Broadway play. Courtesy The New York *Times* Archives

7 War Correspondent

Working in Harm's Way

For the war correspondent, Nora Ephron writes, "the awful truth is that . . . war is not hell. It is fun."[1] Well, at least for some correspondents. Richard Harding Davis, who reported from Cuba in 1898 for the New York *Herald*, fired twenty rounds and scouted the trail during the Rough Riders' first skirmish at Las Guasimas. At the battle of San Juan Hill, he recalled, "I got excited and took a carbine and charged the sugar house. If the men had been regulars, I would have sat in the rear . . . but I knew every one of them, had played football and all that sort of thing, so I thought as an American I ought to help."[2]

Ernest Hemingway became an archetype not only for the correspondent who conveyed a war scene with a novelist's grace but also for the man with machismo who courageously observed— sometimes even participated in—the fighting.[3] At eighteen, Hemingway quit his reporting job at the Kansas City *Star* to experience World War I in northern Italy. He drove an American Red Cross ambulance in 1918 until an exploding Austrian mortar round sprayed him with fragments.[4] From 1920 to 1924, he reported from Europe for the Toronto *Star*, interviewing Mussolini and covering the Greeks' flight from the Turks (some of these reports were later published virtually unchanged as fiction).[5] While covering the Spanish Civil War as a North American Newspaper Alliance correspondent, he instructed Republican recruits in weapons drill.[6] He was one of the "bold vanguard"[7] of World War II correspondents in 1944 who reached Paris before the Allied troops entered on August 25. Hemingway told his friends, "I love combat."[8]

Several generations earlier, the New York *Tribune*'s Albert Deane Richardson, who once said war correspondents "styled themselves the Bohemian Brigade,"[9] did Hemingway one better. He managed to get himself imprisoned. Rushing in 1863 to cover Grant's attacks on Rebel strongholds in Mississippi, he hopped a Union supply tug that was blown up near Vicksburg.

Ernest Hemingway, convalescing in Italy, April 1919. Library of Congress, Prints and Photographs Division

Margaret Bourke-White, the first woman photographer in World War II. Culver Pictures

Albert D. Richardson. Frontispiece from Richardson's *The Secret Service, The Field, The Dungeon, and The Escape* (Hartford, Conn.: American Publishing Company, 1865). Library of Congress, General Collections

Margaret Fuller, America's first woman foreign correspondent, covered the Italian revolution from Rome in 1849. Library of Congress, Prints and Photographs Division

Northern generals did not grieve over the possible demise or capture of Richardson and other journalists listed as missing. General William Tecumseh Sherman dismissed correspondents as "spies and defamers"[10] who are the "direct cause of more bloodshed than fifty times their number of armed Rebels."[11] He had the New York *Herald*'s Thomas W. Knox tried by court martial for spying, establishing the principle that the field commander decided which correspondents could travel with the army. Sherman was sure that the enemy received notice from journalists of the North's intended attack on Vicksburg and other targets, and he felt the press was "false, false as hell"[12] in much of its reporting.

Almost forty years later, Civil War correspondent Henry Villard agreed that Sherman was "entirely right."[13] Villard wrote in his memoirs: "[T]he harm certain to be done by war cor-

respondents far outweighs any good they can possibly do. If I were a commanding general I would not tolerate any of the tribe within my army lines."[14] Historian J. Cutler Andrews's assessment of the correspondents' work was no kinder: "Sensationalism and exaggeration, outright lies, puffery, slander, faked eye-witness accounts, and conjectures built on pure imagination cheapened much that passed in the North for news."[15]

That assessment perhaps explains the response of the Confederate military to Richardson. He was treated as an enemy soldier. Fished from the Mississippi by Rebel soldiers, he was moved from prison to prison. After twenty months, he finally escaped from a North Carolina penitentiary and walked twenty-seven days until he reached Union lines. He telegraphed the *Tribune:* "Out of the jaws of Death; out of the gates of Hell."[16]

The first American woman to report an overseas upheaval was Margaret Fuller. Able to read Latin at the age of six, master of Greek, Italian, Middle English, Oriental scripture, German epic poetry, and Icelandic saga by her twenties, she edited the transcendentalists' *Dial* magazine at thirty. In 1844, she accepted Horace Greeley's offer to write for the New York *Tribune*, reporting on the blind, the poor, prostitutes, and prisons. A year later, she completed *Woman in the Nineteenth Century*, the first major book on feminism by an American.

In 1846, she left for Europe, becoming the first regular female foreign correspondent. She contributed weekly letters to the *Tribune* on Goethe, Carlyle, and the Brownings. Then she became enamored of Italian republicanism, covering the uprisings in 1848–49. She, her new Italian husband, and their infant son left Italy for the United States in 1850. They died when their ship capsized in a storm. Fuller was forty. Greeley described her as "the loftiest, bravest soul that has yet irradiated the form of an American woman."[17]

Fuller's twentieth-century equivalent, Marguerite Higgins, a twenty-five-dollars-a-week cub reporter at the New York *Herald Tribune*, wrote home to her parents in 1942: "It's a splendid feeling to be on the *Herald* staff . . . . I plan to take Spanish, Russian, and maybe even Chinese lessons. You see I'm still determined to be a foreign correspondent."[18] Higgins, who already spoke French and had studied German, was assigned to Europe in 1944 and by March 1945 was covering the war. Her front-line reports—datelined "With the 7th Army" or "On the Road to Munich"—were followed by coverage of the Dachau and Buchenwald concentration camps, the Nuremberg war trials, and Goering's suicide. She was named Berlin bureau chief in 1946, in time for the Berlin blockade and the airlift.

Higgins earned a Pulitzer Prize—the first won by a woman for overseas reporting—for her coverage of the 1950–53 Korean war. She almost had been prevented from covering Korea. Another *Herald Tribune* correspondent, Homer Bigart, her chief rival, had tried to have her transferred. He reportedly had told her in front of other correspondents and army officers "that she'd better get out of Korea or he'd 'bring the house down on her.'"[19] General Walton H. Walker also had ordered Higgins out of Korea.

Marguerite Higgins, first woman Pulitzer Prize winner for overseas reporting, was honored in 1951 for her coverage of the Korean War. Wide World Photos, Inc.

She had appealed to General Douglas MacArthur. At first he had supported Walker: "There are no facilities at the front for ladies." She had challenged him: "Nobody worries about powder rooms in Korea."[20] MacArthur had relented.

Higgins reported as a *Newsday* columnist from Vietnam during ten trips there.[21] Leishmaniasis, a rare tropical disease she contracted in Vietnam, killed her in 1966 at age forty-five. Even in death, discrimination remained an issue. Richard Kluger's definitive history of the New York *Herald Tribune* included as much about Higgins's appearance—"a voluptuously curved, unmistakably adult body"[22]—and her sexual behavior as it did about other reporters' journalistic achievements.

Nevertheless, Julia Edwards, in *Women of the World*, a balanced history of female foreign correspondents, felt compelled to quote *Herald*

Tribune correspondent Stephen White's summary of the charges against Higgins: "She was a dangerous, venomous bitch and a bad reporter."[23] But perhaps Keyes Beech, Chicago *Daily News* correspondent in Korea and Vietnam, deserves the last word: "She had more guts, more staying power, and more resourcefulness than ninety percent of her detractors. She was a good newspaperman."[24]

Picture-making journalists—combat artists and photographers—gave a new kind of reality to the heroics and horror of war. Winslow Homer appeared to capture the Civil War in "Sharpshooter on Picket Duty," "Prisoners From the Front," and "War News." But while Homer did make brief visits to the front, his Civil War, for the most part, says Gordon Hendricks, "was fought in his New York or Belmont studio."[25]

The greatest Civil War "Special Artist" was Alfred Waud, depicted in Homer's "War News" and teamed with Homer to make sketches for *Harper's.* Trained at Royal Academy schools in London, Waud came to the United States in 1850. From the First Battle of Bull Run in 1861 to Lee's surrender at Appomattox Court House in 1865, Waud positioned himself to capture the best view. Bayonet charges drawn by Homer[26] and Waud show the differences between a romanticized rendering and reportage. Homer depicts soldiers using their bayonets, when actually soldiers preferred to use their rifles' butt ends as weapons in close combat. On Waud's "Bayonet charge of the New York Excelsior Bridge," the artist takes pains to scribble what he knows from his own observation and what comes from others' description. "[S]cenery *truthful*," he writes, underlining "truthful."[27]

News photographers occasionally have captured in their work images that endure as symbols of the human spirit as well as of human strife. Robert Capa, who believed that "if your pictures aren't good enough, then you aren't close enough,"[28] took a front-line photo during

Civil War combat artist Alfred R. Waud sketches men of the First Maine Regiment. Wood engraving, after Winslow Homer, in *Harper's Weekly,* June 14, 1862. Library of Congress, Prints and Photographs Division

DEATH IN SPAIN: THE CIVIL WAR HAS TAKEN 500,000 LIVES IN ONE YEAR

Robert Capa's controversial "Moment of Death" photograph, taken during the Spanish Civil War. Magnum Photos/Life Magazine

the Spanish Civil War that ranks as the most famous—and most controversial—war photograph ever. "Death of a Loyalist Soldier" was captioned in *Life* magazine: "Robert Capa's camera captures a Spanish soldier the instant he is dropped by a bullet through the head in front of Cordoba."[29] O. D. Gallagher, a correspondent who shared a room with Capa at one point during the war, said the photo was a deliberate fake— "Franco's troops were dressed in 'uniforms' and armed and they simulated attacks and defence."[30] Others who worked with Capa insisted the photo was not faked. Capa went on to take memorable photos in World War II, the Israeli

War for Independence, and the French war in Indochina. He was killed there in 1954 when he stepped on a land mine.[31]

Associated Press photographer Joe Rosenthal's "Iwo Jima" became World War II's equivalent of Capa's "Death of a Loyalist Soldier." In 1945, after seventy-two days of bombing and shelling, U.S. Marines invaded the island of Iwo Jima to clean out twenty-three thousand Japanese soldiers from caves and underground fortifications. Finally, amidst sniper fire, Rosenthal photographed six Marines straining to raise a large American flag atop Mount Suribachi. "In a way," said Rosenthal, "it is a

William Mauldin's World War II cartoons celebrated the common foot soldier. United Feature Syndicate

The GI's buddy, Ernie Pyle. Library of Congress, Prints and Photographs Division

picture of a miracle. No man who survived . . . can tell you how he did it. It was like walking through rain and not getting wet . . . ."[32]

That same year, General George Patton's troops pushed into Germany, reaching Buchenwald only two hours after the Nazis' departure. *Life* magazine's Margaret Bourke-White, the first woman photographer in the war, took pictures of a group of men in concentration-camp uniforms behind barbed wire. Not one of the men reacted, as would normally happen, to the burst of light from the camera's flash. They had died, it seemed, even before their malnourished bodies had been consumed by the furnaces. "Using the camera," Bourke-White wrote, "was almost a relief. It interposed a slight barrier between myself and the horror in front of me."[33] Her photos helped the world realize the murderous meaning of Hitler's Final Solution.

Cartoonist William Mauldin and columnist Ernie Pyle represented a different kind of World War II chronicler—the celebrator of the common GI. Mauldin's cartoons of Joe and Willie, the unshaven footsloggers, reflected his desire to "make something out of the humorous situations which come up even when you don't think life could be any more miserable."[34] He captioned his cartoon of tired German prisoners being escorted through the rain and mud by equally tired U.S. infantrymen: "'Fresh, spirited American troops, flushed with victory, are bringing in thousands of hungry, ragged, battle-weary prisoners . . . .' (News item)."[35]

Pyle, a syndicated columnist with Scripps-Howard, focused on U.S. soldiers' names and home towns, linking American readers to the individual soldier fighting and dying for them faraway.[36] His Pulitzer Prize-winning column on the death of Captain Henry Waskow from Belton, Texas, recorded the goodbyes of soldiers who had served with him. One took the dead man's hand and held it in his for five minutes, saying nothing, just studying Waskow's face. "Finally he put the hand down. He reached over and gently straightened the points of the cap-

The press and government: friends or foes?

In peace or war, what should be the relationship between the press and government?

After Watergate, some journalists said the relationship had become overly adversarial. "The First Amendment is not just a hunting license," said Wes Gallagher, Associated Press general manager, in 1975. "We must put before the public ways and means of strengthening the institutions that protect us all—not tear them down."[1]

But others saw the relationship as far from adversarial—indeed, as alarmingly incestuous. They said journalists gave information to the Central Intelligence Agency. They described the press as government's fourth branch and noted the increasing rate at which people moved back and forth between jobs in journalism and government.

Stephen Hess of the Brookings Institution reported that eleven members of the New York *Times*'s Washington bureau were veterans of federal posts, some policy-making, in recent administrations.[2] Leslie Gelb worked at the Defense Department, then covered national security affairs for the *Times*, then joined the State Department as director of political-military affairs, and then returned to national security coverage for the *Times*.[3]

William L. Rivers, a former Washington correspondent, suggested that the Washington press corps was becoming a shadow government: "In a sense the two governments—the official government and the national news media—increasingly form part of a single, symbiotic unit . . . a double-mirror effect, in which each side responds to what the other is doing, while at the same time adjusting itself to the other side's anticipated needs."[4]

In war, a symbiotic relationship between the journalist and government may sometimes be difficult to avoid, as the World War II experience of William L. Laurence suggests. Laurence, science writer of the New York *Times*, repeatedly submitted articles about atomic energy, uranium, and atomic weapons to the govern-

ment's office of press censorship. Laurence recalled, "Story after story . . . was returned with the request not to publish."[5] The government worried about what the enemy might learn from Laurence's stories.

In 1945, the *Times* received a request from General Leslie R. Groves for Laurence to work with him as "the official historian of the atomic-bomb project."[6] Laurence was allowed to visit secret cities involved in the production of the bomb—Oak Ridge, Tennessee, Richland, Washington, and Los Alamos, New Mexico—but forbidden to publish anything or reveal his whereabouts to anyone, even his wife. To allay her fears about dangerous duty, Laurence was ordered to tell her that he was traveling to London on a top-secret project. To lend credence to the lie, the *Times* ran a story datelined London with Laurence's byline.

At General Groves's request, Laurence prepared four possible press releases about the upcoming test of the first atomic bomb near Alamogordo, New Mexico, including one release in which he explained away the death of scientists observing the test as having "nothing to do with the explosion."[7] The lie was necessary, General Groves explained, so that the true nature of the explosion—an atomic-bomb test—would not be made public. Laurence also wrote what became the basis of President Truman's half-hour radio address following Hiroshima.

Laurence was proud not only to be part of one of the biggest stories in history, but also, as he wrote, "to be of some service to the nation."[8] General Groves and the government were also of service to Laurence. He was the only journalist permitted to witness—from a U.S. plane miles above—the dropping of an atomic bomb on Nagasaki.

Laurence's unusual relationship with the government and his coverage of Nagasaki raise a question about possible future wars. Will only journalists working for the military—giving up their news jobs for secret government employment—have full access to the facts?

William Laurence (left), with Leslie R. Groves, of the Manhattan Project. From Laurence's book *Dawn Over Zero: The Story of the Atomic Bomb* (New York: Alfred A. Knopf, 1946).

Terror in Vietnam, as captured by AP photographer Horst Faas. Associated Press

tain's shirt collar, and then he sort of rearranged the tattered edges of the uniform around the wound, and then he got up and walked away down the road in the moonlight, all alone."[37] Pyle died in action, shot by a Japanese sniper on the island of Ie Shima in 1945.

In Vietnam, as in Korea, Pyle's brand of journalism—what one correspondent criticized as morale-building propaganda[38]—became more difficult for American journalists; they found it hard to commit themselves—and their reporting—to the slowly escalating U.S. war effort. Their own experience told them that the U.S. government's pronouncements about Vietnam were, at best, ignorantly optimistic. David Halberstam of the New York *Times* recalled that, during the early days of U.S. involvement, "in Saigon the journalists very quickly came to the

conclusion that the top people in the embassy were fools or liars or both."[39]

Journalists such as Halberstam and the Associated Press's Horst Faas, both veterans of the Congo war, saw themselves as independent professionals, not necessarily sharing the viewpoints of their U.S. government sources. The correspondents resisted criticism that sooner or later, recalled *Esquire* correspondent Michael Herr, every correspondent heard: "My Marines are winning this war, and you people are losing it for us in your papers."[40]

The early correspondents, while they saw the Communists as the enemy, thought the U.S. government had adopted self-defeating tactics and had given in to wishful thinking. "It was a classic example," Halberstam wrote, "of seeing the world the way we wanted to, instead of the way it was."[41]

But *Times* editors in New York were uneasy with Halberstam's reporting in 1963. His articles suggested the United States was losing the war. Secretary of State Dean Rusk used State Department press conferences to charge Halberstam with inaccuracy. In Saigon, Marguerite Higgins, on tour for *Newsday*, disputed what he was reporting. Neil Sheehan, a Vietnam war correspondent for United Press International and later the New York *Times*, said Halberstam "was fighting for his professional life . . . ."[42]

The attacks on Halberstam were part of an assault upon a small, pessimistic group of American correspondents. The White House, the Pentagon, *Time*, and Hearst publications took the offensive, Halberstam recalls, assailing the correspondents for being too young, too left-wing, and too cowardly. The correspondents' sources, of course, were the very American and Vietnamese officers in the field who watched the decline of the war effort.

When President Kennedy tried nudging Arthur Ochs Sulzberger into reassigning Halberstam to some story other than Vietnam, the *Times* publisher not only refused but delayed a two-week vacation Halberstam had scheduled.

Sulzberger wanted to make sure it did not appear the *Times* was bowing to Kennedy's pressure.[43] Later Halberstam's reporting would be proven accurate by events, and, on at least one occasion, even the State Department would admit that its official version was wrong and that Halberstam's version was essentially right.

The professionalization of the correspondent showed itself differently in the work of Faas, the Pulitzer Prize-winning photographer who by 1966 had become picture editor for all AP photographers and free-lancers in Vietnam. He methodically planned his coverage, assessing carefully the combat skill of the soldiers he might accompany. He designed special attire with a waterproof container for his cameras. But he also benefited from luck.

David Halberstam in Vietnam. Photo by Horst Faas, Associated Press. Courtesy of Random House

He was disconsolate in June 1965 when a flat tire prevented him from jumping aboard the first wave of ten relief helicopters headed for Dongxoai, which had been taken by Viet Cong the night before. But most of the two hundred South Vietnamese troops in the first wave—and most of those in the second wave—were soon casualties. The third and fourth waves landed. Faas accompanied the fifth wave. When he arrived, it looked as if the South Vietnamese position was going to be overrun. But he shied from jumping on an exposed rescue helicopter. Viet Cong groundfire killed virtually everyone on the chopper. Faas: "The decision not to go aboard was experience."[44]

Faas was also experienced in the business of photojournalism, having sold photos for the Keystone picture agency. He demanded more than dead bodies: "You show *how* they were killed."[45] Free-lancer Catherine Leroy, with no previous war experience, recalls visiting Faas: "My visual education came very quickly."[46]

It was not coincidence that three of the most powerful images of Vietnam—what historian Susan D. Moeller called "the three photographic icons of the war"[47]—were taken by AP photographers. In 1963, Malcolm Browne photographed a Buddhist monk as he burned himself to death to protest persecution. Eddie Adams captured the moment in 1968 when the national police chief executed a man identified as a Viet Cong terrorist. In 1972, Huynh Cong ("Nick") Ut photographed a burned South Vietnamese child as she fled napalm dropped by mistake from South Vietnamese aircraft.

The wire-service photographers were not trying for flashy feature spreads or photographic symbols of the Vietnam War as atrocity. They were just attempting to keep up with the breaking news—and to take the photos that would meet Faas's test by showing *how* people were dying. In satisfying his standard, they created enduring images of Vietnam—indeed, of war itself.

8 Broadcast Journalist
Expanding the World of News

The nature and delivery of news have been transformed by the electronic media. Radio and television have shrunk the world and brought selected bits of it into the living room, bedroom, and kitchen of virtually every home in the United States. Many Americans feel they have personally experienced almost every dramatic news event for the last half-century—whether it be the assassination of President John F. Kennedy, the war in Vietnam, Neil Armstrong's moon walk, or the Challenger disaster.

Before television, in the 1930s and 1940s, radio could claim it was the nation's major source of national and world news. Writing in 1937 about a typical American community (Muncie, Indiana), Robert and Helen Lynd concluded that "radio was a more important channel of national political news to Middletown than were the local newspapers."[1] President Franklin D. Roosevelt believed that the New Deal's chief method of reaching the American public was radio. And, as the nation headed into World War II, he warned the networks against the broadcast of "false news."[2]

The broadcasting companies got the message: They were to avoid controversy and opinion. Lenox Lohr, the president of NBC, even announced before the Federal Communications Commission in 1940 that the First Amendment did not exist for radio: "I object to people saying [that there is] freedom of speech over the air. I don't think there is any such thing."[3] The next year, the FCC held that "the broadcaster cannot be an advocate."[4]

It was in this environment that radio journalists—most of them trained on newspapers—broadcast their fifteen-minute news and commentary programs. They explained to an anxious nation the Depression, the New Deal, and the progress of World War II.

Radio news had begun in 1920 as a child of newspapers. The earliest regular radio newscasts were broadcast summaries from the Detroit *News* over its experimental station, 8MK. They were used as teasers to increase readership of the *News.* Elton M. Plant, a seventeen-year-old office boy, sang as well as announced. The station made clear its pride in broadcasting 1920 primary-election results: "The sending of the election returns by the Detroit *News* radiophone on Tuesday night was fraught with romance and must go down in the history of man's conquest of the elements as a gigantic step in his progress."[5]

Elton Plant, office boy at experimental radio station 8MK in Detroit, sang as well as announced. © 1920, The Detroit *News*

Walter Cronkite, elder statesman of journalism, chosen in a public opinion poll as most respected American. CBS Photo

Less than two years later, Hans von Kaltenborn—a Phi Beta Kappa graduate of Harvard and a veteran of the Spanish-American War—broadcast a news commentary over WVP, a station operated by the Army Signal Corps on Bedloe's Island, New York. In 1923, he began regular half-hour news analyses over WEAF, a New York station owned by the American Telephone and Telegraph Company.

An associate editor of the Brooklyn *Eagle*, Kaltenborn had been giving "Talks on Current Topics" in the *Eagle* auditorium. He brought an outspokenness to WEAF that the ownership found threatening. When Kaltenborn criticized Secretary of State Charles Evans Hughes, Hughes called WEAF and demanded Kaltenborn be silenced. AT&T, which had a policy of "constant and complete cooperation" with government, encouraged Kaltenborn to leave. He resumed broadcasting on New York's WOR.

In 1930, when the *Eagle* asked him, at age 52, to take a reduction in pay, he quit and went to work full-time at CBS as a one-hundred-dollars-a-week radio commentator. In a style that Harry Truman enjoyed imitating, Kaltenborn sprinted through the news at up to two hundred words a minute, enunciated precisely, and pronounced words by his own rules: "Russia" was RUSH-she-uh.

Kaltenborn traveled to Europe, interviewing Hitler and Mussolini and producing transatlantic broadcasts on the Spanish Civil War. The world's first war coverage by radio began: "(Sound of machine guns) Those are the isolated shots which are being exchanged by the front line sentinels on both sides of this Civil War. It is part of the battle of Irun."[6]

Kaltenborn returned home to his own battle. CBS insisted that he stop expressing his opinions, which had kept his newscasts, for the most

Pioneer newscaster H. V. von Kaltenborn sprinted through the news at two-hundred words a minute. Culver Pictures

part, unsponsored. Kaltenborn moved to NBC and in 1941 helped form the Association of Radio News Analysts. As its first president, he advocated the right of news analysts to state their opinions without using such smokescreen phrases as "It is said . . . ." or "There are those who believe . . . ." He continued regular radio broadcasts until, at age 75 in 1953, he retired. Occasionally he would be asked to appear on television, but he regarded the new medium "as a bastard art" of chalk marks to stand on and cameras to stare at: "It makes me sick."[7]

Another pioneer of radio, Floyd Gibbons, was the first daily network newscaster. He began his career as a seven-dollars-a-week Minneapolis *Daily News* police reporter in "The Front Page" tradition. He delivered a baby, cut a telephone line to scoop the competition, and described a 1911 auto race from inside the winning car. As a Chicago *Tribune* correspondent, he covered Pancho Villa in Mexico, then moved on to Europe for World War I, where a machine gun bullet blew out his left eye. His white linen eye patch became a trademark.[8]

In researching *The Red Napoleon*—his novel about a Communist plan to take over the world through miscegenation—Gibbons visited NBC to obtain information about how a radio correspondent would cover a battle from a plane. Gibbons made such an impression that in 1929 NBC hired him to do a half-hour show, "The Headline Hunter;" that program led to a remote broadcast—the first—of the landing of the German dirigible *Graf Zeppelin*. During the broadcast, he wore a twenty-four-pound shortwave transmitter tied to his chest.

Gibbons, like Kaltenborn, crammed a lot of words into every broadcast. He was clocked at 203 words a minute, which prompted the joke that once when his secretary sneezed while Gibbons was dictating, he had to repeat three thousand words.

His breezy style—he was likely to end a midnight broadcast, ". . . and I'll buzz around this old town for a handful of hot bulletins for you

Famed as an oft-wounded war correspondent before turning to radio newscasts, Floyd Gibbons was also known for his rapid-fire delivery. Culver Pictures

folks west of the river"—was deliberate. "Excitement is news," he explained. "I find out what interests me in the news. I take an incident and try to dramatize it into a human story . . . ."[9]

Gibbons's broadcast philosophy came out of his newspaper experience in Minneapolis and Chicago: "I'm something like a reporter telling his city editor about a story. You know how you shoot it in, the high spots; that's all a city editor wants to know—'two dead, gas on, a note.' He wants a vivid, realistic description, the important facts, and wants it quick. That's the way I try to put my stuff out over the air."[10]

In 1930, *Literary Digest* hired Gibbons to broadcast its poll results on Prohibition and the news six nights a week. The series was not renewed because reportedly one night Gibbons got drunk and serenaded the publisher of the *Literary Digest*, an outspoken advocate of temperance. Gibbons was replaced by Lowell Thomas, who preferred a more dispassionate approach to the news.

Orson Welles in press conference after "War of the Worlds" broadcast, 1938. Culver Pictures

After graduating in two years with both a B.S. and an M.A. from the University of Northern Indiana, Thomas had worked for Colorado papers and accumulated two more degrees from the University of Denver. A job as a teacher of public speaking and a love of adventure—living with the Eskimos in Alaska, reporting World War I, covering T. E. Lawrence in Arabia—led to a career as a public lecturer and author (with another writer's help, he wrote fifty-five books). On the side, he narrated seventeen years of Fox Movietone newsreels, and appeared in about forty feature-length nonfiction movies.

When Thomas became Gibbons's radio replacement in 1930, he launched a broadcast career that covered almost fifty years. By 1935, Thomas claimed a radio audience of twenty million. A 1939 poll ranked him first among radio news commentators. Thomas, however, "had a million dollar voice but not a nickel's worth of news,"[11] said NBC newswriter A. A. ("Abe") Schecter, who did the legwork for Thomas. The Thomas-Schecter relationship foreshadowed the working partnership in television between the reporter-cameraman team and the presenter—an anchor person—who reads and shows the news collected by others.

Schecter was NBC's one-man reporting staff in the early 1930s. Virtually anyone in the country except the president, Schecter discovered, would respond to a telephone call "from NBC." Working out of a storage room that doubled as NBC's carpentry shop, Schecter got the judge in the famous rape-murder trial of the "Scottsboro boys" to accept calls that allowed Thomas to scoop newspapers.[12]

While, for the most part, radio segregated news from entertainment, there was evidence of how the medium—and television to follow—could marry fact and fantasy in colorful but confusing ways. Beginning in 1931, "The March of Time" offered reenactments of the news of the week. Actors played Huey Long, Franklin D. Roosevelt, and other prominent people. Sometimes the reenactments were inventions—the equivalent of today's docudramas.

Most notably, in 1938, Orson Welles presented an update of H. G. Wells's drama, "The War of the Worlds," with the Martian invasion of New Jersey reported by fictional radio news bulletins. Panic ensued. But the wife of H. V. Kaltenborn ridiculed the panic: "Why, how ridiculous. Anybody should have known it was not a real war. If it had been, the broadcaster would have been Hans."[13]

Actually, the broadcaster probably would have been Edward R. Murrow. From 1938 to the end of World War II, Murrow broadcast from a bomber over Germany, from the Maginot Line, and from London under German bombing, the "blitz." The reports were all the more dramatic for their understatement. *Time* said Murrow's London reports contained "no bunk, no journalese, no sentimentality."[14] But clearly Murrow sided with the British—their "muddling through," and "their dying with dignity."[15] In detailing the destruction—"a man pinned under wreckage where a broken gas main sears his arms and face"[16]—Murrow made America realize that the 1938 fantasy of "War of the Worlds" had become 1940 fact. The world was coming to an end, not with a whimper, but with airborne time bombs, parachute flares, and incendiary explosives.

After the war, Murrow returned to New York and took over direction of the CBS news operation. Television news was just beginning. On NBC, John Cameron Swayze was broadcasting the "Camel News Caravan," and Lawrence Spivak was producing "Meet the Press." Murrow, drawing upon talent hired mostly during World War II, put together an outstanding news team—Eric Sevareid, William Shirer, Howard K. Smith, Douglas Edwards, Charles Collingwood, and Don Hollenbeck. He also developed new programs for CBS: on television, "See It Now" and "You Are There," and "People to People" (with Murrow as homes-of-the-famous host, not journalist, asking the Duchess of Windsor to play jacks); on radio, "Hear It Now," "As Others See Us," and "CBS Views the Press," the first time the electronic media dared critique the press. To head the critique, Murrow selected Hollenbeck, a gifted writer and veteran newspaperman who had worked for The Associated Press, New York's *PM*, and NBC. The program was a critical success. *Variety* raved: "[T]he first stanza went off like a howitzer with Hollenbeck

The CBS "World News Roundup" team in 1955. Edward R. Murrow at desk (right) moderates talks with (from left) Charles Collingwood, Ned Calmer, Winston Burdett, Eric Sevareid, William Shirer, Larry Lesueur, David Schoenbrun, Howard K. Smith, and Richard C. Hottelet. CBS photo

Geraldo Rivera: the future of television news?

Does the career of Geraldo Rivera, as some critics contend, parallel the descent of television news—from Murrow-style seriousness and sense of mission to the trivialization of trash journalism?

Rivera began in 1970 as a muckraking reporter for New York's WABC-TV's "Eyewitness News." Rivera—half Jewish, half Puerto Rican—was hired, he says, because ABC wanted to employ a Puerto Rican.[1] But WABC got more than a token member of a minority group. Rivera's reports on migrant labor, drug addiction, elderly care, and conditions at Willowbrook State School for the Mentally Retarded were powerful journalism.

The Willowbrook exposé in 1972 represented Rivera at his pushy best. He played by his own rules ("I believe in throwing my weight on the side of the weaker"),[2] not by the traditional rules of journalistic fairness. He dismissed objectivity as "a word that was made up by some journalism professor."[3]

Shoving his way into Willowbrook's wards, an outraged Rivera filmed naked children lying untended in their own waste. He told his audience: "This is what it looked like, this is what it sounded like. But how can I tell you how it smelled? It smelled of filth, it smelled of disease, and it smelled of death."[4]

Suddenly, Rivera was a star. A special on Willowbrook won television's top journalism awards. Offers poured in from television and motion picture companies. He hosted ABC's "Good Night America," worked as traveling correspondent for ABC's "Good Morning America," and, in 1978, became a featured reporter on ABC's "20/20."

But, in 1985, ABC did not renew Rivera's contract. He began doing syndicated specials, including a two-hour broadcast in 1986 entitled "The Mystery of Al Capone's Vaults." Television critics attacked Rivera, but the show's ratings—33.4 percent of 87.4 million households—made it the best-watched syndicated show in history.

Geraldo Rivera. Courtesy "Geraldo"

A year later, Rivera began to host "Geraldo," a syndicated talk show that has brought him such nicknames as "The Great Panderer"[5] and "the Peck's Bad Boy of television news."[6] During one episode of "Geraldo" his nose was broken by an airborne chair.

Tom Shales, television critic of the Washington *Post*, cast a skeptical eye on the topics of "Geraldo" episodes— "Is swinging sexual suicide?" "Serial killers," "Kids who kill," "Battered women who kill," and male strippers. Shales wrote, "Eventually, Geraldo will surely get around to male strippers who kill."[7]

Shales worries that this type of talk show reflects the cheapening of television news: "Broadcasting seems to be going about the unenviable business of diseducating America—of hyping all that is trivial and frivolous, and hiding all that is real and relevant."[8]

But Rivera, while acknowledging there is a lot of Walter Winchell and "having fun" in what he does, describes his critics as ivory-tower elitists. He says talk shows "democratize real life."[9] Geneva Overholser, editor of The Des Moines (Iowa) *Register*, says, however, that to refer to the talk shows "in the lofty language of democratization of television is hogwash."[10]

Rivera, nevertheless, recalls the national-news monopoly once enjoyed by the three networks: "They reflected philosophy drawn from a narrow slice of American society."[11] Van Gordon Sauter, former president of CBS News, agrees, describing current news programs of the networks and their affiliates as airing "identical news in an identical fashion with identical anchors."[12]

Sauter defends the Rivera-style talk show as good journalism as well as great fun. By the end of 1989, however, declining ratings prompted headlines like "Twilight for 'Geraldo.'" And a public opinion poll showed that those who rated Rivera as not believable had jumped 48 percentage points—from 26 percent in 1984 to 74 percent.

lobbing the critical shells squarely at the editorial mastheads of the country's most powerful dailies."[17]

Some of the dailies responded angrily. And their Red-baiting reply was part of the story of perhaps the most important newscast in television history. Nick Kenny, a New York *Mirror* columnist, reacted to "CBS Views the Press" by agreeing with J. Edgar Hoover's description of CBS as the "Communist Broadcasting System." Kenny described Hollenbeck as "that Stalinbeck lad who makes listeners see Red when he shoots his weekly arrows at the 'capitalistic press.'"[18] William Randolph Hearst, Jr., owner of the New York *Journal-American*, complained to top CBS executives, trying to have Hollenbeck censored or taken off the air. "We took a lot of flak on 'CBS Views the Press,'" said Frank Stanton, then president of the network.[19] Ned Calmer, another CBS news commentator, said Hollenbeck "was very courageous in expressing his views . . . at a time when everybody was frightened."[20] Dozens of journalists and entertainers were blacklisted, and CBS instituted a loyalty oath. Stanton says CBS never sought to remove Hollenbeck. But in 1950 he was switched to hosting a new five-days-a-week "CBS News of America" program, and Douglas Edwards replaced him at "CBS Views the Press." That effectively gutted the program. Hearst got his wish.

Four years later, Murrow's half-hour "See It Now" broadcast on Senator Joseph McCarthy presented film clips in which McCarthy was shown scoffing at Dwight Eisenhower, attacking "Alger, I mean Adlai" Stevenson, calling General Ralph Zwicker, who was a hero of Normandy and the Bulge, "a disgrace to the Army."[21] The clips were damning, but the show's impact came from Murrow's closing: "This is no time for men who oppose Senator McCarthy's methods to keep silent . . . . The actions of the junior senator from Wisconsin have caused alarm and dismay amongst our allies abroad and given considerable comfort to our enemies, and whose fault is that? Not really

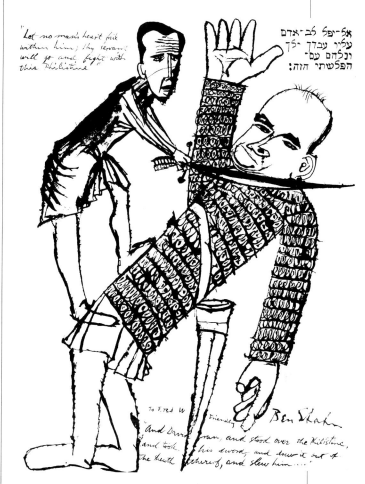

Ben Shahn drawing depicts Edward R. Murrow's attack on Senator Joseph R. McCarthy on *See It Now* as David slaying Goliath. Courtesy Fred W. Friendly

his. He didn't create this situation of fear; he merely exploited it, and rather successfully. Cassius was right: 'The fault, dear Brutus, is not in our stars but in ourselves.'"[22]

Hollenbeck came on the air in New York a few seconds after Murrow finished. Before beginning his WCBS evening news report, he said, "I don't know whether all of you have seen what I just saw, but I want to associate myself and this program with what Ed Murrow has just said, and I have never been prouder of CBS."[23] Jack O'Brian, the radio and television critic for Hearst's *Journal-American*, described the broadcast as a "hate-McCarthy telecast." He praised CBS's removal of "lefties" at lower levels. Why not Hollenbeck and Murrow next? Two weeks later, O'Brian devoted almost his entire column to Hollenbeck and Murrow: "We have discovered the newscasts and telecasts generally of Edward R. Murrow and Don Hollenbeck, to name the leading CBS leaners-to-the-left, develop a peculiarly selective slant in most of their news work."[24]

A worried Hollenbeck—suffering from a duodenal ulcer, drinking too much Cutty Sark, smoking four packs a day, trying to recover from his third failed marriage—went to Murrow about O'Brian's attack. Murrow told him not to worry—ride it out. Days later, Hollenbeck was found dead from gas asphyxiation in his apartment kitchen, a suicide. "All that vilification, Jack O'Brian, it got to him," Murrow said.[25] Murrow closed his "See It Now" broadcast with a tribute to "an honest reporter." He also arranged to have CBS stop employing a Hearst subsidiary to film "See It Now."

To this day, television news worries not only about accurately reporting events but also about shaping or even creating them. Politicians design and schedule speeches and votes at the national party conventions in anticipation of television coverage. Protesters wait for the television cameras to arrive before picketing. Terrorists orches-

trate news conferences and other pseudo-events to meet the medium's requirements. But perhaps no event has provoked more research and writing about television's role than the war in Vietnam.

At first, television coverage was primarily what the television journalists called "bang bang"—action shots of the fighting—and no one could accuse television of opposing the war. But even "bang bang" influenced the public debate in the United States. In 1965, an hour-long report from Vietnam by Morley Safer, the CBS correspondent, showed "Zippo jobs" by U.S. Marines who set ablaze the homes of Vietnamese peasants. That view of the U.S. soldier refuted the Johnson Administration's description of the war. Safer's report, correspondent David Halberstam later wrote, "was like watching a live grenade going off in millions of people's homes. Watching American boys, young and clean, *our boys*, carrying on like the other side's soldiers always did, and doing it so casually. It was the end of the myth that we were different, that we were better."[26]

The conversion of Walter Cronkite—elder statesman of journalism, most respected American—symbolized a transformation in television's coverage of the war. Cronkite had access to the U.S. military's top brass when he visited Saigon in 1965. He listened respectfully to their analyses. But he was troubled by their estimates of the extent and length of the war. Would the war be completed as easily and as quickly as they predicted? In 1968, the stalemated war and the Tet offensive lured Cronkite back to Vietnam.

Returning home, Cronkite, the model of journalistic impartiality, wrote and broadcast a half-hour news special in which he said the United States was not winning and needed to think of getting out, negotiating "not as victors, but as honorable people who lived up to their pledge to defend democracy and did the best they could."[27] President Johnson reportedly told one aide that if he had lost Cronkite—if Cronkite now opposed U.S. involvement in Vietnam—

Morley Safer in Vietnam. CBS photo

then the Administration had lost the American public.[28]

In the post-Cronkite era of television news, it is difficult to think of the broadcast journalist as an old-fashioned reporter. Contemporary television news emphasizes the performer—the personality of the presenter. One public opinion survey noted that eighty percent of the audience choose their network news programs because of the personality of the anchor. While print journalists may choose to chide their television peers for being merely entertainers, television journalists can respond that polls indicate the typical American rates the television journalist twice as believable as the print journalist.

Barbara Walters, Ed Bradley, and Sam Donaldson illustrate not only the television journalist as a personality, but also the diversity of today's broadcast journalists.

Walters, the consummate interviewer, has reason to feel at home talking with the world's celebrities. Her father, Lou Walters, founded and operated New York's Latin Quarter nightclub. After Sarah Lawrence College (where she thought of becoming an actress), Walters flirted with teaching and worked as an advertising agency secretary. She started in television as assistant to the publicity director of WRCA-TV, NBC's New York station. She then moved into producing and writing for shows that always seemed to go off the air. "Each show always had to have one female writer," she once wrote. "They would fire the whole staff, hire a new producer, and he would hire me as the one female writer."[29]

From a position as a "Today" show writer, she began conducting on-camera interviews, transforming what had been previously a position for a "Today girl"—a woman expected to smile sweetly, read commercials, and otherwise decorate the set. The public liked her intelligence before the camera. But people did not see her hard work behind the camera. She spent two years, for instance, seeking an interview with Secretary of State Dean Rusk.

Barbara Walters interviews Henry Kissinger. Associated Press photo. Courtesy D.C. Public Library

Some of her assignments echoed the "stunt girl" stories of old. She once worked as a Playboy bunny. But her strength was the interview. She even wrote a book, *How to Talk with Practically Anybody About Practically Anything.* In 1976, she moved from NBC to ABC as co-host with Harry Reasoner of the "Evening News." The move created controversy, recalled television critic Ron Powers: "Her position (as the first regular anchorwoman in the history of network television), her salary ($1 million a year under a five-year contract), and her public image as celebrity-in-her-own-right (highest rated substitute host of the 'Tonight Show Starring Johnny Carson,' . . .) all blended into a single and powerful symbol of TV news's drift toward entertainment."[30]

Walters regarded the grumbling by men about her salary, her credentials, and her personality—she was accused of being aloof, cold, and aggressive—as the result of her being "the *first* woman to really go in there and ask some tough questions."[31] Yet, the Walters/Reasoner "Evening News" program never dented the nightly news-ratings lead of NBC and CBS. Walters moved to co-hosting "20/20" and her own interview specials.

Larry Speakes, former White House press secretary for Ronald Reagan, described her interviews as the best of those conducted by network correspondents: "I always treated her with a healthy respect, not only because of her skill, but because I felt she was something of a shark. She would pretend to be friendly, and then save up some real zingers with which to end an interview."[32]

Of Sam Donaldson, ABC's longtime White House correspondent who now co-hosts ABC's "Prime Time Live," Speakes writes: "Foremost . . . for being obnoxious . . . . But I found Sam to be the brightest television reporter to cover the White House. He covered it by instinct . . . . One tactic I warned the President to look out for during press conferences was that Sam was very prone to shout misquotes or misstatements at you to try to get you to comment. Donaldson is very smart, and I'm sure it was a deliberate effort on his part to distort things in order to provoke an answer . . . . In spite of Sam's shenanigans, our analysis consistently showed that Sam and ABC were the fairest and straightest of the networks."[33]

Donaldson—despite his nicknames, "the human bullhorn" and "shoot from the lip"—consistently won polls of fellow journalists as Washington's best all-around television news correspondent. Born in El Paso, Texas, he earned a reputation as a model cadet at New Mexico Military Institute, and graduated from Texas Western College in El Paso, where he worked part-time as a disc jockey for a 250-watt AM station. After college he established a local Young Republicans chapter, spent two and a half years in the Army, and worked as an announcer for Dallas and Washington television stations. He joined ABC's Washington bureau in 1967.

His coverage of the Senate Watergate hearings in 1973 brought him wide attention. By 1977, he was covering the White House. "It's my job to ruffle feathers. Docile reporters may produce 'better stories' from the White House point of view, but not from the public's."[34]

Sam Donaldson. Rhoda Baer photo

He mixed adversarial assertiveness with instinct. In March 1979, for instance, the White House was claiming that President Carter's peace talks with Egyptian President Anwar el-Sadat and Israeli Prime Minister Menachem Begin were inconclusive. At the Cairo airport, Donaldson shouted to Carter above the noise, "Mr. President, is it peace?" Carter hesitated and answered, "I think I'd better stick to the statement because it's been approved by President Sadat and Prime Minister Begin." Donaldson continued: "But it sounds like peace—if the Israeli cabinet agrees?" Carter said, "Right."[35]

Ed Bradley projects an image that is the opposite of Donaldson's—that of the sensitive, compassionate interviewer. He bears the burden of being the leading African American network correspondent. He would like the networks to escape from the habit of thinking first of minority correspondents for stories involving minorities. But some of his finest reporting has involved minority issues.

He returned, for instance, to his hometown of

Philadelphia—he began his career there in 1963 doing unpaid news spots—to conduct a two-hour report entitled "Blacks in America: With All Deliberate Speed." The 1979 documentary, which won Emmy and duPont-Columbia awards, looked at the progress in the quarter-century since the Supreme Court's 1954 school desegregation decision. It contrasted the progress in the South—the increase in integrated schooling, voter registration, and political influence of African Americans—to the unemployment and other challenges facing blacks in Philadelphia.

Bradley's entry into television journalism helps to explain his later success. He landed a position at WCBS in 1967 by rejecting a news director's request that he send tapes of interviews he had done in Philadelphia. "You won't learn enough about me that way," Bradley said.[36] Borrowing a tape recorder, he rushed out to report on an anti-poverty program. His tape got him the job.

By 1972, he was reporting for CBS from Vietnam and Cambodia. Wounded by mortar fire, he nevertheless returned the following year to cover the Communist takeover of the two countries. Later he did "CBS Reports" segments on Vietnamese boat people and starving Cambodian refugees in Thailand. The segment on the Vietnamese opened with Bradley wading into the South China Sea to pull refugees in a flimsy fishing boat to shore.

Bradley moved rapidly at CBS from presidential-campaign correspondent in 1976 to White House correspondent to anchorman of the "CBS Sunday Night News" to correspondent for "CBS Reports" and then, beginning in 1980, to "Sixty Minutes" correspondent. He traveled one-hundred thousand miles and visited about fifty cities in his first year for "Sixty Minutes." That seemed in keeping with his image as a journalistic throwback to the trenchcoat-clad newspaper correspondent who moved from war to war.

Television newspeople, like their print counterparts, make it impossible to believe in one

Ed Bradley in Vietnam. CBS, Courtesy D.C. Public Library

stereotypical American journalist. Their diversity should be reassuring. Freedom of the press cannot mean much where only one press—or one kind of journalist—exists. Journalists do not fit Walter Lippmann's concept of flies on the wall, observing everything in a totally detached, totally neutral manner. Rather, journalists make news. They use their eyes and ears and ideas to shape and reshape an interview or a press release or a tidbit of leaked information into news. So a free society needs a variety of journalists, if only to ensure that the news they make—when considered collectively—moves the public closer to the truth.

The Journalist of Fiction

Fun-house mirror reflection of reality

Tales about journalists have a way of overpowering the reality of journalists' careers. Not everyone in Dement, Illinois, the setting for *A Family Trust*, Ward Just's 1978 novel, remembers Amos Rising, founder of the Dement *Intelligencer*. But the story about Rising that opens Just's novel lives forever.

Angered because two of his gambling clubs in the Chicago suburbs are under attack from Rising's newspaper, Al Capone sends a young thug to make Rising an offer he cannot refuse: Rising will sell Capone and his associates fifty-one percent of the newspaper, otherwise the mob boss, with unlimited cash, will start a competing paper, cut advertising rates to nothing, and drive the *Intelligencer* out of business.

The conversation turns nasty. Capone's man dismisses the *Intelligencer* as "this shitting little rag."[1] Rising taps his desk leg twice with his foot. Two associates burst from an office next door and pummel Capone's enforcer. He barely escapes, flinging an inkpot through the *Intelligencer* front window on the way out. "All in all, Amos Rising thought, a success."[2]

Just's novel ends with a family friend explaining to Rising's granddaughter that the Capone story "will never die. Well, it didn't happen in quite the way we used to tell it. Funny thing, I can't remember anymore what the truth was. So we'll have to live with the yarn, won't we? We live with the stories we make up. Those are the real stories, more real than the originals."[3]

Such "real stories" of the American journalist appear in the movies, television shows, plays, paintings, cartoons, short stories, and novels that are the subject of this section. Many fictional journalists resemble real people. Walter Burns of "The Front Page" was based on the legendary Walter Howey, the coldly calculating city editor of the Chicago *Tribune* (Ben Hecht said you could tell Howey's glass eye because it definitely was the warmer one).[4] Citizen Kane, the protagonist in Orson Welles's 1941 film classic, owes a debt to William Randolph Hearst.[5] And Clark Kent, Superman's prim alter ego, was modeled on a real-life reporter named Wilson Hirschfeld, who reportedly once remarked that he knew no one with as much integrity as himself.[6]

Fictional journalists, however, are only fun-house mirror reflections of real journalists. Fiction writers can claim—as Ned Calmer argued in an author's note to *The Anchorman* (1970)—that their characters come from "the truer world of the novelist . . . all imaginary, and all true."[7]

Artist John Byrne's statue of Clark Kent/Superman in the offices of DC Comics, Inc., New York City

Jack Lemmon and Walter Matthau starred in the 1974 film version of *The Front Page* (Universal Pictures). Poster, Library of Congress, Prints and Photographs Division

But fiction's truths, like nonfiction's truths, are not entirely true. Just as biography, journalism, and other forms of nonfiction distort reality, create stereotypes, and perpetuate myths, so fiction also produces partial truths.[8]

To make a point about journalism, writers of fiction, many of whom once worked as reporters and editors, construct make-believe newspeople whose actions bizarrely exaggerate reality. Fiction writers also bring to life the archetypal journalist they would like to have been.

Finally, writers explore the myths about the journalist that the society accepts as true. Often the myths contain little truth. H. L. Mencken argued persuasively that no fiction writer has produced an "adequate portrait of the journalist . . . ."[9]

Sometimes the myths provide dangerous illusions that distort Americans' understanding not only of the journalist but also of themselves. Other times the myths, rather than deluding, entertainingly capture an element of the journalist's character.

The myths tell us of not one journalist, but of many. This section of the book examines nine myths of journalism—from the archetypal big-city reporter, the "cross between a bootlegger and a whore"[10] in *The Front Page*, to television's multi-million-dollar anchorwoman, hungry for sex and power as well as a juicy scandal. Whatever their truth, these myths, like the story about Amos Rising, will never die.

President Reagan's doodled remembrance of his role in *Nine Lives Are Not Enough*. Copied from *ASNE Bulletin*

9 Reporter

From *The Front Page* to *The Front Page*

In the opening act of Ben Hecht and Charles MacArthur's *The Front Page*, the Chicago police reporters needle Hildy Johnson, who has just quit reporting forever to marry and to enter advertising. Murphy of the *Journal* says: "I got a dumb brother went in for business. He's got seven kids and a mortgage, and belongs to a country club. He gets worse every year. Just a fat-head."[1]

"Listen to who's talking," Johnson replies. "Journalists! Peeking through keyholes! Running after fire engines like a lot of coach dogs! Waking people up in the middle of the night to ask them what they think of Mussolini. Stealing pictures off old ladies of their daughters that get raped in Oak Park. A lot of lousy, daffy, buttinskis, swelling around with holes in their pants, borrowing nickels from office boys! And for what? So a million hired girls and motormen's wives'll know what's going on . . . . [Y]ou'll all end up on the copy desk—gray-headed, hump-backed slobs, dodging garnishees when you're ninety."[2]

Johnson's angry retort, however accurate, belies his love of reporting. By play's end, you know he'll be back in harness soon. Johnson's passion for reporting symbolizes the playwright's nostalgia for "the lusty, hoodlumesque half drunken caballero that was the newspaperman of our youth."[3] The play's amusing portrait of the reporter—as wittily irreverent cynic and conniver determined to scoop the competition—has endured. The generation of real journalists dating from the 1960s may combine, as James Boylan writes, "the individualism and flair of

The Front Page (that is, of yellow journalism) with the ideology and seriousness of 'professionalism.'"[4] But usually the professionalism gets left out of contemporary fiction, leaving *The Front Page* elements to define the journalist of today.

The continuing impact of *The Front Page*

Ben Hecht and Charles MacArthur collaborated on *The Front Page,* a favorite of audiences for over sixty years. This playbill is from 1986. Playbill ® is a registered trademark of Playbill Incorporated, N.Y.C. Used by permission

PLAYBILL®

LINCOLN CENTER THEATER AT THE VIVIAN BEAUMONT

THE FRONT PAGE

Robert Redford and Dustin Hoffman visit the Main Reading Room of the Library of Congress in *All the President's Men* (Warner Brothers, 1975.) Movie still photo by Stanley Tretick

Pat O'Brien and Adolphe Menjou starred in the original
film version of *The Front Page*. (United Artists, 1931.)
Movie still, courtesy of New York Public Library

His Girl Friday, yet another film version of the play *The
Front Page,* featured Rosalind Russell as a female Hildy
Johnson. (Columbia, 1940.) Hand-tinted movie still,
courtesy of the Brian Ann Zoccola-Irv Letofsky Collection

should not be a surprise. The 1928 play became
a hit film in 1931. Other Hollywood versions followed: Rosalind Russell played a female Hildy
Johnson in *His Girl Friday* (1940), Jack Lemmon
acted the original part in a 1974 edition, and
Kathleen Turner portrayed Hildy Johnson as a
television reporter in *Switching Channels* (1988).
A 1949–50 television series—"The Front Page"
set in a small town—cast CBS newsman John
Daly as unscrupulous editor Walter Burns.
Windy City, a musical version of the play, opened
in 1982 with Dennis Waterman as Hildy Johnson.

New York revivals of the *The Front Page* sell
out every generation—1946, 1968, and 1987—
and productions, amateur and professional, annually reintroduce the rascally reporters to new
audiences across the country. The play's influence has extended to hundreds of newspaper
movies and novels and plays in which reporters
wear hats indoors, hide whiskey flasks in bottom
desk drawers, wisecrack about cops, judges, and
editors, especially editors, and display an all-
consuming devotion to The Story.

Not that the reporter didn't exist in American fiction prior to 1928. The success of the
nineteenth-century penny press focused attention on the reporter who gathered the news. By
1871, a writer for *Lippincott's Magazine* could
argue that "for the majority of readers it is the
reporter, and not the editor, who is the ruling
genius of the newspaper."[5]

The reporter piqued the public's interest.
"There are few things concerning which the
general public is more curious, and about which
it knows less," Edwin Shuman wrote in his how-
to guide, *Practical Journalism*, "than the inside
of a metropolitan newspaper office."[6] Fiction
romanticizing the work of the big-city reporter
began to fill the void. The year 1890 saw the
publication of the first novel devoted to reporting—Kirk Munroe's *Under Orders: the Story
of a Young Reporter*—and a short story that was
probably the most popular nineteenth-century
fiction about the reporter.

Under Orders often reads like a simple blurb for journalism. "A first-class, well-trained reporter is one of the brightest, smartest, and best-informed men in the city," says Van Cleef, of the New York *Phonograph.* "He knows everybody worth knowing, and every thing that is happening or about to happen."[7] He also plays amateur detective. *Phonograph* reporter Myles Manning, the novel's hero, not only reports on an important railroad strike at Mountain Junction but discovers that villainous Ben Watkins plans to set fire to the railroad company office, making it appear strikers were to blame. Manning stops Watkins and achieves at novel's end a position as "foreign writer" for an influential illustrated magazine.

Richard Harding Davis's short story "Gallegher: a Newspaper Story" (1890) sold more than fifty thousand copies when published in book form. It recorded the exploits of Gallegher, a Philadelphia *Press* office boy in whom "the detective element was abnormally developed."[8] Gallegher helps capture Hade, a notorious murderer. By lying to the police and stealing a horse-drawn carriage, Gallegher gets the story back to his paper before deadline . . . and before the competition. He proclaims, "I beat the town."[9]

Fiction from the early twentieth century painted a less upbeat picture of the reporter's life. Henry Beeker, the "reliable reporter"[10] in Ben Ames Williams's *Splendor* (1927), has no illusions: "I've been in the newspaper game long enough to know that most of the men who stick to it either die from overwork or go crazy or take to drinking or something."[11] Beeker's paper demotes him to the reference department.

Regret, in newspaper novels, often takes the form of a reporter's disappointment at not having tried to write the Great American Novel. In fact, Clyde Brion Davis, a newspaperman, wrote a novel entitled *"The Great American Novel—"* (1938). Despite his father's warning that newspapermen are "a drunken, shiftless lot of deadbeats,"[12] Homer Zigler becomes a reporter—and a drunken, shiftless deadbeat. His existence

"News," Isamu Noguchi's 1938 sculpture on the facade of the Associated Press building, New York City. Courtesy Associated Press

echoes a reporter's line in Thomas Wolfe's "Gentlemen of the Press": "Christ! Maybe some day I'll write a book myself—about all the poor hams I've known in this game who were going to write a book—and never did. What a life!"[13]

But the public failed to be fascinated by the newspaperman trying to become a serious writer. "There are two kinds of newspapermen," Ben Hecht explains in his novel *Erik Dorn* (1921), "those who try to write . . . and those who try to drink themselves to death. Fortunately for the world, only one of them succeeds."[14] The public responded, however, to the reporter who was a doer.

Isamu Noguchi's mammoth 1938 sculpture on the facade of the Associated Press building in New York captured the rushing movement—the energy and action—of the reporter. So did much fiction about the reporter as spy, adventurer, and, most importantly, amateur detective.

The reporter and the detective both were considered hard-working and highly moral, even when breaking the law.[15] Both insisted on remaining loners and working by their own idiosyncratic rules.[16] And both mixed with high-hatters and the hoi polloi; they, like the heroes of Vern Partlow's song "Newspapermen" (1943),

Nine Lives Are Not Enough, a 1941 B picture starring Ronald Reagan as a brash reporter-photographer, managed to capture nearly every cliché of newspapering. (Warner Brothers, 1941.) Movie poster, courtesy of the Brian Ann Zoccola-Irv Letofsky Collection

"wallow[ed] in corruption, crime, and gore."[17] To put the reporter and detective together in one person made for an ideal protagonist.

George Harmon Coxe, a former newspaperman, banged out mystery novels at the rate of three a year about newshounds, including photographers Kent Murdock and Jack "Flash" Casey, who worked as amateur detectives. Casey became the hero of a radio show, two motion pictures, and a television series with Darren McGavin. Heavy-drinking and handsome, "Flash" was given a personality that fitted many reporter-detectives. Coxe's description: "a quick impatience, especially with bores and phonies, a touch of irascibility too often quick to surface, a sharp and cutting tongue, frequently regretted, to express displeasure when some wrong, real or fancied, had been done, especially to those who lacked weapons to defend themselves."[18]

"Flash" Casey had plenty of company. Ronald Reagan starred as a boastful reporter-photographer in *Nine Lives Are Not Enough* (1941): "On the strength of my story and my story alone, he's behind bars."[19] Even Ernest Hemingway wrote a reporter-detective story (fortunately for Hemingway's literary reputation, the story remains unpublished).[20] The pulp magazines (including *Front Page Stories* and *Newspaper Adventure Stories*) featured Theodore Tinsley's Jerry Tracy, "a Broadway wiseguy" gossip columnist,[21] Fred Mac Isaac's tramp reporter Addison Francis "Rambler" Murphy, and Richard Sale's breezy Joseph "Daffy" Dill. A typical Daffy Dill story opens: "When I came into the city room of the New York *Chronicle* I felt lower than a flounder's flatside, and I had a hangover that would have done credit to the old Romans of Bacchus' day."[22]

For children, board games—"Five Star Final" and "Scoop!"—and such stories as Mildred Benson's *Dangerous Deadline* (1957),[23] Norton Jonathan's *Dan Hyland Police Reporter* (1936),[24] and Walter R. Brooks's tales about Freddy the Pig[25] married reporting to sleuthing. Crime-solving comic-book superheroes—not

The reporter's top priority—winning a Pulitzer Prize

The easiest way for a novelist to show a journalist's independent contrariness is to have the character denigrate the Pulitzer Prize. In *Del-Corso's Gallery* (1983), novelist Philip Caputo conveys the attitude of Harold Bolton, a Pulitzer-winning bureau chief in Saigon: "[T]hose journalistic medals were given out by the sort of men Bolton despised, pompous editors who made Rotary Club speeches about the first amendment and the mission of a free press in a democracy."[1]

But in the typical novel about the press, the Pulitzer Prize is the Holy Grail. The young, ambitious reporter dreams that today's assignment—however routine it may appear—will bring him a story worthy of the Pulitzer. Elliott Chaze writes in *Tiger in the Honeysuckle* (1965): "Publishers liked kids who said Golly-Moses when offered eighty a week and who liked to run out in the middle of the night and cover fender bendings and who thought you could win the Pulitzer prize with a really crackling account of an overnight freeze."[2]

The Pulitzer often is a more powerful lure than money. A news source in Carole Nelson Douglas's *The Exclusive* (1986) tempts reporter Liz Jordan: "I've, uh, got a story for you. . . . It just might be your ticket to a Pulitzer."[3] In Garry Trudeau's "Doonesbury" comic strip, a weary reporter refuses to quit journalism because, he says, "I'm only two leaks away from a Pulitzer Prize."[4]

The Pulitzer Prize also dominates the thoughts of newsroom has-beens who want to make up for mediocre careers. In Michael Malone's *Dingley Falls* (1980), A. A. Hayes daydreams about winning a Pulitzer "in recognition of his quiet decades as the editor of a small-town weekly. . . ."[5] In a mystery novel, when an older reporter starts talking about winning a Pulitzer, he can be counted a sure-fire candidate for the morgue. "All my life I wanted to win the Pulitzer Prize," says reporter Merrill McDaniels in Tony Hillerman's *The Fly on the Wall* (1971). "Wanted somebody to pay attention to me."[6] Six pages later, somebody does, and McDaniels winds up dead.

In earlier generations, fiction portrayed reporters as motivated by the big story, the "game" of journalism, and the by-line on Page One that might bring a bigger paycheck or at least a pat on the back. But today every good reporter (even Lois Lane)[7] wins a Pulitzer or lusts for one. A soon-to-be-killed reporter in Jeff Millar's *Private Sector* (1979) tells her reporter/lover, "Win the Pulitzer for the Gipper."[8]

In the journalism of the real world, the Pulitzer has assumed almost the same importance. Newspaper promotion departments spend thousands of dollars touting their entries for the Pulitzer Prize. "It has gotten to the point where many papers have large segments of the staff devoted to nothing but trying to win Pulitzer Prizes,"[9] writes Dave Barry, a Miami *Herald* humor columnist and winner of a Pulitzer.

Pulitzer Prize medal. Courtesy, The Washington *Post*

Barry jokes about Pulitzer entries—multi-part, million-word stories like "Death From Below: How 10,000 Americans Each Year Are Killed By Their Own Plumbing"—that bore readers and waste a lot of trees and staff time. His tongue-in-cheek solution is to have newspapers, whenever they feel like it, print stories claiming they have won Pulitzer Prizes. "What the hell? The public won't know," Barry says. "They don't read that stuff anyway."[10]

only Superman (Clark Kent)—chose newspeople as their mortal identities. The roster of those superheroes reads like a guest list for a Halloween party: The Black Fury, The Ray, Bob Phantom, Captain Zero, The Crimson Avenger, The Destroyer, Elastic Lad, The Fox, Megaton Man, Miss America, Mr. A., Patriot, Son of Vulcan, Spider-Man, Spider-Ham, The Sword, and The Wasp.[26]

The Watergate reporting by The Washington Post's Robert Woodward and Carl Bernstein gave birth to *All the President's Men* (1975), a movie promoted as "The Most Devastating Detective Story of This Century." Novelists soon flooded bookstores with Washington investigative reporters, invariably winners of Pulitzer Prizes. Drew Pearson had previously provided Hap Hopper, a comic-strip crusader, but now Les Whitten, Jack Anderson's ferret, created Aubrey Warder of the Washington *Eagle*.[27] The Washington Post's Lawrence Meyer answered with reporter Paul Silver of the Washington *Herald*.[28] And Marc Olden created Harker, a Washington reporter for the New York *World-Examiner*, who had won two Pulitzers.[29] Perhaps the most blatant cloning of Woodstein occurred in Jeff Millar's *Private Sector* (1979). Millar's "perfect couple"—CBS TV's John Harland and The New York *Times*'s Molly Rice—saved the U.S. government from being taken over by two hundred mega-corporations.[30]

Molly Rice represented a growing interest in the woman gumshoe reporter stereotype. Minority reporters, however, rarely appeared in fiction.[31] African Americans were usually the victims of white reporters—as in Langston Hughes's "Name in Print"[32]—or journalistic Tontos to white Lone Ranger reporters and editors.

An exception—reporter Max Reddick in John A. Williams's *The Man Who Cried I Am* (1967)—works for a left-liberal New York newspaper and then a national newsmagazine where he is "a new Negro employee, a pioneer, a 'first

Negro first.'"[33] Reddick began his career on the *Harlem Democrat*, interviewing Moses Lincoln Boatwright, a Harvard-educated African American who is finally executed for murdering and cannibalizing a white man. Boatwright had refused to tell white reporters the parts of the man he had eaten. Reddick receives a note from Boatwright written the afternoon before his execution: " . . . I took the heart and the genitals, for isn't that what life's all about, clawing the heart and balls out of the other guy?"[34]

In Arthur Hailey's *Overload* (1979) African American reporter Nancy Molineaux of the *California Examiner* stalks terrorists and Golden State Power and Light officials. She remains as independent and autonomous as any of her white male predecessors. "I know you prefer being a loner, and you've gotten away with it because you get results," growls Molineaux's city editor. "But you can push that game too far." Molineaux shrugs: "So fire me."[35]

While reporters have continued to be portrayed positively, cynicism toward all institutions—the press as well as Congress, religion, and business—has spawned fictional reporters who subvert the social order instead of defending it. Sometimes these anti-heroes or non-heroes lie to uncover the truth, but often they lie to lie. Sometimes they pursue the murderer, but occasionally they murder. In Jim Thompson's *The Nothing Man* (1954), Clinton "Brownie" Brown of the Pacific City *Courier* commits—or thinks he commits—the Sneering Slayer murders.[36] In the film *Al Capone* (1959), Keely, a sleazy reporter based on the Chicago *Tribune*'s Jake Lingle, works for the Chicago mobster, double-crosses him, and winds up a corpse.[37]

Roger Simon's *Wild Turkey* (1974) presents a fictional version of *Rolling Stone* journalist Hunter S. Thompson. Gunther Thomas, "the renowned Ph.D. in guerrilla journalism,"[38] smokes joints and lies through his bourbon breath. "I'll be back in twenty minutes . . . ," he says,[39] returning in thirteen months. Thompson

Pulp magazines quickly exploited the popularity of the reporters in Hecht-MacArthur's play *The Front Page*. *Newspaper Adventure Stories* magazine. Courtesy San Francisco Academy of Comic Art

wrote *Fear and Loathing in Las Vegas* (1971), which follows Raoul Duke on assignment with his three-hundred-pound Samoan lawyer Dr. Gonzo. Duke rents a red Chevrolet convertible, the Great Red Shark, and fills the trunk with acid, mescaline, cocaine, uppers, downers, and screamers. Duke plans to cover a motorcycle and dune-buggy race as if it were the ultimate story, a Second Coming, "the American Dream"[40]—a search for "[f]ree lunch, final wisdom, total coverage."[41]

But Duke never actually reports anything,

instead pumping himself full of drinks and drugs: "Why bother with newspapers . . . . Agnew was right. The press is a gang of cruel faggots. Journalism is not a profession or a trade. It is a cheap catch-all for fuckoffs and misfits—a false doorway to the backside of life, a filthy piss-ridden little hole nailed off by the building inspector, but just deep enough for a wino to curl up from the sidewalk and masturbate like a chimp in a zoo-cage."[42]

Gregory Mcdonald's Irwin Maurice Fletcher, the investigative reporter who stars in nine best-selling whodunits and two movies, represents the contemporary reporter. In *Fletch* (1974), the first novel in the series, Mcdonald's reporter works undercover as a beach bum on a drugs-amid-the-dunes investigation. He also tries to fathom millionaire Alan Stanwyk who, for fifty thousand dollars and a plane ticket to South America, wants Fletch to murder him.

To solve the two mysteries, Fletch, who describes himself as a liar with a magnificent memory, breaks all of journalism's rules. He pads his expense account with penicillin treatments for sex with strung-out druggies. He masquerades as a doctor, an insurance investigator, and reporter Bob Ohlson from the competing *Chronicle-Gazette*. In the end, Fletch cracks the drug ring, discovers Stanwyk is a murderer, and leaves the country with two attaché cases filled with three million dollars in tens and twenties.

Despite the drugs and other reminders of contemporary America, Mcdonald laces the Fletch mysteries with *Front Page* fun. Fletch skewers Clara, his news editor, with acerbic one-liners reminiscent of Hildy Johnson's assaults on Walter Burns. A police chief's routine questions also prompt wisecracks from Fletch. Police chief: "Do you live alone?" "Except for a pet roach." "And what do you do for a living . . . ?" "I'm a shoeshine boy."[43] The portrayal of Fletch, like that of many fictional newshounds, owes less to real reporters than to the newsroom reprobates of *The Front Page*.

See Porcupine, in Colours, just Portray'd,
Urg'd by old Nick, to drive his dirty trade;

Veil'd in darkness, acts the assassins part,
And triumphs much to stab you to the heart.

''See Porcupine, in Colours, Just Portray'd,'' 1799 engraving. William Cobbett, who wrote under the name ''Peter Porcupine,'' was perhaps the most venomous editor/printer in the history of American journalism. Courtesy, The Historical Society of Pennsylvania

10 Editor

From Peter Porcupine to Lou Grant

America's most famous newspaper editor—subject of a wax-museum exhibit—only worked at his trade for five years. On television, no less. From 1978 to 1982, Lou Grant served as Los Angeles *Tribune* city editor, loved by public and press alike.

In some ways, the "Lou Grant" show did not challenge the age-old stereotype of the hard-boiled city editor. The show also failed to reproduce faithfully the real city editor's daily desk-bound routine. For example, as David Shaw, press critic of the Los Angeles *Times*, noted, "A big-city editor does not go out on story assignments."[1]

But Lou Grant's version moderated the image from the first generation of talkies where the miscreant city editor destroyed reputations and drove reporters to suicide.[2] Grant had integrity. "You hired me for being a man of strong opinions!" he shouted at his publisher. "You didn't say they had to be yours!"[3] Grant's integrity, moreover, was not paired with the sadism characteristic of the fictional city editor from the '30s—"this mythical agate-eyed Torquemada," in Stanley Walker's words, who "invents strange devices for the torture of reporters."[4]

If the city editor represents the big-city press of the twentieth century, a very different editor symbolized the nineteenth-century press. That editor—responsible for the entire paper—ridiculed people in stories and participated in partisan politics. Embodiments of those journalistic sins first made their appearance in Hugh Henry Brackenridge's *Modern Chivalry*, Part II (1804 and 1805),[5] the earliest American novel about the editor.

Brackenridge created Peter Porcupine, an editor whose personal attacks on Paul Polecat offend half the village. The other half defends Porcupine. A town meeting tries to decide the dispute. Speeches in defense of Porcupine's press freedom and scurrility meet with a persua-sive counter-argument—that abuse by the press, not press freedom, is the real issue. The town meeting moves to permit the continued publication of Porcupine's newspaper, but recommends that another paper be begun as competition. Porcupine, however, leaves town in a hurry, threatened not only by the potential competition but by arrest for libel and overdue bills.

In a commentary that accompanied the novel, Brackenridge, a knowledgeable journalist instrumental in establishing the Pittsburgh *Gazette*, explained *Modern Chivalry* as an attack on *the* symbols of press scurrility—William Cobbett, a Britisher who departed the United States one step ahead of a libel suit, and J. T. Callender, sentenced under the Alien and Sedition Act of 1798.

America's most famous fictional editor on television—Lou Grant. Courtesy "Lou Grant," MTM Enterprises, Inc.

Brackenridge also created an unnamed radical editor who argues that his paper, *Twilight*, must invade privacy and find fault to satisfy subscribers: A "newspaper is a battery, and it must have something to batter at."[6] But Captian Farrago, governor of the district served by the paper, argues for less bile and more balance: "I had no idea of shackling the press, but only of suggesting such hints, as might conduce to its credit, and the good of the community."[7]

A vituperative press was not just a creature of Brackenridge's imagination. U.S. newspapers from 1790 to 1820, says historian James Melvin Lee, demonstrated that "the new freedom of the press promoted not truth but calumnies and falsehoods."[8] Not surprisingly, pre-Civil War novelists followed Brackenridge's example. They portrayed the American editor as Peter Porcupine. In fact, James K. Paulding used the name again as the moniker for an editor in *The Diverting History of John Bull and Brother Jonathan* (1812). Peter Porcupine, the partisan blackguard, is echoed in other pre-Civil War editors— jail-worthy Janson in Frederick William Thomas's *Clinton Bradshaw* (1835), hypocritical Captain Kant in James Fenimore Cooper's *Homeward Bound* (1838), Steadfast Dodge in Cooper's *Home as Found* (1838), the unnamed liar who edits the *Crater Truth-Teller* in Cooper's *The Crater* (1847), and Augustus Postlethwaite Tompkinson, Eliphalet Fox, and Virgil Philpot in John Pendleton Kennedy's *Quodlibet* (1840). The editor during and after the Civil War stopped being synonymous with the sins of the partisan press. First, the newspaper became more complex, not just a soapbox for the editor, but an advertising medium for merchants, and a source of up-to-the-hour news for readers. Second, the reporter and publisher/owner established themselves as more visible symbols of a rapidly growing business— a giant industry with highspeed presses and armies of advertisers and millions of readers. Third, the editor no longer performed every function. He couldn't possibly write articles and editorials, set type, and run the press. Specialization meant a more limited role for the editor, who now often directed only the newsroom.

Some fiction written during and after the Civil War continued to portray editors as patronage-hungry partisans. Scatchal and Scourage, the editors in John Ferguson Hume's *Five Hundred Majority* (1872), line their pockets with Tammany bribes. Henry Sedley, author of *Dangerfield's Rest; or, Before the Storm* (1864), describes the press as "too much under the control of men who, entirely blackened and disgraced themselves, have been seldom happy unless hard at work begriming and traducing all who come within their sphere, that none may be distinguished as being above their own dirty level."[9]

But most post-Civil War novels depicted the big-city editor, for the first time, as worrying about beating the competition to a news story, and conducting himself as a responsible professional who sets high standards for his reporters.

The novels frequently were written by editors who viewed newspaper work with affection. Bayard Taylor, a Horace Greeley protegé at the New York *Tribune*, described two editors in *John Godfrey's Fortunes; Related by Himself. A Story of American Life* (1867). The first editor, the New York *Daily Oracle*'s Mr. Brandagee, represents an earlier generation of unscrupulous villains. But Mr. Clarendon, of the New York *Daily Wonder*, who hires the novel's hero, symbolizes the new editor. Thoughtful, decisive, and street-smart, Clarendon demands of his reporters "a plain style, exact adherence to facts, and above all—quickness."[10] Clarendon also pursues thorough coverage of New York, employing a city editor (mentioned for the first time in an American novel).

Speed—beating the competition—became a major responsibility for the new editor. In Harriet Beecher Stowe's *We and Our Neighbors* (1873), the wife of Harry Henderson, a New York editor, writes that "the demands of this New York newspaper life are terribly exhausting. It's a sort of red-hot atmosphere of hurry and competition . . . [N]ews-papers jostle each other, and run races, neck and neck, and everybody connected with them is kept up to the very top of his speed, or he is thrown out of the course."[11]

The editor also had to fend off advertisers and other businesspeople who wanted to corrupt him. *The Money Captain* (1898) by Will Payne, financial editor of the Chicago *Daily News*, pits Hamilton J. Leggett, editor of the Chicago *Eagle*, against Archibald Dexter, the city's gas baron. Leggett accuses Dexter of bribing the city council; Dexter retaliates by having Leggett arrested for criminal libel, vowing to send him to the penitentiary. Attacked by one of his bribery cohorts, Dexter dies of heart failure. Leggett covers the *Eagle*'s front page with a damning obituary ("Archibald Dexter, Arch Corruptionist") and, in the last edition, adds an editorial-page item pointing to Dexter's corpse as valuable for "illuminating its epoch."[12]

But however well the editor responded to corruption, however speedy his staff, he was doomed toward the end of the nineteenth century to become primarily a background character. In Kirk Munroe's *Under Orders: the Story of a Young Reporter* (1890)—dedicated to John Bogart, city editor of the New York *Sun*, and written by a former *Sun* newsman—the editor still plays an important role. The story's Bogart-like city editor, Joe Haxall, encourages cub reporters, disciplines the tardy, and defends his staff against unfair criticism. He foreshadows the

Board game "Five Star Final," © 1937. Courtesy Laurence Paddock, editor, *Daily Camera*, Boulder, Colorado. Photo by Reid Baker, Library of Congress

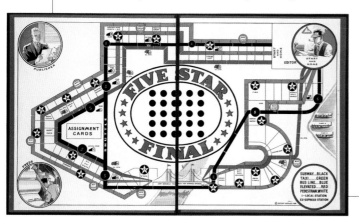

Edward G. Robinson plays the tough managing editor in *Five Star Final.* (Warner Brothers, 1931.) Courtesy The Irv Letofsky Papers in The Elwyn B. Robinson Department of Special Collections, Chester Fritz Library, University of North Dakota

gruff-on-the-outside, caring-on-the-inside city editors of 1930s fiction and film. But the reader knows that Haxall is merely a foil for the boy reporter, the story's hero.

Nevertheless, the hard-boiled editor—following *The Front Page*'s success as a Broadway play in 1928 and as a movie in 1931—became a staple of twentieth-century American mythology. In Silas Bent's *Buchanan of The Press* (1932), as in many novels, a stranger with "the look of a nervous and irascible man" enters the newsroom. Reporter Luke Buchanan "knew enough about newspaper offices to know that this man would be his boss, for this was the City Editor."[13] The movie industry also gave viewers tough-guy editors galore—Edward G. Robinson in *Five Star Final* (1931), Clark Gable in *After Office Hours* (1935), and Spencer Tracy in *Libeled Lady* (1936).

Even the comics perpetuated the stereotype of the editor who, through teeth tightly gripping a cigar, screams at his staff, "Is this a paper or a rest home?! Heads are gonna roll!"[14] Perry White, Clark Kent's ornery editor, found his way into comics, radio, television, and motion-

Does an editor have a duty to be irresponsible?

In 1970, Daniel Ellsberg called New York *Times* correspondent Neil Sheehan with an offer to provide the Pentagon Papers—the classified Defense Department history that helped explain the course of U.S. involvement in Vietnam.

Should Sheehan's editor have told him that the *Times* was not interested? A Garry Trudeau cartoon captured how Sheehan might have responded to the prospect of the leak: "But thanks anyway, Mr. Ellsberg."

The newspaper editor, in fiction and fact, stands at the center of an important debate about freedom of the press.

Must a free press also be a responsible press? Or does a free press, obligated to reveal even material the government stamps secret, have a duty to behave in ways that many would judge irresponsible?

After the *Times* published three daily installments of the Pentagon Papers in June 1971, the Justice Department won a temporary restraining order prohibiting publication of the remainder of the series. The government lawyers contended that continued publication would bring "immediate and irreparable harm" to the "national defense interests of the United States and the nation's security."[1]

The U.S. Supreme Court voted 6 to 3 that, in this case, the right to a free press came first. In a concurring opinion, Justice Hugo L. Black said: "Only a free and unrestrained press can effectively expose deception in government. . . . [F]ar from deserving condemnation for their courageous reporting, *The New York Times, The Washington Post* and other newspapers should be commended for serving the purpose that the Founding Fathers saw so clearly."[2]

The late Howard Simons, managing editor of the Washington *Post,* looked at the Pentagon Papers case through the eyes of a thirty-year veteran of Washington: "[I]t is difficult to work there without bumping into a secret. By one estimate, there are 20 million documents classified every year, some of them newspaper clippings. I learned that secrecy labels are attached to many of these documents, not to protect a true secret, but to avoid embarrassment or to cover up a cost overrun or an abuse of power, or to stifle criticism or to avoid public scrutiny. Or simply out of habit."[3]

But after the Pentagon Papers, after Watergate, after other press-government confrontations, a number of journalists asked whether the press was irresponsibly harassing government. In a 1982 speech, Michael J. O'Neill, then editor of the New York *Daily News* and president of the American Society of Newspaper Editors, told the Society that "we should make peace with the government; we should not be its enemy. . . ."[4]

O'Neill looked at the press and saw an institution with "an adversarial mindset." He contended: "Our assignment is to report and explain issues, not decide them. We are supposed to be the observers, not the participants, the neutral party, not the permanent political opposition."[5] Sociologist-senator Daniel Patrick Moynihan wrote of the press growing "more and more influenced by attitudes genuinely hostile to American society and American government."[6]

But other journalists responded that real news does not come easily. "News," as Lord Northcliffe reportedly said, "is something someone wants to suppress."[7] To get it, a journalist must be willing to reconcile himself to being labeled irresponsible, live with the threat of a lawsuit, and take solace in the words of Hippolyte de Villemessant, founder of *Le Figaro,* who stated in 1866: "A journalist whose writing does not stir up either a duel or a lawsuit is a bad journalist."[8]

Cartoonist Garry Trudeau comments on the Pentagon Papers case. Copyright 1971, G. B. Trudeau; courtesy Charles W. Bailey

Spider-Man cartoon strip (1977), with the stereotypical boss editor. Spider-Man: TM © 1989, Marvel Entertainment Group, Inc. All Rights reserved.

picture serials. In an early episode of a 1940 movie serial, White (played by Pierre Watkin, formerly editor of the Sioux City *Tribune* and Sioux Falls *Argus*) responds according to form. When Superman's rescue of a woman receives a *Daily Planet* banner headline ("Man from Sky Saves Girl"), White bellows at his staff: "Of all the stupid stories that have come across my desk, this is the worst . . . . It's a case of mass hysteria and that's how I want it played. Now get out of here, all of you."[15]

The tough-guy stereotype required two traits of an editor. First, he had to believe that getting the story was all that mattered. His reporters counted for nothing. Journalism ethics existed only as an oxymoron.

Second, the editor had to be so malevolent that his staff prayed for his early demise. Reporters sometimes responded to the editor's criminal behavior with public deference. But privately reporters spewed only disrespect and derision. One reporter described his editor as "sort of a cross between a ferris wheel and a werewolf—but with a lovable streak, if you care to blast for it."[16] Another reporter barked: "All editors are idiots. There are no exceptions."[17]

George Bancroft played an iron-willed editor in *Mr. Deeds Goes to Town* (1936). When he be-

rates his staff to the point of degrading them, one reporter momentarily loses his temper and shouts a profanity. The honking horn of a passing car prevents Bancroft from hearing the words. "What did you say?" Bancroft shouts. "Er . . . I said," the frightened reporter stammers, quickly looking at the editor's ceiling, "you've got dirty plaster."[18]

A few tough editors survived into the '50s. In *Deadline, USA* (1952), Humphrey Bogart created the role of Managing Editor Ed Hutcheson, who launches a campaign against a Mafia leader (a hit man falls into the printing press and finds himself all over page one). But Hutcheson fails to save his paper. It dies.

A generation ago, editors became paper-pushing newsroom bureaucrats who conferred with lawyers, carried out the publisher's orders, and consoled reporters. Editors faded into fiction's woodwork. Clark Kent's editor was demoted to adorning a Super Heroes cookbook with "Perry White's Great Caesar's Salad."[19]

Perhaps by the '50s the end of an era had arrived. Newsroom bosses lacked luster as leaders and as leading men. In *Francis Covers the Big Town* (1953), Gene Lockhart played editor to a talking mule. Editor Sam Gatlin (Jack Webb) in *—30—* (1959) came across, typically, as dully responsible and deadpan (or, rather, as dead).

Humphrey Bogart as a crusading managing editor of a doomed newspaper in *Deadline USA*. (20th Century Fox, 1952.) Courtesy The Irv Letofsky Papers in The Elwyn B. Robinson Department of Special Collections, Chester Fritz Library, University of North Dakota

"Morning papers." Painting by J. G. Brown, 1899. Copley Newspapers, Inc., Courtesy The James S. Copley Library, La Jolla, California

11 Newspaper Carrier

Journalism's Hero

Neither the eighteenth-century newspaper carrier nor today's version is fiction's favorite. Eighteenth-century carriers—Boston printer's apprentice Benjamin Franklin[1] and New York *Gazette and Mercury* printer's apprentice Lawrence Sweeney (haughtily dismissed by a competing paper as "the egregious and clamorous Lawrence Sweeney")[2]—made the history books for being first. And today's carriers, a vanishing breed of child warriors, earn our sympathies. Facing muggers and worse, they deliver papers in even the most robbery-ridden neighborhoods.

But in between the printer's apprentices and the home-delivery carriers, there were the ebullient newsboys and newsgirls who shouted their wares on the street. The greatly outnumbered girls greeted a newspaper-sponsored carrier excursion, from which they were excluded, with smiles, according to an 1881 *Harper's Weekly* cartoon. They sold all their papers that day: "A day of rejoicing for the newsgirls."[3] They also developed their own sales techniques. Little Annetta, a teary, three-year-old Chicagoan, literally gave her papers away, earning more in tips, her sister said, "than all of us together."[4]

Newsboys and newsgirls alike were known for their effective, enthusiastic salesmanship. "So entirely absorbed do these urchins become in their vocation," stated *Leslie's Weekly* in 1856, that they continue their cries, "along an entire block of buildings in which every house is closed and not a possible purchaser in sight."[5] But newsies, as their fictional image captured, were much more than salespeople. In an 1866 novel for children, Luke Darrell, fourteen-year-old Chicago newsboy, is advised to pursue a college education and a literary career. Recalling his

"Extra." Painting by John George Brown. From the Collection of Dr. and Mrs. Kenneth Blau

A newsie shouts the headlines for the Philadelphia *Sunday Press*. Poster, Library of Congress, Prints and Photographs Division

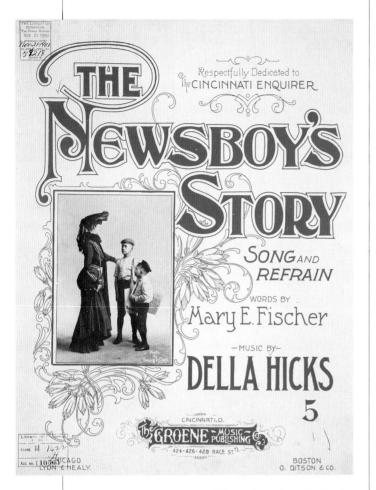

"The Newsboy's Story," 1892, dedicated to the Cincinnati *Inquirer*. Sheet music. Library of Congress, Music Division

afternoons hawking the *Evening Journal*, Luke chooses instead to become a farmer. He laughs, "My *calling* may be said to have been a *literary* one for nearly five years."[6]

The literary work of the newsboy, whom historian Frank Luther Mott has called the "humblest of our journalists,"[7] required ruthlessly editing the paper's contents into a few, often brief words—for example, "Railroad accident. Twenty lives lost."[8] Then the newsboy hit the street, heralding his headline. If his headline—or the headline he lifted from the paper's front page—captured the public, he sold out. Harry Golden, editor of *The Carolina Israelite*, recalled barking headlines from the corner of Delancey and Norfolk Streets in New York: "I could sell 100 papers a day; with a good headline, 150."[9]

A visitor to the United States a century ago criticized newsboys as the "controlling editors in American journalism," their "opinions in turn shaped by the prevailing interests of the public."[10] No doubt the newsboys knew the importance of developing a headline the public would buy. In an 1892 C. S. Reinhart drawing, an illiterate newsboy hands a regally dressed gentleman a paper: "Read me sumpin to holler, Boss."[11] When a newsboy dies "frozen through" because that night his papers didn't sell and he had no home, the heroes of "The Roosevelt Bears get out a newspaper" (1907) invent stories—ten feet of snow in July, ten thousand killed by mosquitoes, a nineteen-foot man—that guarantee every newsie will sell out and a newsboy home will be built.[12] The ends to which a newsboy will go to invent a salable headline are capsulized in the story, perhaps apocryphal, about the sly street waif who bellows: "Twenty-two people swindled." The tempted reader pays the newsboy a penny, looks for the swindle story, and, when he cannot find it, turns to complain. The newsboy, who is now a half block away, shouts "Twenty-*three* people swindled."[13]

But the image of the newsboy that survived was not that of a sly huckster. The newsie symbolized America at its active, persevering, freedom-loving best.

Paintings, sheet music, fruit box labels, movies, statues, children's fiction—all suggested the image of the noble newsboy conveyed in Mark Twain's *A Connecticut Yankee in King Arthur's Court* (1889). When a boy begins trumpeting the first issue of the Camelot *Weekly Hosannah and Literary Volcano*, the Yankee declares that "one greater than kings had arrived—the newsboy."[14]

The newsboy represented a young America. The nation, like the newsie, was filled with energy and potential. With that energy and potential, the future would be bright. Both the newsie and the nation would grow in strength and independence as they matured. Boston newsboy Ned Nevins, the hero of Henry Morgan's 1866 novel, has no father, no education,

The real newsie: more hardship than heroism

The newspaper carrier of fiction is best known for heroism, not handicaps and hardships. In comic books, newsboy Billy Batson shouts "Shazam" and becomes Captain Marvel, "the world's mightiest man . . . powerful champion of justice."[1] Freddy Freeman, disabled newsboy, transforms himself into Capt. Marvel, Jr., "the famed flying foe of evil."[2]

But the early newsies of fact often were homeless waifs, hawking newspapers to survive. They slept huddled together in abandoned stairwells, packing cases, and wooden barrels. Unscrupulous saloonkeepers solicited their business, feeding them liquid lunches of whiskey at three cents a glass.

The New York *Sun* of the mid-nineteenth century charged children sixty-seven cents for one-hundred papers.[3] The carriers sold the papers for a penny apiece, but were not reimbursed for unsold copies. In order not to lose their investment they were forced to stay on the street selling, regardless of weariness or the weather.

Ballads and broadsides captured their plight. "The Newsboys" describes the midnight chill on a deserted street in December: "A poor ragged boy . . . shivers with cold as each blast sweeps him by, His shrill treble voice on the night air is stealing, 'Five o'clock Herald! one cent sir, please buy.' "[4]

Church organizations established newsboy lodging-houses in many cities. In lower Manhattan, where an estimated forty thousand deserted children lived, a six-pence lodging-house provided food and a bed, evening school, a gym, and even a bank.[5] At one lodging-house, a boy who had deposited twelve dollars received an overcoat worth ten dollars as a prize for the largest deposit.[6]

But for every child who found shelter in a newsboy lodging-house, hundreds were forced to fend for themselves on the street.

Lewis Wickes Hines photograph: "Girls coming through alley. The smallest girl has been selling for 2 years. Hartford Conn. Mar. 1909." Library of Congress, Prints and Photographs Division

The Boston *Herald,* like many other newspapers, used the newsboy as a company emblem. Coin plate. Courtesy Loren Ghiglione

and no money. But he supports his sick mother by picking coal at a dump and by hustling newspapers. He explains his hard work, "I want to be free,—that is, what mother calls self-reliant . . . ."[15] By going to night school, leading a principled life, and working hard as a newsboy, he will achieve independence.

The newsboy also symbolized four important changes in American life. First, Americans in the nineteenth century turned away from military and political heroes and began developing heroes in commerce.[16] The heroes were local. In paintings, they did not wear classical garb but the clothes, however tattered, of the city streets.[17] In fiction, they did not speak the refined language of the well-educated but the vernacular. These new American heroes sought glory on the battlefield of trade. Writing in 1843, Joseph C. Neal said, "Our clarion now, more potent than the Fontarabian horn, is the shrill voice of the news-boy."[18]

Second, rural society was giving way to the

urban. The newsboy of fiction often had left the farm to seek opportunity in the city. There the pint-sized pioneer of the urban frontier found not only opportunity but a different and dangerous way of life. A whole subgenre of early movies developed around newsboys being struck by a car or truck.[19] Newsboys also boozed; an ad for a 1930s magazine, *Newspaper Adventure Stories,* tells the tale of newsboy Lucian Senox, "demoted to the reportorial staff, where he made less money but got more gin."[20] In *John Ellard, The Newsboy* (1860), Philadelphia newsies not only drink, but swear, chew tobacco, and frequent gambling saloons. They are in constant danger of being cheated, robbed, even murdered. The Philadelphia newsies, however, have the heroic toughness to survive: "For quickness and shrewdness, newsboys as a class excel all others."[21]

Third, conditions in the immigrants' crowded slums raised the question of whether America's faith in the individual was only so much rhetoric. The newsies of fiction demonstrated that— despite poverty and privation—one could live by a code, a clear notion of individual honor and individual justice. Horatio Alger, Jr., whose 117 novels sold millions of copies, explained the theme of his six children's stories about the newsboy: "[H]is history will at least teach the valuable lesson that honesty and good principles are not incompatible even with the greatest social disadvantage. . . . "[22] Alger's newsie always pays his debts. He doesn't sell papers in another newsboy's territory. He doesn't cheat customers, either by selling yesterday's unsold papers as today's or by returning less than the correct change. And he metes out newsboy justice to those who don't play fair.

Fourth, the newsboy represented the transition to a modern, mass-distribution, big-city journalism of high-speed typesetting and printing, circulation-hungry publishers, and first-with-the-story reporters. The emphasis was on speed. The carrier in William Gropper's "Newsboy" (1945)[23] streaked across the cartoon. Sheet

"The Newsboy," carved and assembled wood, 1879. This 42″ high trade sign originally hung outside the front office of the Pawtucket (Rhode Island) *Record*. Courtesy the Michael and Julie Hall collection. Photo by Thomas B. Wendell

music—"Newsboy Galop," "Newsboy Polka," and "Newsboy Schottische"—suggested fast feet. Inevitably, when The Boston *Herald*,[24] The Pawtucket (Rhode Island) *Record*,[25] or another newspaper chose a newsboy as its emblem, it depicted a carrier racing down the street and shouting the contents of the paper he held in his upraised hand.

The newsboy's feet and mouth moved quickly; if his ethical sense was not as developed, that could be blamed on the journalism he repre-

sented. As Rube Goldberg's cartoons indicated, publishers churned out money-making extras that failed to distinguish between the momentous and the trivial.[26] Rufus, the essentially honest newsboy hero of Alger's *Rough and Ready; or, Life Among the New York Newsboys* (1869), is not above "manufacturing news to make his papers sell."[27] Alger excuses this ethical lapse by noting that Rufus "was only imitating the example of some of our most prominent publishers."[28]

Despite the occasional lapse, the ethics and achievements of the fictional newsies are such that they come across not only as the most commendable of journalists but also as mythic figures—self-reliant survivors of city life who are truly American heroes.[29]

"No Place for a Nice Girl." Painting by Dean Cornwell, 1956. Courtesy Chicago Press Veterans Association

12 Newswoman

Tough and Tormented

The ten veteran newsmen—unbuttoned vests, opened collars, loosened ties—dominate the smoke-filled, paper-littered newsroom. In a corner sits a young woman, a candidate for a reporter's job. Her sorrowful face, slouched shoulders, and clasped hands tell of her isolation. Though she has her back to the newsmen, she feels their stare. Or do they glare? The young woman's presence, it appears, threatens them.

Perhaps that is not the story behind Dean Cornwell's "No Place For A Nice Girl." But the 1956 painting reflects generations of newsroom rejection. It also raises a question: Can a newswoman be both what the culture asks of a stereotypical "nice girl" (passive, sweet, content, virtuous, marriage-minded) and what journalism expects of her (alert, ambitious, and Amazon aggressive)?

Not until the 1890s could someone write of "women regularly employed on a daily newspaper."[1] A few newswomen—Margaret Fuller, Elizabeth Cochrane (Nellie Bly), Winifred Black (Annie Laurie), D. G. Croly (Jenny June)—achieved fame. But most were confined to promotional stunts, "sob sister" human-interest stories, or "women's news" coverage. They were not permitted to write on important topics—men's topics—for instance, "politics, finance, and even baseball (O crucial test!)."[2] They received few front-page assignments or top newsroom positions. No surprise, then, that little early fiction featured newswomen.[3]

The fiction that did, however, perpetuated stereotypes. In Victorian America, newspaper work—indeed, most work except housework—was for men. A woman should marry, then keep her house clean and her family happy. If a woman were so unfeminine—and so uncaring of husband and children—as to attempt newspaper work, she could expect ridicule.[4] Myra Mold, the dedicated editor in David Ross Locke's *A Paper City* (1879), faces the charge that because of her work she has neglected her husband, children, and home.[5]

To become a journalist, a woman needed the strongest of excuses. A dead husband and starving children to feed might do. But even then only the most foolish of women admitted in polite society that they scribbled for a living. Helen Harkness, the heroine of William Dean Howells's *A Woman's Reason* (1883), worries about her Boston friends discovering she writes for a newspaper.[6] The widow who produces a newspaper column in Rebecca Harding Davis's *Frances Waldeaux* (1897) stops writing for fear her son will learn of her trade.[7]

Linda Watkins played a reluctant woman reporter in *Sob Sister.* (Fox, 1931.) Promotion from *Film Daily*, April-June 1931

Victorian sensibilities called for a lady-like "nice girl" to place marriage before career. In Rebecca Harding Davis's "Earthen Pitchers" (1874), Philadelphian Jane Derby pens a successful woman's column and letters from Paris and Rome (written, of course, from Philadelphia).[8] But her main motives are to marry the man she loves and have his children. Helen Fisbee replaces hospitalized John Harkless as editor of the Carlow County *Herald* in Booth Tarkington's *The Gentleman from Indiana* (1900). Fisbee, who "can turn off copy like a rotary snow-plough in a Dakota blizzard,"[9] triples the circulation of the *Herald* and takes it daily. But in the end, she appears ready to marry Harkless and abandon her career for his.

The newswoman who tried to have both career and marriage walked a tightrope. If she were judged insufficiently compassionate, she, by definition, stopped being a lady—a woman worthy of marriage. If she were judged too compassionate, she risked being typecast as too soft— not enough like a man—to be a journalist. In Elizabeth Garver Jordan's *Tales of the City Room* (1898), reporter Ruth Herrick knows success is hers if she can discover whether a woman murdered her husband. The woman confesses to Herrick, explaining that her husband had attacked her aged mother. Herrick says, "I am going to forget this interview. I am going to let you have the chance which a fair trial will give you."[10] The woman is acquitted. Herrick's managing editor concludes, "Strange how Miss Herrick failed on that case . . . . But, after all, you can't depend on a woman in this business."[11]

The devoted newswoman ready to put aside all thought of marrying[12] was not rewarded, however, for her single-mindedness and self-assertion. Those traits counted only as character flaws. In Gertrude Atherton's *Patience Sparhawk and Her Times* (1897), Miss Merrien, a reporter for the New York *Day*, does what is expected of her to survive in journalism, including faking a story. Her editor loads her with bottom-of-the-barrel assignments—interviews on "What would

Sara Payson Willis ("Fanny Fern") Parton, 1864. Library of Congress, Prints and Photographs Division

you do if you knew that the world was to end in three days?" He refuses to train her for the editorship she deserves. Eight or ten years is all that a poorly paid, overworked newswoman can stand, Miss Merrien says. "About six out of every ten newspaper women either go to the wall or to the bad."[13]

Perhaps no nineteenth-century novel portrayed the newswoman's plight more powerfully than *Ruth Hall: A Domestic Tale of the Present Time* (1855), a roman à clef by Fanny Fern (Sara Payson Parton), herself a successful journalist. Elizabeth Cady Stanton, the famous suffragist, applauded *Ruth Hall*—*Ruthless Hall* as one reviewer called it[14]—as the first novel by a female to portray a woman's life honestly.[15] Hall lives in a world of malevolent males. Her father, to save money, pushes her to marry at sixteen. Her husband dies of typhoid fever, leaving her and their two children in poverty. When she decides— reluctantly, of course—to enter journalism, penny-pinching male editors reject her work or pay only fifty cents an article.

Her writing, however, brings acclaim and makes her newspaper editor wealthy. She asks for a raise. "There it is," the editor says, smiling, "women are never satisfied. The more they get, the more grasping they become."[16] But John Walter, a smart New York editor, hires Hall to write exclusively for his paper. Hall earns a fortune. And a collection of her newspaper pieces—a book like Fern's own *Fern Leaves from Fanny's Portfolio* (1853)[17]—makes her famous. At novel's end, while "strong-minded" Hall may choose to wed Walter, marriage is not inevitable. But her independence, from malevolent and

Dinah Mason, the hard-boiled, sleuthing film critic of Richard Sale's novelette. Courtesy Bernard A. Drew

marvelous males alike, and her self-respect are certain.[18]

The twentieth century—the era of World War I, the Nineteenth Amendment, and the Great Depression—brought an increasingly self-confident newswoman to comic strips, movies, short stories, and novels. Frank Godwin's comic strip about Constance Kurridge began in 1927 as the story of an attractive socialite who goes to picnics and masquerade parties. In 1934, however, Connie starts working as a *Daily Buzz* reporter. She handles a robbery, a disappearing scientist, and a baffling kidnapping "like a veteran."[19]

Film portrayed the able, adventurous newswoman as early as Thomas Edison's *The Reform Candidate* (1911). Indeed, movie historian Deac Rossell writes, "continuing throughout the 1920s and coming to full flower in the 1930s, the newspaper film genre was the only place where an actress could portray a role that stood on an equal footing with men."[20] While the young female reporter on a real newspaper might be restricted to the "women's page" and "society" news, the film newswoman did everything. Joan Crawford captured mobsters (including Clark Gable) in *Dance, Fools, Dance* (1931); Mae Clarke got the bad guy and a front-page scoop in *The Final Edition* (1932); Glenda Farrell as Torchy Blane, heroine of nine movies, chased murderers around the world in *Fly-Away Baby* (1937); and Bette Davis nabbed the killer in *Front Page Woman* (1935), which was based on a Richard MacAulay story entitled, ironically, "Women are Bum Newspapermen."

Short stories by William Allen White and Jack London were not atypical of popular-magazine fiction. White's "Society Editor" (1906) lionized a hard-working Miss Larrabee. Other newswomen—the less worthy ones who wore white stockings and low shoes and read their own unpublished short stories—regarded the society editor's "wide-shouldered shirtwaist and melodramatic openwork hosiery with suspicion and alarm."[21]

Positive images of the newswoman: exceptions to the rule

Only rarely does contemporary fiction portray a woman journalist as a whole human being. In Caryl Rivers's *Girls Forever Brave and True* (1986), Peg Morrison, a Pulitzer Prize-winning Washington journalist, no longer tries "to be just like the men."[1]

Morrison understands the dilemma faced by every woman journalist: "If I try to be macho, flaunting my nonexistent balls, I'm a bitch and a castrating woman. I can't get into the old boy network, but God forbid if I bat my eyelashes to get lunch with an undersecretary. They say I made it on my back. If I admit I actually *feel* something about a story, I'm an overemotional broad. How do I win?"[2]

Even the detective novel—a genre that, historian Kathleen Gregory Klein claims, chooses not to allow women to function as competent, independent heroes[3]—now features an occasional woman reporter who, without a man's help, solves crimes and successfully makes her way in the world.

The woman reporter in earlier detective fiction inevitably shouted her independence but proved her dependence. In Paul Gallico's "Solo Job" (1937), Sally "Sherlock" Holmes, New York *Standard* reporter, rebuts the claim of her night editor and fiancé that she's "just a girl": "No. No, Ira, I'm not. I'm a reporter. . . . I've always worked alone. I can stand on my own feet, Ira. I won't let what we are to each other change what we are to ourselves."[4] But she escapes death at story's end only because her fiancé has her tailed. "Always watch over me," she tells him. "It is what you're here for."[5]

Nevertheless, Samantha Adams, the Atlanta *Journal-Constitution* reporter-detective in Alice Storey's *First Kill All the Lawyers* (1988), nails the murderer and, perhaps to illustrate her independence, resists a fling with her first lover: "Now she was grown-up."[6] Free-lance reporter Louisa Evans deals honestly with her divorce and her workaholic behavior in Jane Johnston's *Paint Her Face Dead* (1987). And Nyla Wade, a small-town reporter with "a Mickey Spillane heart underneath a Doris Day facade,"[7] solves the murders and forth-rightly confronts her sexual identity in Vicki McConnell's *The Burnton Widows* (1984).

A few fictional news-women, at least, are beginning to be portrayed as something other than unfulfilled unfortunates in need of a man.

Lois Lane finds new purpose and independence in this 1967 representation of her character. Lois Lane is a trademark of DC Comics Inc. © 1968.

In "Amateur Night" (1906), London's plucky Edna Wyman, twenty years old, heeds an editor's advice to "make yourself indispensable;"[22] by story's end she earns a position as a newspaper writer. The hardboiled pulp fiction magazines of the 1930s featured short stories about Whitman Chambers's Katie "Duchess" Blayne, police reporter for *The Sun*, and Richard Sale's Dinah Mason, film critic of the New York *Chronicle*. Both women proved as capable as any male sleuths.[23]

Novels of the 1920s and 1930s offered other variations on the theme of woman as competent journalist. Esther G. Hall's *Haverhill Herald* (1938) and Clarence Kelland's *Contraband* (1923) developed the small-town stereotype. Carol O'Farrell succeeds with the weekly *Herald*, founded by her father, despite those who say that "newspaper work doesn't seem suitable for a girl."[24] In *Contraband*, Carmel Lee inherits the Gibeon (Maine) *Free Press* and crusades successfully against liquor smuggler Abner Fownes, who holds a chattel mortgage on the paper. Lee: "Everybody said I couldn't run a paper. But I can. I *can*."[25]

Still infecting much fiction, though, was the notion that women lacked the toughness to be real journalists. Perhaps small-town editors or big-city "woman's page" writers. But not police reporters or foreign correspondents. The worn-out woman reporter in Edna Ferber's *Dawn O'Hara, The Girl Who Laughed* (1911) is ordered to bed by her doctor: "Newspaper reporting, h'm? . . . That's a devil of a job for a woman . . . . can't you pick out something easier—like taking in scrubbing, for instance?"[26]

To succeed, fictional newswomen had to become "men," denying their womanhood, or they had to exist only in relation to men.[27] This was increasingly evident in the fiction and film images of the 1940s. Beauty, dependence, irrationality—"feminine" traits—are more important. In movies, girl-next-door types usually do not become newswomen. Brassy blondes or clever flirts do.[28]

Katharine Hepburn and Spencer Tracy co-starred in *Woman of the Year*. Hepburn played a world affairs pundit, Tracy a sports columnist (MGM, 1941). Movie still. University of Southern California Cinema-Television Library

These newswomen use their wiles to snare men: reporter Rosalind Russell remarries Cary Grant, her editor and former husband, in Howard Hawks's *His Girl Friday* (1940); sob sister Barbara Stanwyck captures Gary Cooper in *Meet John Doe* (1941), and syndicated newswoman Katharine Hepburn finally makes a good marriage mate for sports reporter Spencer Tracy in *Woman of the Year* (1942). Comic-strip beauties Brenda Starr and Lois Lane, both superb reporters, pine for men. Starr pursues her Mystery Man.[29] Lane longs for Superman.[30] Tears come to her eyes in "Assignment: Heartbreak!" when Superman puts his arm around Wonder Woman. Lane asks, "Does he think *I'm* made of *steel?*"

"Portrait of a Lady" (1941) by Martha Gellhorn, a talented war correspondent married to Ernest Hemingway from 1940 to 1946,[31] profiles Ann Maynard, a World War II correspondent in Finland after the Russian invasion. Dressed in a ski suit that "exaggerated . . . her not looking like a woman,"[32] Maynard reports from the front. Her stereotypical macho obsession with her work as a correspondent ("I am here where no one has been")[33] is replaced, irrationally, almost overnight, with a crazy urge to be

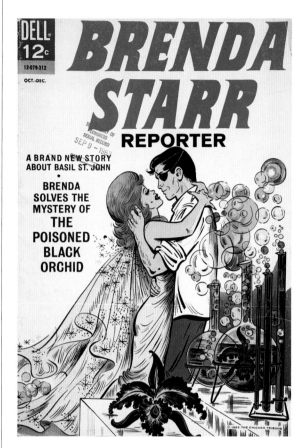

Dale Messick's Brenda Starr was an outstanding reporter obsessed by her love affair with "The Mystery Man," Basil St. John. The Chicago *Tribune*

Anna Hastings stirred up passions and politics in the halls of Congress. Cover, Allen Drury's *Anna Hastings,* (New York, Warner Books, 1977)

not only loved but owned by Lieutenant Lahti, a Finnish aviator. He treats her like a "high-class whore."[34] But when he is shot down she describes his death as if it entails hers: "And now I will never have anything . . . . I have lost everything I wanted . . . ."[35]

The contemporary newswoman, while regularly cast as a tough, talented pro, often bears the burden of being depicted as an emotionally empty Super Bitch or Super Whore.[36] Bitchiness even characterizes comic-strip newswomen. In "Dick Tracy" reporter Wendy Wichel growls: "The public should be reminded that no police officer in history has killed in the line of duty as often as Dick Tracy!"[37]

Promiscuity, like bitchiness, is used as an excuse in the soft-porn fiction of today to explain away newswomen's success.[38] Newswomen writhe as well as write, sleeping with their sources and their editors. The archetypal Super

Whore is a blond female television journalist. Jeff Millar's *Private Sector* (1979) provides ABC News's Trish Denning ("beige pantsuit, two buttons too many open at the neck"),[39] Allen Drury's *Mark Coffin, U.S.S.* (1979) features Lisette Grayson ("the Hill's most famous bedroom newslady"),[40] and Michael Barak's *The Phantom Conspiracy* (1980) offers Rachel Burke ("the blond, curvaceous CBS reporter [who] knew how to use her advantages").[41]

Even women publishers—fictional clichés popular after Katherine Graham became publisher of the Washington *Post*—usually are portrayed negatively, as unfulfilled and unfeeling. For every admirable Margaret Pynchon, the publisher of the Los Angeles *Tribune* on television's "Lou Grant,"[42] there are at least three man-killers. In Diana Davenport's *The Power*

Eaters (1979), Hilda Doral, publisher of America's most powerful evening paper, murders her stepson to obtain her publishing empire.[43] Myra Pell, of Warren Adler's *Henderson Equation* (1979), institutionalizes her husband and then brings him home to sit next to the family's trophy guns. He shoots himself in the mouth.[44] In *Anna Hastings: The Story of a Washington Newspaperperson!* (1977), Allen Drury's heroine pushes her paper to be the most principled and the most aggressive anywhere ("Anna's a better man than both of you . . . . And tougher").[45] To keep that reputation, she publishes an exposé about her husband, who then commits suicide. She adopts the motto for the paper of: "The Truth—Regardless!"[46]

Joan Mellen, after studying "new" movies of the sixties and early seventies, concluded that they did not provide new, positive images; the newswoman and other professional women who have replaced family and home with career are, however talented in their work, "empty, disintegrated and alienated."[47] Megan Carter (Sally Field) in *Absence of Malice* (1981), Tony Sokolow (Sigourney Weaver) in *Eyewitness* (1981), Kimberly Wells (Jane Fonda) in *The China Syndrome* (1979), and other newswomen in movies confirm Mellen's conclusion.

Perhaps the same can be said of newswomen in all of fiction. They are expected to hunger for a good man or a family as much as for a good story. If they don't, they are dismissed as unfulfilled—women who might as well be men. If they do pursue men, they are rejected as women not serious about their career—dependent women who rely on men for self-fulfillment.[48] Fiction, for the most part, still suggests that the best place for a woman is not in the newsroom.

In *Absence of Malice,* Sally Field portrayed an idealistic but misguided reporter (Columbia, 1981). Library of Congress, Prints and Photographs Division

Sigourney Weaver in *Eyewitness* played yet another woman journalist whose career is "empty, disintegrated and alienated" (20th Century Fox, 1981). Movie poster, Library of Congress, Prints and Photographs Division

13 Scandalmonger
Seller of Sensationalism and Sleaze

When Emile Gauvreau, managing editor of the New York *Mirror*, completed his second novel, *The Scandal Monger* (1932), worried staff members presented him with a Luger automatic. They expected Gauvreau might require it.[1] The book-jacket blurb for *The Scandal Monger* promised an exposé of, in the patois of the publicist, "glorified Peeping Toms who . . . are terrorizing the metropolis. To feed the insatiable appetite for scandal they do not hesitate to break up homes, blast reputations, wreck men and women's lives."[2]

Gauvreau's solicitous staff knew the novel was really about one scandalmonger—the *Mirror*'s Walter Winchell. Winchell had threatened to quit if the novel was not suppressed. And the Broadway columnist—with his automatics and his armed bodyguards—provoked fear. What would Winchell do about publication of *The Scandal Monger*?

The novel hatchets Roddy Ratcliffe—named after the rodent—whose "scavenging beak"[3] and "slimy eyes"[4] symbolize the gossip columnist's prying, parasitic work. A prima donna without a sense of ethics—but with a talent for sleaze and "slanguage," as he names his new argot—Ratcliffe echoes Winchell in minute detail. Winchell had started as a vaudeville dancer; so too, Ratcliffe. Winchell had written a column in which he had an ocean liner landing at the "port of Paris"; Ratcliffe repeats the same impossibility of geography. Winchell had printed a prediction of a gangster's execution; Ratcliffe does the same, raising questions about Winchell's ties to the mob. In the end, Ratcliffe, the five-thousand-dollars-a-week columnist and radio commentator, loses everything and goes crazy.

Hedda Hopper interviews Gene Tierney under the watchful gaze of 20th Century Fox mogul Darryl F. Zanuck. Photo by Ralph Crane for *Life,* 1946. Courtesy Black Star

Gauvreau also had written Winchell into his first novel, *Hot News* (1931). Columnist Wanda Winthrop (real name Walooska Vladekowsky)—"he-woman" spewing "amazing gibberish of scrambled lingo"[5]—keeps her ear to the gutter. She also destroys people: "In a year's time Wanda's column of inside gossip caused seventy-five divorces . . . ."[6]

But Winchell never harmed Gauvreau.

Other writers of novels and movies also tried to exploit the public's interest in scandal and its personification, Winchell. The word "scandal" found its way into a string of Hollywood film titles: *Scandal for Sale, Night Club Scandal, Scandal Street, Design for Scandal*, and three newspaper movies called *Scandal Sheet*. Ed Sullivan and other syndicated scandalmongers never could equal for venality their movie counterparts: Douglas Fairbanks, Jr. in *Love is a Racket* (1932), Ned Sparks in *Crusader* (1932), and Lew Ayres in *Okay, America* (1932). But Winchell tried—by playing himself in *Wake Up and Live* (1937) and *Love and Hisses* (1938). In a four-year period, George Jean Nathan claimed, twenty-seven plays and forty-three movies included characters patterned after Winchell. He even

Real-life scandalmonger Walter Winchell played himself in *Love and Hisses.* (20th Century Fox, 1938.) Movie still. New York Public Library

achieved song celebrityhood in "I Want to Be in Winchell's Column."[7]

Winchell was not the only scandalmonger fictionalized by Hollywood. Two of the *Scandal Sheet* movies depicted Charles "Hardboiled Charlie" Chapin, city editor of the New York *Evening World*. Chapin, a sadistic slave driver, once bragged, "I was myself a machine, and the men I worked with were cogs."[8] He boasted of firing 108 staffers. Once, Irvin S. Cobb, then on the *World*'s staff, learned Chapin was ill. Cobb spoke for the entire newsroom: "I trust it's nothing trivial."[9] Chapin murdered his wife and died in Sing Sing Prison. In the 1931 *Scandal Sheet*, the editor discovers his wife is having an affair with a banker and kills him. Sent to prison, the editor runs the inmate newspaper. In the 1952 version, the editor murders his wife and waits for the investigative reporters on his staff to nail him.

Winchell and Chapin, of course, did not give birth to newspaper scandal. It had been on the American scene for almost two-hundred and fifty years. In 1690, when Boston's Benjamin Harris produced his first and only issue of *Publick Occurrences*, he made sure to include on his front page a tearjerker about a tragic old man, "of somewhat a Silent and Morose Temper,"[10] who was driven by the Devil to hang himself.

Early fiction focused on Paul Pry characters who infringed upon people's privacy. But not until the late nineteenth century did novelists begin to create fictional equivalents of yellow journalists. The stereotype of the scandalmonger started to take shape. First, the scandalmonger not only infringed upon privacy, he stomped it to death. Second, if he could not find titillating news, he created it. Third, he callously disregarded the damage done to those he besmirched.

Henry James's *The Reverberator* (1888) introduced the society paper's European correspondent, George M. Flack, who tries to win the heart of Francina Dosson by smearing the family of her fiance, Gaston Probert. Flack publishes information that violates the confidence of the naive Dosson, and he regularly invades people's privacy: "I'm going for the secrets, the *chronique intime*, as they say here; . . . Now what I'm going to do is to set up the biggest lamp yet made and to make it shine all over the place. We'll see who's private then!"[11]

In Miriam Michelson's *A Yellow Journalist* (1905), Rhoda Massey, a reporter for the San Francisco *News*, has to overcome being treated like a newswoman freak; "they felt for me all that delightful compound of curiosity and patronizing interest that they annually bestowed on the bearded lady or the two-headed calf."[12] Massey also has to deal with sources who tell one story to her and three different versions to three other reporters from competing papers. One source explains: "'Tain't no lie to lie to a newspaper reporter that gets a livin' by tellin' lies!"[13] But Massey succeeds anyway: "I love a secret! There's only one thing more fascinating than to know what nobody else knows; and that is to give

"The Great American Interviewer," *Puck*, March 1877. Courtesy New York Public Library

THE GREAT AMERICAN INTERVIEWER.

He starts with energy only known to the true American.   He urges on his wild career. "Who cares, who dares."   "Diphtheria? Eh?"   "You overheard their conversation?"

Impersonation: should reporters ever lie about their identity?

One controversial technique among reporters has been to impersonate a police officer, a prisoner, or a waitress, experiencing first-hand a story that might otherwise be lost or less dramatic.

In 1978, the Chicago *Sun-Times* operated a saloon—reporters worked as bartenders, photographers snapped pictures of payoffs to city officials—a ruse that resulted in a revelatory twenty-five-part series. A Pulitzer Prize jury nominated the series for an award. The objections of two Pulitzer advisory board members—Eugene Patterson and Benjamin Bradlee—prevented the Chicago *Sun-Times* from winning. Bradlee, executive editor of the Washington *Post,* explained: "How can newspapers be for honesty and integrity when they themselves are less than honest in getting a story? We instruct our reporters not to misrepresent themselves, period."[1]

Yet impersonation always has been a part of journalism, from Nellie Bly in the late nineteenth century posing as a madwoman to gain admission to Blackwell's Island Insane Asylum, to Gloria Steinem in the 1960s lying about her identity to obtain a job as a Playboy Bunny.

One of the most useful forms of impersonation—in both fiction and fact—has involved a reporter briefly becoming a person of a different race. Lois Lane, Clark Kent/Superman's sidekick, became black for twenty-four hours in a comic-book story entitled "I am curious (black)!"[2]

Three decades ago John Howard Griffin, a white working in Fort Worth, Texas, as a staff writer for *Sepia,* chemically darkened his skin and traveled the South for four weeks as an itinerant black. Griffin's account became a magazine series, then a book, *Black Like Me,* that sold twelve million copies in fifteen languages, and finally a 1964 movie starring James Whitmore.[3]

Actor James Whitmore recreated the real-life ordeal of journalist John Howard Griffin in the film *Black Like Me.* (Contintental Distributing, Inc., 1964.) Library of Congress, Prints and Photographs Division

Griffin found restaurants, rest rooms, water fountains, beaches, and jobs closed to him. "No use trying down here," an Alabama plant foreman told him. "We're gradually getting you people weeded out. . . . We're going to do our damndest to drive everyone of you out of the state."[4]

At the end of the four weeks, Griffin found himself looking in the mirror at his black self with compassion: "I knew I was in hell. Hell could be no more lonely or helpless. . . . I heard my voice, as though it belonged to someone else, hollow in the empty room, detached, say: 'Nigger, what you standing up there crying for?' "[5]

Though many journalists today define impersonation as off limits, even some of its critics permit passive posing. At Bradlee's Washington *Post,* Athelia Knight wrote a 1984 series based on bus trips with other visitors to Lorton Reformatory in Virginia. Bradlee justifies Knight's participation in the trips, which revealed how visitors smuggled drugs to inmates: "There is no pose. There may be no sign around the reporter's neck, but at no time did . . . Athelia Knight lie."[6]

Jerry Thompson, who went underground for thirteen months in 1979–1980 to report on Ku Klux Klan activities, disagrees with a ban against impersonation. His paper, the Nashville *Tennessean,* had used traditional methods to report on the Klan. But the coverage, Thompson says, proved unsatisfactory. It read like a Klan press release, with Klan leaders "getting out the message that they want to get out." Infiltration, Thompson says, was "a last resort, . . . the only way."[7]

Thompson's reporting may have been the kind "60 Minutes" Executive Producer Don Hewitt had in mind when he said: "Misrepresentation is probably not a good idea, but in specific cases it's a sensational idea."[8]

it away in a glorious, self-conscious, jubilating scoop."[14]

Yellow journalism was succeeded in the 1920s and 1930s by jazz journalism—tabloids that created fake photographs, "composographs," and ran columns by Winchell, Louella Parsons, and other tattlers. *Newspaper Adventure Stories*, a 1930s thriller pulp magazine, plugged its next issue by promising "the peeper king of Manhattan tabloids."[15]

Although jazz journalism in fiction had a short life, scandalmongers continued to thrive. To film makers, the line between a scandalmonger's character assassination and actual assassination with a gun was without significance. At least sixteen movies portrayed journalists as killers. Other films in the 1930s cast newspeople as picture snatchers and bribe takers.

Hunsecker (Burt Lancaster), the New York gossip columnist in *The Sweet Smell of Success* (1957), degraded as effectively as the '30s slingers of slime. But by the '50s the scandalmonger stood less for a type of journalist and more for a sick, sensation-seeking society.

In *Ace in the Hole* (1951), Billy Wilder, once described as a misanthrope with a mind full of razor blades, presents Chuck Tatum (Kirk Douglas), banished by eleven big-city papers to small-town scribbling for the Albuquerque (New Mexico) *Sun-Bulletin*.[16] Sent to report a rattlesnake tournament, Tatum hears of Leo Minosa (Richard Benedict) trapped in a tunnel three hundred feet below ground. Tatum recalls the 1925 case of Floyd Collins, an explorer entombed for eighteen days in a Kentucky cave. His story made front-page headlines nationwide. One reporter "crawled in for the story," Tatum remembers, "and came out with the Pulitzer Prize." Tatum extracts a promise of an exclusive on the Minosa story from his former boss in New York. Then he cynically arranges to prolong the rescue attempt. Minosa's sluttish wife (Jan Sterling) says to Tatum, "I've met a lot of hardboiled eggs in my life . . . but you, you're 20 minutes."

Ordinary citizens flock to the scene of Minosa's ordeal. The first family to arrive, Mr.

and Mrs. Federber (Frank Cady and Geraldine Hall)—"Mr. and Mrs. America," an announcer says—want their children to participate in the death watch. The father explains, "This is very instructive." A crowd of three thousand applauds Tatum, whose writing mimics the worst human-interest reporting of the tabloids. Tatum says, "The way they [the readers] like it is the way I'm going to play it." He knows how the story should end—"It's a better story if we're not too late"—but Minosa dies before rescuers can reach him.

Ace in the Hole bombed at the box office. Paramount changed the movie's title to *The Big Carnival*."[17] Some critics raved, but others labeled it "ruthless" and "unAmerican." Journalists were defensive. Bosley Crowther of the New York *Times* attacked the film as "a distortion almost as vicious as the journalistic trickery."[18] But Wilder, who had once been a crime reporter, said, "The day I read the reviews, I was on Wilshire Boulevard and . . . someone was run over by a car in front of me. A news cameraman came and took a picture. I said to him, 'Come on, let's

Front Page Stories, a 1930s pulp magazine, reflected the wide-open tabloid style of jazz journalism. Courtesy San Francisco Academy of Comic Art

help this man. He's dying.' But the cameraman replied, 'Not me, boy. I've got to get my pictures in.' And off he went."[19]

The contemporary treatment of scandalmongering suggests that the problem goes deeper. The villains have become the institutions of journalism: sensationalizing newspapers, magazines, broadcast stations, and television networks. *Slander* (1957), for example, exposes the *Confidential*-style smear magazine.

Art focuses not on the journalist's face, but on journalism's institutional face—in the case of newspapers, the front page. Andy Warhol draws page one of the September 20, 1958, New York *Journal American*.[20] Conrad Atkinson paints the front page of the New York *Daily News*, the *Village Voice*, and other papers.[21] Page one of a tacky tabloid becomes a ubiquitous symbol, evident in Warhol's "A Boy for Meg" (1961),[22] the cover art for Arnold Sawislak's newspaper novel *Dwarf Rapes Nun; Flees In UFO* (1985), and the performance costumes of Ellen Rothenberg.[23] To make a production of Sheridan's "School for Scandal" appear contemporary, an actress reads the *National Enquirer* on stage. The bold headlines more than hint at the gossipy contents.

Popular music sends a similar message. "Candle In The Wind," a musical tribute by Elton John and Bernie Taupin to Marilyn Monroe, scolds the press that "hounded" her even after death. In Don Henley's song "Dirty Laundry," journalists cry: "Come and whisper in my ear . . . . We love dirty laundry." The refrain shouts: "Kick 'em when they're up. Kick 'em when they're down. Kick 'em all around."[24]

Between the Lines (1977), *Wrong Is Right* (1981), *Medium Cool* (1969), and *Network* (1976) also tackle the issue of institutional responsibility—responsibility for sensationalism and for other forms of media murder. Haskel Wexler's *Medium Cool* depicts a television cameraman covering the protest demonstrations at the 1968 Democratic National Convention. John (Robert Foster), the journalist, and his equipment only exist as tools of the network, which works with other powerful institutions—here the

Kirk Douglas as a jaded, down-and-out reporter in *Ace in the Hole* (Paramount, 1951). Movie still. Irv Letofsky Papers in The Elwyn B. Robinson Department of Special Collections, Chester Fritz Library, University of North Dakota

FBI and the CIA—to destroy the innocent. In *Network*, cynical executives use news commentator Howard Beale (Peter Finch), a mad messiah, to build ratings. Terrorists, with the support of the executives, finally assassinate Beale on camera.

Novels like John Katzenbach's *In the Heat of the Summer* (1982)—the source for the movie *The Mean Season* (1985)—and Linda Stewart's *Panic on Page One* (1979) question newspapers' motivation. In *Panic on Page One*, the Los Angeles *Tribune*, formerly a serious sheet, faces extinction. To save the paper, the new publisher, Harrison "Trip" Crawford, hires Vince Perrino, a drunken columnist, to egg on a serial killer. The paper's circulation soars. Perrino describes journalists and others "makin' their buck on a fucked-up, crazy, psychotic creep. Hey listen— it's the new American Dream."[25]

The novel begins and ends with words published in 1835 by Alexis de Tocqueville: "In order to enjoy the inestimable benefits that the liberty of the press ensures, it is necessary to submit to the inevitable evils it creates."[26]

"The New England Editor." Painting by Thomas Hart Benton, 1946. Museum of Fine Arts, Boston

14 Small-Town Editor
Love and Hate Give Way to Nostalgia

When Norman Rockwell visited the office of country editor Jack Blanton, the *Saturday Evening Post* treated the resulting painting as if it represented unromanticized reality. Blanton, the editor of the *Monroe County Appeal*, Paris, Missouri, "is shown batting out a last-minute editorial," the *Post* wrote. "Peering over Blanton's shoulder is the *Appeal*'s printer, Paul Nipps, whose experienced eye is gauging the number of printed lines the editorial will take up." And so, name by name, detail by detail, the *Post* described the painting, as if it were a photograph documenting the world of a small-town editor in April 1945.

But the painting idealized the country editor's office. That is Rockwell coming through the door. He loved the editor's office so much that he made himself a part of it.[1] The office brought the community together. It served as what William Allen White, the famous Kansas editor, called the town's "social clearinghouse."[2]

Nostalgia for the small-town editor's world—nostalgia occasionally mixed with a touch of nastiness—has colored the country editor's image since at least the 1930s. The editor, filled with common sense and compassion, represents the wisdom of the ages even when, as with young John Boy of television's "The Waltons," he is barely old enough to vote.

Television has given us not only the nauseatingly noble editor of the *Blue Ridge Chronicle*, but also John O'Hara's small-town journalists in the 1976 "Gibbsville" dramatic series.[3] Art has offered Thomas Hart Benton's image of the pencil-in-hand "New England Editor" (1946). And Hollywood has provided many a small-town Socrates—ranging from Will Rogers as the editor of a one-man newspaper in *Life Begins at Forty* (1935) to James Cagney as an itinerant crusading reporter in *Johnny Come Lately* (1943)—and a wagon train of westerns about pistol-packing editors.

"The Country Editor." Painting by Norman Rockwell, 1946. The Curtis Publishing Company

Will Rogers starred as the folksy editor of a one-man newspaper in *Life Begins at Forty* (Fox, 1935). Movie still, New York Public Library

Mystery writers have supplied small-town sleuths. Fredric Brown builds his classic *Night of the Jabberwock* (1950) around the plight of the genial, fifty-three-year-old editor of the weekly Carmel City *Clarion* ("of course there wasn't any real news in it, but then there never was"). Editor Doc Stoeger feels compelled, when finally faced with real news, to kill not one but five great stories. Otherwise he might damage or even destroy the lives of several townspeople. He says, "But I'm not proud of myself—the only thing is that I'd have been ashamed of myself otherwise."[4]

Garrison Keillor, host of American Public Radio's "A Prairie Home Companion" from 1974 to 1987, created editor Harold Starr of the *Herald-Star*, which serves the imaginary town of Lake Wobegon, Minnesota. The *Herald-Star* keeps a near-perfect past alive at Christmas by printing a generation-old photo of Main Street at night, "snowy, the decorations lit, and underneath, the caption 'O little town of Wobegon, how still we see thee lie.'"[5] Keillor's

small-town editor puts in news items and eliminates others to perpetuate the image of the community that townspeople want. The most interesting local news—the terrible truth you'll get from waitress Dede while eating a leisurely lunch at the Chatterbox Cafe—doesn't find its way into the *Herald-Star*.

Many novelists, also nostalgic, have preferred to focus on country editors who turned their backs on the big city. William Brinkley's *Peeper* (1981) features Daniel Baxter, owner of the Martha (Texas) *Clarion*, who operates as editor, photographer, and Linotype operator. Previously a White House correspondent, Baxter explains: "A lot of people think I copped out, but I know life is better for me here [in Martha], away from bigness and crowds of people."[6]

The best-known country editor in comic strips, a bird named Shoe, perpetuates the image of the small-town curmudgeon. Jeff Mac-Nelly, creator of the "Shoe" strip, got his first journalism job on the *Newspaper*, a twice-weekly serving Chapel Hill, North Carolina. MacNelly says that Jim Shoemaker, his editor there, "resembles to a shocking degree" Marty Shoemaker, the cigar-smoking, sneaker-wearing bird who serves in the comic strip as the *Tattler-Tribune*'s editor-in-chief. The *Tattler-Tribune*'s staff includes: Cosmo ("Perfesser") Fishhawk, the somnolent but sage reporter who pens an investigative series on dental floss abuse; Muffy Hollandaise, the preppy cub reporter (she plays tennis with a Calvin Klein racket); and Loon, who photographs dog-catches-Frisbee clichés and serves as circulation manager (the title that goes with being the paper's newsboy).

Perfesser, the small-town reporter, symbolizes MacNelley's resistance to the change that engulfs twentieth-century America. MacNelly, who dismisses the word processor as "sort of a fad that will go away,"[7] has Perfesser sabotage his word processor; Shoe says to his star reporter, "In the march of progress, Perfesser, you are athlete's foot."[8]

Before the small-town journalist became a

nostalgic symbol of a simpler, pre-computer America, he represented the U.S. press at both its best and worst. "The Country Printer," Philip Freneau's 1791 poem, portrayed the jack-of-all-trades printer, the eighteenth-century equivalent of the country editor, as a respected member of the community. Readers "know him well"[9] and accept his inadequacies. The printer relies on the thrice-weekly stage and its passengers for news. If "[a]ll is not Truth . . . that travellers tell,"[10] the readers tolerate the inaccuracies repeated by the printer. The printer/journalist acts as self-censor, emphasizing local people's good qualities and concealing ill "from vulgar sight!"[11] He can be counted on to defend freedom of the press—to "favour freedom's sacred cause"[12]—and to uphold the community's values.

But small-town journalists, like their big-city counterparts, soon were attacked in real life and in fiction for their political partisanship and for what Alexis de Tocqueville called their "open and coarse appeal"[13] to the passions of their readers. They abandoned principles, de Tocqueville wrote, "to assail the characters of individuals, to track them into private life and disclose all their weaknesses and vices."[14]

Charles Dickens, relying on an 1842 visit to the United States, echoed de Tocqueville. In *The Life and Adventures of Martin Chuzzlewit* (1843-44), Dickens introduced General Cyrus Choke. Choke speaks on behalf of a small-town paper, the *Watertoast Gazette*, and sells Chuzzlewit on investing in Eden, an uninhabited frontier swamp advertised as a "flourishing city." Two reporters for the *Gazette*, assigned to write about Chuzzlewit, prove to be dimwits: "One of them took him below the waistcoat; one above."[15] When Chuzzlewit opens his mouth to speak, the

"Shoe," Cartoon strip by Jeff MacNelly. Courtesy Tribune Media Services, Inc.

Illustration from *Editorial Wild Oats*, by Mark Twain (New York, Harper & Brothers, 1905). Library of Congress, General Collections

above-waistcoat reporter drops to one knee, "looking in at his teeth, with the nice scrutiny of a dentist."[16]

Other fiction from the 1830s and 1840s—by James Russell Lowell and James Fenimore Cooper—aimed similar jibes at the small-town journalist. Lowell's *The Bigelow Papers* (1848), a collection of satiric verses by Yankee farmer Hosea Bigelow and other residents of the village of Jaalam, attacks the nation's two thousand edi-

tors, including the editor of the local *Independent Blunderbuss*: "Nine hundred and ninety-nine labor to impress upon the people the great principles of Tweedledum, and the other nine hundred and ninety-nine preach with equal earnestness the gospel according to Tweedledee."[17] Cooper's Steadfast Dodge, the mentally inactive editor of the *Active Inquirer*, represents equality gone daffy. In the name of people's rights, he hypocritically uses the paper "to pour out his vapidity, folly, malice, envy, and ignorance."[18]

Much fiction about the small-town journalist focused on the nation's westward movement. Fighting to survive, the frontier editor boomed his community and kept his readers happy, or else. Criticism of his work came not only in the form of verbal abuse but in bareknuckle attacks and pistol-whippings. In Mark Twain's "Journalism in Tennessee," for example, the new associate editor of the *Morning-Glory and Johnson County Warwhoop* has a finger shot off and two teeth knocked out. Then he is shot six times, thrown out a window, and scalped. He resigns, telling the paper's editor almost apologetically, "Vigorous writing is calculated to elevate the public, no doubt, but then I do not like to attract so much attention as it calls forth."[19]

The frontier editor also schemed and cheated. In *Westward Ho!* (1832), James Paulding, who worried that newspapers would "fall into the hands of unprincipled demagogues,"[20] created a slimy demagogue, Zeno Paddock. His paper, the *Westward Sun*, serves the Kentucky settlement of Dangerfieldville, population five hundred. A pretentious blackmailer, Paddock finally leaves journalism to run a hotel and sell whiskey to boatmen. In *A Paper City* (1879), David Ross Locke, who used the pseudonym Petroleum V. Nasby, portrayed the editors in a frontier Illinois village as bribe-taking liars. When a dishonest land developer gives an editor a half-dozen lots and the promise of a printing contract, the editor endorses a wildcat bank designed to rob the townspeople.

William Allen White: the mythic small-town editor

William Allen White's *In Our Town*—a fictional account of life in a small town—helped perpetuate the image of White as the archetypal country editor.

To the American public, the editor-owner of the Emporia (Kansas) *Gazette* symbolized courage as well as kindness, embodying the virtues of the nation's small-towns. In 1924, when both candidates for governor refused to repudiate Ku Klux Klan support, White ran as an anti-KKK candidate.

White also challenged Gov. Henry Allen's use of a new compulsory arbitration law to ban the display in store windows of signs that read: "We are for the striking railroad men 100 per cent." White sympathized with local strikers. He put one of the banned signs in his office window, altered it to read "49 percent," and declared that he would boost the number one percent every day the railroad shopmen's strike remained nonviolent.[1]

Threatened by Gov. Allen with arrest, White wrote "To an Anxious Friend," an eloquent defense of free speech that won a Pulitzer Prize. The editorial began: "You tell me that law is above freedom of utterance. And I reply that you can have no wise laws nor free enforcement of wise laws unless there is free expression of the wisdom of the people—and, alas, their folly with it. But if there is freedom, folly will die of its own poison, and the wisdom will survive."[2]

White's generous spirit showed itself in his fiction. At the end of *In Our Town,* he called for a community of compassion that would leave everyone—in words that foreshadowed those of President George Bush—"much kinder . . . much gentler."[3]

But White was more complicated than the public image of the courageous, compassionate editor. The struggling four-page paper he bought in 1895 for three thousand dollars brought him "an independence that money could not buy."[4] White wanted not only independence but also success for his paper and for himself. He sought to establish himself as a leading citizen, spearheading the establishment in 1899 of a local street fair, campaigning for a new YMCA and a new railroad, and founding the Current Club, a men's discussion group.

Biographer Sally Foreman Griffith attributes a nervous breakdown in 1901 to "increasing conflicts among the various roles that he aspired to play."[5] Those roles included not only editor and small-town booster, but novelist ("I do not seem able to write a novel"),[6] activist in Republican politics, and entrepreneur.

The national media embraced White, the small-town editor. Proclaiming "An American Institution is 70," *Life* magazine celebrated White in 1938 as "a living symbol of small-town simplicity and kindliness and common sense."[7]

White did not object to his portrayal as exemplar of small-town virtue. In his first editorial in 1895, he had written that "the new editor hopes to live here until he is the old editor, until some of the visions which rise before him as he dreams shall have come true."[8] True to his word, White remained editor of the *Gazette*, involved in improving Emporia, until his death in 1944.

A REAL AMERICAN GOES HUNTING.

In his 1924 campaign for the governorship of Kansas, William Allen White wrote, "I want to be governor to free Kansas from the disgrace of the Ku Klux Klan." Library of Congress, Prints and Photographs Division

At the end of the nineteenth century and the beginning of the twentieth, two conflicting visions of the small-town journalist took hold. The Edgar Howe school of newspaper fiction saw the small-town paper as a dark prison cell, acceptable only to those satisfied with leading lives of desperation. The William Allen White school of fiction wrote upbeat stories about country living and happy small-town journalists who, in White's words, "get more than our share of fun out of life."[21]

For writers such as Booth Tarkington, Wilbur Nesbit, Roy Stannard Baker, Alice Hegan Rice, and Michael Foster, small-town journalism was not something to denigrate but to idealize. Nowhere is the William Allen White viewpoint stated more clearly than in Foster's 1937 novel about Shelby Thrall, a New York editor who forsakes big-city journalism for the editorship of a country weekly. The novel—entitled *American Dream*—ends with Thrall addressing a soliloquy

A *Life* magazine article called William Allen White an "American Institution." Photo Bernard Hoffman, *Life* Magazine © 1938, 1966 Time Inc.

to a country chipmunk: "The American Dream. Whatever it has been, was lost in corruption: befouled by the hands of the grabbers, and peddled by the shouters through noisy streets and dirty marble corridors, and lost . . . . But . . . maybe somewhere—in the little lamplit homes along quiet streets . . . the dream might still be living."[22] Thrall's family, "emigrants to the future," find their dream alive in small-town journalism.

Howe's *The Story of a Country Town* (1885), however, depicted the small town as a depressing place that defeats its inhabitants, including the editor of its newspaper. The plot relies heavily on Howe's own life story. Howe's father, incapacitated by the Civil War, put out the *Union of States* in Bethany, Missouri, having traded a Methodist preacher's pulpit for the editor's inkwell. After two years as an editor, he deserted his family. Edgar, then thirteen, couldn't support himself working as a *Union of States* printer. After bouncing from paper to paper, he decided to establish his own. He succeeded on his third attempt—in Atchison, Kansas—filling his *Globe* with "gab, gossip, and paid locals."[23]

Working days as editor and publisher of the *Globe*, Howe wrote *The Story of a County Town* at night. The characters, appropriately, live in a world of dreary darkness. Rev. John Westlock, owner of the Twin Mounds (Missouri) *Union of States*, sneaks out of town with a widow. His son, Ned, takes over the weekly but soon learns the difficulty of overcoming the townspeople's malice and envy. "[I]f I said a good word for any of them, it was proved beyond question immediately that he was a very unscrupulous, a very ridiculous, a very weak, and a very worthless man."[24] Soon Ned longs "to give away the establishment."[25]

William Dean Howells, a native of the small-town Midwest, said Howe's novel captured "the grim truth of the picture."[26] Howells himself used small-town weeklies as the backdrop for the beginning and end of *A Modern Instance* (1882), a novel about the disintegration of a marriage.

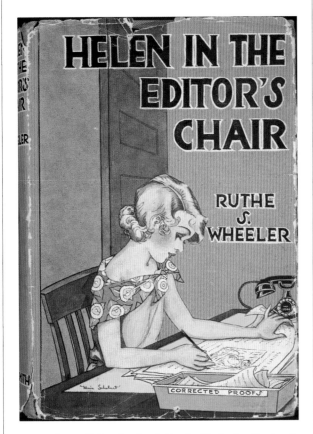

Cover from *Helen in the Editor's Chair,* by Ruthe S. Wheeler (Chicago: Goldsmith Publishing Co., 1932). Courtesy Loren Ghiglione

Bartley Hubbard edits the weekly *Free Press* in the decaying Maine village of Equity, a name belied by reality. Eventually he works for Boston newspapers, abandons his wife and daughter, and turns up in Whited Sepulchre, Arizona, where he publishes a scandalous Sunday paper. A target of Hubbard's leering lines retaliates by killing him. Matthew 23:27: "Woe unto you, scribes and Pharisees, hypocrites! for ye are like unto white sepulchres, which indeed appear beautiful outward, but are within full of dead men's bones, of all uncleanness."

The attack on the small town and its editor intensified. In *Spoon River Anthology* (1915), Edgar Lee Masters told the stories from the grave of 244 former residents of a country town, including Coolbaugh Whedon, editor of the Spoon River *Argus*. Whedon takes "every side of every question,"[27] perverts truth, and ruins local reputations to gain power and profit.

In his 1920 novel, *Main Street*, Sinclair Lewis presented Loren Wheeler's Gopher Prairie *Weekly Dauntless* as the Minnesota town's cheerleader. Whether the local amateur baseball team wins or loses, the paper's message remains the same: "Boost, Boys, and Boost Together—Put Gopher Prairie on the Map—Brilliant Record of Our Matchless Team."[28] The paper always has a well-meaning, neighborly word for everyone, making it, says an observer, "so confoundedly untrue."[29]

Main Street was a literary phenomenon, a best-seller. The novel's success made it difficult for Americans to continue seeing the small town as the soul of the nation, and the country editor as something more than a megaphone for people in the sticks. Americans realized that the nation's power and prestige—as well as most of its population—now resided in or near its cities. No longer could anyone say with a straight face, as Woodrow Wilson did in 1896, "the history of a nation is only a history of its villages written large."[30] Big-city papers, not country weeklies, excited the imagination. Young journalists left small-town papers to find better pay and greater visibility on metropolitan dailies. Those who stayed behind became symbols in American fiction of eccentric individualism—of loyalty to the community, to traditional values, to place, and to one's opinion, however quirky.

Sam Linkum, the New York newsman in Herbert Mitgang's *The Montauk Fault* (1981), sees the small-town paper as a soapbox. "After all, that's how it all began, having your independence in print and letting the other fellow have his. . . . We've seen what's happened to most of the big press. It's been tainted by the same hardsell bland that rules the tube. End of speech."[31] The small-town editor is intentionally out of touch. He rejects common wisdom, technological change, journalism's worship of objectivity, society's emphasis on money, and the city's quickening pace. For that reason, America views the country editor with nostalgic, if occasionally patronizing, affection.

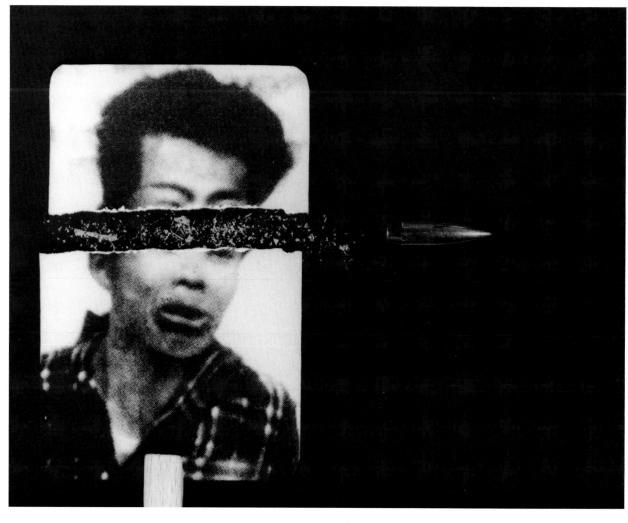

15 War Correspondent

From Adventure to Angst

In the beginning—long before Vietnam—the war correspondent played the role of daredevil adventurer.[1]

Nineteenth-century fiction about the correspondent was the excuse for a boy-gallops-horse, boy-fights-baddies, boy-gets-glory romance.[2] Rudyard Kipling's *The Light That Failed* (1899), the model for this kind of fiction, featured adventure-seeking Dick Heldar, British illustrator, who winds up in Khartoum because "there was a row, so I came."[3] Heldar suffers a sword slash and loses his sight. But he also shoots and kills a number of Arabs. His final words are, "Put me, I pray, in the forefront of the battle."[4] He dies in the arms of a veteran correspondent, the recipient of the "crowning mercy of a kindly bullet through his head."[5]

The American war correspondent was equally principled, patriotic, and courageous.[6] He exuded optimism and idealism. A man of action, he relished the adventure that came with being a war correspondent. Perhaps the most stereotypical American correspondent-as-adventurer appeared in Stephen Crane's *Active Service* (1899). The novel drew upon Crane's coverage of the Greco-Turkish War of 1897 (where he was not above posing for studio photos as a daring chap in a rented uniform, sitting atop papier-mâché rocks).[7]

Crane's hero, Rufus Coleman of the New York *Eclipse*, pursues Marjory Wainwright, his true love, to Greece. Her father, a professor of Greek, and her mother have taken her abroad to prevent her marrying the "scalawag" journalist.

Eddie Adams' photograph, "Vietcong executed" (1968), was the subject of Karl Baden's photo collage *Moment of Division* (After Harold Edgerton/Eddie Adams), 1988. Photo collage, courtesy Howard Yezerski Gallery and Loren Ghiglione; Adams photo, AP/Wide World

The Wainwright family becomes lost in the Turkish war zone, which is peopled by "ferocious Albanians." Coleman rides on horseback to rescue the family. "He was on active service, an active service of the heart, and he felt that he was a strong man ready to conquer difficulty even as the olden heroes conquered difficulty . . . . He, too, had come out to fight for love with giants, dragons, and witches."[8] At novel's end, of course, the professor harrumphs his consent to Marjory's marriage to Coleman.

Not all the fiction before World War I portrayed the war correspondent as hero. Occasionally he was viewed with a skepticism that took the form of satire or farce. Crane's "The Lone Charge of William B. Perkins" (1899) opens: "He could not distinguish between a five-

Stephen Crane in Athens, May 1897. The inscription is to Sam S. Chamberlain, managing editor of the New York *Journal*. Collection of Stanley and Mary Wertheim

War correspondents now question their role everywhere

After Vietnam, whether the war portrayed is in Southeast Asia, the Middle East, or Central America, disillusionment inevitably colors the fictional depiction of the U.S. correspondent.

Sometimes the correspondent sacrifices himself and others to the big story or photo. *The Killing Fields* (1984) focuses on the relationship between Sydney Schanberg (Sam Waterston) of the New York *Times* and Dith Pran (Haing S. Ngor), a photojournalist who served as his interpreter in Cambodia. Schanberg, despite the growing presence of the murderous Khmer Rouge, encourages Pran to stay in Cambodia. By the time Schanberg leaves, he cannot get Pran out of the country. In Tom Stoppard's 1978 play, *Night and Day,* the idealistic Jacob Milne and other journalists die because of "bloody ego." A bystander explains: "You're all doing it to impress each other and be top dog the next time you're propping up a bar in Beirut or Bangkok. . . ."[1]

But more often fictional correspondents—in portrayals that many real journalists dismiss as "fundamentally false"[2]—fail because they have become, through their work, morally bankrupt. Photojournalist Richard Boyle (James Woods) in Oliver Stone's *Salvador* (1986) is, at 42, a whoring, boozing, drug-gulping, out-of-work has-been. He claims he was the last American journalist out of Cambodia. That could be a lie, but Boyle clearly tells the truth when he confesses, "I kind of weasled around in my life." In *Under Fire* (1983), combat photographer Russell Price (Nick Nolte) travels to Nicaragua in 1979 to report on what another cynical correspondent calls "a neat little war." Price espouses neutrality: "I don't take sides, I take pictures." Eventually, however, he abandons the journalist's code and fakes a photo. He wants to help the guerrillas. He hopes to save lives: "I think I finally saw too many bodies."

Post-Vietnam novels about the war correspondent often suggest that the journalist, if he does his job, sacrifices his own humanity. Much of the romance has gone out of his work. The adventure has given way to alienation and emotional death. In *DelCorso's Gallery* (1983), Philip Caputo alludes to the dashing correspondents of yesteryear; the epigraph quotes Kipling on those "who have the lust to go abroad at the risk of their lives and discover news." But combat photographer Nicholas DelCorso, who is not above staging a massacre photo, feels no pride. Shooting photos of Vietnamese civilians being butchered was "as though he had murdered them with his camera."[3] At novel's end, after DelCorso has photographed another massacre in Lebanon, he is shot. "He felt utterly abandoned now, utterly alone."[4] It "seemed he had something important to say, something he desperately needed to say." He whispers, "Shit," then dies.[5]

It is not certain, however, that Hollywood will keep turning out movies about sensitive correspondents who bemoan war's waste, cruelty, and devastation. Americans prefer war heroes to search and destroy—not to search their own souls. The American heart, D. H. Lawrence wrote, "is hard, isolate, stoic, and a killer."[6] It favors fictional correspondents who, instead of rejecting war, rejoice in the enemy's destruction.

In *Under Fire,* Nick Nolte plays an American journalist caught up in the human drama and danger of the 1979 Nicaraguan revolution. (Orion, 1983)

Frederic Remington, "The War Correspondent," 1904.
Courtesy of William Ruger; photograph courtesy of
Gerold Wunderlich & Company, New York

inch quick-firing gun and a nickel-plated ice pick, and so, naturally, he had been elected to fill the position of war correspondent."[9] Sent to Cuba, the whiskey-besotted Minnesota *Herald* correspondent borrows a rifle and opens fire on a Spaniard who turns out to be a dried palm branch. Perkins boards a departing ship, "wearing a countenance of poignant thoughtfulness."[10]

War correspondent Richard Harding Davis's *The Galloper*, a 1906 play about coverage of the Greco-Turkish War, tweaked know-nothing newsmen who, explained an Athens bureau chief, "as soon as they reached Athens . . . put on revolvers and khaki yachting caps and called themselves war correspondents. And then they lost themselves in those mountains, and they haven't found the Greek army and the whole Greek army can't find them."[11] Copeland Schuyler, a foppishly elegant New York wastrel, wearing a gray felt hat with a white puggree, pre-

tends to be superstar correspondent Kirke Warren, a veteran of six wars. Schuyler survives threats from five hundred insurgents, Warren's divorced wife, and bloodthirsty bullies who want to make the correspondent's fourth duel his last. He not only escapes death but wins the girl and finds one million dollars in pearls.

World War I—as British writer Evelyn Waugh's *Scoop* (1937) suggested—hardened the humor. In *Scoop*, world-famous U.S. correspondent Wenlock Jakes reports an African revolution where there is none. His colleagues follow suit. A week of the press corps' accounts of the make-believe revolution foments a real one.

World War I brought machine guns and massed artillery fire. "It's different from anything I knew," a correspondent in Will Levington Comfort's *Red Fleece* (1915), a World War I novel, insists. "It's so damn businesslike. Something's come over the world. War was more like a picnic before. I never saw it like this. I believe we've gone crazy."[12]

The craziness of World War I for the correspondents—the censorship, the travel restrictions, the trench warfare where, as Mary S. Mander explained, "there was nothing to see"[13]— forced upon fiction writers a new vision of irony and isolation, fragmentation and futility. The correspondent who evaded censorship and reported the truth sometimes risked his career. Will Irwin's unvarnished account of the sixteen-day battle of Ypres caused the British and French to blacklist him. His press credentials were cancelled; he could not resume work as a war correspondent for two years.[14]

Between World Wars I and II, Hollywood had to settle for a foreign correspondent—a distinct second to a war correspondent—to provide U.S. viewers with overseas adventure. In *Clear All Wires* (1933), Lee Tracy, who starred in nine newspaper movies, played a correspondent who took on agents of an unnamed foreign power; in *I'll Tell The World* (1934), correspondent Tracy found a lost dirigible and saved a queen from assassination.[15]

Often Hollywood used the correspondent to wake up America to the Nazi threat.[16] Alfred Hitchcock dedicated *Foreign Correspondent* (1940) to "those forthright ones who early saw the clouds of war while many of us at home were seeing rainbows."[17] New York police reporter Johnny Jones (Joel McCrea) is supremely ignorant about World War II ("What war?"). But, outfitted with a correspondent's moniker (Huntley Haverstock) and bowler-and-umbrella wardrobe, he heads for Europe. He uncovers a Nazi spy ring, participates in a death-defying car chase, and walks away from a trans-Atlantic plane crash. Rescued by a ship, Haverstock telephones his paper. "He wouldn't phone if it weren't a story,"[18] his boss says, ordering the presses to be held. In the end, Haverstock gets the girl as well as the story, and "The Star-Spangled Banner" plays in the background.

Movies about the Pacific theater also sent the message that, while the real World War II correspondent perhaps only reported the war, the fictional correspondent fought it. In *Malaya* (1949), correspondent James Stewart helps the U.S. government defeat the Japanese by smuggling out rubber. In *Blood on the Sun* (1945), Nick Condon (James Cagney), a U.S. journalist in pre-World War II Tokyo, gets even for the murder of U.S. reporter Ollie Miller (Wallace Ford) and his wife Edith (Rosemary De Camp). The Millers had been trying to smuggle out Premier Tanaka's plan of world conquest. Condon succeeds, mounting a judo attack on his Japanese foes. When Tokyo's police chief beseeches Condon to forgive him for not pursuing the murderers of the Millers, the incensed correspondent responds, "Yes, forgive your enemies. But first, get even!"[19]

The first feature-length Hollywood film about Vietnam was little more than an update of the patriotic World War II movies. In John Wayne's *The Green Berets* (1968), the U.S. Special Forces defeat the Viet Cong and extol the virtues of the war. Correspondent George Beckworth (David Janssen) asks questions that

mark him as less than a true believer. Green Beret Wayne, who talks as if he is in the middle of another Western, lectures Janssen: "Out here due process is a bullet." Another Green Beret finally corners Janssen: "That's what it's all about . . . . You gonna stand there and referee or you gonna help us?" Janssen converts, and, rifle in hand, runs to the aid of the Green Berets.

However such World War II-movie clichés may seem a generation later, Michael Herr recalls that, as a correspondent in Vietnam, he occasionally played the correspondent's part from the movies: "Things got mixed."[20] As he and another reporter prepare to sprint closer to the action, he asks a Marine, "Listen, we're going to cut out now. Will you cover us?"[21]

But after *Green Berets*, both film and fiction began to present a different picture of the correspondent and of the U.S. role in Vietnam.

The portrayal of the war photographer had special significance. The camera had become, in James Agee's words, "next to unassisted and weaponless consciousness, the central instrument of our time."[22] Said to reproduce life, the camera in Vietnam achieved the status, ironi-

In *Foreign Correspondent,* director Alfred Hitchcock awakened audiences to the dangers of coming war (United Artists, 1940)

cally, of mythic instrument of death, literally shooting people. Artists incorporated photos of death in their Vietnam prints and paintings; superimposed across the top of one My Lai massacre photo is a correspondent's question to a soldier about those murdered: "And babies?" Across the bottom, the soldier's answer: "And babies."[23]

In A. J. Quinnell's *The Snap* (1983), the Nikon FTN of U.S. photojournalist David Munger is displayed as a museum piece—"no one was ever allowed to touch it"[24]—on a pedestal of death. Michael Herr, whose hallucinatory prose captured the flavor of Vietnam, recalled twenty young correspondents listening to the lines of a song by the Mothers of Invention, "Trouble Comin' Every Day," as if it were an anthem for the war: "And if another woman driver gets machine-gunned from her seat / They'll send some joker with a Brownie and you'll see it all complete."[25] Poet Gerald Lange wrote about seeing on television a South Vietnamese raise a pistol to the head of a Viet Cong and then quickly—"too quickly"—shoot him to death, the camera capturing:

> the violent contortion of the facial muscles
> the slow stiffness of the dying limbs
> the blood squirting to equilibrium
> christ[26]

No surprise that the correspondent wondered about his work. Ward Just, who covered Vietnam for the Washington *Post*, questioned in his fiction the journalist's commitment to the values of his profession. In the title story of *Honor, Power, Riches, Fame and the Love of Women* (1979), a Just character says: "Reporters, so secure in the cocoon of their professional neutrality, are especially fond of the word 'commitment.' They do not appreciate the double meaning."[27]

The correspondent is a prisoner of the war, "all dissolution, failure, hackneyed ironies, and guilt . . . ."[28] In *The American Blues* (1984), Just's narrator, a famous Vietnam correspond-

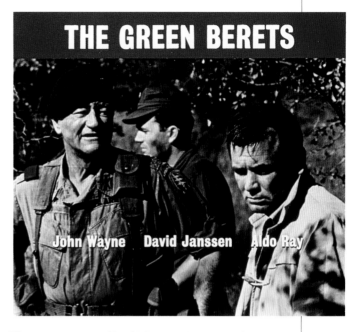

War correspondent David Janssen learns patriotism in John Wayne's *The Green Berets.* (Warner Brothers, 1968.) Movie poster, The Brian Ann Zoccola-Irv Letofsky Collection

ent, struggles with writing a history of the war. But he cannot finish. Perhaps it's more appropriate for the history of Vietnam not to end: "[F]inal chapters and grand endings were inherently suspect, as the last breath of discredited romanticism."[29]

The romantic view of the fictional correspondent as adventurer gives way in the treatment of the Vietnam correspondent to a portrait of a conscience-ridden zombie, demoralized and even demented. The photojournalist in Quinnell's *The Snap* is going insane from the mind games Vietnam has played on him. In Amlin Gray's *How I Got That Story*, a 1980 play about covering a war in Am-bo Land (Vietnam), the correspondent not only abandons his job at the Trans Pan Global Wire Service but also loses his mind. He ends up as a "Yankee dressed up like a gook."[30]

Vietnam correspondents resemble the soldiers who escape death from an airstrike in Just's *Stringer* (1974). While they survive, they are "now without sense," their brains and hearts empty of what once made them human. They too are dead. "Worse perhaps."[31]

16 TV Journalist
The Journalist as Celebrity

The most thought-provoking fictional portrait of the television journalist exists, ironically, in the nonfiction art of Robert Heinecken. "1984: A Case Study in Finding an Appropriate TV Newswoman (A CBS Docudrama in Words and Pictures)" (1985), a satirical series of photographs, pretends to document Heinecken's participation in CBS's search for a new morning newswoman.[1] In a set of three photos, the top picture shows Jane Pauley's televised face, the bottom Bryant Gumbel's face, and the middle a superimposed composite of the two. After enjoying the humor of the hermaphroditic composite, the viewer realizes how the center image captures the artificial, ambiguous quality of television. Does the viewer see a man or a woman? A white person or a person of color? The image emphasizes the indistinguishable quality of the television journalist.

Not surprisingly, perhaps, the first generation of fiction about television journalism—from the 1950s and 1960s—focused on the medium itself, not the people who report television news. Novels explored how television perverted the process of electing a president, or how Congress and other governmental agencies, with their licensing power over television, menaced the independence of the networks. David Levy, an NBC vice president who lost his job after an appearance before a Senate subcommittee, fictionalized his experience in *The Chameleons* (1964). A headline-seeking senator pressures Steven Lane, president for network television of Federal Broadcasting Company, to become a sacrificial lamb or a lying chameleon. Lane is forced to resign from FBC.[2]

During the 1960s, art also focused on the medium—the screen on which the news appeared, not the person who gathered or presented it. Vija Celmins's "T.V." (1965) shows a television set floating in empty space. On the screen, an airplane explodes, the victim of a terrorist bomb or of enemy missile fire. But the dull gray tones and the detached presentation deaden the subject, as if television discourages the viewer from responding with feeling to real tragedy. Is it a fictional, made-for-television air disaster or the news? The painting, like television itself sometimes, doesn't provide a clue.[3]

"Seven A.M. News," by Alfred Leslie, 1976–78. Courtesy of Joseph Shein, Philadelphia

Jane Pauley-Bryant Gumbel composite from the traveling exhibition "1984: A Case Study in Finding the Appropriate TV Newswoman (A CBS Docudrama in Words and Pictures)" by Robert Heinecken

The anchorperson: symbol of what's wrong with television news?

The news anchorperson—a beautiful bimbo at the local level and a charismatic, entertaining nonjournalist at the network level—is fiction's favorite symbol of television news.

Fiction emphasizes elements of the standup comic and the Hollywood sex symbol in its portrayal of the news anchor. Max Headroom, a parody of the network anchor, bursts onto the screen: "[T]his is Max Headroom on Bigtime Television and what I want to know is: Don't eskimos ever get bored with their weather forecasts."[1] Or the glamorous, egotistical anchor makes you aware that he is more important than the news he presents. In a *New Yorker* cartoon, a handsome, blow-dried anchor smilingly reports: "A recent survey showed that ninety-five per cent of the nation's high-school students had never heard of Costa Rica, but they all knew about yours truly."[2]

The importance to real-world television of the anchor, regardless of journalistic abilities, is only slightly less dramatic. An appealing anchor brings higher ratings which, in turn, bring more advertising dollars. The network basks in the anchor's celebrity status. Peter J. Boyer writes: "Howard K. Smith once observed that being chosen as a network anchor was 'like being nominated for president,' which is true enough, except that network anchors are a little more rare (there have been only eighteen of them)."[3]

The celebrity anchor—the personification of influence and financial success—also represents power, or at least the appearance of power. CBS's Dan Rather, who earns four million dollars a year, ranked tenth—ahead of Henry Kissinger and Vice President George Bush—in a 1984 survey of "prominent citizens" who were asked to select the most influential Americans.[4] The only Americans regarded as more influential were nine elected or appointed office holders, including the president.

What networks seek in an anchor, say industry insiders, has little to do with journalism. Walter Cronkite complains about the choice of "the young and beautiful, but inexperienced and callous."[5] Liz Trotta, a correspondent for NBC News and then CBS News, contends that "most news executives are looking for 'personalities'—and so it follows that journalistic skills are optional. It is enough if the personality gives the *appearance* of being a journalist."[6]

In both fiction and fact, the networks seem willing to replace the journalist with an anchor who is not a journalist. Lucille Kallen has a character in a 1984 novel say: "According to television, an ordinary reporter was a thing of the past; today you were an anchorperson with an extensive wardrobe or you were nothing."[7] Networks in the world of fact appear to be defining news by the standards they apply to anchors. One network executive says: "We like stories that have wiggle. Sexy stories. Iran has wiggle. Defectors for the Bolshoi have wiggle. Stories about government agencies have *no wiggle*."[8]

On accepting a George Polk Award in 1982, Ted Koppel read a poem: "No matter how an anchor tries/ his function is to symbolize./To spice the viewer's evening meal/ With equal parts of sex appeal/ and evidence that we are free—by oozing credibility." But an important question is whether the typical anchor really oozes credibility or something else that ultimately could undermine television's credibility.

"*A recent survey showed that ninety-five per cent of the nation's high-school students had never heard of Costa Rica, but they all knew about yours truly!*"

Gahan Wilson cartoon in *The New Yorker*, April 24, 1989

Often art depicted television as a blank screen. Andy Warhol emphasized the commercial nature of everything about television, including its presentation of news, in "$199 Television" (1960).[4] And May Stevens, in "Prime Time" (1967),[5] paints a blank-screen television looking over the shoulder of a silent man, the passive viewer, as if the television set were the Big Brother of George Orwell's *Nineteen Eighty-Four*.[6]

In Alfred Leslie's "7:00 A.M. News" (1976-78), the screen is not blank, but its tableau of crisis seems equally ominous.[7] A solitary woman stares upward as if hypnotized. The tragic events depicted in her newspaper and on her television set have numbed her into a stupor. In Mark Kostabi's "Goya TV" (1982), a television replaces the executioners in the famous Spanish poster "Third of May."[8] Edward Kienholz's "The Eleventh Hour Final" (1968) depicts the television set as tombstone for the dead in Vietnam—"This Week's Toll: American Dead—217, American Wounded—563, Enemy Dead—635, Enemy Wounded—1291."[9]

Early feature films denigrated television journalists. That's not surprising. Fearing competition from the new medium, Hollywood denied television's existence, refusing to depict an American living room with a television set. Of seventeen movies through 1974, two-thirds presented television newspeople as silly, insensitive, or unscrupulous.[10] In *Cold Turkey* (1971), radio comedians Bob Elliott and Ray Goulding portrayed "Paul Hardly" and "Walter Cronic" as blunderbuss network newscasters. In *Man Afraid* (1957), *The Love Machine* (1971), *The Omega Man* (1971), and *Extreme Closeup* (1973), repulsive television journalists invaded privacy and drove people to suicide.

The '70s cult of personality—the celebrityhood granted Walter Cronkite, Barbara Walters, and others—generated fiction and film about television news stars. Some portrayals echoed fiction about newspapering, with the investigative reporter's pen and pad replaced by minicam

Assignment **(New York: The Dial Press, 1981)**

and mike.[11] The escapist fare of the '70s and '80s, however, required that television reporters not only solve murders but travel the globe in search of terrorists and other world-class monsters. In *Wrong Is Right* (1982), Patrick Hale (Sean Connery) investigates terrorists in Marseilles and Rome, the CIA in Washington, and a possible assassination plot in North Africa. Robert Branker, a network newsman who looks "remarkably like a Hollywood version of a great white hunter,"[12] discovers in Laurence Leamer's *Assignment* (1981) that the U.S. government and even his own network are promoting a giant cocaine industry in Peru. In William Stevenson's *Eclipse* (1986), Scott Talbot, "America's favorite newsman,"[13] works with U.S. and

ROBERT B. PARKER

A SPENSER NOVEL

A SAVAGE PLACE

A Savage Place (New York: Delacorte Press, 1983)

Ted Baxter is the bumbling newscaster on "The Mary Tyler Moore Show." "The Mary Tyler Moore Show," MTM Enterprises, Inc.

Israeli intelligence to save the world from terrorists who could bring about the Fourth Reich. And, closer to home, TV newsman Benson Stryker learns at the end of Chuck Scarborough's *Stryker* (1978) that he has been transformed into a murderer to stop President Nixon from destroying all the networks.[14]

Newspaper fiction's stereotypical hero reeks of rumpled masculinity. He mutters profane wisecracks while a cigarette dangles from the corner of his mouth. But fiction and film about television journalists rely on femmes fatales: Polly Bishop, whose "huge eyes and . . . rakish cheekbones" suggest Audrey Hepburn,[15] in Thomas Gifford's *The Glendower Legacy* (1978); VV Cameron, "a slender body oozing confidence at every pore,"[16] in Edward Stewart's *The Great Los Angeles Fire* (1980); Jane Fonda as Kimberly Wells ("Keeps 'em panting without offending the wives")[17] in *The China Syndrome* (1978), and Candy Sloan, the blond investigative reporter for KNBS-TV ("Live Action News") who wears "skin-tight jeans with someone's name on the butt and spiked heels."[18] To help detective Spenser in Robert B. Parker's *A Savage Place* (1981), she uses her "feminine wiles."[19] That gets her killed.

Several novels—Carole Nelson Douglas's *The Exclusive* (1986), Danielle Steel's *Changes*

(1983), and Cara Saylor Polk's *Images* (1986)—ask whether a television newswoman can be true both to journalism and to herself. In *The Exclusive*, Liz Jordan, who eventually quits network news for public television, suspects early in her television career that her father, a country editor, is right: "TV was no place for a journalist, and certainly it was no place for a lady."[20] But most fiction ignores the ethical issues and exaggerates the glamour, portraying the typical newswoman as a cross between Barbara Walters and a lifesized Barbie doll. In the Barbara/Barbie category, Kate Sinclair (of James Brady's *Nielsen's Children*) and Hattie Connors (of Al Morgan's *Anchorwoman*)—both thirty-five years old, both stunningly beautiful, both welcome (perhaps too welcome) at the White House—bulldoze their way to the top.

The Barbara/Barbie archetype is known best for her nonjournalistic achievements—her multimillion-dollar salary, her picture on the cover of *Time* magazine, and her power, sexual as well as social. The book-jacket blurb for Muriel Dobbin's *Going Live* (1987) promises "sexual and professional passion." The blurb begins: "A spellbinding novel about three eager, talented women on the fiercest, fastest track of all—TV broadcasting . . . . [T]heir peers wonder which one will become the first solo female news anchor."[21]

In Ron Nessen's *The Hour* (1984), Pamela Ganderson of CBN admits why she chose television news over a newspaper career: "More money and fame."[22] Such values pervade all television news in these portrayals. Edward Kienholz's assemblage, "Six O'Clock News" (1964), fills the news anchor's spot with a toy Mickey Mouse head—television news as mindless, "Mickey Mouse" material.[23] Ted Baxter, the newscaster on television's "The Mary Tyler Moore Show," and Tom Grunick (William Hurt), the aspiring anchorman in James Brooks's *Broadcast News* (1987), send the same message. So does television's parade of parodies—"Not Necessarily the News," "Our Planet

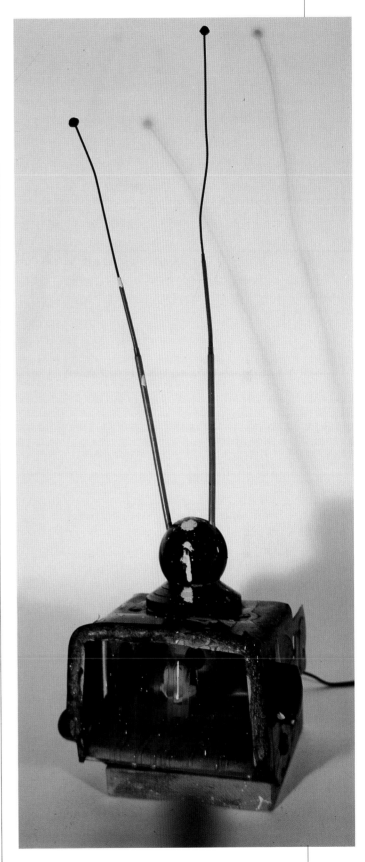

Six O'Clock News, Edward Kienholz, 1964. Mixed media including light, glass, and fiberglass. Collection of William N. Copley

Tonight," "Over Here, Mr. President," "Stop-watch," "The Generic News," and "The Week-end Update," a segment on "Saturday Night Live." There Baba Wawa (Gilda Radner) inter-rupts her interview of Betty Ford and Rosalyn Carter: "Neither of you truly deserves to be First Lady.... Who does...? Me, Baba Wawa, first lady of TV .... Plus I have a terrific person-ality."[24]

Parodying television journalists is difficult because the journalists insist on parodying them-selves. ABC's Diane Sawyer poses as a Marilyn Monroe seductress in *Vanity Fair*.[25] Geraldo Rivera conducts an on-air brawl/interview with white supremacists and has his nose broken.[26] The fictional accounts of broadcast journal-ists—like the self-parodies and parodies—offer three indictments of television news.

First, integrity counts for nothing. *Anchor-man* (1970), by CBS correspondent Ned Calmer, chronicles the departure from a national network of honest anchor Hedley Johns. Forced "to

choose . . . between his conscience and his job,"[27] he has no option but to resign. Lloyd Garner, his successor, is saved from the same choice only because a sniper doesn't miss. In Nessen's *The First Lady* (1979), the White House seeks the source of an erroneous story broadcast by GBC News correspondent Phyllis Thornberg. When Thornberg will not name the source, the White House offers as bait an exclusive interview with the president and the destruction of a file about a Thornberg sexual indiscretion. If Thornberg refuses to reveal the source, the White House will take the file to newspaper re-porters: "[T]hey look down on you as more movie star than reporter."[28] Thornberg buckles, obtaining the file and her interview with the president.

Second, ratings rule the news. Nessen's vet-eran anchorman Mitch Crawford knowingly lies about a contact lens sterilizer, describing it as a killer. Crawford confesses: "I was under a lot of pressure to do a tough piece, an extra-tough

William Hurt portrays a network television news correspondent in *Broadcast News* (20th Century Fox, 1987). Movie still. Courtesy University of Southern California Cinema-Television Library

Gilda Radner and Chevy Chase on "Weekend Update" of NBC's "Saturday Night Live." NBC Photo

piece, to get the ratings up."[29] In *Network* (1976), anchorman Howard Beale (Peter Finch) gains a reprieve for his career when he announces his plan to kill himself on air, and his ratings skyrocket. People at WKRLD Channel 3 in Edward Gorman's *Murder Straight Up* (1986) exterminate a suicidal teenager to increase the impact of their teen-suicide series.

Third, to demand anything other than entertainment and show-business hype from television news—to ask for the intelligence, honesty, and fairness expected of print journalists—is to invite disappointment. In Barbara Gordon's *Defects of the Heart* (1983), Jessica Lenhart of New York's independent station WPTN cares too much about capturing the truth in her news documentaries. "Your idealism, while attractive," her boss warns her, "may work against you."[30] She finds television twisting her into a sensation seeker. While working on a report about a dangerous anti-miscarriage drug, she visits a family with a little boy on crutches. He has lost one leg. Lenhart recognizes, "to her horror, that she wished he could be more pathetic, more damaged . . . . [S]he was seized by an even grimmer truth . . . . [W]hat kind of woman have I become, that I am disappointed not to find this family drowning in despair? What have I done to feed the monstrous maw of television?"[31] Eventually she quits. She has no choice.

Orson Welles as a caricature of William Randolph Hearst in *Citizen Kane.* **Courtesy University of Southern California Cinema-Television Library**

17 Owner

Small-town Hero, Big-city Villain

When William Randolph Hearst learned that R.K.O. would portray him in *Citizen Kane* as a controlling, conniving tycoon, he showed the world why. A Hearst loyalist offered R.K.O.'s president $842,000, the production and post-production cost of Orson Welles's 1941 classic, if he would destroy the negative and all prints of the movie.[1] Hearst ordered his papers not to review *Citizen Kane*.[2] He also banned reviews of other R.K.O. movies.[3] R.K.O. at first could not find movie houses—except its own—that would book *Citizen Kane*.

The movie, significantly, begins with Charles Foster Kane's death. So the viewer knows how the two hours of Kane's life to follow will end—in solitary, helpless futility. But the life itself remains an ironic puzzle. Is the viewer expected to both love and hate Kane? Or just love to hate him? Welles, who played Kane, described him as "at once an idealist and a swindler, a very great man and a mediocre individual."[4]

Kane symbolizes fiction's portrayal of the media owner. His independence brings applause, his villainy jeers. Fiction admires the owner's insistence on being his own boss, on doing things his way. But it despises the things he chooses to do. Kane announces his Declaration of Principles—"I will also provide them with a fighting and tireless champion of their rights as citizens, and as human beings"—but the Declaration, like Kane himself, is a cynical lie.[5] When Jed Leland (Joseph Cotten), Kane's truthful alter ego, tries to write an honest review of the "hopelessly incompetent" operatic debut of Kane's second wife, he cannot in his drunken stupor complete it. Kane finishes the review without softening the criticism. He makes sure the review is printed. Then he fires Leland.

The earliest portrayals of the newspaper owner date from the late nineteenth century. The newspaper had become a big, expensive business. Ownership had shifted from the editor in the newsroom to the publisher in the counting room.

Typically the publisher represented rapacious capitalism—"Wall Street, Washington, social coteries, the manipulating few."[6] Henry Francis Keenan's *The Money-Makers* (1885) provides "thinly veiled pictures" of railroad magnate Amasa Stone and other capitalists.[7] Alfred Carew, an honest editor, opposes a protective tariff, supports labor unions, and pursues a scandal involving Aaron Grimstone, a corrupt capitalist. To silence Carew, Grimstone buys the paper and fires him.

A friend warns Carew that Grimstone's kind "are not men to be balked by one newspaper, or a dozen. When a newspaper opposes them they find means of buying it out."[8] But Carew starts another paper, the *Free Press*. Grimstone does everything he can to foil Carew; he delays *Free Press* postal deliveries, prevents purchase of wire-service news, and files libel suits. Carew, however, proves victorious.

In the nineteenth century, the problem of reconciling private ownership with public responsibility normally presented itself in the form of evil individuals, easily identifiable: Mr. Goldstick (named that because he measures everything by its dollar value), the publisher in Harriet Beecher Stowe's *My Wife and I* (1871); Mr. Mushington in Ellen Glasgow's *The Descendant* (1897); banker Abner Hildreth in George Eggleston and Mary Bacon's *Juggernaut* (1891); Mr. Stoller, the vulgar viper of a newspaper owner in William Dean Howells's *Their Silver Wedding Journey* (1899); Mr. Witherby, "the countingroom incarnate"[9] who owns "a journal without principles and without convictions, but with interests only,"[10] in Howells's *A Modern Instance* (1882) and *The Quality of Mercy* (1892).

During the early twentieth century, Hollywood movies chose to portray the publisher as nineteenth-century novelists had depicted him.

Among the ruthless villains, mad for money or power, were Oscar Apfel playing publisher Hinchcliffe in *Five Star Final* (1931), Berton Churchill in *Scandal for Sale* (1932), Otto Kruger in *Scandal Sheet* (1939), and Edward G. Robinson in *Unholy Partners* (1941).

But twentieth-century fiction focused on the newspaper owner's independence as well as his villainy. His autonomy symbolized both the independence of the United States as a nation, and the editorial independence of the advertising-supported newspaper from political parties and their corrupting subsidies.[11]

Autonomy is a key component of the American dream. The more autonomous the newspaper owner, and the more he can determine his own success, the more the public admires him. For that reason, the country always has had a soft spot for the editor-owner of the small-town paper, the one-man band who sells the ads, writes the stories, prints the paper, and then distributes it too. In children's literature and comics, everyone from Mickey Mouse to Freddy the Pig gets to run his own newspaper.

The country editor-owner, unlike the big-city editor, does not see himself as tainted if he works at the business-side goal of making money. Alan Mabry, the editorial-writing reformer in Hodding Carter's *The Winds of Fear* (1944), finds pleasure in charting advertising linage. "Knowing what kind of business they were doing told him how well he was paying his way . . . . [H]e enjoyed the triumph of selling a two-by-five to someone like Jerry Travis who hadn't taken space in the *Salute* in two years."[12] Equally important, a financially healthy paper owned by the editor, not someone else, improves his chance of being an independent journalist. Mabry reflects, "It's because the paper's ours . . . . Nobody is independent, but this is about as near to it as a newspaperman can get."[13]

The trick is not pushing independence to the point of insolvency. The country editor-owner—like Judson Welling of the New Athens (Nebraska) *Telegraph* in Frederic Babcock's *Hang Up the Fiddle* (1954)—keeps himself "always poor enough to prove his honesty."[14] But the crusading country editor risks sliding beyond poverty into bankruptcy. Randall Gerrard, the owner of a Mississippi Delta weekly in Charlaine

Mickey Mouse Runs His Own Newspaper, a miniature book by Walt Disney (Racine, Wisconsin: Whitman Publishing Co., 1937). Courtesy Loren Ghiglione

Owners seek to take over the world

The possibility that by the year 2000 less than a dozen international media conglomerates will dominate the world has generated a string of "conspiracy" novels.

Throughout Jeff Millar's *Private Sector* (1979) runs the question of who—really, what—will buy the New York *Times.* Molly Rice, a *Times* investigative reporter, worries about the demise of real journalism: "The *Times* is the Lone Ranger . . . . Everything else is turning into show business. The . . . conglomerates. They all seemed to be called . . . 'Twenty-Second Century Communications Group,' and you never see them, or know who they are, except for the lawyer clones who announce the sale at a press conference."[1] The *Times* later is sold for nine-hundred million dollars to a "Swiss bank account,"[2] part of a secret conspiracy of two hundred giant corporations worldwide buying the media to take over the U.S. government.

In Jack Anderson's *Control* (1988), foreign companies again infiltrate American media. Catlett Communications buys television stations, film studios, and publishing companies, aided by eight-hundred million dollars from The Consortium, a group of Korean, Japanese, and "nationalist-conservative" German investors.[3] In Michael Thomas's *Hard Money* (1985),[4] The Consortium is called EmpCom Holdings; five hundred giant corporations raise nine billion dollars to take over a telecom-munications conglomerate and push the conservative agenda of Eldon Erwitt, a Reaganesque president.

The Cold War begins a new stage in David Aaron's *Agent of Influence* (1989). At the rate of three-hundred million dollars a year, the Soviets subsidize a prestigious but profitless European media conglomerate owned by French mogul Marcel Bresson. Bankrolled by the USSR, Bresson plots a takeover of News/Worldweek, an eight-billion-dollar company that controls America's most influential news media.[5]

Bresson's puzzling life—no known relatives, no real estate, no fixed address, except for a yacht docked at Monte Carlo—prompts an investigation by a reporter (eventually murdered) and by a Congressional committee that worries about "how much foreign ownership of American business is consistent with our national sovereignty and well-being."[6]

Bresson, a KGB/CIA double agent born of Chinese parents and raised in the Soviet Union, dies mysteriously. And News/Worldweek defeats the takeover attempt, though at novel's end the company receives a new hostile takeover offer from a Japanese media company, Ashahi Shimbun.

Bresson's ominous warning lingers: "Nations . . . are dangerously overarmed anachronisms. The earth will be ruled by global corporate organizations. And the key to global economic and political power is the media."[7]

During the white heat of the Yellow Journalism war between the New York *World* and the New York *Journal,* the owners of the New York *Times* chose an ethically pure and "decent" approach, as indicated in this 1896 advertising poster. Library of Congress, Prints and Photographs Division

Harris's *Sweet and Deadly* (1981), adopts the motto: "Crusaders lose advertising revenue."[15] In Arthur Gordon's *Reprisal* (1950), Lester Crowe, the stooped, fiftyish editor of the Hainesville (Georgia) *Courier*, recalls a crusading editorial he had written when he was younger: "We got a brick through the plate-glass window, and wrapped around the brick was a note saying the next mistake we made they'd burn us down. They would have, too."[16]

The threat to independent owners, however, does not come primarily from brick throwers. As larger and larger corporations purchase newspapers, magazines, and broadcast stations of all sizes, the individual owner gives way to the corporate owner. Fiction, in turn, idealizes the independent owner. Good or bad, he serves his community in a way that a corporation cannot. "Control must be in a single pair of hands," says a character in a typical newspaper novel. "No successful newspaper was ever run by a committee."[17]

In fiction's romanticized reality, the suspect corporation usually fails in its effort to buy the independently owned publication or station that it pursues. In Richard Powell's *Daily and Sunday* (1964), the Knudsen chain ("its individual papers were too much alike, as if they were boxes of assorted cookies distributed under a national brand")[18] does not succeed in purchasing the employee-owned *Mail*. In Arthur Miller's *Final Edition* (1981), unscrupulous national media czar Samuel Bradbury (whose "philosophy is to milk the last penny out of every property he purchases")[19] fails to take over J. P. Hargrove's Bay City *Times*. Margaret Pynchon (Nancy Marchand), the owner/publisher of the Los Angeles *Tribune* on television's "Lou Grant," haughtily rejects a media mogul's offer for her newspaper: "My God, we're not talking about a side of beef."

But a few novels suggest a different reality. In Ward Just's *A Family Trust* (1978), the children and grandchildren of Amos Rising, founder of the Dement *Intelligencer*, agonize about selling the Midwest daily. Eventually they accept the offer of the Dows group, though they agree with the grandson who describes the Dows executives as "assholes."[20] And Anna Murdoch, whose husband, Rupert, runs one of the world's largest real media empires, writes in soap-opera style about the crisis facing Yarrow McLean ("the only publisher in New York with balls," says a union boss).[21] McLean must decide between passing on her company to unfit children—a fourth generation filled with "greed, and disloyalty and hatred"[22]—or selling. She sells to another media conglomerate.

Conspiracy assumes an increasingly large role in fiction and films—in such movies as *A Flash of Green* (1985), *Network* (1976), *Wrong Is*

Don Wright cartoon on media takeover, Miami *News*, 1985

In 1901, the owners of the Washington *Evening Star* commissioned Frederick Dielman to depict "Journalism" in seven lunette paintings for the new *Star* building. This painting, "Diffusion of Intelligence," shows journalism the way newspaper owners often choose to view their business—as sending forth a winged genius of enlightenment. Library of Congress, Prints and Photographs Division

Right (1981), and *The Parallax View* (1974). Ownership often takes the form of a shadowy giant corporation—a newspaper chain, a communications conglomerate, or a multinational media empire—manipulated from afar by foreigners whose real goals are shrouded in secrecy.

The action in fiction about journalism has shifted, writes William McKeen, "from the newsroom to the board room."[23] Journalism's independence and integrity depend almost completely on the value system of the media owner. Elliot Weyden, the lover of owner Yarrow McLean in Murdoch's *Family Business*, sulks. News reports about Weyden's ownership of a brothel and his father-in-law's mob ties have forced him out of the presidential race. "Journalism stinks," he tells McLean. "You're in a rotten business . . . . You build people up, and then you tear them down . . . . You don't know about loyalty or decency."[24]

Then Weyden asks the make-or-break question: "Would you have published the story—if you'd gotten it first, if one of your reporters had come up with it—*and you're my woman*—would you have published it?" McLean "loved him too much to lie to him. 'Yes,' she said."[25] Publication of the truth comes first, she explains. "[T]hat's what I'm there for and you just have to live with that because if I kowtow to every poor bastard who thinks he's getting the rough end of the stick, I may as well print out toilet paper."[26]

For the most part, the owner today remains a villain that fiction writers love to humble. In Richard North Patterson's *Private Screening* (1985), a psychotic terrorist humiliates newspaper magnate Colby Parnell on national television, pushing him to kill himself. In Colin Watson's *Coffin Scarcely Used* (1981), publisher Marcus Gwill is found electrocuted, his mouth stuffed with marshmallows.

But the owner, whether a heel,[27] a smut artist,[28] a compulsive collector of corporations,[29] or a sensation-mongering Citizen Kane, can redeem himself at least partially by remaining loyal to the press's avowed mission: the pursuit of the truth.

TV:2000

Edited by ISAAC ASIMOV, CHARLES G. WAUGH,
and MARTIN HARRY GREENBERG

A CHOICE COLLECTION OF SUPER SCIENCE FICTION STORIES

Includes top writers
such as Eric Frank Russell,
Robert Silverberg,
Theodore Sturgeon and others.

FAWCETT CREST 20433-2 • $2.95

In *TV: 2000*—a collection edited by Isaac Asimov, Charles G. Waugh, and Martin Harry Greenberg (New York: Ballantine Books, 1982)—as in other science fiction, the journalist often works in a surreal world. Courtesy Loren Ghiglione

The Journalist of Tomorrow

Into the world of science fiction

An American journalist concerned about the future of the news media might want to remember one disturbing episode of "The Twilight Zone," a 1960s television show. Arriving from the Other Planet, aliens promise Earth's population a globe free of war and poverty. The aliens begin to implement dramatic reforms. Earth's skeptics are reassured when they finally decipher the title of a book by the intruders: *To Serve Man*. At program's end, as Earthlings who have accepted an invitation to visit the Other Planet are about to depart, a translator enters and screams: "Don't go! I've decoded more of *To Serve Man*! It's a cookbook."[1]

The intruders taking over American media are not from other planets. They are from other countries. Hachette SA, a French company that produces more magazines than any other firm in the world, now publishes the *Encyclopedia Americana* as well as twelve U.S. magazines. Bertelsmann AG, a German company, owns not only Doubleday, Bantam Books, and other U.S. publishing houses, but also American magazines and RCA and Arista records. Thomson Corp., the Canadian firm, publishes 116 U.S. dailies, more than any other newspaper chain.

If, as Henry Luce said, the twentieth is "the American century,"[2] the twenty-first—at least for the news media—could be the global century. The American journalist—like the American book publisher and the American magazine editor—could wind up working for one of five to ten mammoth media corporations controlling the world's most influential newspapers, magazines, and television stations.

But media ownership is not the only uncertainty for the American journalist of the future. How will tomorrow's journalist use—or be used by—robots and computers? With broadcast and print media possibly merging into electronic publishing, will the First Amendment rights of print or the more restricted rights of broadcast prevail? Will the pressure for news that can be marketed worldwide lead to glitzy (or grisly) mini-reports that entertain more than they edify?

Predictions often miss the mark. But thinking about the U.S. journalism of the future—about its definitions of news, its degree of freedom, its ethical standards, and its technology—still serves a useful purpose. Such thinking suggests a range of possibilities for the kind of journalist—perhaps not an American, perhaps not even a human—who will be reporting on the life of the United States in the twenty-first century and beyond.

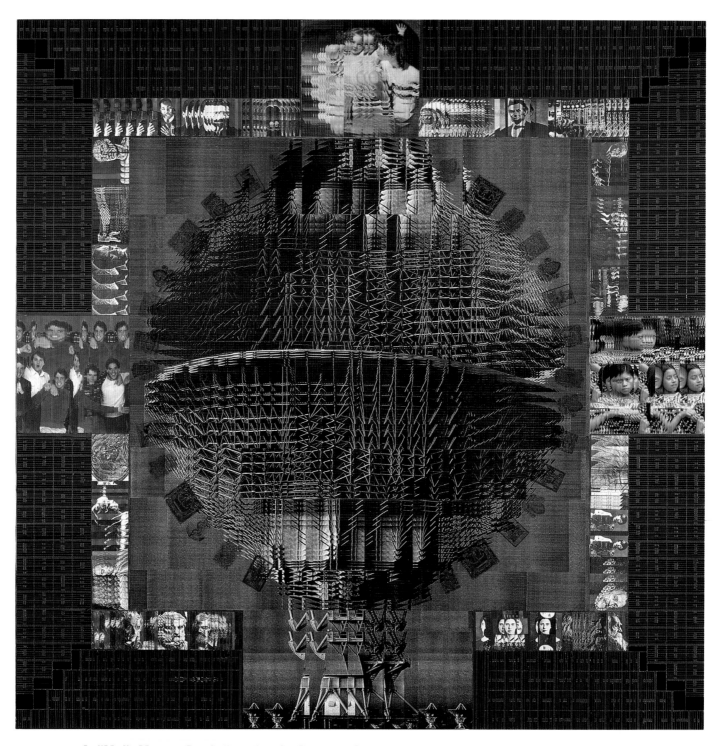

In "Media Message People," a collage by Samuel E. Gallo, the media are symbolized by the spherical center section, which suggests a world interconnected by media networks as complex as the human nervous system. Printers' marks surround the sphere. The human elements are represented in the three square panels at the edges of the collage. Along the outer band, portraits of famous people are accompanied by the people's messages written in a computer code used to translate words into binary numbers. Courtesy Gannett Center for Media Studies

18 "Today's Fiction—Tomorrow's Fact"?

Who is the journalist of the future? To begin by asking that question of science fiction writers, not futurists, journalists, philosophers, or scientists, may seem likely to provide no more insight than calling on crystal-gazer Jeane Dixon. Furthermore, many science fiction writers disavow any interest in prediction. They characterize their descriptions of future journalists as only critiques of contemporary reporters and human foibles.

But science fiction writers—even those who produce third-rate literature—broaden and deepen our sense of the possibilities of change. Alvin Toffler, the author of *Future Shock*, describes science fiction as a sociology of the future—"a mind-stretching force for the creation of the habit of anticipation."[1] Some science fiction writers proclaim: "Today's fiction—tomorrow's fact."[2] And specialists at the Massachusetts Institute of Technology's Media Lab—inventors of futuristic communications machines—attach importance to the ideas of such science fiction writers as Isaac Asimov, William Gibson, and Fred Pohl.

The Media Lab's Marvin Minsky, an expert in artificial intelligence, says science fiction writers "try to figure out the consequences and implications of things in as thoughtful a way as possible. A couple of hundred years from now, maybe Isaac Asimov and Fred Pohl will be con-

French family watches television news, as foreseen in 1882 by Parisian lithographer Albert Robida. Note loudspeaker just below the screen. Photo from The Bettmann Archive

sidered the important philosophers of the twentieth century, and the professional philosophers will almost all be forgotten, because they're just shallow and wrong, and their ideas aren't very powerful."[3]

Science fiction suggests three types of journalists in the future: the human journalist who, like his twentieth-century predecessors, makes his living from investigating and reporting the news; the nonhuman journalist—a robot, computer, or other device—that supplements, even replaces, the human journalist; and the consumer of news who uses the technology of the future to become his own journalist.

The most prosaic of the three—the human who works as a professional journalist—echoes the reporter who stars in murder mysteries, spy novels, and other fiction. He will do anything to get the big story. The journalist in *Special Bulletin* (1983), *Countdown to Looking Glass* (1984), and other end-of-the-world films risks death.[4] In the best of the lot, *The Day the Earth Caught Fire* (1962), Peter Stenning (Edward Judd) of the *Daily Express* calls his office with the scoop— movie reporters always bark stories into a phone— as the earth careens toward the sun.

Occasionally the independent, irreverent renegade journalist discards the story of the century once he gets it. In Ray Bradbury's "The Toynbee Convector" (1988), reporter Roger Shumway obtains an exclusive interview with the only man to have traveled ahead in time and to have brought back photos, films, and sound cassettes— evidence that encouraged contemporary humanity to build a glorious future. The man tells Shumway that he really perpetuated a fraud. But Shumway, thinking about what the man's lie has created, decides to keep the truth to himself.[5]

Science fiction writers distinguish between newspaper reporters and television journalists. Newspaper reporters still look for the truth, as they did in the old days of the twentieth century. Asimov relies on the narrator of his short story "The Billiard Ball" (1967), a reporter for the *Tele-News Press*, to explain Einstein's general theory of relativity.[6] The plot of "The Silly Season" (1950), written by C. M. Kornbluth, who had once been a journalist, turns on the willingness of editors, short of news during the summer, to report alleged sightings of shining domes, black spheres, and flying saucers. Then when black pits—perfectly circular holes—open up and devour people, the public refuses to believe the "newspaper hysteria."[7] The press has become the boy who cried wolf. The wolves turn out to be Martians who take over the earth and rule by "yoke and lash."[8]

The newspaper journalist usually exists in science fiction as an anachronistic skeptic, a narrator whom the reader can believe. In Ed Naha's *The Paradise Plot* (1980), home subscribers to News Satellite Network receive their news—"a constantly droning telex-print-out" of headlines[9]—twenty-four hours a day via cable hookups. The public also watches television commentator Tony Safian—metallic blue hair, "chin of granite, head of meat."[10] But it is Harry Porter of the only remaining U.S. paper, the *Herald-Times-News*, who offers the most credible reports. Known to champion the underdog, he also saves Island One, the first human colony in space, from mass murderers and the Children of Light, deadly mutants with telepathic tentacles.[11]

Reporting only the facts can put the newspaper journalist of science fiction at a disadvantage. In R. A. Lafferty's "Magazine Section" (1985), John T. Woolybear, who has written outrageous but true stories for newspapers' Sunday magazine sections for forty years, cannot place his articles anymore.[12] Printing today's reality is not good enough for the New York *Times* in Robert Silverberg's "What We Learned from This Morning's Newspaper" (1972)—the *Times* publishes news that won't occur for nine days.[13] In Len Jenkin's *New Jerusalem* (1986), investigative reporter Faber finds his skills unneeded. Since readers no longer want reality, newspapers fire their reporters. Or they force the reporters to become "inventors" who manufacture fiction—

How will future journalists define news?

In two sets of playful wooden sculptures, William Accorsi explains the traditional definition of news. In the first sculpture, an ordinary calamity occurs—dog bites man. No news there, normally.

The second sculpture captures man biting dog. That's unusual enough to be news.

But in the journalism of the future, will man-bites-dog suffice? Judging from the definition of news used increasingly by today's trash journalists, will the man have to be an AIDS-infected Hollywood superstar who not only bites the dog but then cooks it to death, slices it into bite-sized pieces, and feeds it to homeless children on Sunset Boulevard?

Journalism's taste for glitzy celebrities, grisly tragedies, and the believe-it-or-not bizarre is no longer confined to supermarket tabloids and television talk shows. As newspaper readership slides about one percentage point a year—in 1967, 73 percent of U.S. adults read a paper every day, twenty-one years later only 51 percent did—even the most serious journalists are concerned about reaching and retaining readers.

James K. Batten, president and chief executive officer of Knight-Ridder, Inc., one of the nation's most respected media companies, believes the newspaper industry must "develop a new and fierce commitment to publishing newspapers that strain to please and satisfy our customers every day."[1]

To some, the attempt to please readers translates into show biz gossip, shorter articles, numerous photographs, and more charts and other eye-catching graphics. But many journalists worry about sacrificing the depth and detail needed day after day to report—and to understand—the issues most important to the world's future.

In the science-fiction movie *The Day the Earth Caught Fire,* a record heat wave and other environmental oddities push journalists into providing continuing and complete front-page coverage. The real-world summer of 1988 brought similar oddities: unrelenting pollution and acid rain, and the hottest temperatures worldwide in the 120 years records have been kept.

But real journalists for the most part saw the greenhouse effect—the world's warming from gases pumped into the atmosphere—and other environmental happenings during the summer of 1988 as weather stories not deserving of sustained coverage, certainly not sustained coverage on Page One.[2]

The front page of the future undoubtedly will carry the kind of news that makes the front page today—political contests, wars, and other good-guy/bad-guy conflicts, especially those involving celebrities. But less certain is daily coverage on Page One of complex environmental crises—even if those crises threaten the very existence of a future.

Sculptor William Accorsi's whimsical 1989 interpretation of the old joke about the definition of news: "Dog bites man—no news. Man bites dog—news." Courtesy Loren Ghiglione. Photo by Reid Baker, Library of Congress

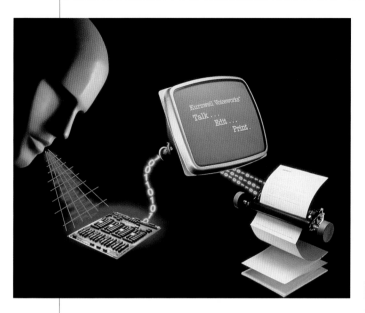

Although only in development and perhaps twenty years from actual use, voice-activated typewriters are seen by inventor Raymond Kurzweil as the tools of tomorrow's reporters. Courtesy Kurzweil Applied Intelligence

"names of nonexistent winners of nonexistent lotteries, details of the imaginary sex lives of imaginary popular entertainers."[14] Faber is retained as the paper's last honest reporter, "perhaps to be pointed out as a vestigial organ."[15]

Most journalists in science fiction work for intergalactic television networks. The television journalist—even television itself—falls victim to a variety of manipulative forces. Not just the Soviets (Brian Garfield's *Deep Cover*)[16] or the Nazis who won World War II and now rule America (Philip K. Dick's *The Man in the High Castle*),[17] but virtually every powerful institution, from advertising[18] to the new world order, seeks to enslave television news. Usually the new world order smacks of George Orwell's *Nineteen Eighty-Four* (1949), with Big Brother journalism monitoring or misinforming everyone. To keep the human race penned in underground tanks, the world's ruling elite in Philip K. Dick's *The Penultimate Truth* (1964) spreads "pure lie" in every news report.[19] Each report describes nonexistent, never-ending nuclear wars above ground. The protagonist in Joan Vinge's "Media Man" (1976) is a mouth-for-hire: "willing to say

anything, sell anything, without question, for the highest bidder."[20] In Norman Spinrad's *A World Between* (1979), the Institute of Transcendental Science attempts to use the media on Pacifica, the galaxy's preeminent electronic democracy, to enslave a bliss-filled utopia.[21]

Science fiction repeatedly pits the television journalist against human privacy and dignity. In Frank Javor's "Interview" (1963), Lester V. Morrison of the intergalactic network "technically augments" the reaction of a woman whose only child was just killed. He uses four receptors attached to the woman's body—invisible to viewers and painful to the woman—to cause the dramatic, emotional response on camera he wants from her.[22] Television cameras in Bruce Sterling's *The Artificial Kid* (1980) hover over staged streetfights, and teen-agers are killed onscreen for audience enjoyment.[23] In *Death Watch*, a 1979 movie based on D. G. Compton's *The Continuous Katherine Mortenhoe* (1974), network boss Vincent Ferriman (Harry Dean Stanton) implants a miniature camera in the head of Roddie the reporter (Harvey Keitel) so that everything he views is transmitted to millions of television watchers. Disease has been all but conquered in this future world. To thrill the jaded television audience, Roddie films the last days of a medical aberration, Katherine Mortenhoe (Romy Schneider), dying of an incurable disease. Eventually he realizes he no longer is a journalist: "I was a reporting device."[24]

Science fiction's second type of journalist—the machine as journalist—is best represented by the intelligent robot. In *Prelude to Foundation* (1988), Asimov's Chetter Hummin, a journalist "sick of gathering together all the nonsense from every world,"[25] turns out to be R. Daneel Olivaw. The R. stands for robot.

Science fiction anticipates technology that would permit tomorrow's journalist to report from beyond today's time and space. The physicist in Asimov's "The Dead Past" (1956) builds a truth-telling chronoscope, which can locate and recreate images of events from the past 125

Reporting or distorting reality?

Will the journalism of tomorrow present an accurate—or distorted—image of reality?

Journalists for generations have used tedious cut-and-paste techniques to alter photographs.

But the arrival of still video photography permits journalists to store an image in digital form inside a computer, call up the image on the computer's screen and easily alter or delete parts of it. The image also can be merged with other images—a bald-headed man in a banker's suit can be given the spikey hairstyle, beard, tattoos, muscles, and leather vest of a barroom brawler.

Since the technology produces no original negative, evidence of ethically questionable photo editing does not exist. "Who is to say what is real and what isn't," asks Frank S. Folwell, assistant director of photography at *USA Today.* "It raises a lot of troubling questions."[1]

Instances abound of published photographs about which those questions can be raised. An Asbury Park *Press* editor deleted a person from a news photo and filled in the hole by electronically duplicating part of a nearby wall.[2] The St. Louis *Post-Dispatch* electronically removed a can of Diet Coke from a picture of Pulitzer Prize-winning photographer Ron Olshwanger and his wife.[3]

Such incidents have led publications to develop policies that ban electronically altered photos. The *Post-Dispatch,* while still permitting traditional cropping, now prohibits the use of its Scitex machine to move, alter, add, or subtract elements in news photographs. At

The St. Louis *Post-Dispatch,* which now has a policy against electronically altering photos, once removed a Coke can from a picture of Pulitzer Prize-winning photographer Ron Olshwanger and his wife. Courtesy St. Louis *Post-Dispatch*

the *National Geographic,* which moved a Great Pyramid at Giza to fit into a vertical magazine cover, digital systems no longer are used "to delete anything that's unpleasant or add anything that's left out."[4]

The issue also exists for broadcast journalists. In a 1987 *Journal of Mass Media Ethics* article, Don E. Tomlinson envisioned the possibility of television news producers "re-creating" an event they could not capture on camera—simulating, for example, the Soviet downing of Korean airliner flight 007.[5]

In 1989, possibility became reality. A new CBS program, "Saturday Night with Connie Chung," used James Earl Jones and other prominent actors in dramatic reenactments of news events. Also in 1989, ABC News aired a TV report on an American diplomat's alleged spying activities. The viewer saw two realistic photographs—actually simulations—of a man resembling the diplomat passing a briefcase to another man. At the same time, an ABC correspondent narrated: "It was not until earlier this year that [the diplomat] was videotaped handing over a briefcase to a known Soviet agent on the streets of a European capital."[6] The staged photographs—accidentally, said ABC, not labeled a simulation—raised the possibility of digital systems being used to develop simulations.

Some newspapers and magazines continue to succumb to "improving" on what they photograph. "People used to be able to look at photographs as depictions of reality," says Jack Corn, the Chicago *Tribune's* director of photography. "Now that's being lost."[7]

years.[26] T. L. Sherred's "E for Effort" (1947) presents a technology that films the past, creating holographic images of the French Revolution and other events.[27] In Stanislaw Lem's *The Futurological Congress* (1971), television has been replaced by physivision: "[S]trange people, not to mention dogs, lions, landscapes and planets, pop into the corner of your room, fully materialized and indistinguishable from the real thing."[28]

Television news has always provoked questions about the reality of what it presents. The nature of a visual medium—to entertain, to dramatize, to create daydreams for the masses—influences its news content. The world of fantasy merges with the world of fact.[29] For many people what appears on television becomes reality.[30] In a 1970 *New Yorker* cartoon, a rain-soaked father who is changing a flat tire on the family car explains to his two children, "Don't you understand? This is *life*, this is what is happening. We *can't* switch to another channel."[31]

Science fiction writers have focused on the ability of television and computers (which Timothy Leary described as the LSD of the '80s) to transform or avoid reality. In Ray Bradbury's "The Veldt" (1950), parents anger their children by threatening to take away their television room. The children use their television room—a giant three-dimensional television set that creates images, smells, and sounds from their imagination—to retaliate. The children imagine that lions devour their parents. The lions do.[32] Laurent Michaelmas, the television journalist in Algis Budrys's *Michaelmas* (1977), takes advantage of a magic megacomputer to access the world's data banks and control the news, not just reporting on corrupt officials but neutralizing them.[33] In William Gibson's *Neuromancer* (1984)—a novel that helped initiate the "cyberpunk" movement in science fiction—a person can plug his brain directly into computer networks. "Artificial intelligences," highly sophisticated computer beings, take the person on wild mental trips.[34]

"Prime Time," by May Stevens, 1967. Oil on canvas. Courtesy Edwin A. Ulrich Museum of Art, The Wichita State University Endowment Art Collection, Wichita, Kansas

In the "cyberpunk" of Gibson and other science fiction writers, the third kind of journalist—the nonjournalist consumer of news as his own journalist—comes into existence. Everyone is his own journalist, creating, stealing, synthesizing the information he wants. The photographer in Gibson's "The Gernsback Continuum" (1981) takes pictures of 1930s futuristic architecture as an "alternate history" to the world of the 1980s. The alternative history becomes disturbingly alive to him. Many people in the United States are said to be living inside their own mental videos drawn from an environment of skin-deep technological images.[35] Science fiction writer J. G. Ballard says, "You're about to see the transformation of the home to a TV studio, in which we're each the star, director, scriptwriter, and audience of our own continuing movies."[36]

In Ballard's *The Day of Creation* (1987), Doctor Mallory, the narrator, dreams of bringing a life-saving river to arid Central Africa. A miracle follows. Mallory's rival, Professor Sanger, a television documentary maker, challenges Mallory's apparent creation. Sanger: "Look at your river—that's a complete invention." Mallory: "A television company might even have thought it up?" Sanger: "Perhaps it did. And the difference? Sooner or later, everything turns into television."[37] Sanger concludes, "The truth is merely the lie you most wish to believe."[38]

What, in summary, should be made of the three kinds of journalists who populate science fiction? Perhaps only that the real journalists of the future—whatever forms they take—will ex-

hibit some of the characteristics of science fiction's journalists. The real journalists, like their make-believe counterparts, will have to resist the manipulators, the dictators, the "inventors" who would obliterate the line between reality and fantasy. They will have to deal not only with Buck Rogers gadgets which expand their capabilities but with some sort of "revolution" that could radically reorder their world and limit their freedom.

Experts cannot agree on what to call the revolution—the communications revolution,[39] the control revolution,[40] the information revolution,[41] the information technology revolution,[42] the computer revolution,[43] the scientific and technological revolution,[44] the third industrial revolution,[45] the electronics revolution,[46] the microelectronics revolution[47]—but they are sure that the post-industrial world is developing revolutionary ways of transmitting information, including information collected by journalists.

What's the form of this information future? Frederick Williams's vision of the twenty-first century is perhaps typical. Every human anywhere on the planet—reminiscent of Dick Tracy—has a wrist-mounted communications device that permits "contact with any other human via a satellite communications network."[48] Each person has access to materials that make him increasingly his own journalist. Interactive television, providing more than one hundred channels, permits people to "talk" to their television sets. They bank, make purchases, and gather information from home. They receive mail electronically. Discs for home players supplement reference libraries. An electronic network connects people to their communities for religious services, university education, work, and play.

Most forecasts assume a continuing convergence of information technologies—television, telephones, computers, and others—and the creation of a single communications system. Neologisms describe the convergence: "telematic" (from a French word that combines computer

Science fiction's portrayal of the journalist sometimes appears to owe a debt to the likes of Dick Tracy, who began using his first wrist two-way radio in 1946. In a 1989 issue of *Life,* Tracy holds up his voice-activated wrist phone with video display—gadgetry comparable to the sci-fi wrist computer, capable of transforming the reporter's spoken words into a typeset article back in the newsroom. Library of Congress, General Collections

and telecommunication technologies); "informatic" (computing plus information, including news content), and "compunications" (computing plus communications). The convergence inevitably involves the digitalization of mass media and telecommunications content—that is, the transmission of coded sounds, images, or data not unlike communication by Morse code, except a million times faster.

The experts do not agree, however, on what the convergence of these information technologies means to the quality of journalism. To oversimplify, the experts split into two camps—optimists and pessimists—on the future of news communication. Consider three aspects:

1. Politics. Some aspects of journalistic information-gathering—for example, the public opinion poll—already seem outdated. QUBE, two-way, locally operated cable channels in Columbus, Ohio, allowed viewers to push a button in their homes to indicate their feelings on public issues. An experiment in Alaska with "Consensor," a little box with two dials that permitted the viewer to indicate not only priority but intensity of feeling, improved on QUBE. Ninety Alaskans—representative of the state's population—used Consensor voting terminals to register their opinions after listening to broadcast journalist Daniel Schorr provide background on such issues as port and road improvements, jails, mass transit, and exploration for natural gas. The results of the Alaskans' "votes" on twenty-two issues were flashed on the home TV screen within one minute. The optimists see electronic plebiscites—as well as cable TV channels devoted to legislative proceedings and teleconferences with elected representatives—as improving democracy. The pessimists look at the convergence of technologies and worry about the misuse of the information collected. They ask whether we're moving toward privacy-threatening centralized data banks, vastly upgraded surveillance capabilities, and *Nineteen Eighty-Four*-style governmental control.[49]

2. Community. The 100-channel cable system, available in stereo to everyone over high-definition, wall-sized televisions, will permit Americans greater access twenty-four hours a day to a larger quantity of news programming. That access could combine with what Yoneji Masuda, president of the Institute for the Information Society, calls a new globalism. People could become more sensitive to the shortage of natural resources, the damage from worldwide pollution, and the need for peaceful coexistence. But "narrowcasting," say the pessimists, will provide so many distracting entertainment possibilities—for those who can afford them—that it

In artist Ray Driver's vision of the journalist of tomorrow, reporters fly their beats wearing 1930s press cards in their hats. Courtesy Ray Driver/*Washington Journalism Review*

is less likely people will view the news. And the pessimists worry about the elderly, the poor, and the marginally literate. Will they be able to take advantage of all channels? And will news—fragmented into different formats with different editorial content to satisfy the interests of different racial, religious, political, and commercial groups—continue to provide the shared knowledge that the public now gets from mass media? Alvin Toffler's prediction in *The Third Wave* of the demassification of the media could result in people vegetating at home in front of their television sets or computers, pursuing their specialized interests, worrying little about public issues, spending less time with their neighbors, and rarely inhabiting public places. John Robinson, director of the Survey Research Center, University of Maryland, reports that society is headed toward a day when people will spend more hours tuned to television sets, video recorders, and other mass media than in conversations with their fellow humans.[50] Perhaps science fiction barely exaggerates the future. In "The Intensive Care Unit" (1977), J. G. Ballard creates a world in which life—including marriage—occurs over television. Humans don't meet in person.[51]

3. Power. Disraeli rewrote the ancient Greeks' maxim that knowledge is power. He said that, as a general rule, the most successful person is the one who has the best information. The same could be said of nations. Marshall McLuhan's "global village"[52] and other futurists' notions of the communications age, the optimists say, accurately predict a planet-wide paradise in which news flows freely to the people of all nations. But pessimists respond that some nations—indeed, some continents and some planets—probably will continue to be primarily communications recipients, dependent on news generated from abroad by transnational companies. The world is not moving toward a "homogeneous 'United States of the World,'" argues Kaarle Nordenstreng. He emphasizes the desire of non-Western nations to protect their sover-

eignty and cultural identity, to regulate the flow of information from Western news media and other transnational corporations, and to create a "new international information order," dismissed by many U.S. journalists as another name for government control and censorship of the press.[53]

The implications of the communications age for journalists are unclear. Today's reporters can be excused for wondering whether the digitalization that comes with the convergence of technologies will render journalists obsolete by the twenty-first century. In a *Washington Journalism Review* attempt to predict the life of a twenty-first-century reporter,[54] Bob Scribe, who covers the police in 2014, frets: "I don't know about my future in this business . . . . I heard the other day that they're working on a new computer that writes better than reporters. They say that one day I'll go out to cover a shooting and all I'll do is call in my notes, real stream-of-consciousness stuff. The computer will write it. I'll be a legman for a computer."[55]

The experts confirm Scribe's worries. "Digitalization makes communication from persons to machines, between machines, and even from machines to persons as easy as it is between persons," communications professor James Beniger explains in *The Control Revolution*. "[A]nd eventually tastes, odors, and possibly even sensations, all might one day be stored, processed, and communicated in the same digital form."[56]

In the future, as Stewart Brand says in his book on the MIT Media Lab, humans will be asking and answering such questions as, "How do we directly connect our nervous systems to the global computer?" But human journalists, Asimov predicts, still will play a key role: "Nothing will substitute for first-hand experience."[57] Benjamin Compaine, formerly executive director of Harvard's Program on Information Resources Policy and now president of Nova Systems, adds, "[Y]ou're not going to have computers or robots go out and get the news . . . ."[58] Christine Urban, president of Urban & Associates, says,

Will future journalists be less free?

Several trends suggest tomorrow's journalist will have less freedom than today's:

1. The recent marriage of Time, Inc. and Warner Communications Inc.—creating the largest media and entertainment combine in the world—foreshadows global conglomerates to which freedom of the press and journalistic standards may be less important. The Time/Warner-style merger raises the question of which set of values will prevail, that of the journalism company or that of the entertainment company.[1]

The importance of the bottom line to the new integrated media and entertainment company also is not clear. When Henry Luce helped start Time Inc., he committed the business not only to making money but also to making, in the words of Jason McManus, *Time*'s editor-in-chief, "a difference in society, in domestic and world affairs and in people's lives."[2] Will the new global Goliaths sacrifice the full use of the First Amendment freedoms involved in doing good to concentrate on doing well?

Will the size of the media megaconglomerates—five to eight such giants may dominate the industry worldwide in a decade[3]—make it easier for the U.S. Supreme Court or the public to attempt to restrict press freedom?[4] Chief Justice Warren Burger, in a 1978 case, singled out "large media conglomerates"[5] for a warning. The public also appears more willing to defend freedom of press for the hometown weekly than for a billion-dollar transnational media conglomerate.

2. Newspaper companies with greater freedom than government-regulated electronic media are increasingly marrying themselves to those media. Newspaper owners look ahead and see the day when subscribers might choose to read the news on a home video screen. If newspapers move from printing to electronic publishing, the distribution of news could be dominated by electronic media. Electronic media are more susceptible to government regulation.

Virtually every president, for example, has tried to manipulate broadcast regulation and licensing to serve his own ends.[6] Angry about the Washington *Post*'s Watergate coverage, President Richard Nixon told staffers: "The main thing is that the *Post* is going to have damnable, damnable problems out of this one. They have a television station. . . . And they're going to have to get [its license] renewed . . . ."[7]

Congress's Office of Technology Assessment also worries about defining freedom of the press legally when print, broadcast, and other media—traditionally accorded different degrees of First Amendment freedom—are no longer distinct. Who is responsible for libel in interactive electronic publishing where anyone with a computer becomes a provider as well as a consumer of news? Electronic publishers, says the Office of Technology Assessment, "may be forced to censor."[8]

3. West German, Australian, Japanese, French, and English companies, under pressure from their home governments, have learned to live with no First Amendment rights and limited press freedom. Now those companies are buying up U.S. media. Kenneth R. Thomson says of Thomson Corp., the new five-billion-dollar international conglomerate, "I can't imagine any publishing company anywhere in the world that would be beyond our ability to acquire."[9]

Jeff MacNelly's "Shoe" comic strip (1989) suggests a question important to the future of journalism: What will be the commitment of the increasingly dominant global media conglomerates to the costly task of reporting the news? Courtesy Tribune Media Services, Inc.

The increasing trend toward foreign firms purchasing American media has prompted at least one U.S. company to shield itself against international raiders. Knight-Ridder, Inc. has adopted a charter amendment that requires 80-percent approval for any sale or merger that the board decides would threaten the quality of the news product or place more than 20 percent of the firm under foreign ownership. No one can predict to what extent, if any, foreign owners will accept less press freedom to maximize the profits of their U.S. media holdings.

4. The U.S. educational system sends the message to the next generation of Americans that freedom of expression is praiseworthy, just don't practice it here. As a result of the U.S. Supreme Court's decision in Hazelwood v. Kuhlmeier (1988), which gave high school administrators control of scholastic journalism, Mark Goodman, director of the Student Press Law Center, says: "We are hearing increasing

reports of school principals and superintendents actually banning certain stories or entire topics from student newspapers and yearbooks. Typically the censored articles involve criticism of school officials or policies or discussion of important social issues like drug abuse or AIDS."[10]

At the university level, liberals—traditionally advocates of free speech—now argue for the suppression of expression they judge objectionable. Students and faculty at Dartmouth seek to ban the *Dartmouth Review*, a conservative weekly.[11] At Stanford and other universities, students put forward rules punishing speech that stigmatizes individuals on the bases of sex, race, sexual orientation, or national origin. Lee Dembart, a Stanford Law School student, writes: "It is distressing that the 'politically correct' view on campus these days seems to favor curtailment of speech."[12]

5. Increasing privatization of schools and other public institutions, a trend toward preventing access to public records, a growing concern in the age of computers about protecting personal privacy—all suggest tomorrow's journalists will be more restricted than today's in their access to information.

Boston University, in taking over management of a public school system in Chelsea, Massachusetts, seeks to suspend application of the state's open meeting and open record laws to certain aspects of its operation of the school system.[13] The U.S. Supreme Court rules unanimously that disclosure of FBI "rap sheets"—which contain information compiled from public records—is an unwarranted invasion of personal privacy. Autopsy reports in Massachusetts are judged medical records, and therefore private, not public, despite the fact that the subjects of the records are no longer alive.

In the computer era, reporters can match data bases to create new information. Legislatures are responding by preventing people from providing data previously available to journalists. Iowa has become the first state to make it a crime for a video store operator to tell anyone what films are being rented by a customer. Experts foresee that the federal government, using national security as justification, might restrict vital information about, say, its own nuclear arms activities—activities that could affect the future of civilization. In the computer age, David Patten, author of *Newspapers and New Media*, concludes, "New efforts to restrict First Amendment freedom will inevitably result."[14]

by Jeff MacNelly

"The way data are manipulated has nothing to do with the essential skills of information-gathering and writing."[59] Through home computers, consumers may have access to large quantities of unprepackaged data. But databases, Urban says, will not replace journalists.

John Diebold, chairman of The Diebold Group, Inc., warns, however, that "our imaginations tend to be bound by the constraints of the past."[60] The vision of tomorrow's journalist held by many members of the media community is cautiously conservative, reminiscent of the 1900 Mercedes-Benz study that predicted worldwide demand for automobiles would never climb above one million, primarily because of the unavailability of chauffeurs.[61]

Somewhat more daring visions of the journalist's future come from John Wooley, president of Vutext, and Mike Greenly, a journalist who is also president of Mike Greenly Marketing. Greenly experimented with computer conferencing—what he calls interactive electronic journalism—as early as the 1984 Democratic convention. He also covered the World Future Society's 1986 conference, "FutureFocus," by connecting himself via personal computer to 2.1 million telex machines around the planet. Linking a personal computer and telexes permits planetwide reader feedback—questions and ideas that transform the reader/spectator into a journalist/participant—and stimulates better journalism, Greenly says.[62]

Wooley predicts not only interactive electronic journalism but a Max Headroom-style computer-generated figure on the screen conducting an effective one-on-one session with each member of the public.[63] "The reporter does the legwork," says Wooley, but the editors "have a more diverse tool kit."[64] They conceive of ways to tailor the presentation of the news—via home computer—to the individual consumer. Graphics, video, printed pages, and a weather map reflect the interests of each person. For the older viewer, the presentation might use a computer-generated Walter Cronkite. For the younger, a computer-generated Clark Kent.

Talk of computer-generated presenters of news may sound like twenty-third century fantasy (in a Superman comic book, Lois Olsen of the Galaxy News Cruiser in the year 2230 uses

In the March 1989 issue of *Heavy Metal*, the illustrated fantasy magazine, a cartoon strip by Juan Gimenez describes the adventures of Leo Roa, employed by the *Starr* newspaper, who sleeps next to a poster of famous World War II correspondent Ernie Pile [*sic*] and dreams of becoming a famous interplanetary correspondent. Courtesy Loren Ghiglione

her shipboard computer to punch up and transmit an image of her ancestor, journalist Jimmy Olsen, Clark Kent's friend from the 1980s).[65] But researchers at MIT's Media Lab already have worked on projects only a step short of Wooley's vision for the future. More than a decade ago, the Media Lab demonstrated a way to transmit a human presence through telephone lines. The Defense Advanced Research Projects Agency had wanted to know how, in event of nuclear attack, the president and other U.S. leaders could hide in different locations but communicate with one another. "Talking Heads," video screens molded into the shape of life-like facial masks, were made to appear to speak with the aid of rear-projected talking faces.[66]

"Talking Heads," however, fall far short of tomorrow's possible robot reporters. Hans Moravec, director of Carnegie Mellon University's Mobile Robot Laboratory, envisions a postbiological future. He contends that within the next century machines "will mature into entities as complex as ourselves, and eventually into something transcending everything we know—in whom we can take pride when they refer to themselves as our descendants."[67] Not only will intelligent robots be able to see, hear, move, and reason, they will be capable of reproducing and improving themselves without human help.[68]

The twenty-first or twenty-second century Woodward and Bernstein could consist of a human reporter teamed with a nonhuman one. The nonhuman one—a "roboreporter"—would take on tasks that it could perform better than any human. Far more sensitive than the human eye and hand, the roboreporter could measure movement to a tenth of a micron and weight to a few micrograms. It could visit other planets to report on worlds that humans could not inhabit.

The reality of the journalist's future, then, may not fall that far short of the fantasy created by Asimov and other science fiction writers. Human reporters will continue to scavenge for

Although *RoboCop* involved law enforcement, some futurists believe robots and artificial intelligence—"roboreporters"—will supersede human journalists. Orion Pictures Corporation, 1986. Courtesy Photofest

the news. But roboreporters will work with human journalists or scoop them. And interactive technologies will encourage passive consumers of news to become active participants—amateur journalists not only reacting to professional journalists' reports but volunteering their own experiences and story ideas to expand an ever-changing body of information. These new reporters—nonhuman professionals and human amateurs—suggest an exciting new chapter in the history of the American journalist.

Acknowledgments

At the risk of forgetting names, I would like to thank— in addition to people acknowledged in the preface, text, and footnotes—hundreds of others who made this book and exhibit possible.

The project benefited from the dedication and ideas of the Library of Congress's experienced exhibits staff: Elna M. Adams, John Adams, John A. Birmingham, Andrew J. Cosentino, Deborah A. Durbeck, Donna Elliott, Tambra Johnson, Monica Lester, Leonard C. Ludes, Christopher J. O'Connor, Gene Edwyn Roberts, Margaret Shannon, and Gwynn E. Wilhelm. Others at the Library who made important contributions are: Francis J. Carroll, head of the newspaper section, Serial and Government Publications Division; Bernard Reilly, head curator, Prints and Photographs Division; Carol Pulin, curator of fine prints, and Elena G. Millie, curator of posters, also of the Prints and Photographs Division; Patrick G. Loughney, curator of the Mary Pickford Theater of the Motion Picture, Broadcasting and Recorded Sound Division; Mary Wolfskill, head of reference and reader services, and reference librarians Charles J. Kelly, Frederick W. Bauman, Jr., and Jeffrey M. Flannery, all of the Manuscript Division; Alan Jabbour, Acting Assistant Librarian for Cultural Affairs, and Jackie Wintle and John Kozar, cultural affairs administrators; Helen Dalrymple, public affairs specialist; Bucky Wall, audiovisual specialist; and John Henry Hass, educational liaison officer.

I owe a personal thanks for the help I received in 1987-88 at the Gannett Center for Media Studies from the Center's excellent staff—Gregory Berzonsky, Wendy Boyd, Esther Chiu, Jane Coleman, Paul Eisenberg, Craig Fisher-Lemay, Shirley Gazsi, Beverly Greenfield, John Polich, Deborah Robinson, Deborah Rogers, and Hunt Williams—and from fellow Fellows Ralph M. Baruch, Asa Briggs, Jane Delano Brown, Ellis Cose, Victoria Fung, Garth S. Jowett, James M. Kinsella, John F. Lawrence, Ernest Leiser, Gerald S. Lesser, Kati Marton, Timothy R. Miller, and Paul F. Perry. Also deserving of personal thanks are research assistants Ann Pryor Ambrecht, Rett Ertl, Justin Friedman, Cheryl Klein, Cameron McWhirter, and Elizabeth Thompson, and the staff at the library of Columbia University's Graduate School of Journalism.

In 1988-89, I was allowed to continue work on this book thanks to a fellowship at Harvard's Joan Shorenstein Barone Center on the Press, Politics and Public Policy. Members of the Center's staff—Nancy Palmer, Maura Barrios, Jody Watson, Chrys Poff, and Kari Nystrom—were very helpful. I also benefited from the suggestions of Ellen Hume, executive director, Gary R. Orren, associate director, Lawrence K.

Grossman, visiting lecturer in the Frank Stanton Chair on the First Amendment, and Center fellows Kiku Adatto, Bernice Buresh, Nicholas Daniloff, Dayton Duncan, Godfrey Hodgson, and Philip van Niekerk.

I also was assisted by the American Society of Newspaper Editors staff: Nancy Andiorio, Elise Burroughs, Mireille Grangenois, Suzanne Jenkins, and Chris Schmitt.

Many archivists, curators, editors, educators, librarians, publishers, and friends contributed suggestions or materials for the exhibit section on the journalist of fact: Andy Aleff, Kenneth W. Andrews, Reid Ashe, Mark Ashton, Phillip H. Ault, H. Brandt Ayers, Ben H. Bagdikian, Tracy Baker, Georgia B. Barnhill, Jeanette Bartz, Mansfield Bascom, Maurine Beasley, Robert Bentley, Harold T. Berc, Mae Berger, William Block, William Bray, Judith W. Brown, William R. Burleigh, Benjamin J. Burns, Brian D. Burns, Betty W. Carter, Hodding Carter III, Jerry Ceppos, Robert C. Christopher, Robert P. Clark, Roger N. Conger, Lawrence S. Connor, Edward Cony, Diane Cooke, Helen K. Copley, Gene Cryer, Larry Dinnean, Michael Emery, Katherine Fanning, George Fattman, Will Fehr, Jean Folkerts, Gary Fong, Helen Forde, Fred W. Friendly, Marianne Fulton, John Griffin, Rebecca F. Gross, Robert J. Haiman, David Halberstam, Robert Hirst, Stevie Holland, Peter Holmes, Fern Ingersoll, Robert W. Jodon, Alex Jones, Gregg K. Jones, Michael Jubb, Bernard Judy, Kent Keeth, Karen M. Kelly, Tom Kelly, Joseph Kingsbury-Smith, Sanders LaMont, Lawrence Landis, Doris Lemert, John M. Lemmon, George R. Lewis, Lionel Linder, Cheryl Lutz, Drake Mabry, Edward Manassah, Robert Karl Manoff, Patrick McCauley, Marcus McCorison, Susan H. Miller, Charles Modlin, Ward Morehouse III, Carl Morris, Ray Moscowitz, Alina Mueller, Jean Mulvaney, Ted M. Natt, Patience Nauta, Paul Neely, Rolfe Neill, David Nord, Herman J. Obermayer, James F. O'Donnell, Herbert O'Keef, William O'Leary, Sandy Oppenheimer, Burl Osborne, Carolyn Park, John C. Pratt, Joseph Pultizer, Jr., John Rothman, Dan M. Ryan, Robert Sanders, Pamela Brunger Scott, Ed Seaton, Clark Secrest, Mrs. Ben Shahn, Martin Silverstein, Earl H. Smith, Sharon Carter Smith, Mary Smyser, Richard Smyser, James Squires, John L. Stallings, Linda Stanley, Donna Stewart, Carolyn J. Strickler, Edmund B. Sullivan, John Sullivan, Arthur Ochs Sulzberger, Rev. Robert Tabscott, William H. Taft, Tom Teepen, Seymour Topping, Joyce Ann Tracy, Sarah Truher, Barbara Vandegrift, Larry Viskochil, Paul David Walker, George B. Waters, Delmar Watson, Anne S. Wells, Wilma Wilcox, William F. Woo, Wendell Wood, and John Zakarian.

Indispensable to the fiction section were Gene Giancarlo, who read literally hundreds of novels and edited a draft of the section, and experts Bill Blackbeard, Howard Good, Otto Penzler, Deac Rossell, Welford D. Taylor, and Steve Weinberg. They gave me ideas, caught errors, and helped me organize the section. Others who assisted are Lynn Barrett, Jeff Bierig, Michael Cart, Bernard Drew, Michael Hall, Donna L. Hanlon, Barrie J. Hughes, Garrison Keillor, Irv Letofsky, Rosalie Miller, Catherine Modica, Marion Reese, Ellen Rothenberg, Marcia Ruth, Nat Sobel, and Dorothy Swerdlove.

The final section on the future of newspapers presented me with the most difficult challenge. My ignorance of science and science fiction knows no bounds. In addition to those acknowledged through quotation and footnote, I would like to thank: Stanley Asimov, Neil Barron, Muriel Becker, Beth Krevitt Eres, Beverly O. Friend, James Gunn, Peter Jasco, Timothy R. Miller, and Frederik Pohl, who read and improved drafts of the chapter; Brad Balfour, Moshe Feder, David Hartwell, Gerald Jonas, David Mead, Sam Moskowitz, Peter D. Pautz, John J. Pierce, Charles Sheffield, Norman Spinrad, Lou Stathis, Marshall Tymm, and Donald Wollheim, who greatly helped my research on the journalist in science fiction; and Elliot Jaspin, Richard Schmidt, William Stephenson, and Nancy Woodhull, who provided valuable ideas about the real journalist's future.

Loren Ghiglione

Notes

Introduction
(pages 3–11)

1. Benjamin Harris, as quoted in Frederic Hudson, *Journalism in the United States from 1690 to 1872* (New York: Harper & Row, 1873), p. 45.

2. *Ibid.*, p. 46.

3. As quoted in Frank Luther Mott, *American Journalism, A History: 1690–1960* (New York: The Macmillan Co., 1962), p. 9.

4. *Ibid.*, p. 10.

5. Mott and other historians insist *Publick Occurrences* was the first American newspaper, though acknowledging that news-sheets were published in Mexico as early as 1541. See *ibid.*, footnote 7, page 6. Lea Ann Brown notes that Harris planned to publish *Publick Occurrences* monthly, "or if any Glut of Occurrences happen, oftener." She concludes: "Acceptance of *Publick Occurrences* as the first American newspaper requires suspending the part of the modern definition which includes a minimum of weekly publication." See Lea Ann Brown, "Benjamin Harris," in *American Newspaper Journalists, 1690–1872 (Dictionary of Literary Biography*, v. 43), ed. by Perry J. Ashley (Detroit: Gale, 1985), p. 282.

6. Stephen Botein downplays the legal significance of the Zenger trial, arguing that it should be understood primarily as "quasi-theater." See Stephen Botein, introduction to *'Mr. Zenger's Malice and Falshood': Six Issues of the New-York Weekly Journal 1733–34* (Worcester, Mass.: American Antiquarian Society, 1985), p. 6.

7. "Roundup: FBI, Police Invade Newsrooms," in *The News Media & the Law*, Vol. 12, No. 4, Fall 1988, pp. 4–5.

8. Floyd Abrams, as quoted in A. E. Dick Howard, "The Press in Court," in Philip S. Cook, Douglas Gomery, and Lawrence W. Lichty, eds., *American Media: The Wilson Quarterly Reader* (Washington, D.C.: The Wilson Center Press, 1989), p. 80.

9. Hadley Richardson Hemingway Mowrer, as quoted in Denis Brian, *The True Gen: An Intimate Portrait of Ernest Hemingway By Those Who Knew Him* (New York: Grove Press, 1988), p. 3.

10. Michael Schudson, "What Is a Reporter? The Private Face of Public Journalism," in James W. Carey, ed., *Media, Myths, and Narratives: Television and the Press* (Newbury Park, Calif.: Sage Publications, 1988), p. 239.

11. David S. Broder, *Behind the Front Page: A Candid Look at How the News Is Made* (New York: Simon and Schuster, 1987), p. 14.

12. See S. Robert Lichter, Stanley Rothman and Linda S. Lichter, *The Media Elite* (Bethesda, Md.: Adler & Adler, Publishers, Inc., 1986), p. 28.

13. William A. Rusher, *The Coming Battle for the Media: Curbing the Power of the Media Elite* (New York: William Morrow and Company, Inc., 1988), p. 11.

14. Ben H. Bagdikian, *The Media Monopoly* (Boston: Beacon Press, 1983), p. ix.

15. As quoted in Eugene H. Methvin, "Mephistophelean journalism," *The Quill*, April 1989, p. 40.

16. Walter Karp, "All the Congressmen's men: How Capitol Hill controls the press," *Harper's Magazine*, July 1989, p. 56.

17. As quoted in "Thrust of literary effort debated," *presstime*, August 1989, p. 40.

18. Louis Banks, "Memo to the Press: They hate you out there," *The Atlantic Monthly*, April 1978, p. 42. See also Aaron Wildavsky, "The media's 'American egalitarians,'" *The Public Interest*, Summer 1987, pp. 94–104.

19. Methvin, *op. cit.*, p. 40.

20. Lowell Weicker, as quoted in James H. Dygert, *The Investigative Journalist: Folk Heroes of a New Era* (Englewood Cliffs, N.J.: Prentice-Hall, 1976), p. vii.

21. Edward S. Herman and Noam Chomsky, *Manufacturing Consent: The Political Economy of the Mass Media* (New York: Pantheon Books, 1988), p. 299.

22. Leon V. Sigal, *Reporters and Officials: The Organization and Politics of Newsmaking* (Lexington, Mass.: D.C. Heath and Company, 1973), p. 126.

23. W. Lance Bennett, *News: The Politics of Illusion*, second edition (New York: Longman, 1983), p. 117. See also Halberstam as quoted in Michael Parenti, *Inventing Reality: The Politics of the Mass Media* (New York: St. Martin's Press, 1986), pp. 52–53.

24. Joseph Kraft, as quoted in Robert C. Christopher, *Crashing the Gates: The De-WASPing of America's Power Elite* (New York: Simon and Schuster, 1989), p. 157.

25. Louis Harris poll cited in Thomas Griffith, *How True: A Skeptic's Guide to Believing The News* (Boston: Little, Brown and Co., 1974), p. 6.

26. James A. Davis and Tom W. Smith, *General Social Survey, Cumulative Code Book, 1972–1976* (Chicago: National Opinion Research Center, July 1976), question 74G.

27. James A. Davis and Tom W. Smith, *General Social Survey, Cumulative Code Book, 1972–1983* (Chicago: National Opinion Research Center, July 1983), question 152G.

28. Sydney Schanberg as quoted in Jane Gross, "Movies and the Press Are an Enduring Romance," *The New York Times*, June 2, 1985, sec. 2, p. 19.

29. J. Paul Leigh, "Estimates of the Probability of Job-Related Deaths in 347 Occupations," *Journal of Occupational Medicine*, Volume 29, No. 6, June 1987, p. 514.

30. David H. Weaver and G. Cleveland Wilhoit, *The American Journalist: A Portrait of U.S. News People and Their Work* (Bloomington, Ind.: Indiana University Press, 1986), p. 12. In fairness to Weaver and Wilhoit, they go on to describe the quoted summary of their 1982–83 national telephone survey of 1,001 journalists as "inadequate, as this chapter will show."

31. Doug Underwood, "When MBAs rule the newsroom," *Columbia Journalism Review*, March/April 1988, pp. 23–30.

32. Christopher, *op. cit.*, p. 159.

33. Ben Bradlee, letter to the author, April 17, 1984.

34. Tom Wolfe, "The New Journalism," in Tom Wolfe and E. W. Johnson, eds., *The New Journalism* (New York: Harper & Row, 1973), p. 3.

35. Dan Rather, as quoted in Timothy Crouse, *The Boys on the Bus* (New York: Random House, 1973), p. 230.

36. Frederick Taylor, letter to the author, April 30, 1984.

37. Charles Anderson, undated 1984 letter to the author.

38. See Ernst Kris, "The Personal Myth: A Problem in Psychoanalytic Technique," in *Selected Papers of Ernst Kris* (New Haven: Yale University Press, 1975), pp. 272–300.

39. See Jay Martin, *Who Am I This Time? Uncovering the Fictive Personality* (New York and London: W.W. Norton & Co., 1988), p. 12.

40. *Ibid.*, p. 25.

41. W. A. Swanberg, *Citizen Hearst* (New York: Charles Scribner's Sons, 1961), p. 105.

42. Sidney Kobre, *The Yellow Press and Gilded Age Journalism* (Tallahassee: Florida State University Press, 1964), p. 56.

43. Maxwell Taylor Courson, "The Newspaper Movies: An Analysis of the Rise and Decline of the News Gatherer as a Hero in American Motion Pictures, 1900–1974," (Ph.D. dissertation, University of Hawaii, 1976), p. 151.

44. Nora Sayre, "Falling Prey to Parodies of the Press," *The New York Times*, January 1, 1975, p. 8.

45. Ron Dorfman, "Journalists Under Fire," *The Quill*, October 1983, p. 13.

46. Harry S. Ashmore, "Cause, Effect, and Cure," *Mass Communications*, occasional paper of the Center for the

Study of Democratic Institutions of the Fund for the Republic, Inc., 1966, p. 33.

47. Norman Isaacs, *Untended Gates: The Mismanaged Press* (New York: Columbia University Press, 1986), p. 99. See also Richard M. Clurman's call for the media to report "energetically and critically on themselves" and to give the public greater access for reply through talk-back programs, ombudsmen, expanded letters-to-the-editor columns, and other devices. Richard M. Clurman, *Beyond Malice: The Media's Years of Reckoning* (New Brunswick, N.J.: Transaction Books, 1988), p. 268.

48. As quoted in William A. Henry, III, "Journalism Under Fire," *Time*, December 12, 1983, p. 77.

49. For a description of a survey at the University of Texas, see John Hohenberg, *A Crisis for the American Press* (New York: Columbia University Press, 1978), p. 27.

50. Walter Lippmann, *Liberty and the News* (New York: Harcourt, Brace & Howe, 1920), p. 76.

51. See Donna A. Demac, *Liberty Denied: The Current Rise of Censorship in America* (New York: PEN American Center, 1988), p. 164.

52. Alexander Hamilton, paper no. 84, in Alexander Hamilton, James Madison, and John Jay, *The Federalist Papers* (New York: Mentor, 1961), p. 514.

THE JOURNALIST OF FACT
(pages 13–17)

1. Edna Buchanan, as quoted in Calvin Trillin, "Covering the Cops," *The New Yorker*, Feb. 17, 1986, p. 39. See also, Edna Buchanan, *The Corpse Had a Familiar Face: Covering Miami, America's Hottest Beat* (New York: Random House, 1987).

2. Ted Gup, "In Maine: A Town and Its Paper," *Time*, Jan. 18, 1988, p. 10.

3. See biographical sheet on Terry Anderson provided by Associated Press, May 1989.

4. Having other kinds of diversity—newswomen as well as newsmen, people of color as well as whites—also is crucial. Kay Mills, of the Los Angeles *Times*: "Having women at all levels of a newspaper, listening to the community with a new perspective, helps the newspaper cover its community more thoroughly, just as having more blacks, more Hispanics, and more Asian-Americans in the newsroom broadens coverage." Kay Mills, "New perspectives, different voices," *The Quill*, April 1989, p. 24.

5. Robert A. Rutland, *The Newsmongers: Journalism in the Life of the Nation, 1690–1972* (New York: The Dial Press, 1973), p. 3.

6. As quoted in Edith O'Keefe Susong, "Reminiscences of 50 years as a newspaper publisher," *The Greeneville Sun*, October 1, 1966, p. 1.

7. *Ibid.*, and June N. Adamson, "Selected Women in Tennessee Newspaper Journalism" (Master's thesis, University of Tennessee, 1971), pp. 92–122.

8. Ira B. Harkey, Jr., *The Smell of Burning Crosses* (Jacksonville, Ill.: Harris-Wolfe & Company, 1967), p. 18.

9. See John Cameron Sim, *The Grass Roots Press* (Ames, Iowa: The Iowa State University Press, 1969), p. 113.

10. See P. D. East, *The Magnolia Jungle: The Life, Times, and Education of a Southern Editor* (New York: Simon and Schuster, 1960).

11. Recent scholarship suggests the story may be apocryphal. See Barbara Belford, *Brilliant Bylines: A Biographical Anthology of Notable Newspaperwomen in America* (New York: Columbia University Press, 1986), p. 104.

12. See Ishbel Ross, *Ladies of the Press* (New York: Harper & Brothers, Publishers, 1936), p. 29.

13. See Catherine L. Covert, "Journalism History and Women's Experience: A Problem in Conceptual Change," *Journalism History*, Vol. 8, No. 1, (Spring 1981), p. 6.

14. The term "First Americans" is used by Jeannette Henry in her foreword to James E. Murphy and Sharon M.

Murphy, *Let My People Know: American Indian Journalism, 1828–1978* (Norman: University of Oklahoma Press, 1981), p. viii.

15. It requires Sally Miller twenty-six chapters—one chapter per ethnic group—to briefly sketch the role of ethnic-press journalists in America. Her list is by no means complete, failing to include the Italian-American press, for example. See Sally M. Miller, ed., *The Ethnic Press in the United States: A Historical Analysis and Handbook* (New York: Greenwood Press, 1987).

16. As quoted in Murphy, *op. cit.*, p. 26. See also Ralph Henry Gabriel, *Elias Boudinot: Cherokee and His America* (Norman: University of Oklahoma Press, 1941).

17. Jean Folkerts and Dwight L. Teeter, Jr., *Voices of a Nation* (New York: Macmillan Publishing Co., 1989), p. 166.

18. As quoted in Felix Gutierrez, "Spanish-Language Media in America: Background, Resources, History," *Journalism History*, Vol. 4, No. 2 (Summer 1977), p. 41.

19. *Ibid.*

20. *Ibid.* See also Juan Gonzales, "Forgotten Pages: Spanish-Language Newspapers in the Southwest," *Journalism History*, Vol. 4, No. 2 (Summer 1977), p. 51.

21. Harry H. L. Kitano, "The Japanese-American Press," in Miller, *op. cit.*, pp. 198–200.

22. Transcript of May 15, 1989, interview of Lucile Bluford by Fern Ingersoll, director of the women in journalism oral history project, Washington Press Club Foundation.

23. Lucile Bluford, as quoted in Diane E. Loupe, "Storming and Defending the Color Barrier at the University of Missouri School of Journalism: The Lucile Bluford Case," a paper presented to the August 1989 meeting of the Association for Education in Journalism and Mass Communciation, p. 20.

1. Street reporter
(pages 19–27)

1. James Stanford Bradshaw, "George W. Wisner—A New Appraisal," unpublished paper on file at the library of Columbia University's Graduate School of Journalism, p. 1.

2. George Wisner, *New York Sun*, May 13, 1834, p. 2.

3. George Wisner, *New York Sun*, January 2, 1834, p. 2.

4. George Wisner, *New York Sun*, October 23, 1833, p. 2.

5. George Wisner, *New York Sun*, August 1, 1834, p. 2.

6. Samuel G. Blythe, *The Making of a Newspaper Man* (Philadelphia: Henry Altemus, Co., 1912), p. 4. See also Ted Curtis Smythe, "The Reporter, 1880–1900. Working Conditions and Their Influence on the News," *Journalism History*, Vol. 7, No. 1 (Spring 1980), pp. 1–10.

7. Will Irwin, *The Making of a Reporter* (New York: G.P. Putnam's Sons, 1942), p. 33.

8. Edwin L. Shuman, *Steps Into Journalism. Helps and Hints for Young Writers* (Evanston, Ill.: Correspondence School of Journalism, 1894), p. 21.

9. Walt Whitman, "The New York Press," *New York Aurora*, March 29, 1842, in Joseph Jay Rubin and Charles H. Brown, eds., *Walt Whitman of the New York Aurora: Editor at Twenty-Two, A Collection of Recently Discovered Writings* (State College: Pennsylvania State University Press, 1950), p. 112.

10. Walt Whitman, "Life in a New York Market," *New York Aurora*, March 16, 1842, in Rubin and Brown, eds., *ibid.*, pp. 20–22.

11. Walt Whitman, "Scenes of Last Night," *New York Aurora*, April 1, 1842, in Shelley Fisher Fishkin, *From Fact to Fiction* (New York: Oxford University Press, 1988), p. 20.

12. See Raymond A. Schroth, *The Eagle and Brooklyn: A Community Newspaper, 1841–1855* (Westport, Ct.: Greenwood Press, 1974), pp. 39–58.

13. Fishkin, *op. cit.*, p. 33.

14. Ishbel Ross, *Ladies of the Press* (New York: Harper & Brothers Publishers, 1936), pp. 61–62. See also Marion Mar-

zolf, *Up From the Footnote: A History of Women Journalists* (New York: Hastings House, Publishers, 1977), pp. 33–34, 37, and Kay Mills, *A Place in the News: From the Women's Pages to the Front Page* (New York: Dodd, Mead & Company, 1988), pp. 25–27.

15. Ross, *ibid.*, p. 65.

16. As quoted in Faye B. Zuckerman, "Winifred Black (Annie Laurie)," in Perry J. Ashley, ed., *American Newspaper Journalists, 1901–1925, Dictionary of Literary Biography*, Vol. 25 (Detroit: Gale Research Co., 1984), p. 17.

17. As quoted in Gay Talese, *The Kingdom and the Power* (New York: The World Publishing Company, 1969), p. 224.

18. *Ibid.*, pp. 224–225.

19. See Meyer Berger, *The Story of the New York Times, 1851–1951* (New York: Simon and Schuster, 1951).

20. See Louis Stettner, ed., *Weegee* (New York: Alfred A. Knopf, 1977), p. 11.

21. *Weegee*, with an introduction by Allene Talmey, (New York: Aperture, Inc., 1978), p. 5.

22. Stettner, ed., *op. cit.*, p. 15.

23. *Ibid.* For a short story that says a great deal about Weegee, see "Retrospective on Weegee," in Judy Lopatin, *Modern Romances* (New York: Fiction Collective, 1986), pp. 25–42.

24. Delmar Watson, ed., *"Quick Watson, the Camera,"* (Hollywood, Calif: Delmar Watson, 1975), p. 26.

25. R. C. Hickman, as quoted in catalogue issued in conjunction with the exhibition "Black Dallas in the 1950s: Photographs from the R. C. Hickman Archive," February 27-May 30, 1987, Barker Texas History Center, University of Texas at Austin.

26. See profile on Michel duCille in "Neighbors" section, *The Miami Herald*, July 30, 1987, p. 12.

27. *Ibid.*

28. See Peter Weitzel, managing editor of *The Miami Herald*, as quoted in Kendall J. Wills, *The Pulitzer Prizes, 1988* (New York: Touchstone/Simon & Schuster, Inc., 1988), pp. 313–314.

29. As quoted in Lou Cannon, *Reporting: An Inside View* (Sacramento: California Journal Press, 1977), p. 294.

30. As quoted in Leonard Downie, Jr., *The New Muckrakers* (Washington: The New Republic Book Company, Inc., 1976), pp. 34–35.

31. *Ibid.*, p. 3.

32. *Ibid.*, p. 5.

33. *Ibid.*

34. *Ibid.*, p. 34.

35. As quoted in Cannon, *op. cit.*, p. 294. Also see Barry Sussman, *The Great Cover-Up: Nixon and the Scandal of Watergate* (New York: New American Library, 1974), and Carl Bernstein and Robert Woodward, *All the President's Men* (New York: Simon and Schuster, 1974).

Alternative reporters (page 23)

1. Robert J. Glessing, *The Underground Press in America* (Bloomington: Indiana University Press, 1970), p. xiv.

2. As quoted in *ibid.*, p. 8. Glessing lists more than 450 underground papers with about five million circulation.

3. As quoted in Kevin Michael McAuliffe, *The Great American Newspaper* (New York: Charles Scribner's Sons, 1978), p. 24.

4. *Ibid.*, p. 28

5. David Armstrong, *A Trumpet to Arms* (Los Angeles: J.P. Tarcher Boston, distr. by Houghton Mifflin, 1981), p. 26.

2. Persuader
(pages 29–37)

1. See Glyndon G. Van Deusen, *Horace Greeley: Nineteenth-Century Crusader* (Philadelphia: University of Pennsylvania Press, 1953), pp. 284–286.

2. William Harlan Hale, *Horace Greeley: Voice of the People*, (New York: Collier Books, 1961), p. 273.

3. Richard Kluger, *The Paper: The Life and Death of The New York Herald Tribune* (New York: Alfred A. Knopf, 1986), p. 92.

4. C. E. Norton, *Correspondence Between Thomas Carlyle and Ralph Waldo Emerson* (Boston: J. R. Osgood and Company, 1883), Vol. II, p. 266.

5. Frank Luther Mott, *American Journalism, A History: 1690–1960* (New York: The Macmillan Co., 1962), p. 341.

6. But Greeley was known to stoop to personal invective. In "Judgment on the Satanic Press," he labeled James Gordon Bennett, publisher of the New York *Herald*, a "low-mouthed, blatant, witless, brutal scoundrel." See Kluger, *op. cit.*, p. 78.

7. *The Rebel*, August 6, 1863, as cited in Joseph Frazier Wall, *Henry Watterson: Reconstructed Rebel* (New York: Oxford University Press, 1956), p. 39.

8. As quoted in Robert K. Thorp, "Henry Watterson," in Perry J. Ashley, ed., *American Newspaper Journalists, 1901–1925, Dictionary of Literary Biography*, Vol. 25 (Detroit, Mich.: Gale Research Co., 1984), p. 326.

9. Paul M. Cousins, *Joel Chandler Harris* (Baton Rouge: Louisiana State University Press, 1968), pp. 108–109.

10. *Ibid.*, p. 109.

11. See Langston Hughes, Milton Meltzer, and C. Eric Lincoln, *A Pictorial History of Blackamericans* (New York: Crown Publishers, Inc., 1983), p. 234.

12. See Joel Chandler Harris, *Free Joe and Other Georgian Sketches* (New York: Charles Scribner's Sons, 1887). Harris's attitude toward race is thoroughly explained in Wayne Mixon, "The Irrelevance of Race: Joel Chandler Harris and Uncle Remus in Their Time," scheduled for publication in the November 1990 issue of *The Journal of Southern History*.

13. As quoted in Cousins, *op. cit.*, p. 148.

14. Leland Huot and Alfred Powers, *Homer Davenport of Silverton: Life of a Great Cartoonist* (Bingen, Wash.: West Shore Press, 1973), p. 69.

15. Stephen Hess and Milton Kaplan, *The Ungentlemanly Art: A History of American Political Cartoons* (New York: Macmillan Publishing Co., Inc.; London: Collier Macmillan, 1975), p. 126.

16. As quoted in *ibid.*, p. 127.

17. Huot and Powers, *op. cit.*, p. 97.

18. *Ibid.*, p. 121.

19. Richard O'Connor, *Heywood Broun, A Biography* (New York: G. P. Putnam's Sons, 1975), p. 78.

20. Walter Lippmann, as quoted in Ronald Steel, *Walter Lippmann and the American Century* (Boston: Little, Brown and Company, 1980), p. 231.

21. John Mason Brown, as paraphrased in John Luskin, *Lippmann, Liberty, and the Press* (University, Alabama: University of Alabama Press, 1972), pp. 176–177.

22. Arthur Krock, *Memoirs: Sixty Years on the Firing Line* (New York: Funk & Wagnalls, 1968), p. 64.

23. As quoted in Steel, *op. cit.*, p. 232.

24. Heywood Broun, "Sacco and Vanzetti," *New York World*, August 5, 1927, as reprinted in John K. Hutchens and George Oppenheimer, eds., *The Best in The World* (New York: The Viking Press, 1973), p. 383.

25. *Ibid.*, p. 389.

26. As reprinted in Heywood Hale Broun, *Collected Edition of Heywood Broun* (New York: Harcourt, Brace and Company, 1941), p. 209.

27. See Dale Kramer, *Heywood Broun, A Biographical Portrait* (New York: Current Books, Inc., 1949), p. 9.

28. Pete Daniel and Raymond Smock, *A Talent for Detail: The Photographs of Miss Frances Benjamin Johnston, 1889–1910* (New York: Harmony Books, 1974), p. 43.

29. *Ibid.*

30. *Ibid.*, p. 17.

31. As quoted in Charles A. Fecher, *Mencken: A Study of His Thought* (New York: Alfred A. Knopf, 1978), p. 10.

32. H. L. Mencken, as quoted by Theo Lippman, Jr., ed., "Introduction," in H. L. Mencken, *A Gang of Pecksniffs* (New Rochelle, New York: Arlington House Publishers, 1975), p. 20.

33. Mencken, as quoted in *ibid.*, p. 19.

34. H. L. Mencken, *A Mencken Chrestomathy* (New York: Alfred A. Knopf, Inc., 1949), p. 624.

35. Lippman, as quoted in Steel, *op. cit.*, p. 23.

36. Charles A. Fecher, ed., *The Diary of H. L. Mencken* (New York: Alfred A. Knopf, 1989), p. xx.

37. H. L. Mencken, "On Journalism," *The Smart Set*, April 1920, as reprinted in Lippman, ed., *op. cit.*, p. 63.

38. H. L. Mencken, *Prejudices: Sixth Series* (New York: Alfred A. Knopf, Inc., 1927), pp. 14–15.

39. Hodding Carter, *Where Main Street Meets the River* (New York: Rinehart & Company, Inc., 1953), p. 3.

40. As quoted in Harry D. Marsh, "Hodding Carter's Newspaper On School Desegregation, 1954–1955," *Journalism Monographs*, No. 92, May 1985, p. 5.

41. Hodding Carter, *The Winds of Fear* (New York: Farrar & Rinehart, Inc., 1944); reprint (New York: Award Books, 1964), p. vii.

42. Marsh, *op. cit.*, p. 6.

43. Hodding Carter, "Liar by Legislation," *The Delta Democrat-Times*, April 3, 1955, p. 1.

No freedom about race (page 34)

1. George D. Prentice, as quoted in Clement Eaton, *The Growth of Southern Civilization, 1790–1860* (New York: Harper & Brothers, 1961), p. 267

2. *Ibid.*

3. Cassius Clay, as quoted in Clement Eaton, *The Freedom-of-Thought Struggle in the Old South* (New York: Harper & Row, 1940, 1964), p. 186.

4. *Ibid.*, p. 188.

5. *Ibid.*, p. 189.

6. Hodding Carter, *Their Words Were Bullets: The Southern Press in War, Reconstruction, and Peace* (Athens: University of Georgia Press, 1969), p. 17.

7. See Harry Golden, *The Right Time: An Autobiography* (New York: G. P. Putnam's Sons, 1969), p. 311. For this and other Golden plans, see Joseph Wershba, foreword to Harry Golden, *Carl Sandburg* (Urbana: University of Illinois Press, 1988), pp. 8–9.

8. For this and other Golden plans, see Joseph Wershba, foreword to Harry Golden, *Carl Sandburg* (Urbana: University of Illinois Press, 1988), pp. 8–9.

3. Crusader
(pages 39–47)

1. As quoted in Charles A. Madison, *Critics & Crusaders* (New York: Henry Holt and Company, 1947–1948), p. 15.

2. As quoted in *ibid.*

3. As quoted in *ibid.*, p. 16.

4. As quoted in *ibid.*, p. 29.

5. As quoted in *ibid.*, p. 33.

6. *Nation*, January 4, 1866, Vol. II, p. 7, as quoted in Frank Luther Mott, *American Journalism, A History: 1690–1960* (New York: The Macmillan Co., 1962), p. 323.

7. Rayford W. Logan in "Introduction" to Frederick Douglass, *Life and Times of Frederick Douglass* (New York: Collier Books, 1962), p. 17.

8. Frederick Douglass, "Valedictory," August 16, 1863, reproduced in *Douglass' Monthly, Vol. 4–5, 1861–1863* (New York: Negro Universities Press, 1969), unnumbered page just before p. 849.

9. Alain Locke, "Foreword" to the Centenary Memorial Subscribers' Edition of the *The Life and Times of Frederick Douglass* (New York: Pathway Press, 1941), p. xix.

10. Douglass, *Life and Times of Frederick Douglass*, p. 261.

11. *Ibid.*, p. 264.

12. As quoted in Jonathan Daniels, *They Will Be Heard* (New York: McGraw-Hill Book Company, 1965), p. 101.

13. As quoted in *ibid.*, p. 108.

14. As quoted in *ibid.*, p. 113.

15. As quoted in *ibid.*, p. 117.

16. Jane Grey Swisshelm, *Half a Century* (Chicago: Jansen, McClurg & Company, 1880), p. 130.

17. Jane Grey Swisshelm, *Letters to Country Girls* (New York: J. C. Riker, 1845), p. 78.

18. Swisshelm, *Half a Century*, p. 164.

19. As quoted in Barbara Belford, *Brilliant Bylines, A Biographical Anthology of Notable Newspaperwomen in America* (New York: Columbia University Press, 1986), p. 29.

20. Ethel Payne, interview by the author, September 13, 1989.

21. *Ibid.*

22. *Ibid.*

23. *Ibid.* See also "Missing Pages," *GF Magazine*, Summer 1989, pp. 12–15, 25, which includes an excerpt about this incident from Wallace Terry's upcoming book entitled *Missing Pages, An Oral History of Black Journalists in America, 1940–1990.*

24. *Ibid.*

25. *Ibid.*

26. *Ibid.* On Payne's career, see also Roland E. Wolseley, *The Black Press, U.S.A.* (Ames: Iowa State University Press, 1990), pp. 259–261.

27. See Albert Bigelow Paine, *Th. Nast, His Period and His Pictures* (New York: The Macmillan Company, 1904; republication, Princeton, N.J.: The Pyne Press, n.d.), p. 140–141; and Stephen Hess and Milton Kaplan, *The Ungentlemanly Art* (New York: Macmillan Publishing Co., Inc.; London: Collier Macmillan Publishers, 1975), p. 95.

28. Mott, *op. cit.*, p. 384

29. As quoted in Hess and Kaplan, *op. cit.*, p. 95.

30. As quoted in *ibid.*, p. 102.

31. Will Irwin, *The Making of a Reporter* (New York: G. P. Putnam's Sons, 1942), p. 165.

32. *Collier's*, April 1, 1911, p. 28.

33. *Collier's*, April 22, 1911, p. 22.

34. As reproduced in Will Irwin, *The American Newspaper*, reprint edition (Ames: The Iowa State University Press, 1969), p. 71.

35. Will Irwin, "The Voice of a Generation," *Collier's*, July 29, 1911, p. 23.

36. A. J. Liebling, *The Wayward Pressman* (Garden City, N.Y.: Doubleday, 1947), p. 5.

37. As quoted in Loren Ghiglione, "(Broad) casting the First Stone," Ph.D. dissertation, George Washington University, 1976, p. 110.

38. As quoted in Raymond Sokolov, *Wayward Reporter* (New York: Harper & Row, Publishers, 1980), p. 3.

39. *Ibid.*

40. See Lloyd Goodrich, *John Sloan* (New York: The Macmillan Company, 1952), pp. 44–45.

41. As quoted in Rebecca Zurier, *Art for The Masses* (Philadelphia: Temple University Press, 1988), p. 46.

42. As quoted in Granville Hicks, with John Stuart, *John Reed: The Making of a Revolutionary* (New York: Macmillan, 1936), p. 260.

43. John Hohenberg, *Foreign Correspondence: The Great Reporters and Their Times* (New York: Columbia University Press), p. 231.

44. As quoted in Loren Ghiglione, "'Every government is run by liars',' " in supplement "The reel journalist vs. the real journalist: Hollywood's image of the newspaperman," *The* (Southbridge, Mass.) *Evening News*, October 17, 1976, p. 7.

45. *Ibid.*

46. As quoted in Leonard Downie, Jr., *The New Muckrakers* (Washington: The New Republic Book Company, Inc., 1976), p. 189.

47. Ghiglione, "Every Government is Run by Liars," *op. cit.*, p. 7.

48. I. F. Stone, *In a Time of Torment* (New York: Random House, 1967), p. 13.

49. *Ibid.*

E. W. Scripps and Joseph Pulitzer (page 45)

1. Pulitzer, for example, was accused of being a hypocrite for applauding a union at his *New York World* but keeping his *St. Louis Post-Dispatch* nonunion. See George Juergens, *Joseph Pulitzer and the New York World* (Princeton: Princeton University Press, 1966), pp. 304–305.

2. As quoted in W. A. Swanberg, *Pulitzer* (New York: Charles Scribner's Sons, 1967), p. 11.

3. As quoted in Frank Luther Mott, *American Journalism: A History: 1690–1960* (New York: The Macmillan Co., 1962), p. 434.

4. See Alan Metcalf, "Great Investigative Crusades of Joe Pulitzer," *Media History Digest*, Spring-Summer 1988, pp. 12–18.

5. As quoted in Juergens, *op. cit.*, p. 289.

6. As quoted in Vance H. Trimble, ed., *Faith in My Star* (Memphis: The Commercial Appeal, 1989), p. 19.

7. As quoted in Eric M. Odendahl and Philip B. Demateis, "E. W. Scripps," in Perry J. Ashley, ed., *American Newspaper Journalists, 1901–1925, Dictionary of Literary Biography*, Vol. 25. (Detroit, Mich.: Gale Research Co., 1984), p. 258.

4. Investigator
(pages 49–55)

1. As quoted in Ishbel Ross, *Ladies of the Press* (New York: Harper & Brothers Publishers, 1936), p. 51.

2. As quoted in Barbara Belford, *Brilliant Bylines: A Biographical Anthology of Notable Newspaperwomen in America* (New York: Columbia University Press, 1986), p. 117.

3. As quoted in Ross, *op. cit.*, pp. 58–59.

4. As quoted in Madelon Golden Schilpp and Sharon M. Murphy, *Great Women of the Press* (Carbondale: Southern Illinois Press, 1983), p. 147.

5. As quoted in Peter B. Hales, *Silver Cities: The Photography of American Urbanization, 1839–1915* (Philadelphia: Temple University Press, 1984), p. 167.

6. As quoted in Donald N. Bigelow, "Introduction" to Jacob Riis, *How the Other Half Lives* (New York: Sagamore Press, Inc., 1957), p. x.

7. As quoted in *ibid.* p. vii. See also Blake McKelvey, *The Urbanization of America, 1860–1915* (New Brunswick: Rutgers University Press, 1963), p. 163.

8. Jacob A. Riis, *The Making of an American* (New York: The Macmillan Company, 1901; reprint, 1964), p. 175.

9. Riis, *How the Other Half Lives*, p. 41.

10. *Ibid.*, p. 38.

11. *Ibid.*, p. 79.

12. See, for example, *Evening Sun*, February 12, 1888.

13. Ida B. Wells-Barnett, *Crusade for Justice: The Autobiography of Ida B. Wells*, edited by Alfreda M. Duster (Chicago: The University of Chicago Press, 1970), p. 64.

14. *Ibid.*, p. 65.

15. As quoted in *ibid.*, pp. 65–66.

16. *Ibid.*, p. 71.

17. As quoted in *ibid.*, p. xxi.

18. As quoted in David Mark Chalmers, *The Social and Political Ideas of the Muckrakers* (New York: The Citadel Press, 1964), p. 47.

19. As quoted in Harvey Swados, *Years of Conscience: The Muckrakers* (Cleveland: The World Publishing Company, 1962), p. 85.

20. *Ibid.*

21. See C. C. Regier, *The Era of the Muckrakers* (Chapel Hill: University of North Carolina Press, 1932; reprint, Gloucester, Mass: Peter Smith, 1957), p. 57, and George E. Mowry, *The Era of Theodore Roosevelt* (New York: Harper & Row, Publishers, 1958), p. 65.

22. Mowry, *ibid.*

23. Marion Marzolf, *Up From the Footnote* (New York: Hastings House, Publishers, 1977), pp. 41–42.

24. As quoted in Oliver Pilat, *Drew Pearson: An Unau-*

thorized *Biography* (New York: Harper & Row, Publishers, Inc., 1973), p. 20.

25. *Ibid.*, p. 25.

26. *Ibid.*, p. 2.

27. Ibid., p. 3.

28. Leonard Downie, Jr., *The New Muckrakers* (Washington: The New Republic Book Company, Inc., 1976), p. 63.

29. *Ibid.*, pp. 62–63.

30. Seymour M. Hersh, *My Lai 4: A Report on the Massacre and Its Aftermath* (New York: Random House, 1970), p. 133.

31. See Seymour M. Hersh, *Cover-Up* (New York: Random House, 1972).

32. As quoted in Downie, *op. cit.*, p. 87.

33. *The New York Times*, December 22, 1974, p. 1.

34. John C. Behrens, *The Typewriter Guerillas* (Chicago: Nelson Hall Inc., 1977), p. 130. See Seymour M. Hersh, "An Absence of Instinct," *The Bulletin of the American Society of Newspaper Editors*, February 1970, pp. 4–9.

35. Hersh, *My Lai 4*, p. 140.

Watch the watchdog? (page 52)

1. Janet Malcolm, "The Journalist and the Murderer, 1—The Journalist," *The New Yorker*, March 13, 1989, p. 38.

2. Eleanor Randolph, "The Critic and The Criticized," *The Washington Post*, March 18, 1989, p. C1.

3. See John Taylor, "Holier Than Thou," *New York*, March 27, 1989, pp. 32–37.

4. Elie Abel, formerly dean of Columbia University's Graduate School of Journalism, has said: "Sooner, rather than later, in one form or another, the News Council will be reinvented. It may be a long wait, though." Abel, as quoted in Norman E. Isaacs, *Untended Gates: The Mismanaged Press* (New York: Columbia University Press, 1986), p. 130.

5. A 1986 study by the Gannett Center for Media Studies in New York concluded that most papers have adopted policies for correcting their mistakes "in fixed places . . . under standing headlines, making them accessible to readers." See D. Charles Whitney, "Begging Your Pardon: Corrections and Corrections Policies at Twelve U.S. Newspapers." Working Paper, Gannett Center for Media Studies, New York, 1986, p. 3.

6. Edwin Diamond, A. Biddle Duke, and Isabelle Anacker, "Can we expect TV news to correct its mistakes?" *TV Guide*, Dec. 5, 1987, p. 8.

7. Jeff Cohen, as quoted in Dom Bonafede, "Taking on the Press," *National Journal*, April 8, 1989, p. 858.

8. As quoted in Richard P. Cunningham, "Re-examining the ombudsman's role," *The Quill*, June 1988, p. 12.

5. Exploiter
(pages 57–63)

1. Charles Dickens, *Martin Chuzzlewit* (Harmondsworth: Penguin Books, 1968), p. 318.

2. As reprinted in Frank Luther Mott, *American Journalism, A History: 1690–1960* (New York: The Macmillan Co., 1962), p. 225.

3. Richard Adams Locke, *The Moon Hoax* (New York: William Gowans, 1859; reprint, Boston: Gregg Press, 1975), pp. ix–x.

4. As reprinted in *ibid.*, p. xii.

5. Mott, *op. cit.*, p. 226.

6. As quoted in Ormond Seavey's introduction to Locke, *op. cit.*, p. xxiii.

7. Jules Verne, "In the Year 2889," *The Forum*, February 1889, pp. 662–677.

8. Edgar Allan Poe, "The Atlantic Crossed in Three Days!," *The [New York] Extra Sun*, April 13, 1844, p. 1.

9. Edward Everett Hale, "The Brick Moon," *The Atlantic Monthly*, October, November and December, 1869.

10. Robert Duncan Milne, "The Passing of the Printing

Press," *The San Francisco Call*, December 18, 1898, p 22.

11. Mark Twain, "From the London Times of 1904," *The Century*, November 1898, pp. 100–104.

12. Richard Kluger, *The Paper: The Life and Death of the New York Herald Tribune* (New York: Alfred A. Knopf, 1986), p. 216. See also Tom Wolfe, "Piping a story straight from the skull," *The Bulletin of the American Society of Newspaper Editors*, No. 643, July/August 1981, p. 17.

13. John J. McPhaul, *Deadlines & Monkeyshines* (Englewood Cliffs, N.J.: Prentice-Hall, Inc., 1962), p. 35.

14. *Ibid.*, p. 36.

15. *Ibid.*, p. 38.

16. John Tebbel, *The Media in America* (New York: New American Library, 1974), p. 336.

17. McPhaul, *op. cit.*, p. 47.

18. *Ibid.*, p. 46.

19. Justin E. Walsh, *To Print the News and Raise Hell: A Biography of Wilber F. Storey* (Chapel Hill: University of North Carolina Press, 1968), p. 2.

20. McPhaul, *op. cit.*, p. 49.

21. Lloyd Wendt, *Chicago Tribune: The Rise of a Great American Newspaper* (Chicago: Rand McNally and Company, 1979), p. 256.

22. Walsh, *op. cit.*, p. 266.

23. *Ibid.*, p. 270.

24. W. A. Swanberg, *Citizen Hearst* (New York: Charles Scribner's Sons, 1961), p. 106. See Ferdinand Lundberg, *Imperial Hearst: A Social Biography* (New York: Equinox Cooperative Press, 1936), pp. 60–61.

25. *New York Journal*, October 4, 1896, as quoted in Mott, *op. cit.*, p. 525.

26. *New York Journal*, October 17, 1896, as quoted in *ibid.*

27. James Creelman, *On the Great Highway* (Boston: Lothrop, Lee & Shepard Co., 1901), p. 178.

28. See Mott, *op. cit.*, p. 527; Oliver Carlson and Ernest Sutherland Bates, *Hearst: Lord of San Simeon* (Westport, Conn.: Greenwood Press, 1936), p. 92; John K. Winkler, *William Randolph Hearst: A New Appraisal* (New York: Hastings House, 1955), p. 146; Mrs. Fremont Older, *William Randolph Hearst*, (New York: Appleton-Century, 1936), p. 200; Creelman, *op. cit.*, pp. 174–76; and Marcus M. Wilkerson, *Public Opinion and the Spanish-American War* (Baton Rouge: Louisiana State University Press, 1932), p. 132.

29. As quoted in Mott, *op. cit.*, p. 530.

30. *Ibid.*

31. Swanberg, *op. cit.*, p. 145.

32. Creelman, *op. cit.*, p. 212.

33. As quoted in William H. Taft, "Bernarr Macfadden," in Perry J. Ashley, ed. *American Newspaper Journalists, 1901–1925, Dictionary of Literary Biography*, Vol. 25. (Detroit, Mich.: Gale Research Co., 1984), p. 189.

34. As quoted in Lester Cohen, *The New York Graphic* (Philadelphia: Chilton Books, 1964), p. 7.

35. *Ibid.*

36. Emile Gauvreau, *My Last Million Readers* (New York: E. P. Dutton and Company, Inc., 1941), p. 105.

37. *Ibid.*, p. 126.

38. Cohen, *op. cit.*, p. 231.

Exploiter or exploited? (page 61)

1. Walter Lippmann, as quoted in Edwin R. Bayley, *Joe McCarthy and the Press* (Madison: The University of Wisconsin Press, 1981), p. 78.

2. *Ibid.*, p. 68.

3. *Problems of Journalism, Proceedings of the American Society of Newspaper Editors 1950* (Washington, D.C.: American Society of Newspaper Editors, 1950), p. 295.

4. Bayley, *op. cit.*, p. 67.

5. *Ibid.*

6. *Ibid.*, p. 70.

7. *Ibid.*, p. 174.

8. *Ibid.*, p. 219.

6. Entertainer
(pages 65–73)

1. Milton Meltzer, *Mark Twain Himself* (New York: Bonanza Books, 1960), pp. 66–67.

2. As quoted in Paul Fatout, *Mark Twain in Virginia City* (Bloomington: Indiana University Press, 1964), p. 196.

3. As quoted in *ibid.*, p. 203.

4. As quoted in *ibid.*, p. 208.

5. As quoted in *ibid.*, p. 16.

6. Mark Twain, "Memoranda," *The Galaxy*, Vol. IX, No. 6, June 1870, p. 858.

7. As quoted in Ishbel Ross, *Ladies of the Press* (New York: Harper & Brothers Publishers, 1936), p. 78.

8. Hartnett T. Kane, *Dear Dorothy Dix: The Story of a Compassionate Woman* (Garden City: Doubleday and Co., 1952), p. 234.

9. Madelon Golden Schilpp and Sharon M. Murphy, *Great Women of the Press* (Carbondale: Southern Illinois University Press, 1983), p. 113.

10. Philip Dunne as quoted in Grace Eckley, *Finley Peter Dunne* (Boston: Twayne Publishers, 1981), p. 9.

11. As quoted in Norris W. Yates, *The American Humorist* (Ames: Iowa State University Press, 1964), p. 88.

12. As quoted in *ibid*.

13. As quoted in Louis Filler, ed., *The World of Mr. Dooley* (New York: Collier Books, 1962), p. 73.

14. As quoted in Eckley, *op. cit.*, p. 34.

15. *Ibid.*, pp. 33–34.

16. As quoted in Yates, *op. cit.*, p. 117.

17. As quoted in Bryan B. Sterling, ed., *The Will Rogers Scrapbook* (New York: Grosset & Dunlap, 1976), p. 185.

18. Arthur P. Dudden, ed., *The Assault of Laughter* (New York: Thomas Yoseloff, Publisher, 1962), p. 421.

19. As quoted in Yates, *op. cit.*, p. 120.

20. As quoted in Yates, *op. cit.*, p. 125.

21. As quoted in Donald Day, ed., *The Autobiography of Will Rogers* (Boston: Houghton Mifflin, 1949), pp. 248–249.

22. Dave Anderson, ed., *The Red Smith Reader* (New York: Random House, 1982), p. 301.

23. Stephen Becker, *Comic Art in America* (New York: Simon and Schuster, 1959), pp. 255–256.

24. Anderson, *op. cit.*, p. 301.

25. *Ibid.*, p. 3.

26. *Ibid.*

27. *Ibid.*, p. 194.

28. *Ibid.*, p. 169.

29. As quoted in Frederick C. Klein, "Ordinary Man, Extraordinary Sportswriter," *Wall Street Journal*, June 18, 1986, p. 24.

30. Anderson, ed., *op. cit.*, p. 16.

31. Dave Camerer, ed., *The Best of Grantland Rice* (New York: Franklin Watts, Inc., 1963), p. 8.

32. *Ibid.*, p. 94.

33. See John Stevens, "The Rise of the Sports Page," *Gannett Center Journal*, Fall 1987, pp. 3–7, and David Quentin Voigt, *American Baseball* (Norman: University of Oklahoma Press, 1966), pp. 6–7.

34. Lowell Reidenbaugh, *Cooperstown: Where Baseball's Legends Live Forever* (St. Louis: The Sporting News Publishing Company, 1983), p. 40.

35. *Ibid.*

36. Ross, *op. cit.*, p. 410.

37. As quoted in George Eells, *Hedda and Louella* (New York: G. P. Putnam and Sons, 1972), p. 21.

38. *Ibid.*, p. 73.

39. Kay Mills, *A Place in the News: From the Women's Pages to the Front Page* (New York: Dodd, Mead & Company, 1988), p. 29.

40. Peter C. Marzio, *Rube Goldberg: His Life and Work* (New York, London: Harper & Row Publishers, 1973), p. 181.

Entertain without offending? (page 68)

1. See Sherwood Anderson, "On Being a Country Editor," *Vanity Fair*, February 1928, p. 70, and "The Country Weekly," *The Forum*, April 1931, p. 208.

2. As quoted in Ray Lewis White, ed., *Return to Winesburg* (Chapel Hill: University of North Carolina Press, 1967), p. 4.

3. See Walter B. Rideout, "Why Sherwood Anderson Employed Buck Fever," in Ray Lewis White, *The Achievement of Sherwood Anderson* (Chapel Hill: University of North Carolina Press, 1966), pp. 128–137, and Welford Dunaway Taylor, ed., *The Buck Fever Papers* (Charlottesville: University Press of Virginia, 1971).

4. White, *Return to Winesburg*, p. 21.

5. Sherwood Anderson, "How I Ran A Small Town Newspaper," manuscript, Newberry Library, p. 9., as quoted in White, *Return to Winesburg*, p. 22.

7. War correspondent
(pages 75–83)

1. As quoted in Philip Knightley, *The First Casualty* (New York: Harcourt Brace Jovanovich, 1975), p. 408.

2. John Hohenberg, *Foreign Correspondence: The Great Reporters and Their Times* (New York: Columbia University Press, 1964), p. 135.

3. Vietnam correspondent David Halberstam wrote about "the journalist in search of self as the Hemingway hero." See David Halberstam, "Letter to my Daughter," as reprinted in John Clark Pratt, ed., *Vietnam Voices* (New York: Viking, 1984), p. 659.

4. See Michael Reynolds, *Hemingway's First War* (Princeton: Princeton University Press, 1976; reprint, New York: Basil Blackwell, Inc., 1987), pp. 4–5.

5. William White, ed., *By-Line: Ernest Hemingway* (New York: Charles Scribner's Sons, 1967), p. xi.

6. Knightley, *op. cit.*, pp. 193, 212–213.

7. Hohenberg, *op. cit.*, p. 362.

8. Carlos Baker, *Ernest Hemingway: A Life Story* (New York: Charles Scribner's Sons, 1969), p. 408.

9. Hohenberg, *op. cit.*, p. 64.

10. General William Tecumseh Sherman, as quoted in Joseph H. Ewing, "The New Sherman Letters," *American Heritage*, July/August 1987, p. 24.

11. *Ibid.*, p. 28.

12. *Ibid.*, p. 34.

13. Henry Villard, as quoted in *ibid.*, p. 41.

14. *Ibid.*

15. J. Cutler Andrews, *The North Reports the Civil War* (Pittsburgh: University of Pittsburgh Press, 1955), p. 640.

16. Richard Kluger, *The Paper: The Life and Death of The New York Herald Tribune* (New York: Alfred A. Knopf, 1986), p. 114.

17. Horace Greeley, as quoted in *ibid.*, p. 61.

18. As quoted in Antoinette May, *Witness to War: A Biography of Marguerite Higgins* (New York: Beaufort Books, Inc., 1983), p. 60.

19. *Ibid.*, p. 158.

20. *Ibid.*, p. 154.

21. Virginia Elwood-Akers, *Women War Correspondents in the Vietnam War, 1961–1975* (Metuchen, N.J.: The Scarecrow Press, Inc., 1988), p. 38.

22. Kluger, *op. cit.*, p. 440. See also Kay Mills, *A Place in the News: From the Women's Pages to the Front Page* (New York: Dodd, Mead & Company, 1988), pp. 326–327.

23. Julia Edwards, *Women of the World: The Great Foreign Correspondents* (Boston: Houghton Mifflin, 1988), p. 195.

24. Kluger, *op. cit.*, p. 447.

25. Lloyd Goodrich writes that "no other artist [than Homer] left so authentic a record of how the Civil War soldier really looked and acted." Lloyd Goodrich, *Winslow Homer* (New York: George Braziller, 1959), p. 13. But Gordon Hendricks questions whether Homer normally was on the scene. Gordon Hendricks, *The Life and Work of Winslow Homer* (New York: Harry N. Abrams, 1979), p. 58.

26. See figure 57 in Julian Grossman, *Echo of a Distant Drum: Winslow Homer and the Civil War* (New York: Harry N. Abrams, 1974), p. 81.

27. See Frederick Ray, *Alfred R. Waud: Civil War Artist* (New York: The Viking Press, 1974), and Paul Hogarth, *The Artist as Reporter* (London: Gordon Fraser, 1986), pp. 36–39.

28. As quoted in Jorge Lewinski, *The Camera at War* (New York: Simon and Schuster, 1978), p. 92.

29. *Ibid.*, p. 90.

30. *Ibid.*, p. 88.

31. See Robert Capa, *Slightly Out of Focus* (New York: Henry Holt and Company, Inc., 1947), *Images of War* (New York: Grossman Publishers, 1964), and Cornell Capa and Richard Whelan, eds., *Robert Capa Photographs* (New York: Alfred A. Knopf, 1985).

32. Sheryle and John Leekley, *Moments: The Pulitzer Prize Photographs* (New York: Crown Publishers, Inc., 1978), p. 20.

33. Vicki Goldberg, *Margaret Bourke-White* (Reading, Mass.: Addison-Wesley Publishing Company, Inc., 1987), p. 291.

34. Bill Mauldin, *Up Front* (New York: Henry Holt and Company, 1945), p. 7–8. See also Bill Mauldin, *The Brass Ring* (New York: W. W. Norton & Company, Inc., 1971).

35. Mauldin, *Up Front*, p. 21.

36. See David Nichols, ed., *Ernie's War* (New York: Simon & Schuster, Inc., 1986), p. xiv.

37. Ernie Pyle, *Brave Men* (New York: Henry Holt and Company, Inc., 1944), p. 107.

38. Charles Lynch, as quoted in Knightley, *op. cit.*, p. 333.

39. As quoted in Daniel C. Hallin, *The "Uncensored War"* (New York: Oxford University Press, 1986), p. 5.

40. Michael Herr, *Dispatches* (New York: Alfred A. Knopf, 1977), p. 229.

41. David Halberstam, *The Making of a Quagmire* (New York: Ballantine Books, 1989), p. 339.

42. Neil Sheehan, "In Vietnam, the Birth of the Credibility Gap," *The New York Times*, October 1, 1988, p. 27. See also Sheehan, *A Bright Shining Lie: John Paul Vann and America in Vietnam* (New York: Random House, 1988), pp. 348–350.

43. Knightley, *op. cit.*, p. 380.

44. As quoted in Betty C. Brown, "The Third War of Horst Faas," *Popular Photography*, March 1966, p. 117.

45. *Ibid.*, p. 116.

46. As quoted in Carol Squiers, "Catherine Leroy," *American Photographer*, December 1988, p. 38.

47. Susan D. Moeller, *Shooting War: Photography and the American Experience of Combat* (New York: Basic Books, Inc., 1989), p. 402.

Press and government (page 81)

1. Wes Gallagher, as quoted in James Boylan, "Newspeople," in Philip S. Cook, Douglas Gomery, and Lawrence W. Lichty, *American Media: The Wilson Quarterly Reader* (Washington: The Wilson Center Press, 1989), p. 68.

2. See Stephen Hess, *The Government/Press Connection* (Washington, D.C.: The Brookings Institution, 1984).

3. See Charles W. Bailey, *Conflicts of Interest: A Matter of Journalistic Ethics* (New York: National News Council, 1984), p. 21.

4. William L. Rivers, *The Other Government: Power and the Washington Media* (New York: Universe Books, 1982), p. 18.

5. William L. Laurence, *Men and Atoms: The Discovery, the Uses and the Future of Atomic Energy* (New York: Simon and Schuster, 1959), p. 95.

6. *Ibid.*, p. 96.

7. *Ibid.*, p. 111.

8. *Ibid.*, p. 113.

8. Broadcast journalist
(pages 85–95)

1. Robert S. and Helen Merrell Lynd, *Middletown in Transition: A Study in Cultural Conflicts* (New York: Harcourt, Brace, 1937), pp. 377–78 (note 5); footnote, p. 386.

2. David Holbrook Culbert, *News for Everyman: Radio and Foreign Affairs in Thirties America* (Westport, Conn.: Greenwood Press, 1976), p. 25.

3. *Ibid.*, p. 26.

4. *Ibid.*

5. Detroit *News*, September 1, 1920, as quoted in Erik Barnouw, *A Tower in Babel: A History of Broadcasting in the United States: Volume I—to 1933* (New York: Oxford University Press, 1966), p. 63.

6. As quoted in Irving E. Fang, *Those Radio Commentators!* (Ames: The Iowa State University Press, 1977), p. 28.

7. *Ibid.*, p. 42.

8. See photo opposite title page, "Headline Hunter Floyd Gibbons at work (1935)," and other photos in Edward Gibbons, *Floyd Gibbons: Your Headline Hunter* (New York: Exposition Press, 1953).

9. Fang, *op. cit.*, p. 57.

10. *Ibid.*

11. *Ibid.*, p. 73

12. See Erik Barnouw, *The Golden Web: A History of Broadcasting in the United States: Volume II—1933 to 1953* (New York: Oxford University Press, 1968), pp. 19–20.

13. As quoted in Fang, *op. cit.*, p. 34.

14. As quoted in *ibid.*, p. 316.

15. As quoted in *ibid.*, p. 317.

16. As quoted in A. M. Sperber, *Murrow: His Life and Times* (New York: Freundlich Books, 1986), p. 168.

17. "Man-bites-dog act slays N. Y. press; dailies reaction big $64 question," *Variety*, June 4, 1947, p. 29.

18. "Nick Kenny Speaking," New York *Mirror*, January 15, 1949, p. 12.

19. Interview of Frank Stanton by author, August 4, 1975.

20. Interview of Ned Calmer by author, August 4, 1975.

21. See Fred W. Friendly, *Due to Circumstances Beyond Our Control . . .* (New York: Vintage Books, 1968), p. 37.

22. Edward Bliss, Jr., ed., *In Search of Light: The Broadcasts of Edward R. Murrow* (New York: Avon, 1967), p. 266.

23. As quoted in Friendly, *op. cit.*, p. 41.

24. Jack O'Brian, "Letters From Readers On Slanted Broadcasts," New York *Journal-American*, June 14, 1954, p. 24.

25. As quoted in Joseph E. Persico, *Edward R. Murrow: An American Original* (New York: McGraw-Hill Publishing Co., 1988), p. 392.

26. David Halberstam, *The Powers That Be* (New York: Alfred A. Knopf, 1979), p. 491.

27. As quoted in Clark Dougan and Stephen Weiss, *The American Experience in Vietnam* (New York: W. W. Norton & Co. and Boston Publishing Co., 1988), p. 190.

28. Halberstam, *op. cit.*, p. 514.

29. As quoted in Judith S. Gelfman, *Women in Television News* (New York: Columbia University Press, 1976), p. 28.

30. Ron Powers, *The Newscasters* (New York: St. Martin's Press, 1977), p. 163.

31. *Ibid.*, pp. 170–171

32. Larry Speakes with Robert Pack, "Beat the Press," *TV Guide*, May 14, 1988, p. 8.

33. *Ibid.*, pp. 6–7.

34. As quoted in "Donaldson, Sam," Charles Moritz, ed., *Current Biography Yearbook 1987* (New York: The H. W. Wilson Co., 1987, 1988), p. 140.

35. Sam Donaldson, *Hold On, Mr. President* (New York: Random House, 1987), pp. 85–86.

36. As quoted in "Bradley, Ed," Charles Moritz, ed., *Current Biography 1988* (New York: The H. W. Wilson Co., 1988, 1989), p. 84.

Geraldo Rivera (page 90)

1. Ron Powers, *The Newscasters* (New York: St. Martin's Press, 1977), p. 183.

2. Nancy Shulins, "Geraldo Rivera's Rules of the Game," *AP Newsfeatures Report*, March 13, 1989, p. 1.

3. As quoted in "Rivera, Geraldo," in Charles Moritz, ed., *Current Biography Yearbook 1975* (New York: The H. W. Wilson Co., 1975), p. 359.

4. *Ibid.*

5. As quoted in Nancy Shulins, "Geraldo struggles with image," *Sunday Telegram*, Worcester, Mass., March 26, 1989, p. A17.

6. As quoted in Shulins, "Geraldo Rivera's Rules of the Game," *op. cit.*

7. Tom Shales, "Where Talk Is Cheap and the Bucks Are Big," *The Washington Post National Weekly Edition*, Nov. 28-Dec. 4, 1988, p. 11.

8. *Ibid.*

9. As quoted in "Who's a journalist? What's 'talk show journalism'?" *The Bulletin of the American Society of Newspaper Editors*, July/August 1989, p. 25. See also Geraldo Rivera, "TV's Wave of the Future," *The New York Times*, Dec. 16, 1988, p. A39.

10. *Ibid.* ("Who's a journalist? . . .), p. 26

11. *Ibid.*, p. 24–25.

12. Van Gordon Sauter, "In Defense of Tabloid TV," *TV Guide*, August 5, 1989, p. 4

THE JOURNALIST OF FICTION
(pages 97–99)

1. Ward Just, *A Family Trust* (Boston: Little, Brown and Co., 1978), p. 5.

2. *Ibid.*

3. *Ibid.*, pp. 343–344.

4. Pauline Kael, "Raising Kane," in *The Citizen Kane Book* (Toronto: Bantam Books, 1974), p. 27.

5. Joseph McBride, *Orson Welles* (New York: The Viking Press, 1972), pp. 33–34.

6. Dennis Dooley, "The Man of Tomorrow and the Boys of Yesterday," in Dennis Dooley and Gary Engle, eds., *Superman at Fifty! The Persistence of a Legend!* (Cleveland: Octavia Press, 1987), pp. 29–30.

7. Ned Calmer, *The Anchorman* (Garden City, N.Y.: Doubleday & Co., 1970), p. iv.

8. Pauline Kael calls these partial truths "false, easy patterns." Kael, *op. cit.*, p. 107.

9. H. L. Mencken, "More Tips for Novelists," *Chicago Tribune*, May 2, 1926, as quoted in H. L. Mencken, *A Gang of Pecksniffs And Other Comments on Newspaper Publishers, Editors and Reporters* (New Rochelle, N.Y.: Arlington House, 1975), p. 116.

10. Ben Hecht and Charles MacArthur, *The Front Page* (New York: Covici-Friede Publishers, 1928), p. 40.

9. Reporter
(pages 101–107)

1. Ben Hecht and Charles MacArthur, *The Front Page* (New York: Covici-Friede Publishers, 1928), p. 40.

2. *Ibid.*, pp. 40–41.

3. *Ibid.*, p. 31.

4. James Boylan, "Newspeople," in Philip S. Cook, Douglas Gomery, and Lawrence W. Lichty, eds., *American Media: The Wilson Quarterly Reader* (Washington: The Wilson Center Press, 1989), p. 62.

5. John Lesperance in *Lippincott's Magazine*, August 1871, Vol. VIII, p. 180.

6. Edwin L. Shuman, *Practical Journalism: A Complete Manual of the Best Newspaper Methods* (New York: D. Appleton and Co., 1903), p. vii.

7. Kirk Munroe, *Under Orders: The Story of a Young Reporter* (New York: G. P. Putnam's Sons, 1890), p. 18.

8. Richard Harding Davis, *Gallegher and Other Stories* (New York: Charles Scribner's Sons, 1891), p. 4.

9. *Ibid.*, p. 57.

10. Ben Ames Williams, *Splendor* (New York: E. P. Dutton & Company, 1927), p. 120.

11. *Ibid.*, p. 469.

12. Clyde Brion Davis. *"The Great American Novel—"* (New York: Farrar Rinehart, 1938), p. 11.

13. Thomas Wolfe, "Gentlemen of the Press," in *The Hills Beyond* (New York: Harper & Row, Publishers, Inc., 1941; reprint, New York: New American Library, 1968), p. 52.

14. Ben Hecht, *Erik Dorn* (New York: The Modern Library, 1921), p. 20.

15. See Lee Wilkins, "Film as an Ethics Text," *Journal of Mass Media Ethics*, Vol. 2, No. 2 (Spring/Summer 1987), pp. 109–113; Steve Weinberg, "The Journalist in Novels," *Journal of Mass Media Ethics*, Vol. 2, No. 1 (Fall/Winter 1986–87), pp. 89–92; Deac Rossell, "Hollywood and the Newsroom," *American Film*, October 1975, pp. 14–18.

16. Robin W. Winks talks about detectives working "sometimes against the grain of society." See Winks, *Modus Operandi* (Boston: David R. Godine, Publisher, 1982), p. 40.

17. See Vern Partlow, "Newspapermen," in Pete Seeger and Bob Reiser, *Carry It On! A History in Song and Picture of the Working Men and Women of America* (New York: Simon and Schuster, 1985), pp. 174–177.

18. Otto Penzler, ed., *The Great Detectives* (Boston: Little, Brown and Company, 1978), p. 43.

19. Alex Barris, *Stop the Presses! The Newspaperman in American Films* (South Brunswick, N.J.: A. S. Barnes and Company, Inc., 1976), p. 41.

20. Item 581, Hemingway Collection, John F. Kennedy Library. See also, Ronald Weber, "Journalism, Writing, and American Literature," Occasional Paper No. 5, April 1987, Gannett Center for Media Studies.

21. Theodore Tinsley as quoted in Ron Goulart, *The Dime Detectives* (New York: The Mysterious Press, 1988), p. 153.

22. Richard Sale, as quoted in *ibid.*, p. 160.

23. Mildred Benson, *Dangerous Deadline* (New York: Dodd, Mead & Company, 1957).

24. Norton Jonathan, *Dan Hyland, Police Reporter* (Chicago: The Goldsmith Publishing Company, 1936).

25. See Walter R. Brooks, *Freddy the Detective* (New York: Alfred A. Knopf, 1932) and *Freddy and the Bean Home News* (New York: Alfred A. Knopf, 1943).

26. See Jeff Rovin, *The Encyclopedia of Superheroes* (New York: Facts on File Publications, 1985.)

27. See Les Whitten, *Conflict of Interest* (New York: Doubleday & Co., 1976).

28. See Lawrence Meyer, *A Capitol Crime* (New York: The Viking Press, 1977) and *False Front* (New York: The Viking Press, 1979).

29. See Marc Olden, *The Harker File: Kill the Reporter* (New York: Signet Book, New American Library, 1978).

30. See Jeff Millar, *Private Sector* (New York: The Dial Press, 1979).

31. See "Murder Between the Pages," in Victoria Nichols and Susan Thompson, *Silk Stalkings: When Women Write of Murder* (Berkeley: Black Lizard Books, 1988), pp. 161–179. For African American reporters in film, see "Mystery in Swing" (1940), "The Red Menace" (1949), and "The Bedford Incident" (1965). Maxwell Taylor Courson, "The Newspaper Movies: An Analysis of the Rise and Decline of the News Gatherer as a Hero in American Motion Pictures, 1900–1974," (Ph.D. Dissertation, Cinema, University of Hawaii, 1976), says (p. 278): "[J]ournalism has enjoyed a whites-only image in Hollywood."

32. See Langston Hughes, "Name in Print," in John A. Williams, ed., *The Angry Black* (New York: Lancer Books, 1962. See also William Branch "A Medal for Willie," in

Woodie King and Ron Miller, eds., *Black Drama Anthology* (New York: Signet/New American Library, Inc., 1972).

33. John A. Williams, *The Man Who Cried I Am* (Boston: Little, Brown and Company, 1967), p. 240.

34. *Ibid.*, p. 65.

35. Arthur Hailey, *Overload* (New York: Doubleday & Company, Inc., 1979), p. 270.

36. Jim Thompson, *The Nothing Man*, in *Hard Core: 3 Novels* (New York: Donald I. Fine, Inc., 1986).

37. Courson, *op. cit.*, pp. 230–232.

38. Roger L. Simon, *Wild Turkey* (San Francisco: Straight Arrow Books, 1974), p. 1.

39. *Ibid.*, p. 2.

40. Hunter S. Thompson, *Fear and Loathing in Las Vegas* (New York: Popular Library, 1971), p. 6.

41. *Ibid.*, p. 23. Elsewhere, Thompson refers to *Fear & Loathing in Las Vegas* as "a victim of its own conceptual schizophrenia, caught & finally crippled in that vain, academic limbo between 'journalism' and 'fiction' . . . 'a vile epitaph for the Drug Culture of the Sixties,' . . ." See Hunter S. Thompson, *The Great Shark Hunt: Strange Tales from a Strange Time* (New York: Summit Books, 1979), p. 109.

42. Thompson, *Fear and Loathing in Las Vegas*, p. 200.

43. Gregory Mcdonald, "Fletch" in *Fletch Forever* (Garden City, N.Y.: Nelson Doubleday, Inc., 1978), p. 117.

Top priority: Pulitzer Prize (page 105)

1. Philip Caputo, *DelCorso's Gallery* (New York: Holt, Rinehart & Winston, 1983), p. 37.

2. Elliott Chaze, *Tiger in the Honeysuckle* (New York: Charles Scribner's Sons, 1965), p. 23.

3. Carole Nelson Douglas, *The Exclusive* (New York: Ballantine Books, 1986), p. 68.

4. As cited in Dan Thomasson, "The 'Good Old Days' of Free Access—and some co-opting—are gone," *The Bulletin of the American Society of Newspaper Editors*, February 1987, p. 11.

5. Michael Malone, *Dingley Falls* (New York: Harcourt Brace Jovanovich, 1980), p. 158.

6. Tony Hillerman, *The Fly on the Wall* (New York: Avon Books, 1971), p. 11–12.

7. Dennis Dooley and Gary Engle, eds., *Superman at Fifty! The Persistence of a Legend!* (Cleveland, Ohio: Octavia Press, 1987), p. 114.

8. Jeff Millar, *Private Sector* (New York: The Dial Press, 1979), p. 149.

9. As quoted in Dave Barry, "Journalism prizes a major problem," *The Bulletin of the American Society of Newspaper Editors*, May/June 1987, p. 35.

10. *Ibid.*

10. Editor
(pages 109–113)

1. David Shaw, "What Killed 'Lou Grant,'" *TV Guide*, July 24, 1982, p. 22.

2. See Robert Sklar, "TV's Lou Grant as press criticism," *Columbia Journalism Review*, January/February 1979, pp. 17–18, and "Telling It Like It Isn't: 'Lou Grant' and David Halberstam," in Edwin Diamond, *Sign Off: The Last Days of Television* (Cambridge: MIT Press, 1982), pp. 146–159; Lee Grant, "Images of the Journalist," *The Bulletin of the American Society of Newspaper Editors*, April 1982, pp. 3–9; Thomas A. Schwartz and David Fletcher, "The Newsperson as TV Character," *Media History Digest*, Spring-Summer 1988, pp. 48–57, 64.

3. As quoted in Susan Heeger, "'Ed Asner' Starring Lou Grant," *Channels*, April/May 1982, p. 60.

4. Stanley Walker, *City Editor* (New York: Frederick A. Stokes, 1934), p. 1.

5. James G. Harrison, "American Newspaper Journalism As Described in American Novels of the Nineteenth

Century (Ph.D. dissertation, English department, Univeristy of North Carolina, Chapel Hill, 1945), p. 13.

6. Hugh Henry Brackenridge, *Modern Chivalry*, Part II, 1804–1805. Claude M. Newlin, ed. (New York: American Book Company, 1937), p. 561. [First collected edition, 1815.]

7. *Ibid.*

8. James Melvin Lee, *History of American Journalism* (Garden City, N.Y.: The Garden City Publishing Co., Inc., 1917), p. 101.

9. Henry Sedley, *Dangerfield's Rest; or, Before the Storm. A Novel of American Life and Manners.* (New York: Sheldon & Co., 1864), p. 145.

10. Bayard Taylor, *John Godfrey's Fortunes; Related by Himself. A Story of American Life* (New York: G. P. Putnam, 1865), p. 212.

11. Harriet Beecher Stowe, *We and Our Neighbors* (Boston: Houghton, Mifflin and Company, 1875), p. 42.

12. Will Payne, *The Money Captain* (Chicago: Herbert S. Stone and Co., 1898), p. 317.

13. Silas Bent, *Buchanan of The Press* (New York: The Vanguard Press, 1932), p. 39.

14. See Marc Fisher, "Whatever happened to the tough-fisted, hard-drinking ME?" *Associated Press Managing Editors News*, April 1985, p. 5.

15. Gary H. Grossman, *Superman: Serial to Cereal* (New York: Popular Library, 1977), p. 42.

16. As quoted in Donald W. McCaffrey, *The Golden Age of Sound Comedy* (New York: A. S. Barnes and Co., 1973), p. 133.

17. Leslie H. Whitten, *Conflict of Interest* (Garden City, N.Y.: Doubleday, 1976), p. 10.

18. Alex Barris, *Stop the Presses! The Newspaperman in American Films* (South Brunswick, N.J.: A. S. Barnes and Company, 1976), p. 164.

19. See Mark Saltzman, Judy Garlan, and Michele Grodner, *DC Super Heroes Super Healthy Cookbook* (New York: Warner Books, 1981), pp. 56–57.

Duty to be irresponsible? (page 112)

1. As quoted in *The Pentagon Papers* (Toronto: Bantam Books, Inc., 1971), p. ix.

2. *Ibid.*, p. 663.

3. Howard Simons, as quoted in Massachusetts Press Association *Bulletin*, January 1988, p. 4.

4. As quoted in David Broder, *Behind the Front Page* (New York: Simon and Schuster, 1987), p. 324.

5. *Ibid.*

6. *Ibid.*

7. As quoted in John Hess, "Who's conning whom?" *The Quill*, May 1989, p. 30.

8. *Ibid.*, p. 33.

11. Newspaper carrier
(pages 115–119)

1. See Barrie J. Hughes, *The World Honors the News Carrier* (Watertown, N.Y.: n.p., 1979), p. 4.

2. Frank Luther Mott, *American Journalism, A History: 1690–1960* (New York: The Macmillan Co., 1962), p. 106.

3. See, "The Newsboys' Excursion—A Day of Jolly Sport," *Harper's Weekly*, October 2, 1875, p. 804.

4. "A mite of a girl who gives papers away and makes it pay," *Chicago Tribune*, October 6, 1888, as quoted in Helen MacGill Hughes, *News and the Human Interest Story* (Chicago: University of Chicago Press, 1940; reprint, New Brunswick, N.J.: Transaction Books, 1981), p. 191.

5. *Leslie's Illustrated Weekly Newspaper*, August 2, 1856, p. 124.

6. Anonymous, *Luke Darrell, The Chicago Newsboy* (Chicago: Tomlinson Brothers, 1866), p. 364.

7. Mott, *op. cit.*, p. 314.

8. For this headline, see the frontispiece for Henry

Morgan, *Ned Nevins, The Newsboy; or, Street Life in Boston* (Boston: Lee and Shepard, 1866).

9. Harry Golden, *The Right Time: An Autobiography* (New York: G. P. Putnam's Sons, 1969), p. 54.

10. Knut Hamsun, *The Cultural Life of Modern America*, trans. Barbara Gordon Morgridge (Cambridge: Harvard University Press, 1969), p. 25, as quoted in Gunther Barth, *City People: The Rise of Modern City Culture in Nineteenth-Century America* (New York: Oxford University Press, 1980), p. 67.

11. C. S. Reinhart, "Read me sumpin to holler, Boss," undated *Harper's Weekly* page in author's collection, p. 665.

12. Seymour Eaton [Paul Piper], *The Roosevelt Bears Go to Washington* (Philadelphia: Edward Stearn & Company, 1907; reprint edition, New York: Dover Publications, 1981), pp. 160–170.

13. Bill Blackbeard, founder and curator, San Francisco Academy of Comic Art, interview, December 6, 1988.

14. Samuel Clemens, *A Connecticut Yankee in King Arthur's Court* in *The Complete Works of Mark Twain* (New York: Harper & Brothers, 1971), p. 255.

15. Morgan, *op. cit.*, p. 12.

16. See "America as Symbol" and "The American Cousin," in Joshua C. Taylor, *America as Art* (New York: Harper & Row, 1976), pp. 1–94.

17. See William Aiken Walker's painting, "Newsboy" (1883), David Gilmour Blythe, "The News Boys" (circa 1846–52), Thomas Le Clear, "Buffalo Newsboy" (1853), Aurelius O. Revenaugh, "Newsboy," (n.d.), Henry Inman, "The Newsboy" (1841), John George Brown, "Morning Papers" (1899) and "Newsboy" (n.d.).

18. Joseph C. Neal, *In Town & About or Pencillings & Pennings* (Philadelphia: Godey & McMichael, 1843), p. 1.

19. See Deac Rossell, "The Fourth Estate and the Seventh Art," in Bernard Rubin, ed., *Questioning Media Ethics* (New York: Praeger Publishers, 1978), p. 282. Newsboy movie titles from the 1920s and 1930s include: "The Cowboy Cop," "For His Sake," "Her Mad Bargain," and "Hush Money."

20. "Be a Reporter and see the world through a keyhole," back-cover advertisement, *Newspaper Adventure Stories*, n.d., (probably 1932).

21. Author unknown, *John Ellard The Newsboy* (Philadelphia: William S. and Alfred Martien, 1860), p. 6.

22. Horatio Alger Jr., *Rough and Ready; or, Life Among the New York Newsboys* (Boston: Loring, [1869]), p. 7.

23. See catalog for "A People in Print: Jewish Journalism in America—June 14-December 31, 1987," (Philadelphia: National Museum of American Jewish History, 1987), p. 77.

24. See possible pass to carriers' 1889 dinner, Hughes, *op. cit.*, pp. 39–40, and pin, Ted Hake and Russ King, *Price Guide to Collectible Pin-Back Buttons 1896–1986* (York, Pa.: Hake's Americana and Collectible Press, 1986), p. 196.

25. See Hughes, *ibid.*, p. 11.

26. See Peter C. Marzio, *Rube Goldberg: His Life and Work* (New York: Harper & Row, 1973), p. 127, and p. 129. For other cartoonists' view of the "Extra" peddler, see: a Charles Schulz "Peanuts" cartoon in Stephen Becker, *Comic Art in America* (New York: Simon and Schuster, 1959), p. 365; a George McManus "Jiggs" cartoon in George McManus, *Jiggs is Back* (Berkeley, Calif.: Celtic Book Company, 1986), p. 57, and a McManus "Nisby the Newsboy" cartoon in Bill Blackbeard and Martin Williams, eds., *The Smithsonian Collection of Newspaper Comics* (Washington: Smithsonian Institution Press and Harry N. Abrams, Inc., 1977), p. 36.

27. Alger, *op. cit.*, pp. 16–17.

28. *Ibid.*, p. 17.

29. When historian Dixon Wecter sought to define the U.S. hero, he found Americans responding to an unexpected set of characteristics. Americans, Wecter noted, seek out "a local boy made good" for elevation to folk-hero status. A prospective hero should be "simple in greatness"; he "must not

lose touch with his birthplace and origins, however humble." Dixon Wecter, *The Hero in America* (New York: Charles Scribner's Sons, 1941), pp. 485–487.

The real newsie (page 117)

1. "Capt. Marvel," February 1940, p.1.
2. "Captain Marvel Jr.," April 1946, p. 1.
3. Peter C. Marzio, *The Men and Machines of American Journalism: A Pictorial History from The Henry R. Luce Hall of News Reporting* (Washington: The National Museum of History and Technology, 1975), p. 48.
4. See sheet music for "The Newsboy," words by George R. Jackson, music by D. W. Boardman, in the collection of the American Antiquarian Society.
5. See "The Newsboys' Lodging-House, New York," two-page spread in *Harper's*, undated, pp. 312–13, in the author's possession.
6. See "The Newsboys," *The New Charitable Monthly*, February 1855, p. 22.

12. Newswoman
(pages 121–127)

1. Helen M. Winslow, "Some Newspaper Women," *The Arena*, XVII, December 1896, p. 127.
2. *Ibid.*
3. See "The Newspaper Woman" in James G. Harrison, "American Newspaper Journalism As Described in American Novels of the Nineteenth Century," (Ph.D. dissertation, English department, University of North Carolina, Chapel Hill, 1945), p. 267.
4. See Joanna Russ, "What Can a Heroine Do? or Why Women Can't Write," in Susan Koppelman Cornillon, ed., *Images of Women in Fiction* (Bowling Green, Ohio: Bowling Green University Press, 1972), pp. 3–20.
5. David Ross Locke (Petroleum V. Nasby), *A Paper City* (Boston: Lee and Shepard, 1879), p. 336.
6. William Dean Howells, *A Woman's Reason: A Novel* (Boston: Houghton Mifflin Co., 1883), p. 347.
7. Rebecca Harding Davis, *Frances Waldeaux* (New York: Harper and Brothers, 1897), p. 14.
8. Rebecca Harding Davis, "Earthen Pitchers," *Scribner's Monthly*, VII (November, 1873 to April, 1874), pp. 73–81, 199–207, 274–281, 490–494, 595–600, 714–721.
9. Booth Tarkington, *The Gentleman from Indiana* (New York: Doubleday & McClure Co., 1900), p. 254.
10. Elizabeth Garver Jordan, "Ruth Herrick's Assignment," in *Tales of the City Room* (New York: Charles Scribner's Sons, 1898), p. 27.
11. *Ibid.*, p. 29.
12. Gertrude Atherton, *Patience Sparhawk and Her Times* (London: John Land, The Bodley Head, 1897), p. 301.
13. *Ibid.*
14. Grace Greenwood, "Fanny Fern,—Mrs. Parton," in James Parton, ed., *Eminent Women of the Age: Being Narratives of the Lives and Deeds of the Most Prominent Women of the Present Generation* (Hartford, Conn.: S. M. Betts, 1868), p. 74.
15. Elizabeth Cady Stanton, "Ruth Hall," *The Una*, February 1855, p. 30.
16. Fanny Fern (Sara Payson Parton), *Ruth Hall: A Domestic Tale of the Present Time* (New York: Mason Brothers, 1855); reprint in Joyce W. Warren, ed., *Ruth Hall and Other Writings: Fanny Fern* (New Brunswick, N.J.: Rutgers University Press, 1986), p. 147.
17. Fanny Fern, *Fern Leaves from Fanny's Portfolio* (Auburn, N.Y.: Derby and Miller, 1853).
18. See Linda Huf, *A Portrait of the Artist as a Young Woman: The Writer as Heroine in American Literature* (New York: Frederick Ungar Publishing Co., 1983), p. 24. See also Warren, introduction to *op. cit.*, p. xx.
19. Bill Blackbeard, ed., *Connie: A Complete Compilation: 1929–1930 Frank Godwin* (Westport, Ct.: Hyperion Press, Inc., 1977), p. 71. Other early comic-strip newswomen—Debbie Dean and Jane Arden for instance—are described in Maurice Horn, *Women in the Comics* (New York: Chelsea House Publishers, 1977).
20. Deac Rossell, "The Fourth Estate and the Seventh Art," in Bernard Rubin, ed., *Questioning Media Ethics* (New York: Praeger Publishers, 1978), p. 244.
21. William Allen White, *In Our Town* (New York: McClure, Phillips & Co., 1906), p. 38.
22. Jack London, "Amateur Night" in *Moon Face* (Chicago and New York: M. A. Donohue and Company, 1906), p. 61.
23. See Bernard A. Drew, ed., *Hard-Boiled Dames* (New York: St. Martin's Press, 1986), pp. 164–205.
24. Esther G. Hall, *Haverhill Herald* (New York: Random House and the Junior Literary Guild Corp., 1938), p. 36.
25. Clarence Budington Kelland, *Contraband* (New York: A. L. Burt Company, 1923), p. 19. A feature film of the same name was released in 1925.
26. Edna Ferber, *Dawn O'Hara, The Girl Who Laughed* (New York: Grosset & Dunlap, 1911), pp. 4–5.
27. See Mary Ellman, *Thinking About Women* (New York: Harcourt, Brace & World Inc., 1968) and Viola Klein, "The Stereotype of Femininity," in R. K. Unger and F. L. Denmark, eds., *Woman: Dependent or Independent Variable* (New York: Psychological Dimensions, 1975).
28. Maxwell Taylor Courson, "The Newspaper Movies: An Analysis of the Rise and Decline of the News Gatherer as a Hero in American Motion Pictures, 1900–1974" (Ph.D. dissertation, Cinema, University of Hawaii, 1976), pp. 76–82.
29. See Dale Messick, *Brenda Starr: Girl Reporter* (Racine, Wisc.: Whitman Publishing Company, 1943) and Norma Lee Browning, "First Lady of the Funnies," *Saturday Evening Post*, Nov. 19, 1960, p. 35: Dale Messick, Brenda Starr's creator, says, "Authenticity is something I always try to avoid."
30. See Joanna Connors, "Female Meets Supermale," in Dennis Dooley and Gary Engle, eds., *Superman at Fifty!: The Persistence of a Legend!* (Cleveland: Octavia Press, 1987), pp. 108–115.
31. See Norberto Fuentes, *Ernest Hemingway Rediscovered* (New York: Charles Scribner's Sons, 1988), p. 58: "Martha Gellhorn, photographed in London by Lee Miller. Hemingway kept this photograph of Martha at Finca Vigia. Their relationship was often fraught because Hemingway could never accept the fact that Martha's writing career was as important to her as he was."
32. Martha E. Gellhorn, "Portrait of a Lady," in *The Heart of Another* (New York: Charles Scribner's Sons, 1941), p. 57.
33. *Ibid.*, p. 70.
34. *Ibid.*, p. 90. The description of her as a "high-class whore," significantly, is repeated on p. 109.
35. *Ibid.*, p. 120–121.
36. Diana M. Meehan develops a Bitch category of television fiction about women in *Ladies of the Evening* (Metuchen, N.J.: The Scarecrow Press, 1983). "Superwhore" originates with Joan Mellen's description of Mrs. Miller in the film "McCabe and Mrs. Miller"; see Joan Mellen, *Women and Their Sexuality in the New Film* (New York: Horizon Press, 1974).
37. Bill Crouch, Jr., ed., *Dick Tracy: America's Most Famous Detective* (Secaucus, N.J.: Citadel Press, 1987), p. 162.
38. A subgenre of sexploitation films features women reporters exposing a nudist colony. See "Diary of a Nudist" in Irv Letofsky, "Real to Reel," *The Bulletin of the American Society of Newspaper Editors*, May/June, 1983, p. 15, and other films listed in Rossell, *op. cit.*, p. 282.
39. Jeff Millar, *Private Sector* (New York: The Dial Press, 1979), p. 89.
40. Allen Drury, *Mark Coffin, U.S.S.* (Garden City, New York: Doubleday & Company, Inc., 1979), p. 194.

41. Michael Barak, *The Phantom Conspiracy* (New York: William Morrow and Co., Inc., 1980), p. 13.

42. See Lee Grant, "Tuning in on 'Lou Grant,'" *The Bulletin of the American Society of Newspaper Editors*, No. 650, April 1982, pp. 3–9. But even Margaret Pynchon has her pushy-publisher side. In a July 13, 1981, episode, she tells Lou Grant, the city editor, about her pet project, a local tree planting, and asks him to get it into the paper: "I don't expect too much. However, I don't expect too little either."

43. See Diana Davenport, *The Power Eaters* (New York: William Morrow and Company, 1979).

44. Warren Adler, *The Henderson Equation* (New York: Pocket Books, 1976).

45. Allen Drury, *Anna Hastings: The Story of a Washington Newspaperperson!* (New York: Warner Books, 1977), p. 35.

46. *Ibid.*, p. 297.

47. Mellen, *op. cit.*, p. 25. For the portrayal of women in fiction, see Dorothy Yost Deegan, *The Stereotype of the Single Woman in American Novels* (New York: King's Crown Press, 1951), which mentions Amanda Keeler, world affairs columnist, in Dawn Powell's *A Time to Be Born* (1942).

48. See Donna Born, "The Image of the Woman Journalist in American Popular Fiction 1890 to the Present," paper presented to the Committee on the Status of Women of the Association for Education in Journalism, annual convention, Michigan State University, East Lansing, August 1981, p. 26.

Positive images (page 124)

1. Caryl Rivers, *Girls Forever Brave and True* (New York: St. Martin's Press, 1986), p. 83.

2. *Ibid.*, p. 84.

3. See Kathleen Gregory Klein, *The Woman Detective: Gender and Genre* (Urbana, Ill.: University of Illinois Press, 1988), p. 1.

4. Paul Gallico, "Solo Job," in Ellery Queen, ed., *The Great Women Detectives and Criminals: The Female of the Species* (Garden City, N.Y.: Blue Ribbon Books, 1946), p. 49.

5. *Ibid.*, p. 64.

6. Alice Storey, *First Kill All the Lawyers* (New York: Pocket Books, 1988), p. 110.

7. Vicki P. McConnell, *The Burnton Widows* (Tallahassee, Fla.: The Naiad Press Inc., 1984), p. 104.

13. Scandalmonger
(pages 129–133)

1. Emile Gauvreau, *My Last Million Readers* (New York: E.P. Dutton & Co., Inc., 1941), p. 181.

2. See Emile Gauvreau, *The Scandal Monger* (New York: The Macaulay Company, 1932).

3. *Ibid.*, p. 26.

4. *Ibid.*, p. 11.

5. Emile Gauvreau, *Hot News* (New York: The Macaulay Company, 1931), p. 227.

6. *Ibid.*, p. 230.

7. Simon Michael Bessie, *Jazz Journalism* (New York: E. P. Dutton & Co., Inc., 1938), p. 152.

8. Charles Chapin, as quoted in Stanley Walker, *City Editor* (New York: Frederick A. Stokes Co., 1934), p. 5.

9. *Ibid.*, p. 4.

10. Benjamin Harris, *Publick Occurrences*, as reprinted in Frederic Hudson, *Journalism in the United States from 1690–1872* (New York: Harper & Row, 1873), p. 45.

11. Henry James, *The Reverberator* (London: Macmillan and Co., 1888) p. 68.

12. Miriam Michelson, *A Yellow Journalist* (New York: D. Appleton and Company, 1905), p. 38.

13. *Ibid.*, p. 77.

14. *Ibid.*, p. 259.

15. "Be a Reporter and see the world through a keyhole," undated back-page ad for *Newspaper Adventure Stories* magazine.

16. See Roger Manvell, "Media Ethics: How Movies Portray the Press and Broadcasters," in Bernard Rubin, ed., *Questioning Media Ethics* (New York: Praeger Publishers, 1978), p. 220.

17. See Myron Meisel, "The Big Carnival," in *Dateline . . . Hollywood*, a guide to The Museum of Fine Arts, Boston film and lecture series, May 1-June 14, 1975, no p.n., and Thomas H. Zynda, "The Hollywood Version: Movie Portrayals of the Press," in *Journalism History*, Vol. 6, No. 1 (Spring 1979), p. 19.

18. Manvell, *op. cit.*, pp. 220–221.

19. Tom Wood, *The Bright Side of Billy Wilder, Primarily* (Garden City, New York: Doubleday & Co., Inc., 1970), p. 106.

20. See Andy Warhol, *Journal American* (1960) in the collection of the Dia Art Foundation, New York, New York.

21. See Conrad Atkinson, "front-page" paintings, Feldman Gallery, New York, New York, January 1989.

22. Sidra Stich, *Made In U.S.A.: An Americanization in Modern Art, the '50s & '60s* (Berkeley: University of California Press, 1987), p. 116.

23. See Arnold Sawislak, *Dwarf Rapes Nun; Flees in UFO* (New York: St. Martin's Press, 1985) and Christine Temin, "The paper chase at the ICA," *The Boston Globe*, June 24, 1988, p. 29.

24. Don Henley and Danny Kortchmar, *Dirty Laundry* (n.p.: Cass County Music and Kortchmar Music, 1982).

25. Linda Stewart, *Panic on Page One* (New York: Delacorte Press, 1979), pp. 214–215.

26. *Ibid.*, p. ii and p. 250.

Impersonation (page 131)

1. As quoted in Tom Goldstein, *The News at Any Cost* (New York: Simon and Schuster, 1985), p. 132.

2. Lois Lane comic book, (Nov. No. 106) on display in a 1988 Smithsonian exhibit.

3. Ernest Sharpe, Jr., "The Man Who Changed His Skin," *American Heritage*, February 1989, pp. 52, 55.

4. John Howard Griffin, *Black Like Me* (New York: New American Library, 1962), p. 98.

5. *Ibid.*, p. 67.

6. Ben Bradlee, as quoted in Nancy Doyle Palmer, "Going After the Truth—In Disguise: The Ethics of Deception," *Washington Journalism Review*, November 1987, p. 21.

7. Jerry Thompson, interview with the author, May 19, 1989.

8. Don Hewitt, as quoted in Palmer, *op. cit.*, p. 20.

14. Small-town editor
(pages 135–141)

1. Norman Rockwell, "Norman Rockwell Visits a Country Editor," *Saturday Evening Post*, May 25, 1946.

2. William Allen White, *In Our Town* (New York: McClure, Phillips & Co., 1906), p. 3.

3. See also "Home Fires Burning" (1989), based on Robert Inman's novel of the same name.

4. Fredric Brown, *Night of the Jabberwock* (New York: Quill, 1984), p. 109. See also Lucille Kallen, *Introducing C. B. Greenfield* (New York: Crown Publishers, 1979); *C. B. Greenfield: The Tanglewood Murder* (New York: Wyndham Books, 1980); *C. B. Greenfield: No Lady in the House* (New York: Wyndham Books, 1982); *C. B. Greenfield: The Piano Bird* (New York: Random House, 1984); *C. B. Greenfield: A Little Madness* (New York: Random House, 1986).

5. Garrison Keillor, *Lake Wobegon Days* (New York: Viking Penguin, 1985), p. 227.

6. William Brinkley, *Peeper* (New York: The Viking Press, 1981), p. 5.

7. Jeff MacNelly, telephone interview with the author, Feb. 23, 1988.

8. Jeff MacNelly, *The Greatest Shoe on Earth* (New York: Holt, Rinehart and Winston, 1984, 1985), p. 78.

9. Philip Freneau, *The Poems of Philip Freneau* (Princeton: The University Library, 1907), vol. III, p. 61.

10. *Ibid.*

11. *Ibid.*, p. 62.

12. *Ibid.*, p. 64.

13. Alexis de Tocqueville, *Democracy in America* (New York: Vintage Books, 1959), vol. I, p. 194.

14. *Ibid.*

15. Charles Dickens, *The Life and Adventures of Martin Chuzzlewit* (New York: Penguin Books, 1982), p. 431.

16. *Ibid.*, p. 432.

17. James Russell Lowell, *Bigelow Papers First Series*, edited by Thomas Wortham (DeKalb: Northern Illinois University Press, 1977), pp. 102–103.

18. James Fenimore Cooper, *Home As Found* (New York: Capricorn Books, 1961), p. 318.

19. Mark Twain, "Journalism in Tennessee," in *Editorial Wild Oats*, (New York: Harper and Brothers, 1905; reprint, New York: Arno Press and The New York Times, 1970), pp. 26–27.

20. Quoted from W. I. Paulding, *Literary Life of James K. Paulding* (New York: Charles Scribner & Company, 1867), pp. 262–263.

21. White, *op. cit.*, p. 7.

22. Michael Foster, *American Dream; A Novel* (New York: William Morrow and Company, 1937), p. 499.

23. E. W. Howe, as quoted in S. J. Sackett, *E. W. Howe* (New York: Twayne Publishers, 1972), p. 22.

24. E. W. Howe, *The Story of a Country Town* (Boston: James R. Osgood & Company, 1885), p. 230.

25. *Ibid.*, p. 264.

26. William D. Howells, "Two Notable Novels," *The Century Magazine*, XXVIII, August 1884, p. 632.

27. Edgar Lee Masters, *Spoon River Anthology* (New York: Macmillan Publishing Company, 1962), p. 149.

28. Sinclair Lewis, *Main Street* (New York: Harcourt, Brace and Company, 1920), p. 416.

29. *Ibid.*, p. 228.

30. Woodrow Wilson, *Mere Literature and Other Essays* (Boston: Houghton, Mifflin and Company, 1896), p. 214.

31. Herbert Mitgang, *The Montauk Fault* (New York: Arbor House, 1981), pp. 275–276.

William Allen White (page 139)

1. Sally Foreman Griffith, *Home Town News: William Allen White and the Emporia Gazette* (New York: Oxford University Press, 1989), p. 227.

2. William Allen White, *The Autobiography of William Allen White* (New York: The Macmillan Company, 1946), p. 613.

3. William Allen White, *In Our Town* (New York: McClure, Phillips & Co., 1906), p. 363.

4. William Allen White, letter to Charles Gleed, Nov. 16, 1901, as reprinted in Walter Johnson, ed., *Selected Letters of William Allen White, 1899–1943* (New York: Henry Holt and Co., 1947), p. 47.

5. Griffith, *op. cit.*, p. 94.

6. William Allen White, as quoted in *ibid.*, p. 95.

7. "William Allen White of Emporia: An American Institution is 70," *Life*, Feb. 28, 1938, p. 9.

8. "Entirely Personal," *Emporia Gazette*, June 3, 1895, as quoted in *Autobiography of William Allen White*, pp. 260–261.

15. War correspondent
(pages 143–147)

1. Deac Rossell writes: "Slowly, the reporter became a sidebar figure. Instead of a central, gangling, irridescent Lee Tracy, an elegant Adolphe Menjou or a debonair Cary Grant, the reporter became a confused, weak, shirking, falsely liberal David Janssen, a propped-up cardboard figure waiting to be set straight . . . " Deac Rossell, "The Fourth Estate and the Seventh Art," in Bernard Rubin, ed., *Questioning Media Ethics* (New York: Praeger Publishers, 1978), p. 244.

2. Howard Good, "The Image of War Correspondents in Anglo-American Fiction," *Journalism Monographs*, no. 97, July 1986, p. 3. Good's article—and conversations with him—have been major sources of information and ideas for this section of the book.

3. Rudyard Kipling, *The Light That Failed* (Garden City, N.Y.: Doubleday, Page & Co., 1899), p. 21.

4. *Ibid.*, p. 289

5. *Ibid.*

6. See Donald Spoto, *Camerado* (New York: New American Library, Inc., 1978), pp. 1–47.

7. Herbert Mitgang, "Stephen Crane's Shifting Image," *The New York Times*, Dec. 23, 1987, p. C11.

8. Stephen Crane, *Active Service* (New York: Frederick A. Stokes Company, 1899), p. 120.

9. Stephen Crane, "The Lone Charge of William B. Perkins," in *Wounds in the Rain* (New York: Frederick A. Stokes Company, 1900), p. 33.

10. *Ibid.*, p. 41.

11. Richard Harding Davis, *Farces* (New York: Charles Scribner's Sons, 1906), p. 142.

12. Will Levington Comfort, *Red Fleece* (New York: George H. Doran Company, 1915), p. 97.

13. Mary Mander, "the journalist as cynic," *The Antioch Review*, Winter 1980, p. 95.

14. Emmet Crozier, *American Reporters on the Western Front 1914–18* (New York: Oxford University Press, 1959), p. 93.

15. Alex Barris, *Stop the Presses! The Newspaperman in American Films* (South Brunswick, N.J.: A. S. Barnes and Company, 1976), p. 96. The movie "Clear All Wires!" was based on the play of the same name: Bella and Samuel Spewack, *Clear All Wires!* (New York, Los Angeles: Samuel French, 1932).

16. See "Hollywood Goes to War, 1939–1945," in Garth Jowett, *Film: The Democratic Art* (Boston: Little, Brown and Company, 1976), pp. 293–332.

17. James Robert Parish and Michael R. Pitts, *The Great Spy Pictures* (Metuchen, N.J.: The Scarecrow Press, Inc., 1974), p. 184.

18. Barris, *op. cit.*, p. 103.

19. See Parish and Pitts, *op. cit.*, p. 91.

20. Michael Herr, *Dispatches* (New York: Alfred A. Knopf, 1977), p. 210.

21. *Ibid.*, p. 211.

22. James Agee and Walker Evans, *Let Us Now Praise Famous Men* (Boston: Houghton Mifflin Co., 1960), p. 11.

23. Deborah Wye, *Committed to Print: Social and Political Themes in Recent American Printed Art* (New York: The Museum of Modern Art, 1988), p. 68.

24. A. J. Quinnell, *The Snap* (New York: William Morrow and Company, Inc., 1983), p. 81.

25. Herr, *op. cit.*, p. 218.

26. John Clark Pratt, ed., *Vietnam Voices* (New York: Viking, 1984), p. 353–54.

27. Ward Just, *Honor, Power, Riches, Fame and the Love of Women* (New York: E. P. Dutton, 1979), p. 31.

28. Ward Just, *The American Blues* (New York: The Viking Press, 1984), p. 1.

29. *Ibid.*, p. 204. See also Desmond Ryan, "The Hollywood Reporter: Movies That Do a Reel Number on the Press," *Washington Journalism Review*, Sept. 1985, pp. 45–47.

30. As quoted in Frank Rich, "Stage: Echo of Vietnam, How I Got That Story," *The New York Times*, Dec. 9, 1980, p. C9.

31. Ward Just, *Stringer* (Boston: Little, Brown and Company, 1974), p. 138.

Question their role (page 144)

1. Tom Stoppard, *Night and Day* (New York: Grove Press, Inc., 1979), p. 108.
2. Ron Dorfman, "Journalists Under Fire," *The Quill*, October 1983, p. 13. Journalists complain that other film portrayals—*The Year of Living Dangerously* (about a journalist in Indonesia at the time of Sukarno's overthrow), and *Circle of Deceit* (about a journalist covering the civil war in Lebanon)—also mislead the public about the morality of war correspondence.
3. Philip Caputo, *DelCorso's Gallery* (New York: Holt, Rinehart and Winston, 1983), p. 224.
4. *Ibid.*, p. 347
5. *Ibid.*
6. D. H. Lawrence, *Studies in Classic American Literature* (Garden City, N.Y.: Doubleday & Company, Inc., 1953), p. 73.

16. TV journalist
(pages 149–155)

1. See Robert Heinecken, "1984: A Case Study in Finding an Appropriate TV Newswoman (A CBS Docudrama in Words and Pictures)" (Los Angeles: Robert Heinecken, 1985).
2. David Levy, *The Chameleons*. Reissued in paperback as *The Network Jungle* (Canoga Park, Calif.: Major Books, 1976). Other early books—from the 1950s and 1960s—about television's impact include: John Schneider, *The Golden Kazoo* (New York: Holt, Rinehart and Winston, 1956); Lissa Charell, *The Happy Medium* (New York: William Morrow and Co., 1962); Walter Ross, *Coast-to-Coast* (New York: Simon and Schuster, 1962); Harold Robbins, *The Inheritors* (New York: Trident Press, 1969). See Mary Ann Watson, "Facts and Fictions: TV History Through the Filter of Fiction," *Television Quarterly*, Vol. XXII, No. IV (1987), pp. 21–36.
3. Sidra Stich, *Made in U.S.A.: An Americanization in Modern Art, The '50s and '60s* (Berkeley: University of California Press, 1987), p. 118.
4. *Ibid.*, p. 121.
5. *Ibid.*
6. Also see the cover of Isaac Asimov, Charles G. Waugh and Martin Harry Greenberg, *TV:2000* (New York: Fawcett Crest, 1982).
7. John Arthur, *Realism/Photorealism* (Tulsa, Okla.: Philbrook Art Center, 1980), p. 49.
8. Marc H. Miller, "Television's Impact on Contemporary Art," catalogue for an exhibit at The Queens Museum, Flushing, N.Y., Sept. 13-Oct. 26, 1986, p. 25.
9. Stich, *op. cit.*, p. 199.
10. Maxwell Taylor Courson, "The Newspaper Movies: An Analysis of the Rise and Decline of the News Gatherer as a Hero in American Motion Pictures, 1900–1974" (Ph.D. dissertation, Cinema, University of Hawaii, 1976), p. 88.
11. Typical is R. R. Irvine's Bob Christopher, investigative reporter for Channel 3 in Los Angeles, who catches murderers in *Horizontal Hold* (New York: Popular Library, 1978), *Freeze Frame* (New York: Popular Library, 1976), *Jump Cut* (New York: Praeger, 1985) and *Ratings Are Murder* (New York: Walker and Company, 1985).
12. Laurence Leamer, *Assignment* (New York: The Dial Press, 1981), p. 4.
13. William Stevenson, *Eclipse* (Garden City, New York: Doubleday and Company, Inc., 1986), p. 3.
14. Chuck Scarborough, *Stryker* (New York: Macmillan, 1978).
15. Thomas Gifford, *The Glendower Legacy* (New York: Pocket Books, 1978), p. 52.
16. Edward Stewart, *The Great Los Angeles Fire* (New York: Simon & Schuster, 1980), p. 72.
17. Burton Wohl, *The China Syndrome* (New York: Bantam Books, 1979), p. 5. Based on the screenplay written by Mike Gray, T. S. Cook and James Bridges.
18. Robert B. Parker, *A Savage Place* (New York: Delacorte Press, 1981), p. 7.
19. *Ibid.*, p. 181.
20. Carole Nelson Douglas, *The Exclusive* (New York: Ballantine Books, 1986), p. 84.
21. See Muriel Dobbin, *Going Live* (New York: E. P. Dutton, 1987). See also the ad campaign run by the San Francisco *Examiner* in which it depicts Barbie and Ken dolls as having "everything it takes to be an award-winning TV news team": M. L. Stein, "Battling Back," *Editor & Publisher*, Oct. 25, 1986, p. 13.
22. Ron Nessen, *The Hour* (New York: William Morrow and Company, Inc., 1984), p. 260. See also Ron Powers, *Face Values* (New York: Delacorte Press, 1979).
23. Stich, *op. cit.*, p. 120.
24. Tape of undated "Saturday Night Live" segments owned by the author.
25. See Michael Shnayerson, "Can Diane Sawyer Have It All?" *Vanity Fair*, Vol. 50, No. 9, September 1987, p. 140.
26. See Albert Scardino, "A Debate Heats Up: Is It News or Entertainment?" *The New York Times*, Jan. 15, 1989, p. H29.
27. Ned Calmer, *The Anchorman* (Garden City, N.Y.: Doubleday & Co., Inc., 1970), p. 35.
28. Ron Nessen, *The First Lady* (Chicago: Playboy Press, 1979), p. 222.
29. Nessen, *The Hour*, p. 240. See also Bill Granger, *Sweeps* (New York: Fawcett Gold Medal, 1980).
30. Barbara Gordon, *Defects of the Heart* (New York: Harper & Row, Publishers, 1983), p. 23.
31. *Ibid.*, p. 180.

Anchorperson (page 150)

1. Steve Roberts, *Max Headroom: 20 minutes into the future* (New York: Vintage, 1985), n.p.
2. Gahan Wilson cartoon, *The New Yorker*, April 24, 1989, p. 45.
3. Peter J. Boyer, "The Light Goes Out," *Vanity Fair*, June 1989, p. 68.
4. See John Corry, "Just What Is The Nature of An Anchor's Influence?" *The New York Times*, May 27, 1984, p. H21.
5. Walter Cronkite, as quoted in Ron Powers, *The Newscasters* (New York: St. Martin's Press, 1977), p. 201.
6. Liz Trotta, "Why the Network Didn't Want My Exclusive on Grenada," *TV Guide*, Feb. 27, 1988, p. 3.
7. Lucille Kallen, *C. B. Greenfield: The Piano Bird* (New York, Random House, 1984), p. 58.
8. Alex Raskin, "All the News That Wiggles," *Channels*, May/June 1984, p. 67.

17. Owner
(pages 157–161)

1. Pauline Kael, "Raising Kane," in *The Citizen Kane Book* (Toronto: Bantam Books, 1971), pp. 5–6. For other fictional treatments of Hearstian newspeople, see William Richard Hereford, *The Demagog* (New York: Henry Holt, 1909) and Gore Vidal, *Empire* (New York: Random House, 1987), and such films as *The President Vanishes* (1934), *Mr. Smith Goes to Washington* (1939), and *Meet John Doe* (1941).
2. See Roy A. Fowler, "Citizen Kane: Background and a Critique," in Ronald Gottesman, ed., *Focus On Citizen Kane* (Englewood Cliffs, N.J.: Prentice-Hall, Inc., 1971), pp. 82–84.
3. W. A. Swanberg, *Citizen Hearst* (New York: Charles Scribner's Sons, 1961), p. 497.
4. Orson Welles, as quoted in Peter Cowie, "The Study of a Colossus," in Gottesman, *op. cit.*, p. 110.
5. Joseph McBride, *Orson Welles* (New York: Viking Press: 1972), p. 45.

6. Henry Francis Keenan, *The Money-Makers: A Social Parable* (New York: D. Appleton and Co., 1885), p. 52.

7. G. Harrison Orians, *A Short History of American Literature* (New York: F. S. Crofts and Company, 1940), pp. 227–228.

8. Keenan, *op. cit.*, p. 39.

9. William Dean Howells, *A Modern Instance* in *Novels 1875–1886* (New York: The Library of America, 1982), p. 413.

10. William Dean Howells, *The Quality of Mercy* (New York: Harper & Brothers, 1892), pp. 151–152.

11. See John J. Pauly, "The Ideological Origins of an Independent Press," paper presented to the American Journalism Historians Association convention, Las Vegas, Nevada, October 1985.

12. Hodding Carter, *The Winds of Fear* (Farrar and Rinehart, Inc., 1944; reprint, New York: Award Books, 1964), pp. 174–175.

13. *Ibid.*, p. 175.

14. Frederic Babcock, *Hang Up the Fiddle* (Garden City, N.Y.: Doubleday and Company, 1954), p. 131.

15. Charlaine Harris, *Sweet and Deadly* (Boston: Houghton Mifflin Co., 1981), p. 92.

16. Arthur Gordon, *Reprisal* (New York: Simon and Schuster, 1950), p. 25.

17. Ward Just, *A Family Trust* (Boston: Little, Brown and Company, 1978), p. 15.

18. Richard Powell, *Daily and Sunday* (New York: Charles Scribner's Sons, 1964), p. 4.

19. Arthur Miller, *Final Edition* (New York: Pinnacle Books, 1981), p. 331.

20. Just, *op. cit.*, p. 341.

21. Anna Murdoch, *Family Business* (New York: William Morrow and Company, Inc., 1988), p. 476.

22. *Ibid.*, p. 578.

23. William McKeen, "Heroes and Villains: A study of journalists in American novels published between 1915 and 1975." (Master of Arts dissertation, School of Journalism, Indiana University, August 1977), p. 69. See also Donald Barthelme, "Financially, the paper . . . ," in *Overnight to Many Distant Cities* (New York: G. P. Putnam's Sons, 1983), pp. 23–25.

24. Murdoch, *op. cit.*, pp. 439–440.

25. *Ibid.*, p. 440.

26. *Ibid.*, p. 441.

27. See the portrayal of Edward Armstead, owner of the New York *Record*, in Irving Wallace, *The Almighty* (Garden City, N.Y.: Doubleday & Co., 1982).

28. See James Brady, *The Press Lord* (New York: Delacorte Press, 1982), p. 261.

29. See the depiction of Joel Eliass, the chairman of The World News Network, in Muriel Dobbin, *Going Live* (New York: E. P. Dutton, 1987).

Take over the world (page 159)

1. Jeff Millar, *Private Sector* (New York: The Dial Press, 1979), p. 97.

2. *Ibid.*, p. 179.

3. Jack Anderson, *Control* (New York: Kensington Publishing Corporation, 1988), p. 330.

4. See Michael M. Thomas, *Hard Money* (New York: Viking Penguin Inc., 1985).

5. See David Aaron, *Agent of Influence* (New York: G. P. Putnam's Sons, 1989).

6. *Ibid.*, p. 349.

7. *Ibid.*, pp. 367–368.

THE JOURNALIST OF TOMORROW
(page 163)

1. As quoted in Norman J. Glickman and Douglas P. Woodward, *The New Competitors* (New York: Basic Books, Inc., 1989), p. 3.

2. Henry Luce, as quoted in Ben H. Bagdikian, "The Lords of the Global Village," *The Nation*, June 12, 1989, p. 807. On Luce's "American Century," see also W. A. Swanberg, *Luce and His Empire* (New York: Dell, 1972), pp. 257–261.

18. "Today's fiction—tomorrow's fact?"
(pages 165–178)

1. Alvin Toffler, *Future Shock* (New York: Random House, 1970), p. 376. The University of Missouri's William Stephenson, upon reading a draft of this chapter, wrote "None of your references touches upon quantum theory and indeterminism—the very proposal to 'foretell the future' runs counter to quantum-theoretical premises, which deal with possibilities, not predictions. The future is basically unpredictable would be a better stand for you to take." Perhaps Stephenson is right.

2. David Hartwell, *Age of Wonders: Exploring the World of Science Fiction* (New York: Walker and Company, 1984), p. 79.

3. Marvin Minsky, as quoted in Stewart Brand, *The Media Lab: Inventing the Future at MIT* (New York: Viking Penguin, 1987), p. 224.

4. See Douglas Menville and R. Reginald, *Future Visions* (North Hollywood, Calif.: Newcastle Publishing Company, Inc., 1985).

5. See Ray Bradbury, "The Toynbee Convector," in *The Toynbee Convector* (New York: Alfred A. Knopf, 1988), pp. 3–15.

6. Isaac Asimov, "The Billiard Ball," reprinted in *Asimov's Mysteries* (Greenwich, Conn.: Fawcett Publications, Inc., 1968), pp. 236–255.

7. C. M. Kornbluth, "The Silly Season," reprinted in Frederik Pohl, ed., *The Best of C. M. Kornbluth* (New York: Ballantine Books, 1976), p. 96.

8. *Ibid.*, p. 99.

9. Ed Naha, *The Paradise Plot* (New York: Bantam Books, 1980), p. 23.

10. *Ibid.*, p. 41; see Naha's sequel, *The Suicide Plague* (New York: Bantam Books, 1982), p. 7: in which Porter admits to himself that "print journalism really didn't stand a chance."

11. For other versions of the journalist as good-guy hero, see such Ron Goulart novels as *Death Cell* (New York: Beagle Books, 1971), *Hawkshaw* (New York: Doubleday, 1972), and *Plunder* (New York: Beagle Books, 1972), and Larry Niven and Jerry Pournelle, *Footfall* (New York: Ballantine Books, 1985). For the journalist as bad guy, see George Thomas, writer for Era magazine in James E. Gunn, *The Listeners* (New York: Charles Scribner's Sons, 1972); and columnist Johnny McKennah in John Dalmas, *The Varkaus Conspiracy* (New York: Tor, 1983).

12. R. A. Lafferty, "Magazine Section," reprinted in Gardner Dozois, ed., *The Year's Best Science Fiction* (Chappaqua, N.Y.: Bluejay Books, 1986), pp. 511–521.

13. Robert Silverberg, "What We Learned from This Morning's Newspaper," reprinted in Robert Hoskins, ed., *Infinity Four* (New York: Lancer Books, 1972), p. 17.

14. Len Jenkin, *New Jerusalem* (Los Angeles: Sun & Moon Press, 1986), p. 10.

15. *Ibid.*, p. 9.

16. See Brian Garfield, *Deep Cover* (New York: Dell Publishing Company, Inc., 1971).

17. See Philip K. Dick, *The Man in the High Castle* (New York: G. P. Putnam's Sons, 1962).

18. See Frederik Pohl, *The Merchants' War* (New York: St. Martin's Press, 1984) and Frederik Pohl and C. M. Kornbluth, *The Space Merchants* (New York: Ballantine Books, 1953).

19. Philip K. Dick, *The Penultimate Truth* (Great Britain: Jonathan Cape Ltd., 1967; reprint, London: Triad Grafton Books, 1987), p. 70.

20. Joan Vinge, "Media Man," reprinted in *Eyes of Amber* (New York: The New American Library, 1979), p. 96.

21. See Norman Spinrad, *A World Between* (New York: Pocket Books, 1979). But in Ernest Callenbach's *Ecotopia* (Berkeley: Banyan Tree Books, 1975; reprint, New York: Bantam Books, 1977), the new country (consisting of Northern California, Oregon, and Washington) outlaws multiple media ownerships and narrowly restricts the quantity of advertising. Smaller, freewheeling media serve each city. Despite the "almost anarchic decentralization" (p. 141), coverage by Ecotopia's journalists beats that by U.S. news media, says *Times-Post* reporter William Weston, the first American allowed to visit Ecotopia in twenty years.

22. Frank A. Javor, "Interview," reprinted in Isaac Asimov, Charles G. Waugh and Martin Harry Greenberg, eds., *TV: 2000* (New York: Fawcett Crest, 1982), pp. 237–241.

23. Bruce Sterling, *The Artificial Kid* (New York: Harper and Row, 1980).

24. D. G. Compton, *The Continuous Katherine Mortenhoe* (London: Victor Gollancz Ltd., 1974), pp. 203–204.

25. Isaac Asimov, *Prelude to Foundation* (New York: Doubleday, 1988), p. 21.

26. Isaac Asimov, "The Dead Past," reprinted in *The Best Science Fiction of Isaac Asimov* (Garden City, N.Y.: Doubleday & Co., 1986), pp. 19–64.

27. See T. L. Sherred, "E for Effort," reprinted in *The Astounding Science Fiction Anthology* (New York: Simon and Schuster, 1961), pp. 280–325.

28. Stanislaw Lem, *The Futurological Congress*, trans. Michael Kandel (Krakow, Poland: n.p., 1971; New York: Avon Books, 1976), p. 73.

29. For a popular treatment, see "Visions of Tomorrow," *Life*, February 1989, p. 67: "And around 2015 holographic TV will project three-dimensional moving images that will put you in the middle" of the action.

30. Martin Esslin, *The Age of Television* (San Francisco, Calif: W. H. Freeman and Company, 1982), p. 62.

31. Robert Day cartoon as reprinted in *ibid.*, p. 63.

32. Ray Bradbury, "The Veldt," reprinted in *The Vintage Bradbury* (New York: Vintage Books, 1965), pp. 13–28.

33. Algis J. Budrys, *Michaelmas* (New York: Berkley Publishing Corp., 1977).

34. William Gibson, *Neuromancer* (New York: Ace Science Fiction Books, 1984).

35. William Gibson, "The Gernsback Continuum," in *Burning Chrome* (New York: Arbor House, 1986), pp. 28–40.

36. J. G. Ballard as quoted in Toby Goldstein, "J. G. Ballard: Visionary of the Apocalypse," *Heavy Metal*, April 1982, p. 40.

37. J. G. Ballard, *The Day of Creation* (Great Britain: Victor Gollancz Ltd., 1987; reprint, New York: Farrar, Straus, Giroux, 1988), p. 57.

38. *Ibid.*, p. 157.

39. Frederick Williams, *The Communications Revolution* (Beverly Hills, Calif.: Sage Publications, Inc., 1982).

40. James R. Beniger, *The Control Revolution: Technological and Economic Origins of the Information Society* (Cambridge, Mass. and London: Harvard University Press, 1986).

41. Donald M. Lamberton, ed., *The Information Revolution*. Annals of the American Academy of Political and Social Science, vol. 412, (Philadelphia: American Academy of Political and Social Science, 1974).

42. Tom Forester, ed., *The Information Technology Revolution* (Cambridge: MIT Press, 1985).

43. Edmund Callis Berkeley, *The Computer Revolution* (Garden City, N.Y.: Doubleday, 1962).

44. Radovan Richta, ed., *Civilization at the Crossroads: Social and Human Implications of the Scientific and Technological Revolution* (White Plains, N.Y.: International Arts and Sciences Press, 1967).

45. G. Harry Stine, *The Third Industrial Revolution* (New York: G. P. Putnam's Sons, 1975).

46. Lawrence B. Evans, "Impact of the Electronics Revolution on Industrial Process Control," *Science* 195 (March 18, 1977), pp. 1146–1151.

47. Tom Forester, ed., *The Microelectronics Revolution* (Cambridge: MIT Press, 1980)

48. Williams, *op. cit.*, p. 268.

49. See Richard Hollander, *Video Democracy: The Vote-from-Home Revolution* (Mt. Airy, Maryland: Lomond Publications, 1985).

50. John P. Robinson, "Will the New Electronic Media Revolutionize Our Daily Lives?" in Robert W. Haigh, George Gerbner, and Richard B. Byrne, eds., *Communications in the Twenty-First Century* (New York: John Wiley & Sons, 1981), p. 64.

51. J. G. Ballard, "The Intensive Care Unit," reprinted in *Myths of the Near Future* (London: Jonathan Cape Ltd., 1982).

52. Marshall McLuhan, *Understanding Media: The Extensions of Man* (New York: McGraw Hill Book Company, 1964; reprint, The New American Library, 1966), p. 93.

53. Kaarle Nordenstreng, "New International Directions: A Non-aligned Viewpoint," in Haigh, Gerbner, and Byrne, eds., *op. cit.*, pp. 192–199.

54. Joe Logan, "2014: A Newspaper Odyssey," *Washington Journalism Review*, May 1989, pp. 36–40.

55. *Ibid.*, p. 40.

56. Beniger, *op. cit.*, p. 25.

57. Isaac Asimov, "The Future of Journalism," speech given at 75th Anniversary Conference, Columbia University Graduate School of Journalism, May 6, 1988.

58. Benjamin Compaine, as quoted in "The Cost of Technology: Information Prosperity and Information Poverty." A conference report by the Gannett Center for Media Studies, Columbia University, 1987.

59. Christine Urban, president of Urban & Associates, Sharon, Mass., interview, May 2, 1988.

60. John Diebold, "Newspapers and Information Technology: Some Strategic Options," paper presented at American Society of Newspaper Editors meeting, Washington, D.C., April 15, 1988, p. 4.

61. Brand, *op. cit.*, pp. 255–256.

62. See Mike Greenly, "Interactive Journalism and Computer Networking: Exploring a New Medium," *The Futurist*, Vol. XXI, No. 2, (March-April 1987), pp. 12–16.

63. See Steve Roberts, *Max Headroom: 20 Minutes into the Future* (New York: Random House, 1986).

64. John Wooley, president of Vutext, interview, May 2, 1988.

65. See *Superman*, Anniversary Issue 400 (New York: D.C. Comics, Inc., 1984).

66. Brand, *op. cit.*, pp. 91–93.

67. Hans Moravec, *Mind Children* (Cambridge: Harvard University Press, 1988), p. 1.

68. *Ibid.*, p. 4.

How will future journalists define news? *(page 167)*

1. James K. Batten, "America's Newspapers: What Are Our Prospects," lecture delivered at University of California, Riverside, April 3, 1989. No. 24 in the Press-Enterprise Lecture series, p. 7.

2. See "Notes and Comment," *The New Yorker*, August 29, 1988, p. 17.

Reporting or distorting? *(page 169)*

1. As quoted in "Ethical Questions That Arise When It's Easy to Doctor Images," *The New York Times*, January 15, 1989, p. F13.

2. J. D. Lasica, "Pictures don't always tell truth," *The Boston Globe*, January 2, 1989, p. 29.

3. See Staci Kramer, "The case of the missing Coke can," *Editor and Publisher*, April 29, 1989, p. 18.

4. Jan Adkins, associate art director of *National Geographic*, as quoted in Lasica, *op. cit.*, p. 31.

5. Donald E. Tomlinson, "Coalesce or Collide? Ethics, Technology and Television Journalism 1991," *Journal of Mass Media Ethics*, Vol. II, Issue 2, Spring/Summer, 1987.

6. As quoted in Steve Weinstein and Diane Haithman, "ABC draws fire for botched simulation," *The Boston Globe*, July 27, 1989, p. 24.

7. Lasica, *op. cit.*, p. 29–30.

Future journalists less free? (pages 174–175)

1. See Richard Pollak, "*Time* + Dallas = ?" *The Nation*, March 27, 1989, p. 401.

2. Jason McManus, "A Letter From the Editor-in-Chief," *Life*, April 1989, p. 4.

3. See Steve Lohr, "Media Mergers: An Urge to Get Bigger and More Global," *The New York Times*, March 19, 1989, p. E7.

4. See Tom Goldstein, *The News At Any Cost: How Journalists Compromise Their Ethics to Shape the News* (New York: Simon and Schuster, 1985), pp. 102–103.

5. As quoted in *ibid.*, p. 103.

6. See Lucas A. Powe Jr., *American Broadcasting and the First Amendment* (Berkeley: University of California Press, 1987).

7. Transcript of September 15, 1972, Oval Office, as quoted in Richard S. Salant, "Selling Out the First Amendment," *Washington Journalism Review*, January/February, 1989, p. 51.

8. U.S. Congress, Office of Technology Assessment, *Science, Technology, and the First Amendment*, OTA-CIT-369 (Washington: U.S. Government Printing Office, January, 1987), p. 23.

9. As quoted in Mary A. Anderson, "Thomson merger plan set for June vote; Knight-Ridder to seek protection from acquisitors," *presstime*, April 1989, p. 94.

10. As quoted in Robert P. Knight, "Here's the view from 'complaint central'," *The Bulletin of the American Society of Newspaper Editors*, February 1989, p. 7.

11. Debbie Wilgoren, "Dartmouth protesters seek ban on distribution of Review," *The Boston Sunday Globe*, May 7, 1989, p. 94.

12. As quoted in Lee Dembart, "At Stanford, Leftists Become Censors," *The New York Times*, May 5, 1989, p. A35.

13. Dana Fulham, "BU request in school takeover worries groups," *The Boston Globe*, May 1, 1989, p. 24.

14. Dave Patten, *Newspapers and New Media* (White Plains, N.Y.: Knowledge Industry Publications, 1986), p. 116.

Selected Bibliography

Aaron, David. *Agent of Influence.* New York: G. P. Putnam's Sons, 1989.

Adamson, June N. "Selected Women in Tennessee Newspaper Journalism." Masters thesis, University of Tennessee, 1971.

Adler, Warren. *The Henderson Equation.* New York: Simon and Schuster, 1976.

Agee, James and Walker Evans. *Let Us Now Praise Famous Men.* Boston: Houghton Mifflin Co., 1960.

Alger, Horatio, Jr. *Rough and Ready; or, Life Among the New York Newsboys.* Boston: Loring, 1869.

American Newspaper Journalists, 1901–1925, ed. by Perry J. Ashley (*Dictionary of Literary Biography.* Vol. 25), Detroit: Gale Research Company, 1984.

American Society of Newspaper Editors. *Problems of Journalism.* Proceedings of the American Society of Newspaper Editors, 1950. Washington: American Society of Newspaper Editors, 1950.

Anderson, Charles. Undated 1984 letter to the author.

Anderson, Dave, ed. *The Red Smith Reader.* New York: Random House, 1982.

Anderson, Jack. *Control.* New York: Kensington Publishing Corporation, 1988.

Anderson, Mary A. "Thomson merger plan set for June vote; Knight-Ridder to seek protection from acquisitors." *presstime,* April 1989.

Anderson, Sherwood. "On Being a Country Editor," *Vanity Fair,* February 1928: 70.

———. "The Country Weekly," *The Forum,* April 1931: 208–213.

Andrews, J. Cutler. *The North Reports the Civil War.* Pittsburgh: University of Pittsburg Press, 1956.

Armstrong, David. *A Trumpet to Arms.* Los Angeles: J. P. Tarcher Boston, distributed by Houghton Mifflin, 1981.

Arthur, John. *Realism/Photorealism.* Tulsa, Okla.: Philbrook Art Center, 1980.

Ashmore, Harry S. "Cause, Effect, and Cure." *Mass Communications.* Occasional paper of the Center for the Study of Democratic Institutions of the Fund for the Republic, Inc., 1966.

Asimov, Isaac. *Asimov's Mysteries.* Greenwich, Conn.: Fawcett Publications, Inc., 1968.

———. *The Best Science Fiction of Isaac Asimov.* Garden City, N.Y.: Doubleday & Co., 1986.

———. "The Future of Journalism." Speech given at 75th Anniversary Conference, Columbia University Graduate School of Journalism, 6 May, 1988.

———. *Prelude to Foundation.* New York: Doubleday, 1988.

Asimov, Isaac, Charles G. Waugh and Martin Harry Greenberg. *TV:2000.* New York: Ballantine Books, 1982.

The Astounding Science Fiction Anthology. New York: Simon and Schuster, 1961.

Associated Press. Biographical sheet on Terry Anderson, May 1989.

Atherton, Gertrude. *Patience Sparhawk and Her Times.* New York: John Land, The Bodley Head, 1897.

Babcock, Frederic. *Hang Up the Fiddle.* Garden City, N.Y.: Doubleday and Company, 1954.

Bagdikian, Ben H. "The Lords of the Global Village." *The Nation,* June 12, 1989: 805–820.

———. *The Media Monopoly.* Boston: Beacon Press, 1983.

Baker, Carlos. *Ernest Hemingway: A Life Story.* New York: Charles Scribner's Sons, 1969.

Ballard, J. G. *The Day of Creation.* Great Britain: Victor Gollancz Ltd., 1987; reprint, New York: Farrar, Straus, Giroux, 1988.

———. *Myths of the Near Future.* London: Jonathan Cape Ltd., 1982.

Banks, Louis. "Memo to the Press: They hate you out there." *The Atlantic Monthly,* April 1978: 35-8+.

Barak, Michael. *The Phantom Conspiracy.* New York: William Morrow and Co., Inc. 1980.

Barnouw, Erik. *A Tower in Babel: A History of Broadcasting in the United States: Volume I—to 1933.* New York: Oxford University Press, 1966.

———. *The Golden Web: A History of Broadcasting in the United States: Volume II—1933 to 1953.* New York: Oxford University Press, 1968.

Barris, Alex. *Stop the Presses! The Newspaperman in American Films.* South Brunswick, N.J.: A. S. Barnes and Company, Inc., 1976.

Barry, Dave. "Journalism prizes a major problem." *The Bulletin of the American Society of Newspaper Editors,* May/June, 1987.

Barth, Gunther. *City People: The Rise of Modern City Culture in Nineteenth-Century America.* New York: Oxford University Press, 1980.

Barthelme, Donald. *Overnight to Many Distant Cities.* New York: G. P. Putnam's Sons, 1983.

Bayley, Edwin R. *Joe McCarthy and the Press.* Madison: University of Wisconsin Press, 1981.

"Be a Reporter and see the world through a keyhole." Back-cover advertisement in *Newspaper Adventure Stories.* Date unknown [1932].

Becker, Stephen. *Comic Art in America.* New York: Simon and Schuster, 1959.

Behrens, John C. *The Typewriter Guerrillas.* Chicago: Nelson Hall Inc., 1977.

Belford, Barbara. *Brilliant Bylines: A Biographical Anthology of Notable Newspaperwomen in America.* New York: Columbia University Press, 1986.

Beninger, James R. *The Control Revolution: Technological and Economic Origins of the Information Society.* Cambridge, Mass.: Harvard University Press, 1986.

Bennett, W. Lance. *News: The Politics of Illusion.* Second edition. New York: Longman, 1988.

Benson, Mildred. *Dangerous Deadline.* New York: Dodd, Mead & Company, 1957.

Bent, Silas. *Buchanan of The Press.* New York: The Vanguard Press, 1932.

Berger, Meyer. *The Story of the New York Times, 1851–1951.* New York: Simon and Schuster, 1951.

Berkeley, Edmund Callis. *The Computer Revolution.* Garden City, N.Y.: Doubleday, 1962.

Bernstein, Carl, and Robert Woodward. *All the President's Men.* New York: Simon and Schuster, 1974.

Bessie, Simon Michael. *Jazz Journalism.* New York: E. P. Dutton & Co., Inc. 1938.

Black Dallas in the 1950s: Photographs from the R. C. Hickman Archive. Barker Texas History Center, University of Texas at Austin, February 27-May 30, 1987.

Blackbeard, Bill. San Francisco Academy of Comic Art. Interview, 6 December 1988.

Blackbeard, Bill, ed. *Connie: A Complete Compilation: 1929–1930. Frank Godwin.* Westport, Ct.: Hyperion Press, Inc., 1977.

Blackbeard, Bill and Martin Williams, eds. *The Smithsonian Collection of Newspaper Comics.* Washington: Smithsonian Institution Press and Harry N. Abrams, Inc., 1977.

Bliss, Edward, Jr., ed. *In Search of Light: The Broadcasts of Edward R. Murrow.* New York: Avon, 1967.

Bluford, Lucile. Interview by Fern Ingersoll, director of the women in journalism oral history project, Washington Press Club Foundation. Transcript of 15 May 1989.

Blythe, Samuel G. *The Making of a Newspaper Man.* Philadelphia: Henry Altemus, Co., 1912.

Bonafede, Dom. "Taking On the Press." *National Journal,* 8 April 1989.

Born, Donna. "The Image of the Woman Journalist in American Popular Fiction 1890 to the Present." Paper presented to the Committee on the Status of Women of the Association for Education in Journalism, Annual Convention, Michigan State University, East Lansing. August 1981.

Botein, Stephen. Introduction to '*Mr. Zenger's Malice and Falsehood': Six Issues of the New-York Weekly Journal 1733–34.* Worcester, Mass.: American Antiquarian Society, 1985.

Boyer, Peter J. "The Light Goes Out." *Vanity Fair,* June 1989.

Brackenridge, Hugh Henry. *Modern Chivalry.* Part II, 1804–1805. Edited by Claude M. Newlin. New York: American Book Company, 1937.

Bradbury, Ray. *The Toynbee Convector.* New York: Alfred A. Knopf, 1988.

———. *The Vintage Bradbury.* New York: Vintage Books, 1965.

Bradlee, Ben. Letter to the author, 17 April 1984.

Bradshaw, James Stanford. "George W. Wisner—A New Appraisal." Unpublished paper on file at the library of Columbia University's Graduate School of Journalism.

Brady, James. *The Press Lord.* New York: Delacorte Press, 1982.

Brand, Stewart. *The Media Lab: Inventing the Future at MIT.* New York: Viking, 1987.

Brian, Denis. *The True Gen: An Intimate Portrait of Ernest Hemingway By Those Who Knew Him.* New York: Grove Press, 1988.

Brinkley, William. *Peeper.* New York: The Viking Press, 1981.

Broder, David S. *Behind the Front Page.* New York: Simon and Schuster, 1987.

Brooks, Walter R. *Freddy and the Bean Home News.* New York: Alfred A. Knopf, 1943.

———. *Freddy the Detective.* New York: Alfred A. Knopf, 1932.

Broun, Heywood Hale. *Collected Edition of Heywood Broun.* New York: Harcourt, Brace and Company, 1941.

Brown, Betty C. "The Third War of Horst Fass." *Popular Photography,* March 1966: 117.

Brown, Fredric. *Night of the Jabberwock.* New York: Quill, 1984.

Browning, Norma Lee. "First Lady of the Funnies." *Saturday Evening Post,* 19 November 1960: 34–35, 87–88.

Buchanan, Edna. *The Corpse Had a Familiar Face: Covering Miami, America's Hottest Beat.* New York: Random House, 1987.

Budrys, Algis J. *Michaelmas.* New York: Berkley Publishing Corp., 1977.

Callenbach, Ernest. *Ecotopia.* Berkeley: Banyan Tree Books, 1975; reprint, New York: Bantam Books, 1977.

Calmer, Ned. *The Anchorman.* Garden City, N.Y.: Doubleday & Co., Inc., 1970.

Camerer, Dave, ed. *The Best of Grantland Rice.* New York: Franklin Watts, Inc. 1963.

Cannon, Lou. *Reporting: An Inside View.* Sacramento: California Journal Press, 1977.

Capa, Cornell, and Richard Whelan, eds. *Robert

Capa: Photographs. New York: Alfred A. Knopf. 1985.

Capa, Robert. *Slightly Out of Focus.* New York: Henry Holt and Company, Inc., 1947.

———. *Images of War.* New York: Grossman Publishers, 1964.

"Capt. Marvel." *Whiz Comics,* February 1940.

'Captain Marvel Jr.' April 1946.

Caputo, Philip. *DelCorso's Gallery.* New York: Holt, Rinehart & Winston, 1983.

Carey, James W. *Media, Myths, and Narratives: Television and the Press.* Newbury Park, Calif.: Sage Publications, 1988.

Carlson, Oliver, and Ernest Sutherland Bates. *Hearst: Lord of San Simeon.* Westport, Conn.: Greenwood Press, 1936.

Carter, Hodding. "Liar by Legislation." *The Delta Democrat-Times,* 3 April 1955.

———. *Their Words Were Bullets: The Southern Press in War, Reconstruction, and Peace.* Athens: University of Georgia Press, 1969.

———. *Where Main Street Meets the River.* New York: Rinehart & Company, Inc., 1953.

———. *The Winds of Fear.* New York: Farrar and Rinehart, Inc., 1944; reprint, New York: Award Books, 1964.

Chalmers, David Mark. *The Social and Political Ideas of the Muckrakers.* New York: The Citadel Press, 1964.

Charell, Lissa. *The Happy Medium.* New York: William Morrow and Co., 1962.

Chaze Elliott. *Tiger in the Honeysuckle.* New York: Charles Scribner's Sons, 1965.

Christopher, Robert C. *Crashing the Gates: The De-WASPing of America's Power Elite.* New York: Simon and Schuster, 1989.

Clemens, Samuel. *A Connecticut Yankee in King Arthur's Court.* In *The Complete Works of Mark Twain.* New York: Harper & Brothers, 1917.

Clurman, Richard A. *Beyond Malice: The Media's Years of Reckoning.* New Brunswick, N.J.: Transaction Books, 1988.

Cohen, Lester. *The New York Graphic.* Philadelphia: Chilton Books, 1964.

Collingwood, Charles. *The Defector.* New York: Harper & Row, 1970.

Comfort, Will Levington. *Red Fleece.* New York: George H. Doran Company, 1915.

Compton, D. G. *The Continuous Katherine Mortenhoe.* London: Victor Gollancz Ltd., 1974.

Cook, Philip S., Douglas Gomery, and Lawrence W. Lichty, eds. *American Media: The Wilson Quarterly Reader.* Washington: The Wilson Center Press, 1989.

Cooper, James Fenimore. *Home As Found.* New York: Capricorn Books, 1961.

Cornillon, Susan Koppelman, ed. *Images of Women in Fiction.* Bowling Green, Ohio: Bowling Green University Press, 1972.

Corry, John. "Just What Is The Nature of An Anchor's Influence?" *The New York Times* 27 May 1984: H21.

"The Cost of Technology: Information Prosperity and Information Poverty." A conference report by the Gannett Center of Media Studies, Columbia University, 1987.

Courson, Maxwell Taylor. "The Newspaper Movies: An Analysis of the Rise and Decline of the News Gatherer as a Hero in American Motion Pictures, 1900–1974." (Ph.D. Dissertation, Cinema, University of Hawaii, 1976.)

Cousins, Paul M. *Joel Chandler Harris.* Baton Rouge: Louisiana State University Press, 1968.

Covert, Catherine L. "Journalism History and Women's Experience: A Problem in Conceptual Change." *Journalism History.* Vol. 8:1 (Spring 1981): 2–6.

Crane, Stephen. *Active Service.* New York: Frederick A. Stokes Company, 1899.

———. "The Lone Charge of William B. Perkins." *Wounds in the Rain.* New York: Frederick A. Stokes Company, 1900.

Creelman, James. *On the Great Highway.* Boston: Lothrop, Lee & Shepard Co., 1901.

Crouch, Bill, Jr., ed. *Dick Tracy: America's Most Famous Detective.* Secaucus, N.J.: Citadel Press, 1987.

Crouse, Timothy. *The Boys on the Bus.* New York: Random House, 1973.

Crozier, Emmet. *American Reporters on the Western Front 1914–18.* New York: Oxford University Press, 1959.

Culbert, David Holbrook. *News for Everyman: Radio and Foreign Affairs in Thirties America.* Westport, Conn.: Greenwood Press, 1976.

Cunningham, Richard P. "Re-examining the ombudsman's role." *The Quill,* June 1988.

Dalmas, John. *The Varkaus Conspiracy.* New York: Tor, 1983.

Daniel, Pete and Raymond Smock. *A Talent for Detail: The photographs of Frances Benjamin Johnston, 1889–1910.* New York, Harmony Books, 1974.

Daniels, Jonathan. *They Will Be Heard.* New York: McGraw-Hill Book Company, 1965.

Davenport, Diana. *The Power Eaters.* New York: William Morrow and Company, Inc., 1979.

Davis, Clyde Brion. *"The Great American Novel—".* New York: Farrar Rinehart, 1938.

Davis, James A. and Tom W. Smith. *General Social Survey, Cumulative Code Book, 1972–1976.* Chicago: National Opinion Research Center, July, 1976.

———. *General Social Survey, Cumulative Code Book, 1972–1983.* Chicago: National Opinion Research Center, July 1983.

Davis, Rebecca Harding. "Earthen Pitchers." *Scribner's Monthly*, VII, November 1873 to April 1874.

———. *Frances Waldeaux.* New York: Harper and Brothers, 1897.

Davis, Richard Harding. *Gallegher and Other Stories.* New York: Charles Scribner's Sons, 1891.

———. *Farces.* New York: Charles Scribner's Sons, 1906.

Day, Donald, ed. *The Autobiography of Will Rogers.* Boston: Houghton Mifflin, 1949.

de Borchgrave, Arnaud, and Robert Moss. *The Spike.* New York: Crown Publishers, Inc., 1980.

Deegan, Dorothy Yost. *The Stereotype of the Single Woman in American Novels.* New York: King's Crown Press, 1951.

Demac, Donna A. *Liberty Denied: The Current Rise of Censorship in America.* New York: PEN American Center, 1988.

Dembart, Lee. "At Stanford, Leftists Become Censors." *The New York Times*, 5 May 1989, A35.

de Tocqueville, Alexis. *Democracy in America.* New York: Vintage Books, 1959.

Diamond, Edwin. *Sign Off, The Last Days of Television.* Cambridge: MIT Press, 1982.

Diamond, Edwin, A. Biddle Duke and Isabelle Anacker. "Can we expect TV news to correct its mistakes?" *TV Guide*, 5 December 1987.

Dick, Philip K. *The Man in the High Castle.* New York: G. P. Putnam's Sons, 1962.

———. *The Penultimate Truth.* Great Britain: Jonathan Cape Ltd., 1967; reprint, London: Triad Grafton Books, 1987.

Dickens, Charles. *The Life and Adventures of Martin Chuzzlewit.* Harmonds- worth, England: Penguin Books, 1968.

———. *The Life and Adventures of Martin Chuzzlewit.* New York: Penguin Books, 1982.

Diebold, John. "Newspapers and Information Technology: Some Strategic Options." A paper presented at the American Society of Newspaper Editors meeting, Washington, D.C., 15 April 1988.

Dobbin, Muriel. *Going Live.* New York: E. P. Dutton, 1987.

Donaldson, Sam. *Hold On, Mr. President.* New York: Random House, 1987.

Dooley, Dennis and Gary Engle, eds. *Superman at Fifty!: The Persistence of a Legend!* Cleveland: Octavia Press, 1987.

Dorfman, Ron. "Journalists Under Fire." *The Quill*, October 1983.

Dougan, Clark and Stephen Weiss. *The American Experience in Vietnam.* New York: W. W. Norton & Co. and Boston Publishing Co., 1988.

Douglas, Carole Nelson. *The Exclusive.* New York: Ballantine Books, 1986.

Douglass, Frederick. *Life and Times of Frederick Douglass.* New York: Collier Books, 1962.

Douglass' Monthly, Vol. 4–5, 1861–1863. New York: Negro Universities Press, 1969.

Downie, Leonard, Jr. *The New Muckrakers.* Washington: The New Republic Book Company, Inc., 1976.

Dozois, Gardner, ed. *The Year's Best Science Fiction.* Chappaqua, N.Y.: Bluejay Books, 1986.

Drew, Bernard A., ed. *Hard-Boiled Dames.* New York: St. Martin's Press, 1986.

Drury, Allen. *Anna Hastings: The Story of a Washington Newspaperperson!* New York: Warner Books, 1977.

———. *Mark Coffin, U.S.S.: A Novel of Capitol Hill.* Garden City, New York: Doubleday & Company, Inc. 1979.

duCille, Michel. Profile in "Neighbors" section, *The Miami Herald*, 30 July 1987: 12.

Dudden, Arthur P., ed. *The Assault of Laughter.* New York: Thomas Yoseloff, Publisher, 1962.

Dunne, Finley Peter. *Mr. Dooley in Peace and in War.* Boston: Small, Maynard and Company, 1899.

Dygert, James H. *The Investigative Journalist: Folk Heroes of a New Era.* Englewood Cliffs, N.J.: Prentice-Hall, 1976.

East, P. D. *The Magnolia Jungle: The Life, Times, and Education of a Southern Editor.* New York: Simon and Schuster, 1960.

Eaton, Clement. *The Freedom-of-Thought Struggle in the Old South.* New York: Harper and Row, 1964. Originally published as *Freedom of Thought in the Old South.* Durham, Duke University Press, 1940.

———. *The Growth of Southern Civilization, 1790– 1860.* New York: Harper and Brothers, 1961.

Eaton, Seymour [Paul Piper]. *The Roosevelt Bears Go to Washington.* Philadelphia: Edward Stearn & Company, 1907; reprint, New York: Dover Publications, 1981.

Eckley, Grace. *Finley Peter Dunne.* Boston: Twayne Publishers, 1981.

Edwards, Julia. *Women of the World: The Great Foreign Correspondents.* Boston: Houghton Mifflin, 1988.

Eells, George. *Hedda and Louella.* New York: G. P. Putnam and Sons, 1972.

Ellman, Mary. *Thinking About Women.* New York: Harcourt, Brace & World, Inc., 1968.

Elwood-Akers, Virginia. *Women War Correspondents in the Vietnam War, 1961–1975.* Metuchen, N.J.: The Scarecrow Press, Inc., 1988.

Emerson, Gloria. *Winners & Losers*. New York: Harcourt Brace Jovanovich, 1972.

Esslin, Martin. *The Age of Television*. San Francisco: W. H. Freeman and Company, 1982.

Evans, Lawrence B. "Impact of the Electronics Revolution on Industrial Process Control." *Science* 195 (18 March 1977): 1146–1151.

Ewing, Joseph H. "The New Sherman Letters." *American Heritage*, July/August, 1987.

Fang, Irving E. *Those Radio Commentators!* Ames: The Iowa State University Press, 1977.

Fatout, Paul. *Mark Twain in Virginia City*. Bloomington: Indiana University Press, 1964.

Fecher, Charles A. *Mencken: A Study of His Thought*. New York: Alfred A. Knopf, 1978.

———. Ed. *The Diary of H. L. Mencken*. New York: Alfred A. Knopf, 1989.

Ferber, Edna. *Dawn O'Hara, The Girl Who Laughed*. New York: Grosset & Dunlap, 1911.

Fern, Fanny. *Fern Leaves from Fanny's Portfolio*. Auburn, N.Y.: Derby and Miller, 1853.

Fiedler, Leslie. *Love and Death in the American Novel*. New York: Dell, Inc., 1969.

Filler, Louis, ed. *The World of Mr. Dooley*. New York: Collier Books, 1962.

Fisher, Marc. "Whatever happened to the tough-fisted, hard-drinking ME?" *Associated Press Managing Editors News*, April 1985.

Fishkin, Shelley Fisher. *From Fact to Fiction*. New York: Oxford University Press, 1988.

Folkerts, Jean, and Dwight L. Teeter. *Voices of a Nation*. New York: Macmillan Publishing Co., 1989.

Forester, Tom, ed. *The Information Technology Revolution*. Cambridge: MIT Press, 1985.

———. *The Microelectronics Revolution*. Cambridge: MIT Press, 1980.

Foster, Michael. *American Dream: A Novel*. New York: William Morrow and Company, 1937.

Freneau, Philip. *The Poems of Philip Freneau*. Vol. 3. Princeton: The University Library, 1907.

Friendly, Fred W. *Due to Circumstances Beyond Our Control. . . .* New York: Vintage Books, 1968.

Fuentes, Norberto. *Ernest Hemingway Rediscovered*. New York: Charles Scribner's Sons, 1988.

Fulham, Dana. "BU request in school takeover worries groups." *The Boston Globe*, 1 May 1989.

Gabriel, Ralph Henry. *Elias Boudinot: Cherokee and His America*. Norman: University of Oklahoma Press, 1941.

Garfield, Brian. *Deep Cover*. New York: Dell Publishing Company, Inc., 1971.

Gauvreau, Emile. *Hot News*. New York: The Macaulay Company, 1931.

———. *The Scandal Monger*. New York: The Macaulay Company, 1932.

———. *My Last Million Readers*. New York: E. P. Dutton and Company, Inc., 1941.

Gelfman, Judith S. *Women in Television News*. New York: Columbia University Press, 1976.

Gellhorn, Martha E. "Portrait of a Lady." In *The Heart of Another*. New York: Charles Scribner's Sons, 1941.

Ghiglione, Loren. "The reel journalist vs. the real journalist: Hollywood's image of the newspaperman," *The Evening News* (Southbridge, Mass.), 17 October 1976.

Gibbons, Edward. *Floyd Gibbons: Your Headline Hunter*. New York: Exposition Press, 1953.

Gibson, William. *Burning Chrome*. New York: Arbor House, 1986.

———. *Neuromancer*. New York: Ace Science Fiction Books, 1984.

Gifford, Thomas. *The Glendower Legacy*. New York: Pocket Books, 1978.

Glessing, Robert J. *The Underground Press in America*. Bloomington: Indiana University Press, 1970.

Glickman, Norman J., and Douglas P. Woodward, *The New Competitors*. New York: Basic Books, Inc., 1989.

Goldberg, Vicki. *Margaret Bourke-White*. Reading, Mass.: Addison-Wesley Publishing Company, Inc., 1987.

Golden, Harry. *The Right Time: An Autobiography*. New York: G. P. Putnam's Sons, 1969.

———. *Carl Sandburg*. Urbana: University of Illinois Press, 1988.

Goldstein, Toby. "J. G. Ballard: Visionary of the Apocalypse," *Heavy Metal*, April 1982: 38–40.

Goldstein, Tom. *The News At Any Cost: How Journalists Compromise Their Ethics to Shape the News*. New York: Simon and Schuster, 1985.

Gonzales, Juan. "Forgotten Pages: Spanish-Language Newspapers in the Southwest," *Journalism History*, Vol. 4, No. 2 (Summer 1977), pp. 50–51.

Good, Howard. *Acquainted with the Night: The Image of Journalists in American Fiction, 1890–1930*. Metuchen, N.J.: The Scarecrow Press, 1986.

———. "The Image of War Correspondents in Anglo-American Fiction." *Journalism Monographs*, No. 97 (July 1986): 1–25.

———. *Outcasts: The Image of Journalists in Contemporary Film*. Metuchen, N.J.: The Scarecrow Press, 1989.

Goodrich, Lloyd. *John Sloan*. New York: The Macmillan Company, 1952.

———. *Winslow Homer*. New York: George Braziller, 1959.

Gordon, Arthur. *Reprisal*. New York: Simon and Schuster, 1950.

Gordon, Barbara. *Defects of the Heart*. New York: Harper & Row, Publishers, 1983.

Gottesman, Ronald. *Focus on Citizen Kane.* Englewood Cliffs, N.J.: Prentice-Hall, Inc., 1971.

Goulart, Ron. *Death Cell.* New York: Beagle Books, 1971.

———. *The Dime Detectives.* New York: The Mysterious Press, 1988.

———. *Hawkshaw.* New York: Doubleday, 1972.

———. *Plunder.* New York: Beagle Books, 1972.

Goulden, Joseph C. *Fit to Print.* Secaucus, N.J.: Lyle Stuart Inc., 1988.

Graff, Gordon. "Ethical Questions That Arise When It's Easy to Doctor Images." *The New York Times.* 15 January 1989.

Granger, Bill. *Sweeps.* New York: Fawcett Gold Medal Books, 1980.

Grant, Lee. "Images of the Journalist." *The Bulletin of the American Society of Newspaper Editors.* April 1982: 3–12.

———. "Tuning in on 'Lou Grant.'" *The Bulletin of the American Society of Newspaper Editors,* April 1983: 3–9.

Greene, Graham. *The Quiet American.* New York: The Viking Press, 1955.

The Greeneville Sun. 1 October 1966.

Greenfield, Jeff. *Television: The First Fifty Years.* New York: Harry N. Abrams, 1977.

Greenly, Mike. "Interactive Journalism and Computer Networking: Exploring a New Medium." *The Futurist,* March/April 1987, Vol. XXI, No. 2: 12–16.

Griffin, John Howard. *Black Like Me.* New York: New American Library, 1962.

Griffith, Sally Foreman. *Home Town News: William Allen White and the Emporia Gazette.* New York: Oxford University Press, 1989.

Gross, Jane. "Movies and the Press Are an Enduring Romance." *The New York Times,* 2 June 1985: sec. 2, p. 19.

Grossman, Gary H. *Superman: Serial to Cereal.* New York: Popular Library, 1977.

Grossman, Julian. *Echo of a Distant Drum: Winslow Homer and the Civil War.* New York: Harry N. Abrams, 1974.

Gunn, James E. *The Listeners.* New York: Charles Scribner's Sons, 1972.

Gup, Ted. "In Maine: A Town and Its Paper." *Time,* 18 January 1988: 10.

Gutierrez, Felix. "Spanish-Language Media in America: Background, Resources, History," *Journalism History,* Vol. 4, No. 2 (Summer 1977), pp. 34–41, 65–68.

Haigh, Robert W., George Gerbner, and Richard B. Byrne, eds., *Communications in the Twenty-First Century.* New York: John Wiley & Sons., 1981.

Hailey, Arthur. *Overload.* New York: Doubleday & Company, Inc., 1979.

Hake, Ted, and Russ King. *Price Guide to Collectible Pin-Back Buttons 1896–1986.* York, Pa.: Hake's Americana and Collectible Press, 1986.

Halberstam, David. *The Making of a Quagmire.* New York: Ballantine Books, 1989.

———. *The Powers That Be.* New York: Alfred A. Knopf, 1979.

Hale, Edward Everett, "The Brick Moon." *The Atlantic Monthly,* October, November and December, 1869.

Hale, William Harlan. *Horace Greeley: Voice of the People.* New York: Collier Books, 1961.

Hales, Peter. *Silver Cities: The Photography of American Urbanization, 1839–1915.* Philadelphia: Temple University Press, 1984.

Hallin, Daniel C. *The "Uncensored War."* New York: Oxford University Press, 1986.

Hall, Esther Greenacre. *Haverhill Herald.* New York: Random House and the Junior Literary Guild Corp., 1938.

Hamilton, Alexander, James Madison and John Jay. *The Federalist Papers.* New York: Mentor, 1961.

Hamsun, Knut. *The Cultural Life of Modern America.* Translated by Barbara Gordon Morgridge. Cambridge: Harvard University Press, 1969.

Harkey, Ira B., Jr. *The Smell of Burning Crosses.* Jacksonville, Ill.: Harris-Wolfe & Company, 1967.

Harris, Charlaine. *Sweet and Deadly.* Boston: Houghton Mifflin Co., 1981.

Harris, Joel Chandler. *Free Joe and Other Georgian Sketches.* New York: Charles Scribner's Sons, 1887.

Harrison, James G. "American Newspaper Journalism As Described In American Novels of the Nineteenth Century." Ph.D. dissertation, University of North Carolina, Chapel Hill, 1945.

Hartwell, David. *Age of Wonders: Exploring the World of Science Fiction.* New York: Walker and Company, 1985.

Hecht, Ben. *Erik Dorn.* New York: The Modern Library, 1921.

Hecht, Ben, and Charles MacArthur. *The Front Page.* New York: Covici-Friede Publishers, 1928.

Heeger, Susan. "'Ed Asner' Starring Lou Grant." *Channels,* April/May 1982: 60.

Heinecken, Robert. "1984: A Case Study in Finding an Appropriate TV Newswoman (A CBS Docudrama in Words and Pictures)." Los Angeles: Robert Heinecken, 1985.

Hemingway Collection. Item 581, John F. Kennedy Library.

Hendricks, Gordon. *The Life and Work of Winslow Homer.* New York: Harry N. Abrams, 1979.

Henley, Don, and Danny Kortchmar. *Dirty Laundry.*

Cass County Music and Kortchmar Music, 1982.

Henry, William A., III. "Journalism Under Fire." *Time*, 12 December 1983: 77.

Hereford, William Richard. *The Demagog*. New York: Henry Holt, 1909.

Herman, Edward S. and Noam Chomsky. *Manufacturing Consent: The Political Economy of the Mass Media*. New York: Pantheon Books, 1988.

Herr, Michael. *Dispatches*. New York: Alfred A. Knopf, 1977.

Hersh, Seymour. "An Absence of Instinct?" *The Bulletin of the American Society of Newspaper Editors*, February 1970: 4–6, 9.

———. *Cover Up*. New York: Random House, 1972.

———. *My Lai 4: A Report on the Massacre and Its Aftermath*. New York: Random House, 1970.

Hess, John. "Who's conning whom?" *The Quill*, May 1989.

Hess, Stephen. *The Government/Press Connection*. Washington: The Brookings Institution, 1984.

Hess, Stephen, and Milton Kaplan. *The Ungentlemanly Art*. New York: Macmillan Publishing Co., Inc.; London: Collier Macmillan Publishers, 1975.

Hicks, Granville, with John Stuart. *John Reed: The Making of a Revolutionary*. New York: Macmillan, 1936.

Hillerman, Tony. *The Fly on the Wall*. New York: Avon Books, 1971.

Hogarth, Paul. *The Artist as Reporter*. London: Gordon Fraser, 1986.

Hohenberg, John. *A Crisis for the American Press*. New York: Columbia University Press, 1978.

———. *Foreign Correspondence: The Great Reporters and Their Times*. New York: Columbia University Press, 1964.

Hollander, Richard. *Video Democracy: The Vote-from-Home Revolution*. Mt. Airy, Maryland: Lomond Publications, 1985.

Holtzman, Natalie F., "The image of women journalists in the American novel, 1898–1957," *Matrix*, Summer 1977 (Vol. 62, No. 4), pp. 24–25, 31.

"Home Fires Burning." Television production, 1989.

Horn, Maurice. *Women in the Comics*. New York: Chelsea House Publishers, 1977.

Hoskins, Robert, ed. *Infinity Four*. New York: Lancer Books, 1972.

Howe, E. W. *The Story of a Country Town*. Boston: James R. Osgood & Company, 1885.

Howells, William Dean. "Two Notable Novels." *Century Magazine* XXVIII (August 1884): 632.

———. *The Quality of Mercy*. New York: Harper & Brothers, 1892.

———. "A Modern Instance." In *Novels 1875–1886*. New York: The Library of America, 1982.

———. *A Woman's Reason: A Novel*. Boston: Houghton Mifflin Company, 1883.

Hudson, Frederic. *Journalism in the United States from 1690–1872*. New York: Harper & Brothers, 1873.

Huf, Linda. *A Portrait of the Artist as a Young Woman: The Writer as Heroine in American Literature*. New York: Frederick Ungar Publishing Co., 1983.

Hughes, Barrie J. *The World Honors the News Carrier*. Watertown, N.Y.: n.p., 1979.

Hughes, Helen MacGill Hughes. *News and the Human Interest Story*. Chicago: University of Chicago Press, 1940; reprint, New Brunswick, N.J.: Transaction Books, 1981.

Hughes, Langston, Milton Meltzer and C. Eric Lincoln. *A Pictorial History of Blackamericans*. 5th revised edition. New York: Crown Publishers, Inc., 1983.

Huot, Leland and Alfred Powers. *Homer Davenport of Silverton: Life of a Great Cartoonist*. Bingen, Wash.: West Shore Press, 1973.

Hutchens, John K. and George Oppenheimer, eds. *The Best in the World*. New York: The Viking Press, 1973.

Irvine, R. R. *Freeze Frame*. New York: Popular Library, 1976.

———. *Horizontal Hold*. New York: Popular Library, 1978.

———. *Jump Cut*. New York: Praegers Press, 1985.

———. *Ratings Are Murder*. New York: Walker and Company, 1985.

Irwin, Will. *The Making of a Reporter*. New York: G. P. Putnam's Sons, 1942.

———. *The American Newspaper*. Reprint edition. Ames: The Iowa State University Press, 1969.

Isaacs, Norman. *Untended Gates: The Mismanaged Press*. New York: Columbia University Press, 1986.

Jackson, George R. (words) and D. W. Boardman (music). "The Newsboy." Collection of the American Antiquarian Society, Worcester, Mass.

James, Henry. *The Reverberator*. New York: Macmillan and Co., 1888.

Jenkin, Len. *New Jerusalem*. Los Angeles: Sun & Moon Press, 1986.

John Ellard The Newsboy. Philadelphia: William S. and Alfred Martien, 1860.

Johnson, Walter, ed. *Selected Letters of William Allen White, 1899–1943*. New York: Henry Holt and Co., 1947.

Johnstone, John W. C., Edward J. Slawski, and William W. Bowman. *The News People*. Urbana: University of Illinois Press, 1976.

Jonathan, Norton. *Dan Hyland, Police Reporter.* Chicago: The Goldsmith Publishing Company, 1936.

Jordan, Elizabeth Garver. "Ruth Herrick's Assignment." In *Tales of the City Room.* New York: Charles Scribner's Sons, 1898.

Jowett, Garth. *Film: The Democratic Art.* Boston: Little, Brown and Company, 1976.

Juergens, George. *Joseph Pulitzer and the New York World.* Princeton: Princeton University Press, 1966.

Just, Ward. *Stringer.* Boston: Little, Brown and Company, 1974.

———. *A Family Trust.* Boston: Little, Brown and Company, 1978.

———. *Honor, Power, Riches, Fame and the Love of Women.* New York: E. P. Dutton, 1979.

———. *The American Blues.* New York: The Viking Press, 1984.

Kael, Pauline. *The Citizen Kane Book.* Toronto: Bantam Books, 1974.

Kallen, Lucille. *Introducing C. B. Greenfield.* New York: Crown Publishers, 1979.

———. *C. B. Greenfield: The Tanglewood Murder.* New York: Wyndham Books, 1980.

———. *C. B. Greenfield: No Lady in the House.* New York: Wyndham Books, 1982.

———. *C. B. Greenfield: The Piano Bird.* New York: Random House, 1984.

———. *C. B. Greenfield: A Little Madness.* New York: Random House, 1986.

Kane, Hartnett T. *Dear Dorothy Dix: The Story of a Compassionate Woman.* Garden City, N.Y.: Doubleday and Company, 1952.

Karp, Walter. "All the Congressmen's Men: How Capitol Hill Controls the Press." *Harper's Magazine,* July 1989: 55–63.

Keenan, Henry Francis. *The Money-Makers: A Social Parable.* New York: D. Appleton and Co., 1985.

Keillor, Garrison. *Lake Wobegon Days.* New York: Viking Penguin, 1985.

Kelland, Clarence Budington. *Contraband.* New York: A. L. Burt Company, 1923.

King, Woodie and Ron Miller, eds. *Black Drama Anthology.* New York: Signet/New American Library, Inc., 1972.

Kipling, Rudyard. *The Light That Failed.* Garden City, N.Y.: Doubleday, Page & Co., 1899.

Klein, Frederick C. "Ordinary Man, Extraordinary Sportswriter." *Wall Street Journal,* 18 June 1986.

Klein, Kathleen Gregory. *The Woman Detective: Gender and Genre.* Urbana: University of Illinois Press, 1988.

Kluger, Richard. *The Paper: The Life and Death of the New York Herald Tribune.* New York: Alfred A. Knopf, 1986.

Knight, Robert P. "Here's the view from 'complaint central'." *The Bulletin of the American Society of Newspaper Editors,* February 1989.

Knightley, Philip. *The First Casualty.* New York: Harcourt Brace Jovanovich, 1975.

Kobre, Sidney. *The Yellow Press and Gilded Age Journalism.* Tallahassee: Florida State University Press, 1964.

Kramer, Dale. *Heywood Broun, A Biographical Portrait.* New York: Current Books, Inc., 1949.

Kramer, Staci. "The case of the missing Coke can." *Editor and Publisher,* 29 April 1989.

Kris, Ernst. *Selected Papers of Ernst Kris.* New Haven: Yale University Press, 1975.

Krock, Arthur. *Memoirs.* New York: Funk & Wagnalls, 1968.

Lamberton, Donald M., ed. *The Information Revolution.* Annals of the American Academy of Political and Social Science. vol. 412. Philadelphia: American Academy of Political and Social Science, 1974.

Langer-Burns, Heidi M., "The Image of Journalists in American Film and Fiction from 1975 to 1987: An Application of Leo Löwenthal's Model," Ph. D. Dissertation, School of Journalism, Southern Illinois University at Carbondale, April 1989.

Laurence, William L. *Men and Atoms: The Discovery, the Uses and the Future of Atomic Energy.* New York: Simon and Schuster, 1959.

Lasica, J. D. "Pictures don't always tell truth." *The Boston Globe,* 2 January, 1989.

Leamer, Laurence. *Assignment.* New York: The Dial Press, 1981.

Lee, James Melvin. *History of American Journalism.* Garden City, N.Y.: The Garden City Publishing Co., Inc., 1917.

Leekley, Sheryle and John. *Moments: The Pulitzer Prize Photographs.* New York: Crown Publishers, Inc., 1978.

Leigh, J. Paul, "Estimate of the Probability of Job-Related Deaths in 347 Occupations." *Journal of Occupational Medicine.* Volume 29, No. 6, (June 1987): 510–518.

Lem, Stanislaw. *The Futurological Congress.* Krakow, Poland: n.p., 1971; New York: Avon Books, 1976.

Letofsky, Irv. "Real to Reel." *The Bulletin of the American Society of Newspaper Editors.* (May/June 1983): 15.

Levy, David. *The Chameleons.* Reissued in paperback as *The Network Jungle.* Canoga Park, Calif.: Major Books, 1976.

Lewinski, Jorge. *The Camera at War.* New York: Simon and Schuster, 1978.

Lewis, Sinclair. *Main Street*. New York: Harcourt, Brace and Company, 1920.

Lichter, Robert S., Stanley Rothman and Linda S. Lichter. *The Media Elite*. Bethesda, Md.: Adler and Adler, Publishers, Inc., 1986.

Liebling, A. J. *The Wayward Pressman*. Garden City, N.Y.: Doubleday, 1947.

———. *The Sweet Science*. New York: The Viking Press, 1956.

Lippmann, Walter. *Liberty and the News*. New York: Harcourt, Brace & Howe, 1920.

Locke, Alain. "Foreword" to the Centenary Memorial Subscribers' Edition of *The Life and Times of Frederick Douglass*. New York: Pathway Press, 1941.

Locke, David Ross (Petroleum V. Nasby). *A Paper City*. Boston: Lee and Shepard, 1879.

Locke, Richard Adams. *The Moon Hoax*. New York: William Gowans, 1859; reprint, Boston: Gregg Press, 1975.

Logan, Joe. "2014: A Newspaper Odyssey." *Washington Journalism Review*, May 1989.

Lohr, Steve. "Media Mergers: An Urge to Get Bigger and More Global." *The New York Times*, 19 March 1989: E1.

Lois Lane comic book. November, No. 106. On display in 1988 Smithsonian exhibit.

London, Jack. "Amateur Night." *Moon Face*. New York: M. A. Donohue and Company, 1906.

Lopatin, Judy. *Modern Romances*. New York: Fiction Collective, 1986.

Loupe, Diane E. "Storming and defending the color barrier at the University of Missouri School of Journalism: The Lucile Bluford case." Paper presented to the August 1989 meeting of the Association for Education in Journalism and Mass Communication.

Lowell, James Russell. *Bigelow Papers First Series*. Edited by Thomas Wortham. Dekalb: Northern Illinois University Press, 1977.

Luke Darrell, The Chicago Newsboy. Chicago: Tomlinson Brothers, 1866.

Lundberg, Ferdinand. *Imperial Hearst: A Social Biography*. New York: Equinox Cooperative Press, 1936.

Luskin, John. *Lippman, Liberty, and the Press*. University, Alabama: University of Alabama Press, 1972.

Lynd, Robert S. and Helen Merrell Lynd. *Middletown in Transition: A Study in Cultural Conflicts*. New York: Harcourt, Brace, 1937.

MacNelly, Jeff. *The Greatest Shoe on Earth*. New York: Holt, Rinehart and Winston, 1984, 1985.

———. Interview by author via telephone, 23 February 1988.

Madison, Charles A. *Critics & Crusaders*. New York: Henry Holt and Company, 1948.

Malcolm, Janet. "The Journalist and the Murderer, 1—The Journalist." *The New Yorker*, 13 March 1989.

Malone, Michael. *Dingley Falls*. New York: Harcourt Brace Jovanovich, 1980.

"Man-bites-dog act slays N. Y. press; dailies reaction big $64 question." *Variety*, 4 June 1947: 29.

Mander, Mary. "The journalist as cynic." *The Antioch Review* (Winter 1980): 91–107.

Marsh, Harry D. "Hodding Carter's Newspaper on School Desegregation, 1954–1955." *Journalism Monographs* No. 92, May 1985: 1–23.

Martin, Jay. *Who Am I This Time? Uncovering the Fictive Personality*. New York: W. W. Norton & Co., 1988.

Marzio, Peter C. *The Men and Machines of American Journalism: A Pictorial History from The Henry R. Luce Hall of News Reporting*. Washington: The National Museum of History and Technology, 1975.

———. *Rube Goldberg: His Life and Work*. New York: Harper & Row Publishers, 1973.

Marzolf, Marion. *Up From the Footnote: A History of Women Journalists*. New York: Hastings House, Publishers, 1977.

Masters, Edgar Lee. *Spoon River Anthology*. New York: Macmillan Publishing Company, 1962.

Mauldin, Bill. *Up Front*. New York: Henry Holt and Company, 1945.

———. *The Brass Ring*. New York: W. W. Norton & Company, Inc., 1971.

May, Antoinette. *Witness to War: A Biography of Marguerite Higgins*. New York: Beaufort Books, Inc., 1983.

McAuliffe, Kevin Michael. *The Great American Newspaper*. New York: Charles Scribner's Sons, 1978.

McBride, Joseph. *Orson Welles*. New York: The Viking Press, 1972.

McConnell, Vicki P. *The Burnton Widows*. Tallahassee, Fla.: The Naiad Press Inc., 1984.

Mcdonald, Gregory. "Fletch," In *Fletch Forever*. Garden City, N.Y.: Nelson Doubleday, Inc., 1978.

McGaffey, Donald W. *The Golden Age of Sound Comedy*. New York: A. S. Barnes and Co., 1973.

McKeen, William. "Heroes and Villains: A study of journalists in American novels published between 1915 and 1975." Master of Arts dissertation, School of Journalism, Indiana University, August 1977.

McKelvey, Blake. *The Urbanization of America, 1860–1915*. New Brunswick, N.J.: Rutgers University Press, 1963.

McLuhan, Marshall. *Understanding Media: The Extensions of Man*. New York: McGraw-Hill Book

Company, 1964; reprint, The New American Library, 1966.

McManus, George. *Jiggs is Back*. Berkeley, Calif: Celtic Book Company, 1986.

McManus, Jason. "A Letter from the Editor-in-Chief." *Life*, April 1989: 4.

McPhaul, John J. *Deadlines & Monkeyshines*. Englewood Cliffs, N.J.: Prentice-Hall, Inc., 1962.

Meehan, Diana M. *Ladies of the Evening*. Metuchen, N.J.: The Scarecrow Press, 1983.

Meisel, Myron. "The Big Carnival." In *Dateline . . . Hollywood*. The Museum of Fine Arts, Boston film and lecture series, 1 May–14 June 1975.

Mellen, Joan. *Women and Their Sexuality in the New Film*. New York: Horizon Press, 1973.

Meltzer, Milton. *Mark Twain Himself*. New York: Bonanza Books, 1960.

Mencken, H. L. *Prejudices: Sixth Series*. New York: Alfred A. Knopf, Inc., 1927.

———. *A Mencken Chrestomathy*. New York: Alfred A. Knopf, Inc., 1949.

———. *A Gang of Pecksniffs and Other Comments on Newspaper Publishers, Editors and Reporters*. Edited by Theo Lippman, Jr. New Rochelle, N.Y.: Arlington House Publishers, 1975.

Menville, Douglas and R. Reginald. *Future Visions*. North Hollywood, Calif: Newcastle Publishing Company, Inc., 1985.

Messick, Dale. *Brenda Starr: Girl Reporter*. Racine, Wisc.: Whitman Publishing Company, 1943.

Metcalf, Alan. "Great Investigative Crusades of Joe Pulitzer." *Media History Digest*, Spring/Summer 1988.

Methvin, Eugene H. "Mephistophelean Journalism." *The Quill*, April 1989.

Meyer, Lawrence. *A Capitol Crime*. New York: The Viking Press, 1977.

———. *False Front*. New York: The Viking Press, 1979.

Michelson, Miriam. *A Yellow Journalist*. New York: D. Appleton and Company, 1905.

Millar, Jeff. *Private Sector*. New York: The Dial Press, 1979.

Miller, Arthur. *Final Edition*. New York: Pinnacle Books, 1981.

Miller, Marc H. "Television's Impact on Contemporary Art." Catalogue for an exhibit at The Queens Museum, Flushing, N.Y., 13 September–26 October 1986.

Miller, Sally M. *The Ethnic Press in the United States: A Historical Analysis and Handbook*. New York: Greenwood Press, 1987.

Mills, Kay. "New perspectives, different voices," *The Quill*, April 1989.

———. *A Place in the News: From the Women's Pages to the Front Page*. New York: Dodd, Mead & Company, 1988.

Milne, Robert Duncan. "The Passing of the Printing Press." *The San Francisco Morning Call*, 18 December 1898.

"Missing Pages." *GF Magazine*, Summer 1989. (Includes excerpt from Wallace Terry's upcoming book, *Missing Pages, An Oral History of Black Journalists in America, 1940–1990*.)

Mitgang, Herbert. *The Montauk Fault*. New York: Arbor House, 1981.

———. "Stephen Crane's Shifting Image." *The New York Times*, 23 December 1987: C11.

Mixon, Wayne. "The Irrelevance of Race: Joel Chandler Harris and Uncle Remus in Their Time." Scheduled for publication in *The Journal of Southern History*, November 1990.

Moeller, Susan D. *Shooting War: Photography and the American Experience of Combat*. New York: Basic Books, Inc., Publishers, 1989.

Moravec, Hans. *Mind Children*. Cambridge: Harvard University Press, 1988.

Morgan, Henry. *Ned Nevins, The Newsboy; or, Street Life in Boston*. Boston: Lee and Shepard, 1866.

Moritz, Charles, ed. *Current Biography Yearbook 1987*. New York: The H. W. Wilson Co., 1987, 1988.

———. *Current Biography Yearbook 1988*. New York: The H. W. Wilson Co., 1988, 1989.

Mott, Frank Luther. *American Journalism, A History: 1690–1960*. New York: The Macmillan Co., 1962.

Mowry, George E. *The Era of Theodore Roosevelt*. New York: Harper & Row, Publishers, 1958.

Muench, James F. "The Ethics of Journalists in Bestsellers: 1960–87." Master of Arts Thesis, University of Missouri-Columbia, August 1988.

Munroe, Kirk. *Under Orders: The Story of a Young Reporter*. New York: G. P. Putnam's Sons, 1890.

Murdoch, Anna. *Family Business*. New York: William Morrow and Company, Inc., 1988.

Murphy, James E. and Sharon M. *Let My People Know: American Indian Journalism, 1828–1978*. Norman; University of Oklahoma Press, 1981.

Naha, Ed. *The Paradise Plot*. New York: Bantam Books, 1980.

———. *The Suicide Plague*. New York: Bantam Books, 1982.

Neal, Joseph C. *In Town & About or Pencillings & Pennings*. Philadelphia: Godey & McMichael, 1843.

Neff, Craig. "Portrait of the Sportswriter as a Young Man." *Gannett Center Journal*, Vol. 1, No. 2. (Fall 1987): 47–55.

Nessen, Ron. *The First Lady*. Chicago: Playboy Press, 1979.

———. *The Hour*. New York: William Morrow and Company, Inc., 1984.

"The Newsboys." *The New Charitable Monthly*, February 1855.

"The Newsboys' Excursion—A Day of Jolly Sport." *Harper's Weekly*. 2 October 1875: 804.

Nichols, David, ed. *Ernie's War*. New York: Simon & Schuster, Inc., 1986.

Nichols, Victoria, and Susan Thompson. *Silk Stalkings: When Women Write of Murder*. Berkeley, Calif: Black Lizard Books, 1988.

"Nick Kenny Speaking." New York *Mirror*. 15 January 1949: 12.

Niven, Larry and Jerry Pournelle. *Footfall*. New York: Ballantine Books, 1985.

Norton, C. E. *Correspondence Between Thomas Carlyle and Ralph Waldo Emerson*. Vol. 2. Boston: R. J. Osgood and Company, 1833.

O'Brian, Jack. "Letters From Readers On Slanted Broadcasts." *New York Journal-American*, 14 June 1954: 24.

O'Connor, Richard. *Heywood Broun, A Biography*. New York: G.P. Putnam's Sons, 1975.

Olden, Marc. *The Harker File: Kill the Reporter*. New York: Signet Book, New American Library, 1978.

Older, Mrs. Fremont. *William Randolph Hearst*. New York: Appleton-Century, 1936.

Orians, G. Harrison. *A Short History of American Literature*. New York: F. S. Crofts and Company, 1940.

Osnos, Peter. "I.F. Stone, a Journalist's Journalist." *The New York Times*, 20 June 1989: A23.

Paine, Albert Bigelow. *Th. Nast, His Period and His Pictures*. New York: The Macmillan Company, 1904; republication, Princeton: The Pyne Press, n.d.

Palmer, Nancy Doyle. "Going After the Truth—In Disguise: The Ethics of Deception." *Washington Journalism Review*, November 1987.

Parenti, Michael. *Inventing Reality: The Politics of the Mass Media*. New York: St. Martin's Press, 1986.

Parish, James Robert, and Michael R. Pitts. *The Great Spy Pictures*. Metuchen, N.J.: The Scarecrow Press, Inc., 1974.

Parker, Robert B. *A Savage Place*. New York: Delacorte Press, 1981.

Parton, James, ed. *Eminent Women of the Age: Being Narratives of the Lives and Deeds of the Most Prominent Women of the Present Generation*. Hartford, Ct.: S. M. Betts, 1868.

Patten, Dave. *Newspapers and New Media*. White Plains, New York: Knowledge Industries Publications, 1986.

Paulding, W. I. *Literary Life of James K. Paulding*. New York: Charles Scribner & Company, 1867.

Pauly, John J. *The Ideological Origins of an Independent Press*. Paper presented to the American Journalism Historians Association convention, Las Vegas, Nevada, October 1985.

Payne, Ethel. Interview by the author, 13 September 1989.

Payne, Will. *The Money Captain*. Chicago: Herbert S. Stone and Co., 1898.

Penzler, Otto, ed. *The Great Detectives*. Boston: Little, Brown and Company, 1978.

A People in Print: Jewish Journalism in America. Catalogue for exhibit June 14-December 31, 1987. Philadelphia: National Museum of American Jewish History, 1987.

Persico, Joseph E. *Edward R. Murrow: An American Original*. New York: McGraw-Hill Publishing Co., 1988.

Pilat, Oliver. *Drew Pearson: An Unauthorized Biography*. New York: Harper & Row, Publishers, Inc., 1973.

Poe, Edgar Allan. "The Moon Hoax." *The New York Sun*, 6 January, 1844.

Pohl, Frederik, ed. *The Best of C. M. Kornbluth*. New York: Ballantine Books, 1976.

Pohl, Frederik, *The Merchant's War*. New York: St. Martin's Press, 1984.

Pohl, Frederik and C. M. Kornbluth. *The Space Merchants*. New York: Ballantine Books, 1953.

Pollak, Richard. "*Time* + Dallas + ?" *The Nation*, 27 March 1989.

Powe, Lucas A., Jr. *American Broadcasting and the First Amendment*. Berkeley: University of California Press, 1987.

Powell, Richard. *Daily and Sunday*. New York: Charles Scribner's Sons, 1964.

Powers, Ron. *Face Value*. New York: Delacorte Press, c1979

————. *The Newscasters*. New York: St. Martin's Press, c1977

Pratt, John Clark, ed. *Vietnam Voices*. New York: Viking, 1984.

Pyle, Ernie. *Brave Men*. New York: Henry Holt and Company, Inc., 1944.

Queen, Ellery, ed. *The Great Woman Detectives and Criminals: The Female of the Species*. Reprint edition. Garden City, N.Y.: Blue Ribbon Books, 1946.

Quinnell, A. J. *The Snap*. New York: William Morrow and Company, Inc., 1983.

Raskin, Alex. "All the News That Wiggles." *Channels*, May/June 1984.

Randolph, Eleanor. "The Critic and The Criticized." *Washington Post*, 18 March 1989: C1.

Ray, Frederick. *Alfred R. Waud: Civil War Artist*. New York: The Viking Press, 1974.

Regier, C. C., *The Era of the Muckrakers*. Chapel Hill,

N.C.: University of North Carolina Press, 1952; reprint, Gloucester, Mass.: Peter Smith, 1957.

Reidenbaugh, Lowell. *Cooperstown: Where Baseball's Legends Live Forever*. St. Louis, Missouri: The Sporting News Publishing Company, 1983.

Reynolds, Michael. *Hemingway's First War*. Princeton: Princeton University Press, 1976; reprint, New York: Basil Blackwell, Inc., 1987.

Rich, Frank. "Stage: Echo of Vietnam, How I Got That Story." *The New York Times*, 9 December 1980: C9.

Richta, Radovan, ed. *Civilization at the Crossroads: Social and Human Implications of the Scientific and Technological Revolution*. White Plains, N.Y.: International Arts and Sciences Press, 1967.

Riis, Jacob. *How the Other Half Lives*. New York: Sagamore Press, Inc., 1957.

———. *The Making of an American*. New York: The Macmillan Company, 1901; reprint, 1964.

Rivers, Caryl. *Girls Forever Brave and True*. New York: St. Martin's Press, 1986.

Rivers, William L. *The Other Government: Power and the Washington Media*. New York: Universe Books, 1982.

Robbins, Harold. *The Inheritors*. New York: Trident Press, 1969.

Roberts, Steve. *Max Headroom: 20 Minutes into the Future*. New York: Vintage, 1985.

Ross, Ishbel. *Ladies of the Press*. New York: Harper & Brothers Publishers, 1936.

Ross, Walter. *Coast-to-Coast*. New York: Simon and Schuster, 1962.

Rossell, Deac. "Hollywood and the Newsroom." *American Film*, October 1975: 14–18.

"Roundup: FBI, Police Invade Newsrooms." In *The News Media & the Law*. Vol. 12, No. 4 (Fall 1988): 4–5.

Rovin, Jeff. *The Encyclopedia of Superheroes*. New York: Facts on File Publications, 1985.

Rubin, Bernard, ed. *Questioning Media Ethics*. New York: Praeger Publishers, 1978.

Rubin, Joseph Jay and Charles H. Brown, eds. *Walt Whitman of the New York Aurora: Editor at Twenty-Two, A Collection of Recently Discovered Writings*. State College: Pennsylvania State University Press, 1950.

Rusher, William A. *The Coming Battle for the Media: Curbing the Power of the Media Elite*. New York: William Morrow and Company, Inc., 1988.

Rutland, Robert A. *The Newsmongers: Journalism in the Life of the Nation, 1690–1972*. New York: The Dial Press, 1973.

Ryan, Desmond. "The Hollywood Reporter: Movies That Do a Reel Number on the Press." *Washington Journalism Review*, September 1985: 45–47.

Sackett, S. J. *E. W. Howe*. New York: Twayne Publishers, 1972.

Salant, Richard S. "Selling Out the First Amendment." *Washington Journalism Review*, January/February 1989: 51.

Saltzman, Mark, Judy Garlan, and Michele Grodner. *DC Super Heroes Super Healthy Cookbook*. New York: Warner Books, 1981.

Sawislak, Arnold. *Dwarf Rapes Nun; Flees in UFO*. New York: St. Martin's Press, 1985.

Sayre, Nora. "Falling Prey to Parodies of the Press." *The New York Times*, 1 January 1975: 8.

Scarborough, Chuck. *Stryker*. New York: Macmillan, 1978.

Scardino, Albert. "A Debate Heats Up: Is It News or Entertainment?" *The New York Times*, 15 January 1989: H29.

Schilpp, Madelon Golden, and Sharon M. Murphy. *Great Women of the Press*. Carbondale, Ill.: Southern Illinois Press, 1983.

Schneider, John. *The Golden Kazoo*. New York: Holt, Rinehart and Winston: 1956.

Schroth, Raymond A. *The Eagle and Brooklyn: A Community Newspaper, 1841–1955*. Westport, Ct.: Greenwood Press, 1974.

Schwartz, Thomas A. and David Fletcher. "The Newsperson as TV Character." *Media History Digest*, Spring/Summer 1988: 48–57, 64.

Sedley, Henry. *Dangerfield's Rest; or, Before the Storm. A Novel of American Life and Manners*. New York: Sheldon & Co., 1964.

Seeger, Pete and Bob Reiser. *Carry It On! A History of Song and Picture of the Working Men and Women of America*. New York: Simon and Schuster, 1985.

Sharpe, Ernest, Jr. "The Man Who Changed His Skin." *American Heritage*, February 1989.

Shaw, David. "What Killed 'Lou Grant.'" *TV Guide*, 24 July 1982: 22.

Sheehan, Neil. *A Bright Shining Lie: John Paul Vann and America in Vietnam*. New York: Random House, 1988.

———. "In Vietnam, the Birth of the Credibility Gap." *The New York Times*, 1 October 1988: 27.

Shnayerson, Michael. "Can Diane Sawyer Have It All?" *Vanity Fair*, Vol. 50, No. 9, (September 1987): 140.

Shuman, Edwin L. *Practical Journalism: A Complete Manual of the Best Newspaper Methods*. New York: D. Appleton and Co., 1903.

———. *Steps Into Journalism; Helps and Hints for Young Writers*. Evanston, Ill.: Correspondence School of Journalism, 1894.

Sigal, Leon V. *Reporters and Officials: The Organization and Politics of Newsmaking.* Lexington, Mass.: D. C. Heath and Company, 1973.

Sim, John Cameron. *The Grass Roots Press.* Ames: Iowa State University Press, 1969.

Simon, Roger L. *Wild Turkey.* San Francisco: Straight Arrow Books, 1974.

Sklar, Robert. "TV's Lou Grant as press criticism." *Columbia Journalism Review,* January/February 1979: 17–18.

Smythe, Ted Curtis. "The Reporter, 1880–1900. Working Conditions and Their Influence on the News." *Journalism History,* Vol. 7, No. 1. (Spring 1980): 1–10.

Sokolov, Raymond. *Wayward Reporter.* New York: Harper & Row, Publishers, 1980.

Speakes, Larry and Robert Pack. "Beat the Press." *TV Guide,* 14 May 1988: 4–10.

Sperber, A. M. *Murrow: His Life and Times.* New York: Freundlich Books, 1986.

Spewack, Bella and Samuel. *Clear All Wires!* New York: Los Angeles: Samuel French, 1932.

Spinrad, Norman. *A World Between.* New York: Pocket Books, 1979.

Spoto, Donald. *Camerado.* New York: New American Library, Inc., 1978.

Squiers, Carol. "Catherine Leroy." *American Photographer,* December 1988: 30–38.

Stanton, Elizabeth Cady. "Ruth Hall." *The Una,* February 1855: 30.

Steel, Ronald. *Walter Lippmann and the American Century.* Boston: Little, Brown and Company, 1980.

Stein, M. L. "Battling Back." *Editor & Publisher,* 25 October 1986: 13.

Sterling, Bruce. *The Artificial Kid.* New York: Harper and Row, 1980.

Sterling, Bryan B., ed. *The Will Rogers Scrapbook.* New York: Grosset & Dunlap, 1976.

Stettner, Louis, ed. *Weegee.* New York: Alfred A. Knopf, 1977.

Stevens, John. "The Rise of the Sports Page." *Gannett Center Journal,* Fall 1987: 1–11.

Stevenson, William. *Eclipse.* Garden City, New York: Doubleday and Company, Inc., 1986.

Stewart, Edward. *The Great Los Angeles Fire.* New York: Simon & Schuster, 1980.

Stewart, Linda. *Panic on Page One.* New York: Delacorte Press, 1979.

Stich, Sidra. *Made in U.S.A.: An Americanization in Modern Art, the '50s and '60s.* Berkeley: University of California Press, 1987.

Stine, G. Harry. *The Third Industrial Revolution.* New York: G. P. Putnam's Sons, 1975.

Stone, I. F. *In a Time of Torment.* New York: Random House, 1967.

Stone, Scott C. S. *Spies.* New York: St. Martin's Press, 1980.

Stoppard, Tom. *Night and Day.* New York: Grove Press, Inc., 1979.

Storey, Alice. *First Kill All the Lawyers.* New York: Pocket Books, 1988.

Stowe, Harriet Beecher. *We and Our Neighbors.* New York: J. B. Ford & Co., 1875.

Superman. Anniversary Issue 400. New York: D. C. Comics, Inc., 1984.

Sussman, Barry. *The Great Cover-Up: Nixon and the Scandal of Watergate.* New York: New American Library, 1974.

Swados, Harvey. *Years of Conscience: The Muckrakers.* New York: The World Publishing Company, 1962.

Swanberg, W. A. *Citizen Hearst.* New York: Charles Scribner's Sons, 1961.

———. *Luce and His Empire.* New York: Dell, 1972.

———. *Pulitzer.* New York: Charles Scribner's Sons, 1967.

Swisshelm, Jane Grey. *Half a Century.* Chicago: Jansen, McClurg & Company, 1880.

———. *Letters to Country Girls.* New York: J. C. Riker, 1853.

Talese, Gay. *The Kingdom and the Power.* New York: The World Publishing Company, 1969.

Tarkington, Booth. *The Gentleman from Indiana.* New York: Doubleday & McClure Co., 1900.

Taylor, Bayard. *John Godfrey's Fortunes; Related by Himself. A Story of American Life.* New York: G. P. Putnam, 1864.

Taylor, Frederick. Letter to the author, 30 April 1984.

Taylor, John. "Holier Than Thou." *New York,* 27 March 1989.

Taylor, Joshua C. *American As Art.* New York: Harper & Row, 1976.

Taylor, Welford Dunaway, ed. *The Buck Fever Papers.* Charlottesville: University Press of Virginia, 1971.

Tebbel, John. *The Media in America.* New York: New American Library, 1974.

Temin, Christine. "The paper chase at the ICA." *The Boston Globe,* 24 June 1988: 29.

Thomas, Michael M. *Hard Money.* New York: Viking Penguin Inc., 1985.

Thomasson, Don. "'Good Old Days' of Free Access— and some co-opting—are gone." *The Bulletin of the American Society of Newspaper Editors,* February 1987.

Thompson, Hunter S. *Fear and Loathing in Las Vegas.* New York: Popular Library, 1971.

———. *The Great Shark Hunt: Strange Tales from a Strange Time.* New York: Summit Books, 1979.

Thompson, Jim. *The Nothing Man.* In *Hard Core: 3 Novels.* New York: Donald I. Fine, Inc., 1986.

Toffler, Alvin. *Future Shock*. New York: Random House, 1970.

Tomlinson, Donald E. "Coalesce or Collide? Ethics, Technology and Television Journalism 1991." *Journal of Mass Media Ethics*, Vol. II, Issue 2, Spring/Summer 1981.

Tremble, Vance H., ed. *Faith in My Star: A selection of his own words that showcases the vision and vitality of E. W. Scripps*. Memphis, Tenn.: The Commercial Appeal, 1989.

Trillin, Calvin. "Covering the Cops." *The New Yorker*, 17 February 1986: 39.

Trotta, Liz. "Why the Network didn't Want My Exclusive on Grenada." *TV Guide*, 27 February 1988.

Turner, Kathleen J. *Lyndon Johnson's Dual War: Vietnam and the Press*. Chicago: University of Chicago Press, 1986.

Twain, Mark. "From the London Times of 1904." *The Century*, November 1898, pp. 100–104.

———. "Journalism in Tennessee." In *Editorial Wild Oats*. New York: Harper and Brothers 1905; reprint, New York: Arno Press and The New York Times, 1970.

———. "Memoranda," *The Galaxy*, Vol. IX, No. 6, (June 1870): 858.

Underwood, Doug. "When MBAs rule the newsroom," *Columbia Journalism Review*, March/April 1988: 23–30.

Unger, R. K. and F. L. Denmark, eds. *Woman: Dependent or Independent Variable*. New York: Psychological Dimensions, 1975.

U. S. Congress, Office of Technology Assessment. *Science, Technology, and the First Amendment*. OTA-CIT-369. Washington: U.S. Government Printing Office, January 1987.

Van Deusen, Glyndon G. *Horace Greeley: Nineteenth-Century Crusader*. Philadelphia: University of Pennsylvania Press, 1953.

Van Riper, Frank. "In the Flicks." and Edward C. Norton. "On the Tube." in "How Hollywood Views the Press." *Nieman Reports*, Vol. XXXIII, No. 4 (Winter 1979): 36–39.

Verne, Jules and Michel Verne. "In the Year 2889." *The Forum*, February 1889.

Vidal, Gore. *Empire*. New York: Bantam Books, 1987.

Vinge, Joan. *Eyes of Amber*. New York: The New American Library, 1979.

"Visions of Tomorrow." *Life*, February 1989.

Voight, David Quentin. *American Baseball*. Norman: University of Oklahoma Press, 1966.

Walker, Aiken. *Newsboy or Post No Bills*, 1883.

Walker, Stanley. *City Editor*. New York: Frederick A. Stokes, 1934.

Wall, Frazier. *Henry Watterson: Reconstructed Rebel*. New York: Oxford University Press, 1956.

Wallace, Irving. *The Almighty*. Garden City, N.Y.: Doubleday & Co., 1982.

Walsh, Justin E. *To Print the News and Raise Hell: A Biography of Wilber F. Storey*. Chapel Hill: University of North Carolina Press, 1968.

Warren, Joyce W., ed. *Ruth Hall and Other Writings: Fanny Fern*. New Brunswick: Rutgers University Press, 1986.

Watson, Delmar, ed. "*Quick Watson, the Camera*." Hollywood, Calif.: Delmar Watson, 1975.

Watson, Mary Ann. "Facts and Fictions: TV History Through the Filter of Fiction." *Television Quarterly*. Vol. XXII, No. IV (1987): 21–36.

Weaver, David H. and G. Cleveland Wilhoit. *The American Journalist: A Portrait of U.S. News People and Their Work*. Bloomington: Indiana University Press, 1986.

Weber, Ronald. "Journalism, Writing and American Literature." Occasional Paper No. 5, Gannett Center for Media Studies, April 1987.

Wecter, Dixon. *The Hero in America*. New York: Charles Scribner's Sons, 1941.

Weegee. New York: Aperture, Inc., 1978.

Weinberg, Steve. "My White Whale, or the Great Newspaper Novel," *The New York Times*, 27 August 1989: Book Review Section, 1, 24–25.

———. "The Journalist in Novels." *Journal of Mass Media Ethics*, Vol. 2, No. 1 (Fall/Winter 1986–87): 89–92.

Weinstein, Steve, and Diane Haithman. "ABC draws fire for botched simulation." *The Boston Globe*, 27 July 1989.

Wells-Barnett, Ida B. *Crusade for Justice: The Autobiography of Ida B. Wells*. Edited by Alfreda M. Duster. Chicago: The University of Chicago Press, 1970.

Wendt, Lloyd. *Chicago Tribune: The Rise of a Great American Newspaper*. Chicago: Rand McNally and Company, 1979.

White, Ray Lewis. *The Achievement of Sherwood Anderson*. Chapel Hill: University of North Carolina Press, 1966.

White, Ray Lewis, ed. *Return to Winesburg*. Chapel Hill: University of North Carolina. 1967.

White, William, ed. *By-Line: Ernest Hemingway*. New York: Charles Scribner's Sons, 1967.

White, William Allen. *The Autobiography of William Allen White*. New York: The Macmillan Company, 1946.

———. *In Our Town*. New York: McClure, Phillips & Co., 1906.

Whitman, Walt. "Life in a New York Market." *New York Aurora*, 16 March 1842.

———. "The New York Press." *New York Aurora*, 29 March 1842.

———. "Scenes of Last Night." *New York Aurora*, 1 April 1842.

Whitney, D. Charles. "Begging Your Pardon: Corrections and Corrections Policies at Twelve U.S. Newspapers." New York: Gannett Center for Media Studies, 1986.

Whitten, Leslie H. *Conflict of Interest.* Garden City, N.Y.: Doubleday & Co., 1976.

Wildavsky, Aaron. "The media's 'American egalitarians'." *The Public Interest*, Summer 1987.

Wilgoren, Debbie. "Dartmouth protesters seek ban on distribution of Review." *The Boston Sunday Globe*, 7 May 1989.

Wilkerson, Marcus M. *Public Opinion and the Spanish-American War.* Baton Rouge: Louisiana State University Press, 1932.

Wilkins, Lee. "Film as an Ethics Text." *Journal of Mass Media Ethics.* Vol. 2, No. 2 (Spring/ Summer 1987): 109–113.

"William Allen White of Emporia: An American Institution is 70." *Life*, 28 February 1938.

Williams, Ben Ames. *Splendor.* New York: E. P. Dutton & Company, 1927.

Williams, Frederick. *The Communications Revolution.* Beverly Hills, Calif.: Sage Publications, Inc., 1982.

Williams, John A., ed. *The Angry Black.* New York: Lancer Books, 1962.

Williams, John A. *The Man Who Cried I Am.* Boston: Little, Brown and Company, 1967.

Wills, Kendall J. *The Pulitzer Prizes, 1988.* New York: Touchstone/Simon & Schuster, Inc., 1988.

Wilson, Woodrow. *Mere Literature and Other Essays.* Boston: Houghton, Mifflin and Company, 1896.

Winkler, John K. *William Randolph Hearst: A New Appraisal.* New York: Hastings House, 1955.

Winks, Robin W. *Modus Operandi.* Boston: David R. Godine, Publisher, 1982.

Winslow, Helen M. "Some Newspaper Women." *The Arena*, Vol. XVII (December 1896): 127.

Wisner, George. *Sun* (New York). 23 October 1833; 2 January; 13 May; 1 August 1834.

Wohl, Burton. *The China Syndrome.* New York: Bantam Books, 1979. Based on the screenplay written by Mike Gray, T. S. Cook and James Bridges.

Wolfe, Thomas. "Gentlemen of the Press." *The Hills Beyond.* New York: Harper & Row, Publishers, Inc., 1941; reprint, New York: New American Library, 1968.

Wolfe, Tom. "Piping a story straight from the skull," *The Bulletin of the American Society of Newspaper Editors*, No. 643 (July/August 1981): 17–18.

Wolfe, Tom and E. W. Johnson, eds. *The New Journalism.* New York: Harper & Row, 1970.

Wolseley, Roland E. *The Black Press, U.S.A.* Ames: Iowa State University Press, 1971.

Wood, Tom. *The Bright Side of Billy Wilder, Primarily.* Garden City, New York: Doubleday & Co., Inc., 1970.

Wye, Deborah. *Committed to Print: Social and Political Themes in Recent American Printed Art.* New York: The Museum of Modern Art, 1988.

Yates, Norris W. *The American Humorist.* Ames: Iowa State University Press, 1964.

Zurier, Rebecca. *Art for the Masses.* Philadelphia: Temple University Press, 1988.

Zynda, Thomas H. "The Hollywood Version: Movie Portrayals of the Press." In *Journalism History.* Vol. 6, no. 1 (Spring 1979): 16–25.

Index

Boldface page numbers denote illustrations